Harnessing AI's Potential to Support Student Success and Teaching Excellence

Juan J. Araujo
Texas Woman's University, USA

Sharla Snider
Texas Woman's University, USA

IGI Global
Scientific Publishing
Publishing Tomorrow's Research Today

Vice President of Editorial	Melissa Wagner
Director of Acquisitions	Mikaela Felty
Director of Book Development	Jocelynn Hessler
Production Manager	Mike Brehm
Cover Design	Jose Rosado

Published in the United States of America by
IGI Global Scientific Publishing
701 East Chocolate Avenue
Hershey, PA, 17033, USA
Tel: 717-533-8845
Fax: 717-533-7115
Website: https://www.igi-global.com E-mail: cust@igi-global.com

Library of Congress Cataloging-in-Publication Data

Names: Araujo, Juan Jose, 1971- editor
http://id.loc.gov/rwo/agents/n2021040633 | Snider, Sharla, 1964- editor
http://id.loc.gov/rwo/agents/n2025019355
Title: Impact of AI usage and deployment in school settings / edited by
Juan J. Araujo and Sharla Snider.
Description: Hershey, PA : IGI Global Scientific Publishing, [2026] |
Includes bibliographical references and index. | Summary: "This book will bring together experts from diverse fields in education to examine the evolution of AI technologies, their practical implementations across disciplines (i.e., bilingual education, curriculum and instruction, early childhood education, language and literacy, and special education), and the ethical, social, and economic challenges they pose"-- Provided by publisher.
Identifiers: LCCN 2025014137 (print) | LCCN 2025014138 (ebook) | ISBN 9798337311227 hardcover | ISBN 9798337311234 paperback | ISBN 9798337311241 ebook
Subjects: LCSH: Artificial intelligence--Educational applications
http://id.loc.gov/authorities/subjects/sh87006783
Classification: LCC LB1028.43 .I44 2025 (print) | LCC LB1028.43 (ebook) |
DDC 370.285/63--dc23/eng/20250501
LC record available at https://lccn.loc.gov/2025014137
LC ebook record available at https://lccn.loc.gov/2025014138

British Cataloguing in Publication Data
A Cataloguing in Publication record for this book is available from the British Library.

Editorial Advisory Board

Sadir Yener, *Sinop University, Turkey*

Table of Contents

Detailed Table of Contents

This chapter explores how artificial intelligence (AI) can support teachers in bridging the longstanding gap between educational research and classroom practice. Rather than positioning AI as a replacement for professional expertise, the chapter frames it as a mediational tool that amplifies teacher agency. Through three vignettes—focused on locating relevant research, interrogating program mandates, and challenging policy directives—the chapter illustrates how various AI tools enable more contextualized and critical engagement with research. Drawing on Vygotsky's cultural-historical theory, it emphasizes how AI can function as a cognitive partner in the professional learning process. The chapter also foregrounds ethical considerations, highlighting the need to examine algorithmic bias, equity of access, and the importance of teacher judgment. Practical steps and a teacher-centered checklist are included to guide responsible use. Overall, the chapter argues for a vision of AI that empowers teachers as co-constructors of knowledge, not passive recipients of policy.

As AI tools enter educational spaces, educators face questions about how to integrate them responsibly, ethically, and with pedagogical integrity. This chapter offers a practice-based exploration of AI use in teacher education, grounded in Critical Digital Pedagogy (CDP). Drawing on the author's experiences as an early-career lecturer at an urban university, the chapter presents illustrative cases that showcase AI in lesson planning, assignment design, student engagement, and ethical dilemmas. It includes critical reflection on how outputs were adapted or reimagined to support humanizing teaching. Broader implications for K–12 and post-secondary educators are addressed, including strategies for designing assignments that resist mechanization, fostering critical AI literacy among students, and navigating emerging concerns around authorship. Rather than offering prescriptive solutions, the chapter invites educators to engage with AI critically and creatively.

This chapter explores the transformative role of Artificial Intelligence (AI) in enhancing STEM education through experiential learning, with a focus on the innovative MagicSchool AI platform. It examines how AI-powered tools streamline teacher productivity by automating administrative tasks, generating personalized lesson plans, and creating interactive, standards-aligned content. The chapter highlights AI's capacity to personalize learning by analyzing student data to address individual needs, while also promoting student engagement through gamification, real-time feedback, and adaptive learning systems. MagicSchool AI's unique multi-model approach and specialized tools empower educators to design immersive project-based learning experiences that connect academic concepts to real-world challenges. By integrating AI with experiential learning principles, this chapter illustrates how educators can foster critical thinking, collaboration, and innovation in K-12 STEM classrooms.

This chapter aims to familiarize teacher educators and college of education professors with generative artificial intelligence (AI). As the final instructors that pre-service teachers encounter before they enter the classroom, it is crucial for teacher educators to grasp the technology that their students will need to master in order to support them effectively. According to Shata and Hartley, while education professors tend to hold positive views on artificial intelligence, student perceptions are considerably more skeptical, despite the numerous advantages AI offers in streamlining and enhancing teacher preparation processes. This chapter will outline innovative strategies that provide compelling arguments for integrating AI into lesson development, ensuring alignment with state standards while fostering engaging content strategies and effective resource curation.

Currently, artificial intelligence (AI) is also transforming education as an effective means of cooperation in content production. This chapter explores the nature of AI not as an augmentation but as a disruptor that is changing the profession of educators. This advancement is made possible by the AI in that it is able to automate routine duties such as learning analytics, construction of assessments, and content development. The chapter draws frameworks and resources that support instruction as it discusses practical implementation of artificial intelligence in the construction of learning resources. Such are interactive simulations that map abstract concepts, multimodal teaching aids that address different types of learners, and intelligent adaptive learning environments that offer learning tailored to the type of the learner profile. The use of intelligent assessment system provides immediate feedback and analysis, which can assist educators/teachers and learners to identify their proficiency and deficits.

Special education teachers face challenges in addressing diverse student needs. This chapter explores how AI enhances both teacher efficiency and student outcomes. AI supports individualized lesson plans, behavioral management, and progress tracking, enabling tailored interventions. Assistive technologies like speech-to-text and adaptive learning platforms personalize instruction, while AI tools such as Magic School AI and Brisk Teaching provide real-time feedback and data-driven insights. This chapter will provide a variety of strategies, tools, and techniques for special education teachers. AI offers powerful tools to enhance efficiency and personalized learning in special education. Future advancements require ongoing teacher development and ethical considerations to ensure AI remains a supportive tool, empowering educators rather than replacing them.

This chapter investigates the use of artificial intelligence (AI) tools in preservice teacher education, with a specific focus on Elementary English Language Arts (ELA). It explores how AI tools can be used to support preservice teachers (PSTs) to create effective lesson plans, develop engaging instructional resources, differentiate instruction, and promote active student participation. The chapter explores tools like ChatGPT, MagicSchool.ai, Brisk, Perplexity, Canva, Diffit, and Curipod and illustrates how they can be used responsibly and effectively, offering valuable insights for educators seeking to integrate AI into teacher preparation programs. The chapter concludes with an overview of PSTs' perspectives on AI, addressing perceived benefits, limitations, and ethical considerations in educational settings, as well as offering a glimpse into the next steps of AI in teacher education.

This study aims to investigate the impact of traditional versus reflective journals, enhanced with artificial intelligence (AI), on developing learner autonomy in writing skills among EFL learners. Following a quasi-experimental design, the data collection involved 36 college students in an English preparatory program. A demographic information questionnaire and the Learner Autonomy Scale (LAS) were used to collect the data. While the control group kept traditional reflective journals after each writing task, the experimental group wrote AI-assisted reflective journals using AI chatbot software for five weeks. The findings revealed that traditional reflective journaling had a negligible impact on students' autonomy. However, the implementation of AI-enhanced reflective journals showed a noticeable change in students' self-evaluation skills.

Preface

"Do not confine your children to your own learning, for they were born in another time"

Chinese Proverb

Welcome to the first edition of *Harnessing AI's Potential to Support Student Success and Teaching Excellence*. In this volume the handbook explores the multifaceted landscape of AI in education, integrating theoretical foundations with real-world applications for inservice and preservice teachers, and the often-overlooked repercussions of usage and its deployment in school settings. This comprehensive edited book brings together experts from diverse fields in education to examine the evolution of AI technologies, their practical implementations across disciplines (i.e., bilingual education, curriculum and instruction, early childhood education, language and literacy, and special education), and the ethical, social, and economic challenges they pose. Through insightful, forward-thinking chapters, the book highlights both the transformative potential of AI and the risks associated with its unchecked advancement, emphasizing the importance of responsible innovation in education. By fostering a nuanced understanding of AI's capabilities and limitations, this collection aims to inform educators, researchers, practitioners, and the public, encouraging a balanced dialogue about the future of technology in society.

The audience for this work ranges from preservice and inservice teachers, higher education professionals who prepare future teachers, curriculum designers who are considering ways to use AI as an instructional tool, and others who are looking for a base text about effective practices and theories relating to AI implementation in the current and future classrooms.

This book can also be a resource for university graduate students who are pursuing degrees relating to learning technologies, language and literacy development, and teacher education preparation.

The impact of this work is crucial as teachers, administrators, and policymakers are looking for what is the right approach for such AI implementation. Teachers, in particular, will be at the forefront of thinking about, implementing, and assessing student learning outcomes. The possibilities seem endless and we both believe that we are on the cusp of a paradigmatic shift (Kuhn, 1970)—a history making transformation of our worldview with respect to what counts as labor, learning, collaboration, and access to knowledge.

Still, teachers will continue to be at the forefront because they foster human connection and emotional intelligence outside of the family unit. Educators create safe and supportive environments in classroom settings that may often be new and different for the students in their care whether you are a preschool student or a lifelong learner taking graduate courses. Teachers are nimble and often see the on-the-run teaching moments that happen in real time and respond in developmentally appropriate ways.

As you read the seventeen chapters, we invite you to take *a look, think, act* approach (Patterson et al, 2010; Stringer, 1996). Look (and read) the chapters and carefully consider what patterns, trends, and ideas you notice as you read the author's works. Think about why these ideas might be bubbling into the surface, and what factors might you consider as a reader, educator, or teacher leader. Take action to adjust or implement some of these ideas, tools, strategies, or frameworks in your day to day activities.

A TARGETED ACCOUNT OF THE INTERSECTION OF AI AND EDUCATION

Over the past couple of years, there has been a shift in the ways students and teachers have engaged with artificial intelligence. Institutions of higher education school districts across the country and around the world have grappled with the use of AI in the teaching and learning of young children and adult learners alike. What is a promising practice? What are good strategies of use? What frameworks are useful when integrating AI in early childhood education, STEM education, and faculty development? And perhaps, most importantly for many of the readers of this work, what are questions we need to ask ourselves as we prepare future teachers to teach the next generation of children in their care.

THE CURRENT HANDBOOK: AN OVERVIEW

Chapter 1, *Locate, Interrogate, and Challenge: The Promise of AI for Connecting Research to Practice for Teachers* explores how artificial intelligence can bridge the longstanding research-practice gap by positioning AI as a mediational tool that amplifies teacher agency rather than replacing professional expertise. The authors describe how educators can use AI tools like Semantic Scholar, Elicit, Perplexity, and ChatGPT to locate relevant research, interrogate program mandates, and challenge policy directives through critical engagement. Following a theoretical grounding in Vygotsky's cultural-historical theory, the chapter demonstrates through three detailed vignettes how teachers can move from passive receivers of research to active participants in knowledge construction by utilizing AI to locate meaningful studies, question the suitability of mandated programs, and advocate for instructional practices grounded in evidence. The authors address ethical considerations including algorithmic bias, equity of access, and the importance of maintaining teacher judgment while providing a practical teacher-centered checklist for responsible AI use. In conclusion, the authors provide practical implementation steps and an ethical framework for responsible AI use that empowers teachers as co-constructors of knowledge rather than passive recipients of policy.

Chapter 2, *AI in Action: Practical Insights and Strategies for Educators* discusses how artificial intelligence can be integrated into teacher education through the lens of Critical Digital Pedagogy while maintaining humanizing, equity-oriented educational practices. The author describes how AI tools can support lesson planning, ethical case analysis, and student engagement while requiring critical evaluation and adaptation to meet diverse student needs. Following a theoretical framework of Critical Digital Pedagogy, this chapter is divided into three key parts: (1) contextual background and implementation strategies for AI integration; (2) eight illustrative cases demonstrating AI use in teacher preparation; (3) critical reflections on the affordances and limitations of AI in educational settings. In conclusion, the author provides broader implications for K-12 and post-secondary educators, advocating for AI as a collaborative tool that enhances rather than replaces the human-centered foundations of quality education.

Chapter 3, *Measuring the Role of AI-Enhanced Learning, A Responsible Framework for Educational Innovation* describes how the AI-Evaluation Quadrant Model (AI-EQM) can provide a comprehensive framework for evaluating AI-supported student work while addressing ethical and social challenges in educational innovation. The authors describe how AI impacts multiple educational domains including language learning, special education, and STEM curriculum design, highlighting both opportunities for personalized learning and persistent implementation challenges. Following a review of current literature and theoretical frameworks, the chapter examines measurement difficulties inherent in AI-enhanced learning environments, particularly in assessing cognitive effort, determining AI contribution levels, and evaluating long-term skill development and learning quality. The authors draw on various learning theories including constructivism, Bloom's taxonomy, and cognitive load theory to demonstrate how the AI-EQM can be applied across educational disciplines while ensuring that AI tools support rather than replace meaningful human learning. In conclusion, the authors provide recommendations for responsible AI integration that prioritizes equity, transparency, and the protection of student agency in educational settings.

Chapter 4, *Integrating AI in Lesson Planning Within an Early Childhood Developmentally Appropriate Framework: ECE, Special Education, & Cultural Contexts* presents how artificial intelligence tools can be integrated into early childhood lesson planning while maintaining alignment with Developmentally Appropriate Practice (DAP) principles and supporting diverse learners' needs. The authors describe how educators can use AI as a collaborative tool for creating developmentally appropriate curricula that address the three core considerations of commonality, individuality, and context. Following a comprehensive review of DAP frameworks and ethical considerations, this chapter is divided into three key parts: (1) theoretical foundations of DAP and AI integration principles; (2) practical scenarios demonstrating varying levels of AI prompt specificity and resulting lesson quality; (3) recommendations for responsible implementation including evaluation rubrics and professional development needs. In conclusion, the authors provide guidelines for positioning AI as a collaborative partner that enhances rather than diminishes the human-centered, relationship-based foundations of quality early childhood education.

Chapter 5, *Empowering STEM Education: Harnessing Magic School AI for Experiential Learning* explores how MagicSchool AI can transform K-12 STEM education by enhancing teacher productivity, enabling personalized learning, and promoting student engagement through experiential, project-based learning approaches. The author describes how AI tools can streamline administrative tasks while supporting hands-on, inquiry-driven activities such as interactive simulations, virtual laboratories, and authentic assessment experiences. Following a review of experiential learning research and AI applications in education, the chapter demonstrates the practical implementation of various MagicSchool AI tools including PBL generators, 5E model lesson plans, Science Labs Generator, Choice Board Generator, and assessment creation tools using a comprehensive water cycle unit as an illustrative example. The author addresses ethical considerations and best practices for responsible AI implementation while emphasizing the integration of digital design tools like Canva to enhance visual appeal and accessibility of AI-generated materials. In conclusion, the author positions thoughtful AI integration as a pathway to more personalized, engaging STEM education that prepares students for technology-driven careers while preserving essential human elements of teaching and learning.

Chapter 6, *Enlightening Educators: Unlocking the Benefits of AI in Faculty Development* contributes to the conversation on how generative artificial intelligence can support teacher educators and college of education faculty in preparing preservice teachers for AI-enhanced educational environments. The author describes how faculty can overcome technological skepticism by understanding AI's benefits in instructional guidance, student engagement practices, and resource curation for diverse educational contexts. Following an examination of faculty attitudes toward AI and current educational frameworks, this chapter is divided into three key parts: (1) AI applications for instructional design including lesson planning and standards alignment; (2) student engagement strategies using tools like Kahoot!, Google Classroom, and literacy applications; (3) scaffolding techniques for diverse learners incorporating Universal Design for Learning and Culturally Relevant Pedagogy. In conclusion, the author advocates for comprehensive professional development that positions AI as a supportive tool rather than a replacement for human teachers, emphasizing the need for continuous learning and ethical implementation in teacher preparation programs.

Chapter 7, *AI as a Collaborative Tool: Redefining Educator Roles in Content Development,* explores how artificial intelligence is fundamentally transforming educator responsibilities from traditional content delivery to facilitation and collaboration within modern learning environments. The authors examine how AI automates routine tasks such as assessment creation, grading, and learning analytics, thereby enabling teachers to focus on higher-order pedagogical functions including critical thinking development, creativity cultivation, and individualized student support. Following a comprehensive literature review, this chapter is divided into three key components: design frameworks supporting AI-human collaboration in educational content development; practical applications including interactive simulations, adaptive learning systems, and intelligent assessment tools; and ethical considerations addressing algorithmic bias, data privacy, and equitable access to AI technologies. The chapter presents detailed case studies from Finnish high schools and university initiatives demonstrating successful AI implementation that preserves human expertise while leveraging technological capabilities. Recommendations are provided for balanced AI integration that strengthens technological efficiency while maintaining essential human elements of empathy, creativity, and ethical judgment in educational practice.

Chapter 8, *AI in the Special Education Toolbox: Strategies, Tools, and Techniques for Teachers*, investigates the transformative potential of artificial intelligence to revolutionize special education practice by addressing critical time management and instructional differentiation challenges. The authors describe how special educators dedicate nearly half their professional time to administrative responsibilities rather than direct student engagement, creating an urgent need for technological solutions that preserve pedagogical relationships while streamlining operational tasks. The chapter describes how AI platforms such as MagicSchool AI, Diffit, and Brisk Teaching enable rapid creation of leveled texts, differentiated assessments, and personalized learning materials that would traditionally require hours of manual development. Grounded in established frameworks including Universal Design for Learning and the ABC Model for assistive technology, the chapter showcases practical implementations ranging from automated DOK-leveled questioning to AI-generated choice boards that accommodate diverse learning profiles and abilities. Successful AI integration must address persistent challenges including digital equity gaps, algorithmic bias risks, and data privacy concerns that disproportionately affect vulnerable student populations. The authors of the chapter advocate for a collaborative human-AI model where technology amplifies educator expertise and efficiency while preserving the essential relational and empathetic foundations that define quality special education practice.

Chapter 9, *Psychological and Developmental Repercussions of Pervasive AI Usage in Schools: A Review of Educational Benefits and Challenges,* explores how widespread AI integration creates profound psychological and developmental impacts on students beyond measurable academic outcomes. The authors examine how students navigate algorithm-monitored learning environments that provide feedback and shape educational pathways, potentially creating dependencies on external validation while undermining intrinsic motivation and self-regulation. Following a comprehensive interdisciplinary literature review, this chapter is divided into six critical areas: (1) learning engagement and inclusion challenges in AI-mediated environments; (2) feedback and performance monitoring effects on student autonomy and creativity; (3) social interaction and collaboration changes in algorithm-guided learning spaces; (4) emotional development implications of AI-driven social-emotional learning systems; (5) identity formation and personal development impacts in technology-rich educational contexts; and (6) emotional resilience considerations when AI systems provide primary emotional support. Findings are shared revealing benefits such as personalized learning pathways and concerning risks including reduced tolerance for uncertainty, over-reliance on machine authority, and diminished authentic peer interactions. The authors advocate for human-centered AI integration that prioritizes student well-being, preserves authentic social relationships, and maintains educational spaces for uncertainty, struggle, and creative exploration that foster genuine intellectual and emotional growth.

Our purpose in taking on this edited book project for the past year was to understand more about how the education field from PK through adulthood is engaging with artificial intelligence in meaningful and productive ways. We were especially interested and eager to learn about how others are engaging in this work as they prepare future teachers and what frameworks educators are building for themselves and others. We hope the chapters in this volume will enrich your understanding of AI and help to build capacity across higher education.

REFERENCES

Kuhn, T. (1970). *The structure of scientific revolutions*. University of Chicago Press.

Patterson, L., Baldwin, S. C., Araujo, J. J., Shearer, R., & Stewart, M. (2010). Look, think, act: Using critical action research to sustain reform in complex teaching/learning ecologies. *Journal of Inquiry and Action in Education*, *3*(3). https://digitalcommons.buffalostate.edu/jiae/vol3/iss3/4

Stringer, E. T. (1996). *Action research: A handbook for practitioners*. Sage Publications.

Acknowledgment

We want to express our sincere gratitude to the authors, colleagues, reviewers, and past students who contributed to this book project. Our gratitude for sharing your expertise with respect to education and interaction of artificial intelligence is immeasurable.

We will be remiss not to forget to thank the staff, in particular Amelia Bucher, at IGI Global for providing us a framework, encouragement reminders, and a timeline that fit with our professional calendars. You are the best!

Special thanks are extended to our families, for believing in us and their encouragement as we engaged in the editing process.

Chapter 1
Locate, Interrogate, and Challenge:
The Promise of AI for Connecting Research to Practice for Teachers

Heather A Cato
https://orcid.org/0000-0002-4278-9113
Texas Woman's University, Denton, USA

Nancy Anderson
Texas Woman's University, Denton, USA

ABSTRACT

This chapter explores how artificial intelligence (AI) can support teachers in bridging the longstanding gap between educational research and classroom practice. Rather than positioning AI as a replacement for professional expertise, the chapter frames it as a mediational tool that amplifies teacher agency. Through three vignettes—focused on locating relevant research, interrogating program mandates, and challenging policy directives—the chapter illustrates how various AI tools enable more contextualized and critical engagement with research. Drawing on Vygotsky's cultural-historical theory, it emphasizes how AI can function as a cognitive partner in the professional learning process. The chapter also foregrounds ethical considerations, highlighting the need to examine algorithmic bias, equity of access, and the importance of teacher judgment. Practical steps and a teacher-centered checklist are included to guide responsible use. Overall, the chapter argues for a vision of AI that empowers teachers as co-constructors of knowledge, not passive recipients of policy.

DOI: 10.4018/979-8-3373-1122-7.ch001

INTRODUCTION

Ms. Carter sits through another district training, taking careful notes. She hears the phrase "research-based strategies" again. Curiosity sparks: Which research? Whose research? Later at home, she searches for studies online, only to hit paywalls or jargon-filled articles that do not resonate. Time runs short, and her lesson plans demand attention. Her genuine curiosity fades into familiar frustration. Ms. Carter is not alone.

Teacher professional development most often focuses on evidence-based practices supported by research. Yet, too often, that evidence feels distant, inaccessible, or irrelevant. The problem is not teachers' lack of interest it is the barriers of access, time, and translation that widen the research-practice gap (Biesta, 2007; Pedró et al., 2019). Bridging this gap demands tools that are not just efficient but empowering. Artificial intelligence (AI) offers this potential.

This chapter explores how AI can support teachers in taking a more active, critical stance toward research. It is not about automating teaching; it is about amplifying teachers' professional judgment. Through AI tools, educators can locate meaningful studies, interrogate the quality and context of research claims, and challenge policies disconnected from classroom realities. AI helps teachers mediate the flow of research not merely as a shortcut to information, but as a catalyst for transforming findings into actionable classroom insights.

Three vignettes ground this exploration, illustrating concrete examples of AI-supported inquiry. Mr. Patel discovers relevant research tailored to his rural students' needs. Ms. Rivera questions the suitability of a mandated phonics program for her multilingual learners. Ms. Chen advocates for instructional practices that honor her AP English students' advanced analytical skills. Each narrative reveals how AI can move teachers from passive receivers of research to active participants in knowledge construction.

However, using AI ethically matters. Algorithms carry biases; fluent summaries can obscure nuance. And uneven access risks widening divides. Ethical considerations ensure AI is a supportive tool, not an authoritative voice. In what follows, we examine AI's promise, possibilities, and pitfalls. Practical guidelines and an ethical checklist are provided to help teachers confidently leverage AI. The goal is not just better-informed decisions: it is professional agency reclaimed and revitalized.

AI AS A TOOL FOR SUPPORTING TEACHER RESEARCH

Today, teachers navigate a policy landscape shaped by mandates, district initiatives, and pre-packaged curricula, all of which are positioned under the banner of being "evidence-based." These top-down directives often frame research as static and universal, promoting a one-size-fits-all approach to teaching. However, the evidence is not neutral. It is socially constructed, and the phrase "what works" can obscure more than it reveals (Biesta, 2007). This framing risks erasing the dynamic realities of classrooms, where students arrive with diverse languages, histories, strengths, and needs realities that demand the interpretive expertise of teachers.

Rather than following scripts, teaching involves actively constructing curriculum tailored to unique classroom contexts. In systems that prize fidelity to "evidence-based" programs, teachers and children benefit from critically engaging with research itself. The term "evidence-based" lacks a singular definition and is warranted in varied, and sometimes contradictory, ways. Teachers benefit from approaching research as co-constructors rather than replicators of knowledge. Critically engaging with research means teachers interrogate assumptions and claims in published studies.

Critically engaging with research aligns with Cochran-Smith and Lytle's (2009) notion of practical epistemology, where professional knowledge arises from inquiry, collaboration, and reflection on lived experience. Within this frame, teachers are not just recipients of externally produced research but active agents in determining what counts as evidence, whose knowledge is valued, and how findings are interpreted.

Yet meaningful engagement with research requires time, access, and tools. Here, artificial intelligence, when used critically, can function as a mediational resource that supports inquiry (Chen, Chen, & Lin, 2020). AI tools can assist teachers in locating relevant studies, identifying contradictions, unpacking theoretical assumptions, and translating dense academic texts into more actionable insights. As Campello de Souza et al. (2024) suggest, AI does not replace human thought; it sharpens it.

Cultural-historical theory offers a generative lens for understanding how such mediation works. Vygotsky (1978) argued that all higher-order thinking is mediated by cultural tools, with language playing a central role. Language is not merely a sign system for expressing thought. Language is a tool that organizes experience, enables reflection, and supports decision-making (Wertsch, 1991). Professional learning unfolds as teachers collaboratively use language and other symbolic systems to make meaning. Through social interaction with texts, colleagues, and tools, external dialogue gradually becomes internalized as what Vygotsky termed inner speech: the internal, reflective talk that guides moment-to-moment pedagogical decisions (Vygotsky, 1986; Daniels, 2001). Inner speech transforms into external social speech as new higher-order culturally connected cognitive tools mediate professional learning.

AI can be part of this circuit of mediation. AI's sign systems, such as text, image, voice, and code, reshape how teachers engage with information. These tools reorganize knowledge, enabling teachers to see patterns, explore tensions, and stretch thinking. For example, a high school English teacher exploring a district-mandated literacy program might use an AI assistant to summarize the cited research base, identify underlying theoretical frameworks, and generate questions to guide discussion with colleagues. In doing so, the teacher moves from implementing a program to interrogating its epistemic foundations, supporting a shift from compliance to agency.

Used thoughtfully, AI tools become more than digital assistants. They become cognitive partners in reflection and dialogue. Interactions with AI can scaffold new forms of teacher inquiry, prompting feedback loops in which ideas are externalized, examined, and revised. In Vygotskian terms, AI may function like a more capable peer with tools, nudging thinking beyond what a teacher could accomplish alone.

Framed this way, AI is not a substitute for human judgment but a mediational tool in the construction of knowledge. It becomes part of a larger mediational system that includes language, tools, peers, and professional communities. Rather than restricting teaching to the faithful enactment of externally sanctioned research, AI, understood within this circuit of mediation, can help amplify teachers' professional and research agency. In doing so, it supports a practical epistemology in which teachers co-create knowledge (Cochran-Smith & Lytle, 2009).

Locate: Making Research Accessible and Relevant

Vignette 1: Mr. Patel's Challenge

Mr. Patel, a seventh-grade English teacher in his fifth year, grew up in a small town where stories wove his family together, sparking his love for reading as a way to connect. Now at a rural middle school, surrounded by fields and far from city buzz, he leans on that passion to reach his students. He thrives on swapping ideas with others, but the nearest teacher network is an hour's drive. His school's curriculum, a loose collection of handouts, offers little structure, and the principal, a former high school basketball coach, is supportive but not much help regarding instruction. Patel's second-period class, all boys, has the energy to spare but no love for books, brushing off reading with shrugs and half-hearted tries.

Hoping to find something that will get them excited, Patel spends evenings scrolling TikTok, watching what other teachers are doing. A post catches his eye—kids in book clubs, picking their stories, arguing plots with grins. It feels right for his boys, but he is eager to ground it in evidence, having seen too many trends fizzle without solid backing. At home, he digs online, but journal articles demand subscriptions, and he knows that with the school's tight budget, there is no way he could convince the principal to spend money on academic research (Pedró et al., 2019). A free study finally loads, but it is too general, offering broad claims about reading groups without showing how to make it work for his all-boy crew. The research-practice gap, where studies feel built for someone else, looms large (Pedró et al., 2019). Without colleagues nearby to toss ideas around, the isolation stings. His notebook is full of scribbles and ideas, proof he is all in, but paywalls and vague findings block his path. Frustration builds, not because he is short on effort, but because research feels like a door slammed shut.

That weekend, still turning over ideas, Patel scribbles "book clubs?" at the top of a fresh planning page. He searches online again, but most results lead to blog posts or paywalled resources with little real research. It feels like another dead end. Then a TikTok catches his eye. A teacher raves about a free AI tool called Semantic Scholar, calling it a game-changer for research. Mr. Patel wonders whether the tool might oversimplify the research or misrepresent findings before trying it, but he is still intrigued by the possibilities. Patel tries it, typing "book clubs for middle school boys." This time, studies roll in, real ones, with summaries he can actually read. One highlights how boy-led book clubs, with choice-driven stories, boost engagement, perfect for his action-loving class (Holmes et al., 2019).

Wanting to go further, he pastes the study into ChatGPT and types, "Based on this research, how could I set up book clubs for my middle school boys who aren't into reading?" He doesn't expect much. Maybe a list of steps he's seen before. Instead, the response is specific. ChatGPT pulls key ideas from the study and shapes them into something he can try: a plan for small groups, suggestions to have students vote on adventure books, and open-ended prompts that spark discussion, like asking What would you do in the hero's shoes? Suddenly, he sees it, his boys debating plot twists, not just skimming pages. That heavy frustration lifts, replaced by a quiet buzz. It's not a full plan yet, but it's a real step. The research finally feels like it is his to shape.

Possibilities: Reimagining Access and Agency Through AI

Mr. Patel's story illustrates a common tension in education: the desire to ground instructional decisions in research collides with structural barriers that restrict access to that research. Engaging with academic literature feels daunting for many educators—not due to a lack of curiosity or professional commitment, but because the system makes evidence hard to reach and use (Biesta, 2007; Pedró et al., 2019). AI, when used strategically, can mediate this disconnect by reshaping how teachers search for, interpret, and apply research in context.

Recent advances in artificial intelligence have produced tools that significantly reduce the friction between teacher inquiry and academic research. Semantic Scholar, for example, allows users to input plain-language queries, such as "book clubs for middle school boys," and receive a curated list of open-access studies relevant to their classroom context (Chen et al., 2020). In Mr. Patel's case, this meant bypassing paywalls and vague overviews in favor of a study that addressed his specific student population and instructional goals. However, locating research is only the first step.

AI tools like ChatGPT support what follows: interpreting findings and transforming them into pedagogical action. When Patel asked how to implement the approach described in the study, the AI offered practical suggestions, including student-led groupings, genre-based choice, and open-ended discussion prompts, that aligned with his classroom's research and realities. Far from automating instruction, the tool supported deeper inquiry and amplified Patel's capacity to act on what he learned.

This interaction reflects what Vygotsky (1978) and Wertsch (1991) describe as mediated cognition: the process by which tools, especially those grounded in language, extend human thinking. AI serves not simply as a digital assistant but as a semiotic tool that invites teachers to externalize their reasoning, test ideas, and refine them in light of new information. In this way, the teacher's question becomes part of a larger dialogue with knowledge itself: dynamic, situated, and open-ended. AI can scaffold the reflective practice that moves teachers beyond intuition, offering conceptual leverage for decision-making grounded in evidence and professional judgment.

Equally important is the way these tools challenge traditional gatekeeping in educational research. The research-practice divide has long privileged certain voices, contexts, and questions, often marginalizing the lived realities of teachers and students outside the academic mainstream (Pedró et al., 2019). AI's ability to personalize access, to help a teacher in a rural classroom find and work with research that speaks directly to their needs, represents a democratizing shift. It creates space for practitioner-driven inquiry, where relevance is determined not by publication prestige but by classroom resonance. Still, this promise depends on critical engagement. AI responses require interpretation, contextualization, and at times, resistance (Christou, 2023). But when used with intention, these tools offer more than convenience; they offer teachers a pathway to reclaim research as a resource they shape, not just receive.

Practical Application: Bringing AI into the Work of Teaching

Artificial intelligence can support teachers not only in locating research but also in making evidence-based inquiry a seamless, integrated part of everyday practice. While the tools are sophisticated, the process does not have to be. By following three practical steps: explore, extend, and evaluate, teachers can make AI a research partner that fits into real classroom rhythms. These steps correspond to three critical movements in research engagement: discovering relevant evidence, making sense of it in context, and assessing its fit for a specific instructional decision. What follows is a model for action grounded in professional autonomy and adaptive expertise.

Step 1: Explore with Semantic Scholar

Start with a question rooted in your classroom. Curiosity, a student challenge, or a claim from a district training might spark this. Type the question into Semantic Scholar using your own words, such as "How to increase engagement for middle school boys in reading," and scan the open-access results. Filter by publication date or field to narrow your focus, and look for studies with titles or abstracts that speak directly to your situation. Even a ten-minute search during a planning period can yield articles that offer fresh insight, confirm your instincts, or spark new instructional ideas. The key is approaching the platform with a specific classroom challenge in mind and using it to surface relevant and usable research.

Step 2: Extend with ChatGPT

Once you have found a promising study, use an AI tool like ChatGPT to help translate it into practice. You might upload the abstract or paste a key section and ask questions like, "How can I use this in a fifth-grade classroom with multilingual learners?" or "What are the main takeaways I should consider for group discussions?" The AI will not replace your judgment. It cannot know your students, but it can help unpack dense language, generate examples, or offer implementation suggestions that serve as a starting point. This step is about extending the reach of research, making it tangible and tailored through dialogue.

Step 3: Evaluate with Professional Judgment

AI tools can provide pathways into research, but they are not arbiters of truth (Christou, 2023). As a final step, evaluate the fit of the research and the AI's suggestions within your own context. Ask: Does this align with my students' needs and identities? Does it complement or challenge what I already know works? Where might I adapt or push back? Consider sharing what you have learned with colleagues, whether through team meetings, informal discussions, or digital collaboration spaces. This step reinforces the idea that evidence-based practice is not about compliance but about conversation, inquiry, and continuous refinement. In this way, AI becomes part of a broader professional ecosystem, not a replacement for expertise but a tool that sharpens it.

From Access to Agency

Professional agency flourishes when teachers can ask their own questions, find research that resonates with their students, and thoughtfully adapt it to their local context. AI tools like Semantic Scholar and ChatGPT are not solutions in themselves, but they are powerful mediators, bridging the longstanding divide between research and practice. For educators like Mr. Patel, these tools make it possible to move from frustration to informed experimentation, reclaiming research as usable, flexible, and rooted in real classrooms. As we turn next to the interrogation process, we deepen this vision. We not only access evidence but learn to question it with critical insight and professional confidence.

Interrogate: Evaluating Credibility and Applicability

Vignette 2: Ms. Rivera's Challenge

Ms. Rivera, in her eighth year of teaching, brings a reflective stance shaped by her first-generation college roots and a deep commitment to equitable literacy. After six years focused on comprehension in fourth grade, she now teaches second grade at a bustling urban school where families speak many languages and stories stretch across cultures. She regularly teaches phonics and sees decoding as essential. She also believes literacy should be connected, joyful, and relevant. That is why she pauses when her district introduces a new scripted phonics program, which is presented as aligned with best practices. While the intent may be solid, the program's structure seems to contradict strategies she has found effective, particularly those that integrate oral language, student talk, and responsive scaffolding. To gain a better understanding, Ms. Rivera pursues the citations listed in the teacher guide. The citations feel thin. One article is paywalled. Another link is to a white paper hosted on the publisher's own website. She tracks down one study, but it is based on a homogenous group of first graders in a suburban district, and the funder turns out to be the curriculum developer (Pedró et al., 2019; Yang & Evans, 2022). She is not looking to reject phonics. She is trying to figure out if this version of phonics instruction fits the multilingual learners in her classroom.

At a professional development webinar about AI tools hosted by a local university, she learns about Elicit and Scholarcy—described as digital coaches that help educators engage with research more confidently. Intrigued, she gives them a try. She begins with Elicit, typing in the name of the phonics program and the question: "What is the evidence supporting this program for diverse second-grade learners?" Elicit returns a range of studies, highlighting which are independently funded and affiliated with the publisher. It flags concerns around limited sample sizes and narrow participant demographics. She also wonders if the studies flagged by Elicit reflect mainstream biases or exclude multilingual perspectives. But it also points her to a broader meta-analysis outlining key features of effective phonics programs across varied populations—including the importance of combining structured practice with oral language development (Holmes et al., 2019; Luckin et al., 2016).

To explore alternative approaches, she copies the meta-analysis into Scholarcy, which breaks the study into key takeaways. Scholarcy surfaces comparisons across phonics models, including synthetic, analytic, and embedded, and lists studies that show positive outcomes when phonics instruction is paired with interactive discussion or culturally responsive materials.

For the first time, Ms. Rivera does not feel like she is chasing evidence. She is engaging with it. One study, in particular, centers on bilingual learners and emphasizes flexible pacing and collaborative reading structures (Zawacki-Richter et al., 2019). She highlights the summary and bookmarks several studies to revisit.

Ms. Rivera shares one of these studies with her grade-level team, proposing a small adaptation: "What if we keep the core lessons but make room for oral storytelling or partner reading during application time?" She is not resisting the mandate. She is shaping it. The tools did not hand her a solution, but they helped her ask smarter questions, challenge unclear claims, and locate practices that resonate with her students. Her goal is not to find a perfect program. It is to make informed decisions that reflect both the research and the learners in her room. That week, she tries a small shift during shared reading, replacing the program's scripted drill with paired storytelling prompts. The room comes alive with talk. Her students, many of whom thrive in conversation, begin using new sounds in their own sentences, evidence of practice and growing confidence.

POSSIBILITIES: SUPPORTING RESEARCH-LITERATE TEACHING THROUGH AI

Teachers have been expected to implement research without meaningful access to it for too long. Studies arrive secondhand, repackaged through curriculum or professional development, often stripped of nuance and disconnected from the realities of daily instruction. Educators like Ms. Rivera want to ground their practice in evidence: contextual, transparent, and adaptable evidence. The problem is not a lack of will; it is a lack of infrastructure for inquiry (Pedró et al., 2019). Artificial intelligence offers a promising path forward: not as a shortcut to truth, but as a tool for reclaiming discernment.

Elicit serves as an entry point to research interrogation. Built to support critical questioning, it helps teachers surface patterns across studies, recognize limitations, and evaluate credibility. In Ms. Rivera's case, it helped clarify that some of the cited evidence was narrow or biased, while pointing her to broader, independent studies that aligned more closely with her context. This aligns with Kou and Gui's (2020) notion of situated explanation. Teachers build understanding not just from what AI shows them, but by relating it to the specific dynamics of their classrooms. Elicit does not replace judgment. It scaffolds it.

Scholarcy, meanwhile, supports breadth and depth. It turns complex studies into structured summaries, extracting methodology, findings, and implications in minutes. For busy educators, this matters. It does not flatten research; it reveals structure, letting teachers locate what matters and apply it thoughtfully. In Rivera's case, it showed her a range of phonics approaches and helped her imagine adaptations. This kind of flexible engagement with research echoes Porayska-Pomsta's (n.d.) argument that AI can enable practitioner-led evidence generation—research not consumed passively, but interrogated and reshaped in practice (Holmes, Porayska-Pomsta, Holstein, Sutherland, & Baker, 2022).

Together, tools like Elicit and Scholarcy act as mediating artifacts, not decision-makers, but thinking partners. As Campello de Souza et al. (2024) describe, generative AI becomes part of a sophotechnic mediation process, where meaning is co-constructed between the human user and the tool. For teachers, this means AI can help illuminate research but also prompt questions, test assumptions, highlight implications for equity or bias, and reveal contradictions. The value lies not just in what AI says, but in how it supports teachers in forming their own professional judgments.

Ultimately, these tools shift the experience of research from static to dynamic, from something teachers are handed to something they actively explore. When used with intention, AI empowers educators to connect scholarly knowledge with the complexity of real-world classrooms. It keeps the question of "what works" alive. This is not a fixed standard, but a continuing conversation grounded in local knowledge, professional experience, and the evolving needs of students.

Practical Application: Using AI to Evaluate With Confidence

Teachers can bring research evaluation into their practice through three clear steps. These are not time-intensive. They are built to fit real-world teaching constraints while still offering depth.

Step 1: Interrogate Claims With Elicit

Go to elicit.org and ask a direct question, such as "Is this program effective for multilingual second graders?" Elicit returns a curated list of relevant studies, highlights the sources of funding, and summarizes each study's key limitations. As you review the results, watch for red flags such as small sample sizes, narrow participant demographics, or studies funded by publishers or curriculum developers. These details matter. They help educators assess whether the research is both credible and applicable to their unique classroom context (Pedró et al., 2019; Holmes et al., 2019).

Step 2: Explore Options With Scholarcy

Upload a key article or study at scholarcy.com. It will generate a summary and highlight other approaches, sample groups, and outcomes. You might see that one study used embedded phonics, while another used synthetic phonics with oral discussion. This helps you compare and consider options that might better fit your students (Zawacki-Richter et al., 2019; Luckin et al., 2016).

Step 3: Bring Insights Into Planning

Use what you have found not as a verdict, but as a guide. Jot down a note or highlight a passage to bring into a PLC or grade-level conversation. Ask: How can we adapt this to fit our students? What might we blend or scaffold? This turns evaluation into collaboration, supporting teacher-led adaptation rather than top-down implementation (Porayska-Pomsta, n.d.).

From Uncertainty to Understanding

Professional judgment expands when teachers are equipped with tools that help them ask sharper questions and compare evidence with care. Ms. Rivera's journey shows how AI can support, not dictate the process of deciding what fits, what to question, and where to adapt. She accepted the role of phonics in early reading but refined how she approached it, drawing on relevant and trustworthy evidence.

In that way, her story mirrors the broader promise of AI in education: not to streamline teachers into prescribed answers, but to support them in building research-informed, context-aware practices. By turning interrogation into insight, Ms. Rivera strengthens her voice and opens space for her students to thrive.

Challenge: Promoting Teacher Agency

Vignette 3: Ms. Chen's Challenge

Ms. Chen, a seasoned 11th-grade AP English teacher, has spent over a decade building a classroom where complex texts spark rich, student-driven dialogue. Her lesson plans reflect deep intentionality and every question, every discussion is rooted in the belief that language shapes thought and that high schoolers rise to meet intellectual rigor. So when her new principal, fresh from the elementary ranks, mandates word walls to boost vocabulary test scores, the mismatch is stark. For Ms. Chen, whose students parse metaphor and subtext with precision, the directive feels out of place, less about instruction, more about optics.

When she asks for the research behind the mandate, she gets vague references to "evidence-based practice," but no sources to explore. Curious but unconvinced, she begins her own search. Many articles are paywalled; others emphasize early literacy or come from vendors with promotional interests (Pedró et al., 2019). Her investigation reveals a stark disconnect: blanket policies fail to address the nuanced needs of advanced learners. Still, Ms. Chen is not looking to reject the mandate outright. She wants to offer something better, grounded in evidence and responsive to her students.

That evening, she remembers a tool a colleague once mentioned: Perplexity. Typing in "vocabulary strategies for high school AP English," she receives a concise overview with linked sources. Several studies mention the value of semantic engagement through discussion, using terms like "dialogic instruction," "Socratic seminar," and "generative vocabulary learning." These phrases resonate—she has seen firsthand how students refine their vocabulary not by memorizing words, but by debating texts and articulating complex ideas.

Wanting to go beyond summary, she turns to Elicit, typing: "Do Socratic seminars improve vocabulary in high school students?" Among the results is a comparative study showing that discussion-based instruction led to significantly higher vocabulary retention than passive strategies like word walls or rote copying, especially for students in honors and AP tracks (Holmes et al., 2019). Another paper notes that word walls may support recognition in early readers but lack the cognitive complexity needed for older students, often functioning as visual clutter rather than instructional tools (Facer & Selwyn, 2021). One study even maps vocabulary development through seminar transcripts, reinforcing her belief that dialogic spaces grow not only comprehension but lexical depth.

She triangulates her findings by asking Perplexity a new question: "Are word walls effective for high school students?" The tool delivers studies showing they are rarely used beyond primary grades and often disengage older learners, particularly when imposed without instructional integration. In contrast, strategies that require active, contextual use of vocabulary in speech or writing consistently outperform static display-based approaches (Luckin et al., 2016; Su & Xie, 2022). With this, her case crystallizes: Socratic seminars are not just a preference—they are a research-supported alternative.

Possibilities: Using AI to Challenge Without Confrontation

Ms. Chen's experience reflects a broader reality: many teachers are expected to comply with initiatives labeled as "research-based" without ever being invited into the conversation about what the research actually says or whether it applies to their students. Top-down mandates often sideline the very professionals best positioned to assess what is needed. In these moments, AI offers more than convenience. AI offers teachers the tools to turn passive compliance into active inquiry (National Education Association, 2024).

Two tools were key to Ms. Chen's process: Perplexity and Elicit. Perplexity is an AI-powered search engine that answers open-ended questions in clear language, citing its sources directly. This makes it ideal for quickly scanning the research landscape on a particular topic such as "vocabulary instruction for AP English students" and identifying key terms, trends, and high-quality references. For teachers without journal access or hours to sift through Google Scholar, Perplexity bridges the gap between curiosity and actionable starting points.

Elicit, on the other hand, is a research assistant built for deeper engagement. It retrieves academic papers in response to specific claims or queries and breaks them down by population studied, methods used, and conclusions drawn. Teachers can use it to test whether a strategy works for their students, spot contradictions across studies, or verify whether something marketed as "evidence-based" is actually supported by independent research. Together, these tools support what Biesta (2007) describes as a shift from "what works" to "what works for whom, in what context, and why."

As teachers interact with AI, posing questions, analyzing responses, and adapting instruction, the tools help facilitate decisions and how evidence is understood. These moments of external exploration become part of teachers' internal reasoning, supporting more reflective and situated practice (Vygotsky, 1978; Wertsch, 1991). Used critically, AI does not just help teachers use research. AI helps teachers challenge research when it is misapplied and adapt it when it holds promise (Kou & Gui, 2020). Rather than receiving mandates as fixed truths, teachers can use AI to develop interpretations grounded in professional expertise and contextual understanding (Campello de Souza et al., 2024).

Crucially, this is not about resisting change. It is about reclaiming the space to shape it. By pairing classroom insight with credible evidence, teachers like Ms. Chen are not just implementing best practices; they are co-authoring them. AI supports this process not by doing the thinking for teachers but by equipping them to think more strategically, skeptically, and confidently about the claims and policies that shape their classrooms (Porayska-Pomsta, n.d.).

Practical Application: Turning Evidence Into Advocacy

Artificial intelligence offers a powerful entry point for teachers who want to critically engage with mandates while staying rooted in professional integrity. By using AI tools strategically, educators can navigate policy demands without defaulting to compliance or resistance. Instead, they can lead with evidence.

Step 1: Scan the Landscape

Begin with a question that reflects the heart of your instructional challenge. In Ms. Chen's case, this was "What are effective vocabulary strategies for AP high school students?" Go to perplexity.ai and type in your question. As you review the results, take note of recurring strategies and terms that may not have surfaced in district PD, such as dialogic instruction or semantic engagement. Perplexity links to its sources, making it easier to trace where claims come from and follow up on unfamiliar ideas.

Step 2: Interrogate and Compare Evidence

Once you have identified a term or approach, for example Socratic seminar, use Elicit to investigate the strength and scope of supporting research. Teachers can ask, "Does this work for students like mine?" or "How does this compare to what I have been asked to do?" Elicit helps clarify which studies support or contradict a given claim, how generalizable the findings are, and what assumptions are built into each approach. As noted by Biesta (2007), this kind of interrogation helps move evidence from something handed down to something interpreted and applied with professional care.

Step 3: Frame Your Proposal With Confidence and Context

Armed with clear findings, you can bring your voice into the conversation. For example write a proposal to an administrator, share a reflection in a PLC, or a pilot lesson grounded in classroom-based adaptation. When teachers bring forward research that is responsive to their students and aligned with instructional goals, it becomes difficult to dismiss their perspective as anecdotal. In this way, AI supports the shift from classroom practitioner to evidence-informed advocate (Porayska-Pomsta, n.d.).

Step 4: Document Sources Used in Decision-Making

Keep a clear record of every study, article, or data point you consulted. Documenting your sources reinforces ethical professionalism and provides transparency when you present your case to colleagues and administrators. Make a file of the PDF's of articles and a hyerlinked bibliography to share and refer to when engaged in professional decision making.

From Compliance to Confidence

Professional agency deepens when teachers are equipped not just to access research, but to evaluate its relevance, interrogate its claims, and reshape mandates that miss the mark. AI tools like Perplexity and Elicit help teachers like Ms. Chen move beyond surface-level implementation, offering pathways to analyze, adapt, and advocate with precision. In her hands, research becomes a lever, not for resistance, but for thoughtful revision. By bringing evidence into conversation with experience, she reclaims the space to teach with integrity. Her story shows that when teachers are equipped to interrogate research, they do not just challenge mandates, they reshape them, aligning decisions with the students they know best.

Currents of Care: Ethics in the Circuit of Mediation

Not every tool is neutral. When teachers use AI to explore research, they are not just asking questions. They are entering systems built on choices. Algorithms reflect decisions about what counts as credible, what gets prioritized, and whose voices are amplified. Some of those decisions are transparent. Many are not. Using AI to delve into research is not just interaction with a machine. It is engagement with a network of assumptions. Ethics, in this space, is not abstract. It shapes how research is located, interpreted, and used.

AI can offer teachers access to studies they would not otherwise find. That access is powerful. But what is retrieved can lean toward dominant methods, familiar funders, or high-profile journals. Tools may surface vendor-backed studies while filtering out smaller, community-based research (Yang & Evans, 2022). If teachers are not aware, AI can quietly tilt the frame (Holmes et al., 2022).

Smooth output is not the same as sound advice. AI tools are designed to be fluent, but fluency can mask bias. A clear summary may still misrepresent the nuance of a study. Some tools confidently deliver answers to questions that deserve more uncertainty. For teachers, the challenge is not to reject AI but to remain the interpreter (Campello de Souza et al., 2024). The outputs do not replace critical thinking and a healthy skeptical approach to interpreting how the study is represented by the AI tool.

There is also the matter of access. AI has potential to close the research-practice gap, but educational institutions have vast differences in infrastructure. Not every teacher has current subscriptions to AI tools or time during the day to explore them. Training in AI use is sparse, and early adopters are often those who invest personal resources to experiment with new tools. Without equitable conditions, even the most powerful technology can widen divides. Ethical reflection means asking more than what a tool can do. It asks: who benefits, who is left out, and why are they left out (Pedró et al., 2019; Su & Xie, 2022).

Ethics lives in the small decisions. A teacher who rephrases a prompt to get multiple perspectives. A team that reviews sources before adapting a program. A moment of pause before sharing student work with a platform. These quiet acts keep professional responsibility at the center. AI can assist. It can expand what is possible. But it should never speak louder than the teacher's insight or drown out the needs of the students in front of them.

Ethical Use of AI for Research: A Teacher's Checklist

The following checklist offers a practical guide to using AI tools ethically in classroom-based research inquiry. It supports teachers in maintaining professional judgment, protecting student privacy, and asking critical questions throughout the research process.

Before You Begin

- **Clarify your purpose**: What am I hoping to learn or understand better?
- **Choose tools intentionally**: Am I using a reputable, transparent platform (e.g., Semantic Scholar, Elicit, Scholarcy, Perplexity)?
- **Check access and equity**: Do I have the time, tech access, and support needed to use this tool fairly and effectively?

While Using AI

- **Read critically, not passively**: Does this output reflect multiple perspectives, or is it narrow in scope?

- **Trace the sources**: Can I identify where the information came from? Who funded or conducted the study?
- **Ask about what's missing**: Whose voices or contexts might be underrepresented here?
- **Check for fluency vs. accuracy**: Does the summary simplify too much? Is it masking nuance or complexity?
- **Protect privacy**: Am I avoiding the use of student names, identifying information, or sensitive classroom data?

After Reviewing AI-Generated Research

- **Cross-check findings**: Have I compared this with other sources or my own professional experience?
- **Discuss with colleagues**: Have I shared or reflected on this insight with others before applying it?
- **Adapt, don't adopt**: How will I tailor this research to fit my students, my context, and my values?
- **Document the process**: Am I keeping track of how I used AI in inquiry to support transparency and reflection?

This checklist is not exhaustive. But it offers a starting point—a way to center care, responsibility, and professionalism in every AI-supported inquiry.

Staying Current: Tools Will Evolve

Artificial intelligence (AI) tools are changing fast. By the time this chapter is published, some may look different or be gone entirely. New platforms will appear. Features will shift. But the core practices, locating, questioning, and adapting research, remain the same. These are habits, not software.

To stay current, follow sources like the American Educational Research Association (AERA) Learning Sciences Special Interest Group (SIG), Education Week's EdSurge, or the International Society for Technology in Education (ISTE) newsletter on AI in education. Join educator networks on Substack or LinkedIn. Set a calendar reminder to revisit your go-to tools each semester. Most of all, stay critical: ask what the tool shows, what it hides, and who it serves. AI will keep evolving. So should we.

Closing: From Access to Empowerment

This chapter has explored the potential of AI as a transformative partner in the professional lives of teachers. By moving beyond passive consumption of research toward active engagement, educators reclaim agency in their instructional decisions. As illustrated in Table 1, *Overview of AI Research Processes*, each vignette, Mr. Patel's journey to locate meaningful research, Ms. Rivera's thoughtful interrogation of program mandates, and Ms. Chen's strategic challenge of instructional policies demonstrates how AI mediates professional practice. AI tools scaffold access, deepen inquiry, and sharpen advocacy, aligning clearly with Vygotsky's cultural-historical perspective on mediated cognition.

However, the integration of AI in teaching practice also necessitates careful ethical consideration. As detailed in the ethical column of the chart, responsible use includes critically tracing sources, checking for biases, ensuring equitable access, and fostering professional dialogue. Ethical engagement underscores that AI is not a replacement for teachers' judgment but a complement, amplifying their ability to act with integrity and responsiveness.

Table 1. Overview of AI Research Processes

Step	Teacher	Context	Challenge	AI Tools	Mediation (Theory in Practice)	Ethical Considerations	Outcome
Locate	Mr. Patel	Rural middle school	Engaging readers	Semantic Scholar, ChatGPT	Scaffolded access; translated research into practice, teacher-led adaptation	Ensured equity of access; clarified purpose	Student-led book clubs
Interrogate	Ms. Rivera	Urban multilingual classroom	Evaluating mandated phonics	Elicit, Scholarcy	Supported critical analysis; surfaced biases and alternatives	Traced sources; critically examined AI summaries; ethical questioning	Flexible phonics strategies
Challenge	Ms. Chen	Suburban AP English	Challenging vocabulary mandate	Perplexity, Elicit	Enabled evidence-based advocacy; clarified contradictions	Cross-checked findings; promoted collegial dialogue	Socratic seminar strategy

Note. Table presents illustrative examples of how AI supports mediation of teacher research practices when used ethically and critically.

REFERENCES

Allington, R. L. (2002). *What really matters for struggling readers: Designing research-based programs*. Allyn & Bacon.

Baker, R. S. J. d., & Siemens, G. (2022). Educational data mining and learning analytics. In Spector, J. M. (Eds.), *Handbook of research on educational communications and technology* (5th ed.). Springer., DOI: 10.1007/978-3-030-23206-8

Biesta, G. (2007). Why "what works" won't work: Evidence-based practice and the democratic deficit in educational research. *Educational Theory*, *57*(1), 1–22. DOI: 10.1111/j.1741-5446.2006.00241.x

Campello de Souza, F. C., Rangel, I. A., & Batista, R. C. (2024). The generative AI revolution and sophotechnic mediation. *AI & Society*. Advance online publication. DOI: 10.1007/s00146-023-01833-3

Chen, L., Chen, P., & Lin, Z. (2020). Artificial intelligence in education: A review. *IEEE Access : Practical Innovations, Open Solutions*, *8*, 75264–75278. DOI: 10.1109/ACCESS.2020.2988510

Christou, P. A. (2023). The use of artificial intelligence (AI) in qualitative research for theory development. *The Qualitative Report*, *28*(9), 2739–2755. DOI: 10.46743/2160-3715/2023.6536

Cochran-Smith, M., & Lytle, S. L. (2009). *Inquiry as stance: Practitioner research for the next generation*. Teachers College Press.

Daniels, H. (2001). *Vygotsky and pedagogy*. Routledge.

Darling-Hammond, L. (2000). Teacher quality and student achievement: A review of state policy evidence. *Education Policy Analysis Archives*, *8*(1), 1. Advance online publication. DOI: 10.14507/epaa.v8n1.2000

Facer, K., & Selwyn, N. (2021). Digital technology and the futures of education—Towards 'non-stupid' optimism. *Educational Research*, *63*(2), 130–141. DOI: 10.1080/00131881.2021.1907327

Holmes, W., Bialik, M., & Fadel, C. (2019). *Artificial intelligence in education: Promises and implications for teaching and learning*. Center for Curriculum Redesign.

Holmes, W., Porayska-Pomsta, K., Holstein, K., Sutherland, E., & Baker, R. S. (2022). The promises and challenges of artificial intelligence for education: A critical review. *Learning, Media and Technology*, *47*(1), 1–20.

Luckin, R., & Cukurova, M. (2019). Designing educational technologies in the age of AI: A learning sciences-driven approach. *British Journal of Educational Technology*, *50*(6), 2824–2838. DOI: 10.1111/bjet.12861

Luckin, R., Holmes, W., Griffiths, M., & Forcier, L. B. (2016). *Intelligence unleashed: An argument for AI in education.* Pearson.

National Education Association. (2024). *The role of artificial intelligence in professional learning.* [White paper]. National Education Association.

National Reading Panel. (2000). *Teaching children to read: An evidence-based assessment of the scientific research literature on reading and its implications for reading instruction.* National Institute of Child Health and Human Development.

Pearson, P. D. (2004). The reading wars. *Educational Policy*, *18*(1), 216–252. DOI: 10.1177/0895904803260041

Pedró, F., Subosa, M., Rivas, A., & Valverde, P. (2019). *Artificial intelligence in education: Challenges and opportunities for sustainable development.* UNESCO. https://unesdoc.unesco.org/ark:/48223/pf0000366994

Peña, E. V., & James, A. L. (2024). Transmediating with AI: Literacies, design, and justice in teacher learning. *Learning, Media and Technology.*

Su, L., & Xie, Y. (2022). Artificial intelligence applications in teacher education: A systematic review. *Journal of Research on Technology in Education.* Advance online publication. DOI: 10.1080/15391523.2022.2078694

Vygotsky, L. S. (1978). *Mind in society: The development of higher psychological processes* (Cole, M., John-Steiner, V., Scribner, S., & Souberman, E., Eds.). Harvard University Press.

Vygotsky, L. S. (1986). *Thought and language* (Kozulin, A., Trans.). MIT Press.

Wertsch, J. V. (1991). *Voices of the mind: A sociocultural approach to mediated action.* Harvard University Press.

Yang, S., & Evans, M. A. (2022). AI-supported personalized learning: A conceptual framework. *Educational Technology Research and Development*, *70*(1), 5–28. DOI: 10.1007/s11423-022-10039-3

Zawacki-Richter, O., Marín, V. I., Bond, M., & Gouverneur, F. (2019). Systematic review of research on artificial intelligence applications in higher education: Emerging trends and research agenda. *International Journal of Educational Technology in Higher Education*, *16*(39). Advance online publication. DOI: 10.1186/s41239-019-0171-0

Chapter 2
AI in Action:
Practical Insights and Strategies for Educators

Christina Salazar
https://orcid.org/0009-0003-0596-5338
University of North Texas, Dallas, USA

ABSTRACT

As AI tools enter educational spaces, educators face questions about how to integrate them responsibly, ethically, and with pedagogical integrity. This chapter offers a practice-based exploration of AI use in teacher education, grounded in Critical Digital Pedagogy (CDP). Drawing on the author's experiences as an early-career lecturer at an urban university, the chapter presents illustrative cases that showcase AI in lesson planning, assignment design, student engagement, and ethical dilemmas. It includes critical reflection on how outputs were adapted or reimagined to support humanizing teaching. Broader implications for K–12 and post-secondary educators are addressed, including strategies for designing assignments that resist mechanization, fostering critical AI literacy among students, and navigating emerging concerns around authorship. Rather than offering prescriptive solutions, the chapter invites educators to engage with AI critically and creatively.

INTRODUCTION: THE PROMISE AND PROBLEM OF AI IN EDUCATION

The emergence of artificial intelligence (AI) tools in education has created a wave of excitement, apprehension, and experimentation. Across K–12 and post-secondary contexts, educators are increasingly encountering AI-generated content in student submissions, exploring AI tools for lesson planning, and grappling with

DOI: 10.4018/979-8-3373-1122-7.ch002

new ethical questions around authorship, learning, and assessment. The promise of AI is compelling: automation of repetitive tasks, rapid access to instructional materials, and new ways to differentiate instruction. Yet this same promise raises profound pedagogical and ethical challenges. If not approached critically, AI can flatten the complex, relational, and equity-oriented nature of education into something mechanical, generic, and depersonalized.

As an early-career teacher educator navigating this landscape in real time, I have found myself both drawn to and wary of AI's growing presence in my instructional planning and classroom practices. I have witnessed firsthand how AI can serve as a catalyst for innovation—generating ideas, modeling language, or saving time on routine tasks. But I have also seen how quickly it can obscure the nuance of student thinking, reinforce deficit perspectives, or erode the meaningful struggle and reflection that are essential to deep learning. The tension is not merely about whether to use AI or not, but how we use it, and more importantly, how we position ourselves in relation to it as educators committed to equity and humanization.

This chapter is written in response to that tension. Its purpose is to offer grounded, practice-based insights into the integration of AI tools in the early stages of a teaching career—insights that are both practical and critically reflective. Rather than providing a checklist of dos and don'ts, I aim to open up the complexities of working with AI in educational spaces. Through a series of illustrative cases drawn from my own teaching in a teacher preparation program, I demonstrate how AI tools can be engaged, resisted, repurposed, and transformed through a critical pedagogical lens. I write not from a position of mastery, but from one of inquiry, experimentation, and reflection.

At the heart of this chapter is the framework of Critical Digital Pedagogy (CDP), which asserts that digital tools are never neutral and that teaching with technology must be rooted in care, context, and justice. CDP encourages us to ask: *Whose knowledge is privileged by AI? Whose labor is made invisible? What forms of thinking are promoted, and which are sidelined?* These questions have guided my exploration and shaped my responses when AI outputs failed to meet the needs of my students or challenged the pedagogical commitments I hold. Throughout the chapter, I examine not just how I used AI, but why I revised it, resisted it, or reimagined it—anchoring my practice in theory and reflection.

This chapter is particularly relevant for educators who are navigating similar crossroads. While my context is post-secondary teacher education, the questions I raise and the strategies I share resonate with the realities of K–12 classrooms as well. Teachers at all levels are facing new pressures to adapt to technologies that are evolving faster than our pedagogical frameworks can catch up. Many educators are encountering a paradox: on the one hand, school systems are pushing for "innovation," often in the form of new technologies; on the other hand, the same systems offer little support for ethical reflection, critical engagement, or long-term planning. This chapter seeks to bridge that gap—not by prescribing a model, but by offering a narrative that invites dialogue, uncertainty, and purposeful experimentation.

In the sections that follow, I begin by outlining the theoretical foundation of Critical Digital Pedagogy and its relevance to AI in education. I then present a detailed account of my own classroom practices, organized into three parts: contextual background, implementation strategies, and illustrative cases. The cases serve as focal points for reflection, each one showcasing a different way I used AI in my work as an early lecturer—ranging from lesson planning to ethical case analysis, from crafting AI-resistant prompts to fostering deeper forms of student thinking. After each case, I include a critical reflection that examines the affordances and limitations of the AI integration and considers what was gained, lost, or transformed in the process.

These cases are not meant to showcase "best practices," but rather *lived tensions*—moments when AI seemed useful but incomplete, efficient but misaligned with the deeper goals of education. In some cases, AI helped me jumpstart planning or surface ideas I hadn't considered. In others, it exposed underlying assumptions in educational discourse that I would have otherwise overlooked. And in many, I had to revise, reject, or reframe the AI output in order to stay true to my students' needs and the values I bring into the classroom. These experiences affirmed the importance of teacher agency, reflective practice, and the capacity to use technology not just *critically*, but *creatively* and *ethically*.

Ultimately, this chapter is a call for intentionality. As educators, we cannot afford to adopt AI passively or allow it to shape our practice without scrutiny. Nor can we ignore its presence or potential. Instead, we must learn to work with AI in ways that center human relationships, affirm student agency, and resist the narrowing of education into predictable, machine-readable formats. The work of teaching—particularly in the service of equity and transformation—is irreducible. It involves navigating contradictions, building trust, and attending to the lived realities of learners in all their complexity. If AI is to have a place in that work, it must be held accountable to these values.

In that spirit, I offer this chapter not as a roadmap, but as a reflection on the road I've taken so far. My hope is that it will resonate with other educators who are experimenting, questioning, and striving to do justice to their students in an era shaped increasingly by automation. By situating AI integration within a critical pedagogical framework, and grounding it in the everyday realities of teaching, I hope to contribute to a broader conversation about how we can navigate this moment with care, clarity, and conviction.

THEORETICAL FRAMEWORK: CRITICAL DIGITAL PEDAGOGY

As artificial intelligence becomes increasingly entangled in educational practices—from grading tools and lesson generators to predictive analytics and tutoring bots—the question is no longer whether AI will be used in classrooms, but *how* it will be used and *to what ends*. Entering this conversation without a theoretical compass risks normalizing uncritical and extractive uses of AI that reinforce harmful ideologies under the guise of "efficiency" and "innovation." For this reason, my approach to AI in education is rooted in Critical Digital Pedagogy (CDP)—a framework that calls us to interrogate the power, politics, and possibilities of digital tools in teaching and learning.

At its core, Critical Digital Pedagogy is concerned with the human, relational, and justice-oriented dimensions of education in the digital age. Grounded in critical pedagogy traditions (Freire, 2005; Giroux, 1994; hooks, 1996) and extended through digital scholarship (Bali, 2014; Stommel & Morris, 2018), CDP positions technology not as a neutral tool but as a product of social, cultural, and ideological forces. It challenges the assumption that digital technologies—especially those shaped by commercial and algorithmic logics—can be simply "plugged in" to classrooms without consequence. Instead, CDP insists that technology use in education must be intentional, reflective, and contextually grounded.

One of the foundational insights of CDP is that technology is never neutral (Lankshear & Knobel, 2015; Selwyn, 2010). Every algorithm is written by someone, for some purpose, and embedded with assumptions about what counts as knowledge, intelligence, success, or appropriate behavior. When we use AI to generate lesson plans, evaluate writing, or create classroom materials, we are not simply outsourcing a task—we are invoking systems trained on vast datasets that reflect dominant cultural norms and structural inequalities. For example, an AI-generated lesson plan may privilege Western-centric examples, assume a standard English register, or rely on narrow behaviorist models of learning. Without a critical lens, such outputs can go unchallenged, subtly shaping educational practices in ways that marginalize students and flatten the diversity of human experience.

This is why teacher agency is a central concept in my approach to AI integration. Rather than positioning AI as a substitute for teacher expertise, I see it as a starting point for inquiry—a spark that can be examined, revised, or rejected based on pedagogical intent and student needs. Critical Digital Pedagogy reminds us that educators are not passive implementers of technology but active meaning-makers who bring context, care, and ethical judgment to their work (Aguilera & Salazar, 2023; Stommel, 2014). The goal is not to eliminate AI from the classroom, but to ensure that its use is always filtered through a lens of professional judgment and social responsibility.

For me, this commitment plays out through a pedagogy that is deeply humanizing. Drawing on the work of scholars like Paulo Freire (2005), bell hooks (1996), and del Carmen Salazar (2013) humanizing pedagogy affirms the full humanity of both students and teachers. It prioritizes relationships, dialogue, cultural responsiveness, and the co-construction of knowledge. In contrast to the extractive and depersonalized logic of many AI systems—which may serve to reduce learners to data points or consumers of content—a humanizing pedagogy views education as a space for connection, transformation, and critical consciousness.

When I engage with AI tools as a teacher educator, I ask: *Does this promote authentic engagement? Does it affirm my students' identities and lived experiences? Does it encourage critical thinking, reflection, or dialogue?* These questions help me distinguish between uses of AI that serve humanizing ends and those that undermine them. For instance, I may use AI to brainstorm example questions for a reading discussion, but I will revise those questions to reflect the cultural contexts of my students, to provoke ethical reflection, or to challenge dominant narratives. Likewise, I may invite students to experiment with AI-generated writing, but then ask them to critique the assumptions behind the language or the values embedded in the feedback.

CDP also foregrounds critical literacy in digital contexts. It urges us to teach students not just *how* to use technology, but *how to read it*—to interrogate its purposes, its histories, and its impacts. This aligns with my goal of helping future teachers become not just skilled technicians, but thoughtful, equity-minded practitioners. In my courses, this often means making AI a subject of inquiry, not just a tool. We examine AI-generated educational content, discuss issues of algorithmic bias, and reflect on the ethical dilemmas posed by machine-mediated decision-making. In doing so, students come to see technology not as an unquestionable authority, but as something they can critique, reshape, and use in service of their values.

Another important tenet of CDP is its resistance to standardization (Aguilera & Salazar, 2023; Stommel, 2014). Much of the educational technology landscape, including AI, is built on assumptions of scalability, efficiency, and uniformity—qualities that often conflict with culturally sustaining pedagogy or trauma-informed practice. AI tools tend to produce "clean," decontextualized outputs, optimized for generic classroom scenarios. What assumptions are made about the composition of a "generic classroom"? Real classrooms are messy. Real classrooms are diverse and unpredictable. They are full of contradiction, joy, resistance, and improvisation. In these spaces, standardization can be not only ineffective but actively harmful, erasing student difference in the name of efficiency.

To resist this, my use of AI is mediated by contextual awareness. For example, when designing assignments, I ask whether AI would be able to complete the task. If the answer is yes, I revise the prompt to require elements of lived experience, moral reasoning, or collaborative creation—dimensions that resist algorithmic replication. This does not mean my assignments are "AI-proof" in a punitive sense, but that they invite a kind of thinking that is fundamentally relational, situated, and embodied. In this way, CDP helps me shift the focus from preventing AI use to cultivating the kinds of learning that AI cannot easily simulate.

Finally, Critical Digital Pedagogy offers a stance of ongoing reflection and revision (Aguilera & Salazar, 2023; Stommel, 2014). It acknowledges that educators are always navigating evolving tools, shifting policies, and competing priorities. There is no final or "correct" way to use AI in the classroom. Instead, there is an ethic of attentiveness—a willingness to pause, question, adapt, and reimagine. As an early-career educator, I have found this orientation both liberating and grounding. It has given me permission to try new approaches, to learn from mistakes, and to remain critically aware of the power dynamics at play in any technological integration.

In this chapter, CDP is not just a theoretical backdrop—it is the lens through which examples are filtered, decisions are made, and reflections are written. Therefore, I here share not just the outcomes of my work with AI, but the uncertainties, missteps, and revisions that shaped those outcomes. It is what prompts me to ask not only *what works*, but *for whom*, *under what conditions*, and *at what cost*.

In the next section, I move from theory to practice, offering a narrative of my AI integration as an early-career lecturer. Through contextual grounding, implementation strategies, and illustrative cases, I demonstrate what it means to teach *with* AI without teaching *through* it—and how to ensure that even as we innovate, we do not abdicate our responsibility to teach with humanity, care, and critical awareness.

CONTEXTUAL BACKGROUND

To understand the nuances of how I integrated AI into my teaching, it is important to first situate my practice. I write from the position of an early-career lecturer in a teacher preparation program at a public urban university. My role includes designing and teaching foundational education courses for undergraduate students—many of whom are preparing for careers in K–12 education. The university serves a diverse student population, including many first-generation college students, working adults, multilingual learners, and students of color. These future educators bring rich lived experiences, cultural knowledge, and varied academic preparation into the classroom. This diversity is a strength and informs all aspects of my pedagogy, particularly my commitment to culturally responsive, humanizing education.

As an early-career faculty member, I teach across multiple formats—including face-to-face, synchronous Zoom, and asynchronous online courses. This variety has shaped my pedagogical choices and highlighted the different affordances and constraints of each modality. For example, in-person courses lend themselves to spontaneous dialogue and relational engagement, while online courses often demand more structured planning and intentional scaffolding to maintain student presence and connection. In all cases, my teaching centers on supporting students to become critically reflective and equity-oriented educators—goals that are not easily standardized or automated.

In this context, AI tools offered both support and provocation. Like many early-career lecturers, I juggle heavy course loads, limited preparation time, and evolving institutional expectations. AI platforms like ChatGPT—and others marketed toward educators—seemed to promise efficiency: quickly generated lesson ideas, rubrics, activities, and feedback. Initially, I turned to these tools to streamline lesson planning, differentiate instruction, and create engagement strategies. However, I quickly found that the outputs, while often technically correct and structurally sound, lacked nuance. They frequently missed the mark in terms of cultural responsiveness, criticality, or developmental appropriateness. More concerningly, some reinforced deficit views of students or assumed universal norms that erased the particularities of the urban classrooms my students were preparing to teach in.

During the time period covered in this chapter, I explored AI across three primary teaching functions:

1. **Instructional Planning**: I used AI to generate drafts of lesson plans, formative assessments, scaffolding strategies, and example activities. These outputs served as early-stage planning aids that I would then revise through a critical lens.
2. **Student Engagement**: I experimented with AI-generated discussion prompts, scenarios, and examples as tools for classroom critique, modeling, or revision. I was particularly interested in engaging students in metacognitive conversations about the role and limits of technology in education.
3. **Assessment Support**: I explored the use of AI to model feedback, self-assessment rubrics, and exemplar student work to guide formative assessment. Again, these tools were used as conversation starters or scaffolds—not as replacements for authentic evaluation.

Throughout, I treated AI as a suggestive—not authoritative—partner. Its contributions required close reading, revision, and often significant reworking to align with the needs of my students and the communities they would go on to serve. My process became iterative: generate, analyze, revise, implement, and reflect. I often found that the most productive uses of AI were not in replacing my work, but in *revealing the assumptions behind it*—especially when AI outputs surfaced dominant educational norms that conflicted with the realities of teaching in diverse urban classrooms.

This recursive process was grounded in the framework of Critical Digital Pedagogy (CDP). CDP guided me to think beyond convenience and efficiency, pressing me to ask whether AI-supported decisions advanced humanizing, inclusive, and critically conscious teaching. It also provided language and tools to help my students—aspiring educators themselves—consider the ethical, relational, and political dimensions of integrating technology into learning spaces.

The illustrative cases that follow emerged from this real-world, ethically charged environment. They reflect both the potential and the pitfalls of integrating AI in teaching. They show how, in an urban university setting where the stakes of education are deeply tied to equity and access, even promising tools must be reshaped with care and critique. My goal in sharing them is not to prescribe a model, but to offer a window into the decisions, missteps, and revisions that defined my journey—and to invite others into a similar process of critical engagement.

Implementation Strategies

My approach to integrating AI into teaching has been grounded in reflection, revision, and criticality, as opposed to automation for its own sake. In this section, I outline the specific instructional moves I made during the planning and implementation stages of my courses. These strategies were shaped by real-time decision-making and filtered through the theoretical lens of Critical Digital Pedagogy (CDP), always with a focus on keeping human relationships, ethical reflection, and contextual relevance at the center of my practice.

Planning Stage

As a new faculty member with multiple course preparations and limited resources, I initially turned to AI as a time-saving tool. In particular, I used ChatGPT and similar platforms to generate baseline lesson plans, content explanations, assignment ideas, and student examples. This application was especially beneficial in asynchronous online courses, where I needed to provide extensive written guidance to maintain student presence and engagement. However, I quickly learned that AI-generated suggestions, though technically complete and structurally logical, often failed to meet the deeper needs of my students or the goals of my course.

To address this, I developed a recursive workflow in my planning process:

1. **Prompting with Purpose**: I used very specific, detailed prompts to generate initial materials from AI. For instance, I might ask, "Generate three culturally responsive discussion questions for pre-service teachers about asset-based in-

struction in urban elementary schools." The more I contextualized the prompt, the more useful the results.

2. **Critical Vetting**: I reviewed all AI-generated outputs for alignment with my values and pedagogical commitments. This involved examining:
   - **Cultural Relevance**: Did the content assume a dominant cultural norm? Did it reflect the linguistic, racial, or socioeconomic realities of my students or the communities they would teach in? Were stereotypes present in responses?
   - **Developmental Appropriateness**: Based on my knowledge of and relationship with my students, was the material tailored to the cognitive and emotional readiness of undergraduate students?
   - **Depth of Thinking**: Did the AI output support critical analysis, or merely surface-level understanding?
3. **Theoretical Revision**: I used knowledge from critical, constructivist, and humanizing pedagogies to revise AI-generated materials. For example, I might replace a behaviorist framing of classroom management with one that emphasized relational accountability and restorative practice.
4. **Student-Centered Design**: Finally, I revised activities to emphasize student voice, collaboration, and authentic connection. When possible, I designed prompts and tasks that AI could not replicate—those requiring personal reflection, community-based inquiry, or ethical decision-making.

This process often took as long as creating materials myself from scratch, especially at first. But over time, it trained me to see AI not as a shortcut, but as a tool for revealing assumptions embedded in "neutral" content; a site for which, through prompting AI, I clarified my own pedagogical intent. The revision process itself became a site of reflection, professional growth, and critical insight.

Instruction Stage

While my primary engagement with AI occurred during the planning phase, I also integrated AI into my instructional practice—particularly to model critique, facilitate dialogue, and adapt to emergent classroom needs.

1. **AI as a Supplement, Not a Replacement**: I used AI to generate examples of student responses or to provide initial definitions of complex terms, but always as a launching point for discussion. For instance, in a class on culturally responsive teaching, I displayed an AI-generated response to a case study and invited students to identify what was missing or problematic. These conversa-

tions surfaced issues of tone, deficit framing, and the invisibility of structural factors—teachable moments that deepened students' critical awareness.

2. **Collaborative Engagement with AI**: In several class sessions, I invited students to co-engage with AI. We examined AI-generated lesson plans or feedback statements and asked: *Who is this written for? What assumptions does it make? How would you change it for your own students?* These activities fostered a metacognitive stance toward technology use—aligning with CDP's emphasis on student agency and critical literacy.
3. **Real-Time Adaptation**: In moments when students expressed confusion or requested clarification, I occasionally used AI in real time to rephrase a concept, generate a different example, or provide a contrasting perspective. However, I always framed this as a *starting point*, and we discussed its usefulness and limitations together. For example, if students were struggling with the concept of "funds of knowledge," I might ask AI to define it, then invite students to critique whether the definition honored the concept's origins and intent.
4. **Multimodal Access and Equity**: In online and hybrid settings, I used AI to create supplementary materials—summaries, translations, and outlines—that helped students with varied languages or learning preferences. I treated these materials as scaffolds, not replacements for class dialogue or reflective practice.

Through all of these practices, I worked to maintain a balance between innovation and integrity. I did not view AI as a panacea or as inherently harmful; rather, I saw it as a powerful, if flawed, tool, one that could support pedagogical goals when used critically, and undermine them when used carelessly. The key was *intentionality*: continually asking what I was trying to teach, whom I was trying to serve, and what kind of thinking I wanted to cultivate.

The strategies outlined above laid the groundwork for the more detailed case studies that follow. Each case represents a moment when I used AI in my teaching, reflected on its impact, and made choices aligned with a humanizing, justice-oriented pedagogy. Together, they form a portrait of what it means to teach with AI not as a neutral assistant, but as a contested and revealing presence—one that demands our most thoughtful, ethical, and imaginative responses.

ILLUSTRATIVE CASES OF AI USE AND CRITICAL REFLECTION

Case 1: Enhancing Lesson Planning

Initial AI Contribution:

In one of my first attempts to use AI in lesson planning, I prompted a generative AI tool to develop a lesson on differentiated instruction for a group of undergraduate pre-service teachers. The AI provided a clean, structured plan that included a definition, a lecture outline, and three example activities. At first glance, it seemed helpful—comprehensive and organized. However, as I reviewed the activities, I noticed a disconnect. The examples were generic, relied heavily on traditional models (e.g., visual vs. auditory learners), and did not reflect current theories or the specific backgrounds and strengths of my students.

Critical Intervention:

I began revising the lesson through the lens of humanizing pedagogy and culturally responsive teaching. First, I removed the rigid "learning styles" language and instead emphasized flexible grouping and multiple means of representation, grounded in Universal Design for Learning (UDL). I replaced the AI's prepackaged examples with scenarios that asked students to draw from their own experiences, consider the sociocultural assets their future students bring, and anticipate how differentiated strategies might be shaped by language, identity, and community.

One change involved reworking an AI-suggested role-play activity. Rather than having students "act out" differentiation styles, something many students felt uncomfortable with, I guided them through a collaborative case study where they analyzed how a teacher adapted instruction for multilingual learners in an urban elementary classroom. This shift honored the realities of the teaching contexts we were preparing for and made space for deeper, reflective thinking.

Outcome:

The revised lesson resulted in strong engagement and critical conversation. Students not only grasped the mechanics of differentiated instruction but also connected it to their values and positionalities. Rather than presenting differentiation as a checklist, the restructured lesson shifted differentiation to a relational and responsive practice.

Reflection:

This case reaffirmed that while AI can be a useful brainstorming tool, its suggestions must be critically revised to reflect pedagogical commitments and local contexts. Through a CDP lens, lesson planning becomes not a product to be optimized, but a practice of care, creativity, and resistance to one-size-fits-all solutions.

Case 2: Navigating Ethical Challenges

Initial AI Contribution:

While preparing a classroom activity on ethical dilemmas in education, I asked a generative AI tool to create a few short case studies for students to analyze and discuss. One of the AI-generated scenarios featured a teacher disciplining a student for "aggressive behavior" without acknowledging any sociocultural or contextual factors. The language used—phrases like "the student is disruptive and needs to be managed"—relied on deficit-based assumptions and framed the child as the problem. The scenario was superficially plausible, but deeply problematic. Furthermore, a few of the case studies appeared to reflect racial stereotypes in the names of example students and their example situations.

Critical Intervention:

Rather than discard the case entirely, I decided to use it as a pedagogical moment. I brought the AI-generated version into class and asked students to read it critically: What was being said? What was not? Whose perspective was centered? How might this story change if we learned more about the student's background, home life, or experiences in school?

We then collaboratively rewrote the scenario. Students reimagined the teacher as someone who paused before reacting, asked questions about the student's needs, and reflected on how systemic pressures and cultural misunderstandings might be shaping classroom dynamics. This new version still contained a dilemma but framed it in a way that called for empathy, inquiry, and self-awareness.

Outcome:

Students were visibly more engaged in this activity than in past ethics discussions. The process of critiquing and rewriting helped them not only unpack their own assumptions but also recognize how language can subtly reinforce power structures. Several students expressed surprise at how easily AI reproduced dominant, punitive frames, even in something as brief as a case study. They walked away with a stronger understanding of both educational ethics and the importance of critically evaluating the framing of technology and neutrality.

Reflection:

This experience highlighted a key risk of using AI in educational planning: the replication of biased norms under a veneer of neutrality. Through a Critical Digital Pedagogy lens, it also became an opportunity. By inviting students into the revision process, I modeled ethical vigilance and collective meaning-making. Technology did not define the conversation—it became the occasion for it.

Case 3: Focus on Desired Learning Outcomes

Initial AI Contribution:

Like many educators navigating the rapid integration of AI into student work, I began to observe a growing pattern: students increasingly turned to generative tools to complete assignments that were originally designed to develop their thinking. This shift became especially evident in open-ended written tasks—reflection papers, teaching philosophy drafts, or scenario responses—where some students relied so heavily on AI-generated responses that the work lost its personal voice, specificity, and formative value.

In response, I decided to test whether certain assignments I had designed could be easily completed by AI. In many cases, the answer was yes. The AI could generate generalized but plausible responses that matched the surface structure of what I asked for—though without depth, context, or insight. I realized that the issue was not just student reliance, but assignment design: I needed to rethink *what kind of thinking* my assignments were asking students to do and how I was creating space to assess it.

Critical Intervention:

I shifted my approach to foreground the learning outcome, not just the task. I redesigned assignments to require *in-class*, real-time thinking or personal connections that AI could not meaningfully replicate. For instance, I replaced some longer take-home reflection papers with short, handwritten exit tickets at the end of class, asking students to respond to prompts like, "What concept today challenged your thinking, and why?" In Zoom-based courses, I emphasized collaborative discussions. In asynchronous courses, I assigned reflective prompts that asked students to connect course content to their own experiences, beliefs, or classroom observations.

Outcome:

This shift led to more authentic engagement and a better understanding of where students actually were in their learning. Because I was gathering insight in real time, on paper, in conversation, or through voice, it became easier to scaffold support, adjust instruction, and track growth. Students demonstrated more ownership of their ideas, and the work felt more grounded in our shared classroom context.

Reflection:

This case reminded me that learning is not in the completion of tasks, but in the process of thinking. AI can mimic outputs, but it cannot replicate the messy, relational, often unfinished work of human learning. A CDP-informed pedagogy pushes us to prioritize learning outcomes and re-center classroom practice as a site of ongoing presence, participation, and formative feedback.

Case 4: Redesigning a Traditional Essay Prompt

Initial AI Contribution:

In my Educational Psychology course, I assigned a paper in which students selected a contemporary educational issue—such as standardized testing, behavior management, or technology use—and analyzed it using course theories. The original prompt asked students to "Choose an educational issue and explain its relevance using theories of learning and development discussed in class." Curious about the extent to which this assignment could be completed using AI, I entered the prompt into ChatGPT. Within seconds, the tool produced a competent, well-organized essay with basic references to Piaget, Vygotsky, and behaviorism. However, it lacked specificity, context, and any sense of the writer's voice or reflection. It became clear that while the structure was sound, the assignment could be completed without meaningful engagement or deep understanding.

Critical Intervention:

Rather than eliminate the assignment, I redesigned it to foreground two goals: (1) cultivate students' ability to synthesize research-based ideas, and (2) require writing that reflects personal experience and judgment. The revised prompt asked students to: *"Choose an educational issue that you have personally observed or experienced (as a student, family member, or future teacher). Analyze it using at least two theories from Educational Psychology, and reflect on how this understanding will inform your future teaching."*

Crucially, I did not leave students to navigate this task alone. I devoted class time to explicitly teaching synthesis: how to pull together findings from different readings, recognize tensions or alignments between theories, and apply them to real-world issues. We practiced these skills in class through a low-stakes formative assessment where students identified a key issue, outlined their theoretical connections, and received feedback—on paper, by hand. This ensured that, even if students later used AI to assist with drafting, they had engaged in the core intellectual work of the assignment with me, in real time.

Outcome:

The final submissions were more specific, thoughtful, and personally invested than previous iterations of the assignment. Students demonstrated stronger conceptual understanding and a more nuanced ability to apply theory to practice. Because I had already observed their synthesis work in class, I was able to trace continuity between their formative thinking and their final papers.

Reflection:

This case clarified that meaningful learning doesn't happen in the final product—it happens in the process. By centering in-class synthesis, scaffolding reflective writing, and requiring contextual application, I created a task that supported deeper thinking—regardless of whether students consulted AI in the drafting stage. From a Critical Digital Pedagogy perspective, this approach honors learning as relational, contextual, and iterative. It doesn't block AI, but it makes AI irrelevant to the most important parts of the work.

Case 5: Designing "Impossible-to-AI" Prompts

Initial AI Contribution:

As I continued refining my assignments in the context of rising AI usage, I began stress-testing them regularly: I would input prompts into AI platforms like ChatGPT to see what kind of responses were generated. What I discovered was unsettling. Even when prompts were detailed or grounded in course readings, AI could often produce technically correct but shallow responses—especially if the task asked for summary, analysis, or explanation without anchoring those skills in context or experience. I realized that many of my prompts were *AI-compatible* because they asked for content knowledge without requiring lived insight, ethical judgment, or authentic synthesis.

Critical Intervention:

I began intentionally designing what I called "impossible-to-AI" prompts—not to create traps or barriers for students, but to refocus my assignments on *the kind of thinking I actually wanted to cultivate.* These prompts required student voice, relational understanding, and contextual reasoning—qualities that generative AI could not reproduce convincingly.

For example, in a unit on motivation and classroom climate, I shifted from a typical "compare-and-contrast" essay to this prompt: *"Think of a classroom you were part of—positive or negative. Describe how it shaped your motivation and sense of belonging. Then, connect your experience to at least two motivation theories from our course. How would you recreate or avoid that climate as a future teacher?"* The emotional specificity and reflective framing demanded insight that AI could not fake.

I also included small in-class writing prompts or structured conversations that scaffolded the larger assignment—ensuring students had already done the core cognitive work by the time they began drafting. These activities helped students connect theory to experience and gave me opportunities to observe and support their thinking as it developed.

Outcome:

Student submissions were more grounded, reflective, and contextually rich. Many shared personal schooling stories—both empowering and alienating—and connected those memories to course theories in complex ways. AI-generated versions of the same prompt, by contrast, felt generic and hollow. The gap between human and machine thinking became visibly clear.

Reflection:

Designing "impossible-to-AI" prompts is not about defeating technology—it's about reclaiming the value of *irreducibly human* learning. Through the lens of Critical Digital Pedagogy, this practice affirms that deep educational work lives in reflection, contradiction, and connection—none of which can be easily automated.

Case 6: Generating Counterexamples With AI

Initial AI Contribution:

As part of a unit on culturally responsive pedagogy, I asked ChatGPT to generate a sample lesson plan intended to support multilingual learners in a third-grade classroom. The result was troubling. While the AI-produced lesson appeared organized and linguistically simplified, it leaned heavily on assimilationist practices—emphasizing English acquisition, suggesting sentence stems that simplified thinking rather than supporting their language development. The approach lacked depth and implicitly framed the students' multilingualism as a problem to be managed rather than an asset to be celebrated.

Critical Intervention:

In this class, we turned this lesson into a counterexample. I presented the lesson plan in class with the context that it had been AI-generated in response to a prompt about multilingual support. I asked students to read it critically, annotating where they saw strengths, gaps, and misalignments with the theories and frameworks we had studied.

In small groups, students identified multiple problems: the lesson reinforced deficit thinking, ignored funds of knowledge, and treated linguistic diversity as an obstacle rather than a resource. I then asked students to revise the plan based on culturally sustaining pedagogy, integrating home language use, community connections, and inclusive classroom routines.

Outcome:

This activity led to discussion about how bias can hide in professional language and how "polished" materials, whether AI-generated or institutional, should never be accepted uncritically. Students expressed surprise at how the AI version looked superficially inclusive while enacting harmful assumptions. Their revised lesson plans were more relational, imaginative, and grounded in students' assets.

Reflection:

This case demonstrated the power of using AI not as a model but as a *mirror*—a way to surface and critique the ideological assumptions baked into "neutral" content. Through a CDP lens, this strategy affirms that critique is a core pedagogical practice. AI didn't teach my students how to be responsive teachers—it gave them something to resist, revise, and reimagine.

Case 7: AI for Generating Ideas—Not Products

Initial AI Contribution:

During a class activity on classroom management, several students asked whether they could use ChatGPT to help brainstorm ideas for their upcoming classroom management plan assignment. Their questions were thoughtful, they weren't looking to copy or offload the assignment, but to get "unstuck" and spark new ideas. Their curiosity surfaced a valuable teaching moment: students were trying to bridge the space between their novice understanding and the level of decision-making expected of future educators.

Critical Intervention:

I responded by framing this tension explicitly: I named the expert-novice gap, explaining that part of their cognitive task in this course was to develop professional judgment and pedagogical reasoning. I told them that while AI might have speed and volume, *they* were building the kind of nuanced, context-sensitive expertise that cannot be generated instantly.

To support that process, I designed an in-class activity in which students used ChatGPT to generate 10 to 15 ideas for building community in a classroom of their choice. Then, in small groups,they evaluated the results: Did the idea reflect culturally responsive practice? Was it developmentally appropriate? Did it build authentic relationships and reflect a meaningful teaching stance?

After critiquing the AI-generated ideas, students selected one and rewrote it to better reflect their values and the specific communities they hope to teach. This activity allowed students to see AI as a source of initial momentum—not as a reliable or final answer.

The formal classroom management plan assignment remained rooted in their personal field experiences, course readings, and in-class drafting. Students completed this work by hand or through supported drafting with formative feedback—ensuring that synthesis, reflection, and ownership remained their's.

Outcome:

Students appreciated the permission to explore AI while being held to rigorous standards of thinking and reflection. They began to view AI not as a shortcut, but as a brainstorm partner whose ideas demanded revision, skepticism, and pedagogical clarity.

Reflection:

This case reaffirmed that inviting students to interrogate AI outputs can support, not bypass, the learning process. A CDP-informed approach doesn't just allow AI use—it equips students to evaluate, revise, and transcend it. By foregrounding the expert-novice gap and naming reflection as a form of expertise, we build classrooms where growth, not efficiency, is the goal.

Case 8: Rethinking Citation and Authorship

Initial AI Contribution:

As generative AI became more visible in educational spaces, I began having conversations with colleagues and other scholars about how its use intersected with academic integrity, intellectual labor, and scholarly authorship. We reviewed policy statements from major journals and professional organizations, many of which had just begun to clarify expectations around AI use in manuscript submissions. These professional conversations helped me recognize that the emergence of AI was not just a classroom management issue—it was reshaping how we understand authorship across the field.

Critical Intervention:

Informed by these disciplinary conversations, I brought the topic into my courses. I asked, "If I revise an AI-generated paragraph to make it sound more like me, do I still have to cite it?" Rather than respond with a simple rule, I invited the class into the same complexity I had experienced with my colleagues. We noted that many policies focused on plagiarism prevention but had little to say about the nuances of collaborative writing or the meaning of authorship.

Outcome:

Students became more thoughtful about the writing process and more critical of "product-based" views of authorship. They had space to see AI as a tool that could blur or clarify what they valued about their own contributions. The transparency we cultivated around these issues reduced anxiety and fostered deeper ethical reasoning.

Reflection:

This case demonstrated how scholarly conversations informed my pedagogy—and how teaching AI literacy is also professional development. From a Critical Digital Pedagogy perspective, the question is not merely whether to cite AI, but how to cultivate students' agency, judgment, and ethical awareness in a world where authorship is being redefined. It's also about modeling that process as an early-career scholar navigating the same uncertainties. AI isn't just a student issue; it's a disciplinary one—and we must approach it as such.

Synthesis and Meta-Reflection

Across the eight illustrative cases presented, a set of throughlines emerges, patterns that reveal not only how I used AI in my teaching, but how I navigated tensions through a pedagogical stance rooted in reflective praxis. The process of integrating AI into my early career practice was never about simple adoption or rejection. It was, and continues to be, an iterative negotiation: between efficiency and integrity, innovation and intentionality, automation and agency. While each case unfolded in a different instructional moment, they collectively reflect three core themes: critical engagement, intentional design, and reflection as praxis.

First, critical engagement was foundational. I never treated AI outputs as ready-to-use products. Whether generating a lesson plan, scenario, or list of strategies, I positioned AI responses as raw material—something to interrogate, reshape, or reject depending on its alignment with my pedagogical commitments. This approach reflects a key tenet of Critical Digital Pedagogy: that educators must act not as passive recipients of technological content, but as active meaning-makers who question how power and ideology operate in digital tools. We must never assume that technology is neutral (Lankshear & Knobel, 2015; Selwyn, 2010). In my classes, AI became a text not just a tool. Students and I read it critically: What assumptions does this response reveal? What values are embedded in its tone or framing? Who is this for, and who is erased? These questions shifted AI from being an invisible assistant to a visible, contestable actor in the learning space.

Second, intentional design became an essential practice. Several of the cases revealed that assignments vulnerable to AI use often shared something in common: they asked students to summarize, restate, or reproduce information rather than synthesize, reflect, or apply it meaningfully. This insight prompted me to reexamine my own assessments—not to make them "AI-proof" in a punitive sense, but to make them more reflective of the kind of thinking I wanted students to do. I asked myself: *Would this task cultivate reflection, connection, or growth? Would it require students to bring something of themselves to the work—something AI cannot replicate?*

This principle reshaped both what I assigned and how I structured class time. I added formative assessments that happened in real time—on paper, in conversation, or in low-stakes drafting. I replaced polished take-home assignments with collaborative analysis, ethical inquiry, and reflective synthesis. These shifts helped preserve the integrity of the learning process, not just the product. They also supported equity: by foregrounding process and voice, I created multiple entry points for students with diverse experiences and literacies.

Finally, the most consistent thread across all of these moments was the reflection as praxis. Drawing on Freirean (2005) traditions and the ethos of Critical Digital Pedagogy (Aguilera & Salazar, 2023; Stommel, 2014), I understood reflection not as an afterthought, but as a core component of teaching and learning. AI's emergence in education surfaced new ethical, pedagogical, and epistemological questions that demanded thoughtful, recursive engagement. In response, I treated my own use of AI as an ongoing inquiry—generating, revising, experimenting, and returning to my values again and again.

This reflective stance extended to my students as well. Rather than simply regulating their AI use, I invited them into the complexity. We talked openly about authorship, bias, ethical gray areas, and the changing nature of academic work. We practiced reading AI critically, but also used it as a mirror to reflect on our own assumptions and aspirations as educators. In this way, AI became part of our shared reflective praxis—something we used not just to complete tasks, but to deepen our awareness of how knowledge is made, positioned, and valued.

Through this recursive work, my understanding of both AI and pedagogy evolved. I began the semester thinking of AI as a productivity tool. I ended it thinking of AI as a provocation—a catalyst for refining my pedagogy, strengthening my assessments, and deepening my students' understanding of what it means to think, learn, and teach in an increasingly automated world.

These cases are not offered as models to emulate, but as artifacts of that reflective work. They show what it looks like to engage AI critically, to design with intentionality, and to teach in ways that affirm human relationships, intellectual struggle, and student voice. They also underscore that reflection is not separate from action—it is what makes our action pedagogical, ethical, and responsive.

Ultimately, the presence of AI in educational settings is not a disruption to reflective practice—it is a reason to double down on it. In the face of technologies that can produce fluent language without understanding, we must ask: *What kind of understanding do we want to cultivate?* My hope is that this reflection encourages educators not only to use AI thoughtfully, but to remain rooted in the deeper questions of teaching: who we are accountable to, what we value, and how we make space for students to do the same.

BROADER IMPLICATIONS FOR K–12 AND POST-SECONDARY EDUCATORS

The illustrative cases and reflections shared in this chapter come from my work in a post-secondary teacher education program, but the insights have relevance beyond higher education. Educators across K–12 and university contexts are increasingly navigating the pedagogical, ethical, and political implications of AI in their classrooms. Whether we are teaching third graders or graduate students, we are being asked, explicitly or implicitly, to decide how, when, and why we will engage with tools that can now generate content, simulate dialogue, and produce writing that looks deceptively human. These decisions cannot be left to chance or driven solely by convenience. They must be grounded in pedagogical values, our commitments, and an awareness of the contexts in which our students live and learn.

This section outlines broader implications of what I learned from my practice for both K–12 and post-secondary educators, organized into three key domains: instructional design and assessment, student engagement and critical thinking, and professional development and ethical responsibility.

Instructional Design and Assessment: Focus on Thought, Not Output

One of the clearest implications from my work is the need to rethink assignment design. Across K–12 and higher education, many traditional assessments (short essays, summaries, "explain this concept" questions) can now be completed by AI in a matter of seconds. This doesn't mean we should eliminate writing, but it does mean we must reconsider what our assignments are really asking students to do. Are we measuring their ability to reproduce content, or their ability to think with, through, and beyond it?

Educators in all settings can begin by identifying the cognitive moves they want students to practice: synthesis, ethical judgment, reflective analysis, critical comparison, application to real-world contexts. Then, design prompts that foreground those moves, not just content reproduction. In K–12 classrooms, this might mean shifting from "Explain what a plant needs to survive" to "Think of a time you helped something grow, what does that story teach us about what living things need?" In a college setting, it might mean replacing "Compare Piaget and Vygotsky" with "How would each theorist explain what happened in your last field placement?"

Assignments should also make space for student experience, perspective, and voice, elements AI cannot authentically reproduce. When students are asked to connect course material to their lived realities, family knowledge, or community experiences, the work becomes not only more human, but more resistant to automation.

Additionally, educators should consider building formative checkpoints into their assignment structure. In my own practice, requiring in-class synthesis, handwritten planning, or collaborative idea development ensured that students had already done the intellectual labor before they began drafting. These strategies also create more equitable access by scaffolding complex thinking and reducing reliance on polished, high-stakes products.

Student Engagement and Critical Thinking: Teach AI as Content, Not Just Tool

Another key implication is the value of teaching AI not just as a tool to be used, but as a subject to be studied. From elementary to post-secondary levels, students are encountering generative technologies that influence how they write, search, and learn. They need support in developing critical digital literacy and an ability to read AI outputs with skepticism, to question embedded assumptions, and to evaluate usefulness in light of their goals and values.

In practice, this means inviting students to analyze, critique, and revise AI-generated content. K–12 teachers might have students rewrite an AI-generated story to better reflect their community. College instructors might assign students to compare a chatbot-generated answer to a scholarly article and reflect on what's missing. These activities help students develop both content knowledge and critical awareness.

Equally important is helping students understand the limits of AI: its training data, its biases, its inability to reflect the nuance of lived experience. By involving students in these conversations, we cultivate not only better writers, but more ethical and discerning learners.

This also means talking openly about ethical use of AI in coursework. Educators at all levels should establish transparent expectations and help students reflect on the difference between support and substitution, between collaborating with tools and outsourcing thinking. The goal is not to trap students, but to help them recognize their own agency and the value of their intellectual labor.

Professional Development and Ethical Responsibility: Model Reflection and Dialogue

For educators themselves, one of the most urgent implications is the need to critically examine our own practices and positions in relation to AI. This includes becoming familiar with how AI works, but also engaging in broader questions: What pedagogies are we advancing through our use of technology? What kinds of learning are we privileging? Who benefits, and who is excluded?

As the cases in this chapter show, AI is not neutral. It reflects dominant ideologies and can reinforce deficit perspectives. Educators, especially those committed to equity, must remain attentive to how these patterns shape the resources we use and the content we assign. In my own work, reflecting on AI outputs led me to revise not only what I assigned, but how I defined rigor, how I structured classroom dialogue, and how I positioned students as knowledge creators.

This work is ongoing and collective. K–12 and post-secondary institutions should provide time, space, and community for educators to explore these issues together. Faculty learning communities, PD sessions, or interdisciplinary workshops can offer opportunities to share AI use cases, surface ethical concerns, and develop strategies for intentional, humanizing integration. These professional conversations also reinforce that AI is not just a classroom issue—it is a scholarly and civic issue, one that intersects with broader conversations about labor, authorship, justice, and access.

In particular, early-career educators and teacher candidates must be supported in navigating this terrain. Rather than asking them to master a new tool, we should invite them to ask the questions that matter: What kind of teacher do I want to be? How do I use technology in a way that reflects care, community, and context? What does it mean to teach with AI without teaching through it?

Shared Responsibility, Shared Possibility

The broader implication of this work is not a list of rules, but a call to intentionality and reflection. Whether teaching second grade or supervising doctoral research, we have an opportunity, and a responsibility, to model what it looks like to navigate AI with clarity, care, and courage.

We must resist narratives that reduce teaching to content delivery and learning to output generation. Instead, we can design classrooms where human thinking is centered, where tools serve rather than steer, and where reflection is treated as rigor. This is not just about staying ahead of technology—it is about staying true to the core of what education is meant to be: a relational, ethical, and transformative practice.

CRITICAL CONSIDERATIONS: RISKS AND ETHICAL CONCERNS

While the previous sections have explored the possibilities of using AI as a pedagogical resource, it is equally important to attend to the risks it presents, especially for educators committed to justice, care, and equity. The accelerating adoption of AI in education often comes with narratives of innovation and efficiency, but without critical scrutiny, these narratives obscure real harms. As both a scholar and a classroom teacher, I've found that even the most promising applications of AI require ethical vigilance. What follows are several key areas of concern that should remain central to how we approach AI integration in educational spaces.

Reinforcing Bias and Inequity

Perhaps the most pressing risk is the way AI systems can reinforce and reproduce social and cultural biases. These tools are trained on large datasets drawn from internet text—datasets that are neither neutral nor inclusive. AI can replicate dominant ideologies, white normativity, implicit language ideologies, and deficit perspectives on race, gender, class, disability, and language. As seen in my own classroom examples, AI-generated lesson plans or case studies often excluded or misrepresented multilingual learners, students of color, and culturally sustaining practices.

This is not a technical glitch, it is a structural issue. Educators who use AI must therefore adopt a stance of *critical review*. Before incorporating AI content, we must ask: Whose knowledge is being prioritized? Whose stories are erased? How does the language position students and communities? Without this kind of reflection, we risk embedding algorithmic bias into our instruction and reproducing the very inequities we seek to challenge.

Diminishing Pedagogical Presence

Another significant concern is the temptation to use AI as a substitute for pedagogical labor. AI's ability to generate explanations, activities, or feedback can be seductive—especially under conditions of time scarcity, large class sizes, or institutional pressure to "innovate." But when these tools are used to automate core pedagogical tasks, we risk devaluing the role of teacher judgment, presence, and responsiveness.

Effective teaching is relational and dialogic. It requires knowing our students, interpreting their needs, and adjusting in real time. AI cannot replace these human dimensions. If we come to rely on AI to handle the complexity of instruction, we may not only erode our own agency, but also offer students a hollowed-out version of education, one that prizes efficiency over connection.

Promoting Quasi-Neutrality

Many technological tools present themselves as "objective," "data-driven," or "bias-free." This branding reinforces a problematic ideology of quasi-neutrality—the idea that technology can exist outside of power or politics. In reality, all educational tools and platforms are shaped by the values, assumptions, and decisions of those who build them.

When educators adopt AI without naming its ideological underpinnings, we risk normalizing its authority. This can lead to classrooms where students are encouraged to trust AI outputs more than their own thinking, or where critical literacy is replaced by compliance with algorithmically generated answers. To counter this, we must create learning environments where technology is always up for discussion, critique, and revision.

Eroding Student Voice and Authorship

The growing presence of AI in student writing raises deep questions about authorship, voice, and intellectual labor. As students experiment with generative tools, sometimes transparently, sometimes covertly, we must respond with more than punishment or panic. We must ask what conditions are leading students to feel disengaged or unsure of their ideas. We must also reframe writing not as product creation, but as meaning-making—a process that cannot be automated.

At the same time, we have to acknowledge how AI reshapes the conditions of authorship. Students need support in navigating these tensions—how to distinguish between inspiration and substitution, how to cite tools transparently, and how to recognize the value of their own contributions. And educators need to lead that work by modeling transparency, discussing ethical dilemmas, and building classroom communities where student thinking is centered.

Data Privacy and Surveillance

Finally, there are serious concerns about student data and institutional surveillance. Many generative AI tools are commercial products with unclear privacy policies. When students use these platforms—especially through institutionally endorsed tools—they may be unknowingly feeding their intellectual labor into corporate systems that profit from their input. Educators must be mindful of what platforms they endorse, how student data is used, and what protections are in place. Transparent communication and consent should be foundational.

The presence of AI in education demands more than digital literacy—it requires critical consciousness. As educators, we must resist treating AI as inevitable or neutral. Instead, we must scrutinize its outputs, question its assumptions, and center our practice in ethical responsibility and humanizing pedagogy. AI can be part of the future of education—but only if we shape that future with care, reflection, and integrity.

CONCLUSION: TOWARD RESPONSIBLE AND HUMANIZING AI INTEGRATION

The integration of AI into education is not a question of if but how—and more urgently, for whom, under what conditions, and to what ends. As this chapter has demonstrated, AI can be a helpful partner in the work of teaching, but only when it is engaged with purpose, critique, and reflection. In the absence of this intentionality, AI threatens to mechanize human learning, reinforce inequity, and erode the pedagogical relationships at the heart of education.

My journey with AI as an early-career educator has not been linear or prescriptive. It has been exploratory, dialogic, and reflective. Through each case presented, I have wrestled with the promises and problems of AI—sometimes using it to jumpstart planning or spark student discussion, and other times rejecting its outputs entirely. What has anchored me throughout is the framework of Critical Digital Pedagogy and a commitment to reflection as praxis. These guiding commitments remind me that teaching is not just content delivery—it is ethical, relational, and deeply human work.

One of the central insights of this journey has been the need to re-center student thinking in all AI-related decisions. AI may generate ideas, language, and structure, but it cannot replicate the struggle, insight, or identity that real learning requires. As educators, our responsibility is to design for that kind of learning: to craft assignments that matter, create space for reflection and revision, and invite students to connect theory with lived experience. This is not only how we resist automation—it is how we honor the complexity and brilliance of our learners.

The cases shared in this chapter are not blueprints. They are moments of tension, growth, and possibility. They demonstrate that integrating AI is not about mastering a tool, but about deepening our stance—our ability to teach with curiosity, care, and criticality. They also show that the presence of AI can be creative when it is used to surface assumptions, provoke inquiry, and refine practice.

As educators, we are facing a moment of transformation. We have the capacity, and the responsibility, to shape how AI is used in our classrooms, our departments, and our institutions. This requires reflection, collaboration, and courage. It requires us to ask hard questions about what we value, what we protect, and what we are willing to change.

Ultimately, this chapter is a call for responsible and humanizing AI integration, an approach that recognizes the potential of technology without surrendering to it. AI can support our work, but it cannot define it. Our teaching must remain grounded in relationships, justice, and care. These are not undertakings that can be delegated to algorithms. These are the work of educators and that work, now more than ever, matters.

REFERENCES

Aguilera, E., & Salazar, C. (2023). *Critical Digital Pedagogy in the Platform Society*. Oxford Research Encyclopedia of Education. DOI: 10.1093/acrefore/9780190264093.013.1888

Bali, M. (2014). *Critical pedagogy: Intentions and realities*. Hybrid Pedagogy.

del Carmen Salazar, M. (2013). A humanizing pedagogy: Reinventing the principles and practice of education as a journey toward liberation. *Review of Research in Education*, *37*(1), 121–148. DOI: 10.3102/0091732X12464032

Freire, P. (2005). Pedagogy of the Oppressed. *Continuum.*

Giroux, H. A. (1994). *Disturbing pleasures: Learning popular culture.* Routledge.

Lankshear, C., & Knobel, M. (2015). Digital literacy and Digital Literacies:-policy, pedagogy and research considerations for education. *Nordic Journal of Digital Literacy, 10*(Jubileumsnummer), 8-20.

Selwyn, N. (2010). Looking beyond learning: Notes towards the critical study of educational technology. *Journal of Computer Assisted Learning*, *26*(1), 65–73. DOI: 10.1111/j.1365-2729.2009.00338.x

Stommel, J. (2014). Critical digital pedagogy: A definition. *Hybrid Pedagogy: The Journal of Critical Digital Pedagogy.*

Stommel, J., & Morris, S. M. (Eds.). (2018). *An Urgency of Teachers: The Work of Critical Digital Pedagogy*. Hybrid Pedagogy Incorporated.

Chapter 3
Empowering STEM Education:
Harnessing MagicSchool AI for Experiential Learning

Michaine S. Ashley
https://orcid.org/0009-0002-3008-6741
Texas Woman's University, Denton, USA

ABSTRACT

This chapter explores the transformative role of Artificial Intelligence (AI) in enhancing STEM education through experiential learning, with a focus on the innovative MagicSchool AI platform. It examines how AI-powered tools streamline teacher productivity by automating administrative tasks, generating personalized lesson plans, and creating interactive, standards-aligned content. The chapter highlights AI's capacity to personalize learning by analyzing student data to address individual needs, while also promoting student engagement through gamification, real-time feedback, and adaptive learning systems. MagicSchool AI's unique multi-model approach and specialized tools empower educators to design immersive project-based learning experiences that connect academic concepts to real-world challenges. By integrating AI with experiential learning principles, this chapter illustrates how educators can foster critical thinking, collaboration, and innovation in K-12 STEM classrooms.

DOI: 10.4018/979-8-3373-1122-7.ch003

INTRODUCING AI IN STEM EDUCATION: FOUNDATIONAL SHIFTS IN PEDAGOGY

Since emerging into the K-12 educational space, Artificial Intelligence (AI) has already begun to profoundly transform STEM education by introducing innovative methods and tools that enhance learning experiences for both teachers and students (Ally, 2019; Damioli et al., 2021; Robins et al., 2022). This integration represents a significant shift from traditional methodology, reshaping how educators learn, teach, conduct research, and innovate in their classrooms (Barsoum et al., 2022). AI-powered platforms are revolutionizing teaching approaches by providing resources that personalize learning experiences based on student needs, backgrounds, and school culture (Cao et al., 2020; Tapalova & Zhiyenbayeva, 2022).

Importantly, these transformative technologies also enable experiential learning by supporting hands-on, inquiry-driven activities-such as interactive simulations, virtual laboratories, and robotics experiments-that allow students to learn STEM concepts through direct experience and experimentation (Akhmetova et al., 2025; Kavitha & Joshith, 2024). Experiential learning, as described by Kolb (2015), emphasizes a cycle of concrete experience, reflective observation, abstract conceptualization, and active experimentation. In the context of STEM education, this translates to students engaging in hands-on inquiry, reflecting on their processes, and applying concepts to solve authentic problems. Project-based learning (PBL) is inherently experiential, as it situates students in real-world contexts where they must apply knowledge, collaborate, and iterate solutions (Kavitha & Joshith, 2024). AI tools further enhance this process by providing adaptive feedback, scaffolding, and personalized resources, making experiential learning more accessible and impactful for diverse learners (Gunawan et al., 2021; Martin et al., 2023).

Recent systematic reviews highlight that AI integration not only personalizes instruction but also facilitates experiential and project-based learning, which are shown to boost student engagement and deepen conceptual understanding in K-12 STEM classrooms (Akhmetova et al., 2025; Kavitha & Joshith, 2024; Martin et al., 2023). These transformative technologies enable pedagogical approaches that combine adaptive learning systems with experiential instruction, creating new possibilities for STEM education.

Systematic reviews further demonstrate AI's multifaceted capacity to enhance science literacy through robotics applications (Martin et al., 2023), improve physics concept mastery via interactive chatbots (Omari et al., 2023), and streamline formative assessment through sophisticated machine learning algorithms (Stanja et al., 2022). These advancements align with evolving educational paradigms that emphasize personalized learning trajectories and data-driven differentiation-approaches that are critical for addressing the diverse needs present in today's STEM classrooms (Chen et al., 2023; Gunawan et al., 2021). As AI tools become more accessible to K-12 educators, they offer unprecedented opportunities to transform traditional instruction into dynamic, responsive learning environments that can adapt to individual student progress while maintaining rigorous content standards.

In addition to AI-powered platforms, digital design tools like Canva are becoming valuable assets in K-12 STEM classrooms. Canva enables both teachers and students to craft visually compelling presentations, infographics, and project materials, which can enhance the communication and clarity of STEM concepts. When used alongside AI-generated lesson plans, assignments, and assessments, Canva streamlines the creation of engaging curriculum resources and helps unify the overall design process. Throughout this chapter, you will find guidance and examples on how to leverage digital design tools such as Canva to further enrich and visually enhance the instructional materials produced with AI.

KEY RESEARCH THEMES IN AI-ENHANCED STEM EDUCATION

Research on the integration of Artificial Intelligence in K-12 STEM education consistently highlights three key themes: enhancing teacher productivity and professional capacity, advancing personalized learning systems, and navigating ethical and implementation challenges. AI tools such as MagicSchool AI have demonstrated significant promise in streamlining administrative tasks, including automated grading and data analysis, thereby allowing educators to devote more time to instructional activities and student engagement (Braaten & Farnsworth, 2024; Azzam & Charles, 2025; Koh & Doroudi, 2023). Furthermore, AI can support instructional design through features like backward planning, which has been shown to improve teacher effectiveness and workload management (Keppler et al., 2024). Despite these advantages, effective integration of AI in classrooms requires robust professional development and ongoing support; a need highlighted by 78% of educators in recent AI-STEM studies (Casal-Otero et al., 2023; Frontline Research & Learning Institute, 2024). Without sufficient training, teachers may struggle to harness the full potential of AI tools, underscoring the importance of targeted capacity-building initiatives.

The second major theme centers on the power of AI to deliver personalized learning experiences. AI-powered platforms such as MATHia leverage real-time data analytics to identify individual student learning gaps and provide targeted interventions, resulting in measurable improvements in math proficiency (Pane et al., 2013). Similarly, Karachi et al. (2018) found that the use of intelligent tutoring systems significantly improved student achievement compared to traditional teaching methods, demonstrating the potential of AI to enhance conceptual understanding in STEM subjects. These adaptive systems align with research indicating that blended learning models, those that combine AI-driven feedback with hands-on experimentation, yield superior retention rates in subjects like biology and chemistry (Kavitha & Joshith, 2024; Gunawan et al., 2021). By enabling teachers to differentiate instruction at a granular level, AI fosters a more individualized and responsive classroom environment (Chen et al., 2020; Li et al., 2023).

However, the third major theme highlights the idea that widespread adoption of AI in STEM education also brings forth persistent ethical and implementation challenges that must be addressed to ensure equitable and effective outcomes. Systematic reviews and empirical studies have identified significant equity gaps in access to AI and educational technology resources, particularly among students from low-income or rural communities, which risk exacerbating existing educational disparities (Patino et al., 2023; Hannan & Eynon, 2025). These disparities are often reflected in differences in device availability, internet connectivity, and access to high-quality digital learning platforms, further entrenching the digital divide in K-12 education.

Privacy concerns related to student data collection and management are another critical issue, as the increasing use of AI-powered platforms in schools necessitates strict adherence to data protection regulations and transparent practices (Hahn et al., 2021; Huang, 2023; Slavin, 2022). The datafication of education has raised important ethical questions about surveillance, consent, and the potential misuse of sensitive student information, making robust privacy policies and clear communication with stakeholders essential. Additionally, teacher reluctance, often stemming from insufficient training and support, remains a significant barrier to effective AI integration in the classroom (Antonenko & Abromowitz, 2022; Kim, 2019; Sun & Yan, 2025). This research highlights that comprehensive professional development and ongoing support are necessary for teachers to build the competencies and confidence required to leverage AI tools effectively. Addressing these interconnected challenges is crucial to ensuring that the benefits of AI in STEM education are realized equitably, ethically, and sustainably, ultimately maximizing positive outcomes for all students.

THREE KEY DIMENSIONS OF AI IN STEM EDUCATION

The influence of artificial intelligence on K-12 STEM education is both far-reaching and nuanced; presenting educators with new opportunities as well as important considerations. As schools increasingly integrate AI-powered platforms and tools, three central areas of impact have emerged: enhancing teacher productivity, enabling personalized learning, and promoting student engagement. Each of these domains reflects the multifaceted ways AI can support instructional practice, from streamlining routine administrative tasks and lesson planning, to tailoring instruction for diverse learners, and fostering interactive, motivating classroom environments.

The following sections examine these three core dimensions in detail, drawing on current research and classroom practice to illustrate how AI is transforming the STEM education landscape for teachers and students alike.

Enhancing Teacher Productivity

The effective use of AI in the K-12 classroom has the potential to significantly enhance teacher productivity and allow educators to focus on instructional activities and increasing student engagement. The use of AI tools offers numerous benefits for streamlining administrative tasks, personalizing learning experiences, and improving overall educational outcomes (Azzam & Charles, 2025; Cao et al., 2020; Tapalova & Zhiyenbayeva, 2022).

One of the primary ways AI enhances teacher productivity is by automating routine administrative tasks, such as grading assignments, generating practice questions, analyzing student performance data, and managing classroom schedules (Braaten & Farnsworth, 2024; Koh & Doroudi, 2023; Yilmaz, 2024). AI tools can also greatly expedite the lesson planning process and content creation for STEM educators by curating relevant content, generating a diverse bank of practice problems, and personalizing learning materials (Gunawan et al., 2021; Nja et al., 2023). A study conducted on backwards planning with generative AI found that teachers felt they were teaching more effectively and successfully completing more work when using AI as a tool for lesson planning (Keppler et al., 2024).

Digital design tools such as Canva further support teacher productivity by enabling the rapid creation of visually engaging lesson materials, infographics, lab instructions, and classroom displays. When paired with AI-generated content, Canva allows teachers to transform text-based outputs into polished, accessible resources that enhance student understanding and interest. For example, a teacher might use an AI tool to generate a set of practice problems or a project outline, then use Canva to design an attractive worksheet or project poster that is visually appealing and easy for students to follow. By integrating Canva into the curriculum design process, teachers can efficiently produce high-quality instructional materials that support both clarity and creativity in STEM education.

Personalized Learning

AI-powered systems can analyze vast amounts of student data, including performance patterns, learning styles, and psychographic profiles, enabling teachers to create custom-tailored curriculums that maximize each student's ability to learn (Li et al., 2023; Sahota, 2023; Qu et al., 2022). This data-driven, student-centric approach allows educators to address the diverse needs of their students more effectively, allowing for more impactful and consistent differentiation through the built-in supports and resources provided (Chen et al., 2020; Murtaza et al., 2022).

This was demonstrated in a study of Carnegie Learning's AI-driven math program MATHia (Pane et al., 2013). MATHia uses AI data analytics to identify areas where students struggle and responds by offering targeted interventions to build up their skills. This approach allows K-12 teachers to target student's specific needs at a detailed, skill-by-skill level for each student in their classroom. AI based tools like this enable teachers to provide more individualized attention, thus fostering a more personalized learning environment (Gunawan et al., 2021; Li & Wong, 2023).

However, the implementation of AI for personalized learning also presents challenges of its own (Qu et al., 2022). Ensuring equitable access to AI technologies across different socioeconomic backgrounds remains a significant concern, as students from low-income or rural communities may lack the necessary resources. This risks creating an even larger divide between wealthy school districts who cannot afford to pay for cutting edge AI-driven platforms (Patino et al., 2023). Additionally, teachers require adequate training and professional development in order to effectively utilize AI tools in their classrooms (Antonenko & Abromowitz, 2022; Wu & Yang, 2022). The availability of training, professional development, and the time in which to complete them can also vary district by district (Frontline Research & Learning Institute, 2024; Patino et al., 2023). Privacy and data security issues are also an important concerns, as schools must adhere to strict regulations to protect student information while leveraging AI's capabilities.

Promoting Student Engagement

The integration of AI in K-12 education has shown significant potential to enhance student engagement by offering innovative approaches to personalized learning, interactive content delivery, and real-time feedback (Holicza & Kiss, 2023; Rui & Badarch, 2022; Vesin et al., 2018). AI-powered adaptive learning systems analyze student performance data in real-time, identifying areas where students are struggling and automatically adjusting the material to match their learning pace (Chen et al., 2020; Jiao et al., 2022; Murtaza et al., 2022).

AI can also enhance student engagement through innovative teaching practices like gamification and interactive learning experiences (Patino et al., 2023). AI-powered platforms can create dynamic, interactive lessons that adapt based on a student's responses, keeping students motivated and encouraging active participation (Gunawan et al., 2021). These AI-driven platforms can integrate game-like elements such as rewards, challenges, and leaderboards, which have been shown to boost student engagement and foster a sense of achievement and healthy competition. In teacher-created games and assignments, AI can help teachers in creating expanded question banks, add in differentiation by leveling questions and answers by student reading levels, and generating customizable in-game options based on student responses (Patino et al., 2023).

Students can also utilize digital design programs such as Canva to create visually compelling posters, infographics, digital reports, and project presentations, allowing them to communicate complex scientific ideas in creative and accessible ways. For example, after completing an AI-personalized assignment or interactive lesson, students can use Canva to visually summarize their findings, design lab reports, or collaborate on group projects. This integration not only reinforces content mastery but also encourages students to take ownership of their learning and develop valuable skills in digital communication and design. Such approaches align with emerging research that highlights the positive impact of AI-enhanced, student-centered learning environments on engagement and achievement.

Research has demonstrated the positive impact of AI-enhanced learning environments on student outcomes and engagement (Gunawan et al., 2021; Rui & Badarch, 2022; Xu & Ouyang, 2022). For example, AI can generate scenario-based simulations or virtual experiments, allowing students to manipulate variables and observe outcomes in a safe, digital environment. Such activities bridge the gap between theory and practice, embodying the principles of experiential learning and authentic assessment (Salinas-Navarro et al., 2024). A Stanford-led study published in the journal Educational Evaluation and Policy Analysis found that an AI-powered feedback tool improved instructors' use of "uptake," a practice where teachers acknowledge, reiterate, and build on students' contributions (Demszky et al., 2023). This study also provided evidence that the teacher's usage of AI tools improved their rate of completing assignments and overall satisfaction with the course.

As AI continues to evolve, its role in K-12 education is expected to become increasingly significant, with potential developments in multi-modal learning that can process and interpret data from various inputs like voice, images, and gestures (Chen et al., 2020; Chiu et al., 2022). This advancement could make learning more accessible and interactive, particularly for younger children or students with disabilities. This chapter will focus on the application of AI in the K-12 STEM classroom and how to leverage various AI tools to enhance teacher productivity, personalize student learning experiences, and promote student engagement in meaningful ways.

MAGICSCHOOL AI IN EXPERIENTIAL LEARNING

Experiential learning has emerged as a powerful approach in STEM education, offering students hands-on, interactive experiences that bridge the gap between theoretical knowledge and practical application (Freeman et al., 2014; Karan & Brown,

2022). This method of "learning by doing" allows students to actively engage with materials, interact with peers, and tackle real-world challenges, fostering deeper comprehension and retention of complex concepts (Prince, 2004; Kotsis, 2024). In STEM fields, where abstract theories can often be daunting, experiential learning proves particularly impactful by demystifying challenging concepts, building problem-solving skills, and igniting curiosity (Bell, 2010; Darling-Hammond et al., 2019; Hmelo-Silver, 2004).

Research has shown that experiential learning in STEM education leads to improved student outcomes across various metrics (Karan & Brown, 2022; Topsakal et al., 2022). This hands-on approach not only enhances understanding but also boosts student engagement and motivation. By actively participating in experiments, projects, and real-world applications, students develop a deeper connection to the subject matter, making STEM concepts more relatable and accessible (Johnson et al., 2014; Hmelo-Silver & Barrows, 2006). Experiential learning has also been shown to foster critical thinking and problem-solving skills by engaging students in real-world scenarios and challenges. This approach encourages them to analyze, question, and apply STEM concepts practically while also creating concrete understandings to which future knowledge and understanding can be anchored to. This process not only deepens their understanding but also cultivates an inquisitive mindset that constantly seeks answers and new possibilities (Pimthong & Williams, 2018; Xu & Ouyang, 2022).

Moreover, experiential learning in K-12 STEM education plays a crucial role in developing 21st-century skills essential for future academic and career success. Through collaborative projects and hands-on activities, students cultivate critical thinking, creativity, communication, and teamwork skills (Bell, 2010; Darling-Hammond et al., 2019).

These experiences also help students develop a growth mindset, encouraging them to view challenges as opportunities for learning and improvement rather than insurmountable obstacles. As the job market increasingly demands STEM-related skills, providing students with practical, hands-on experiences in these fields prepares them for the evolving demands of the workforce and fosters innovation and problem-solving abilities that extend beyond the classroom (Akcan et al., 2023; National Science Board, 2024)

Figure 1 The Impact of Experiential Learning in STEM Education

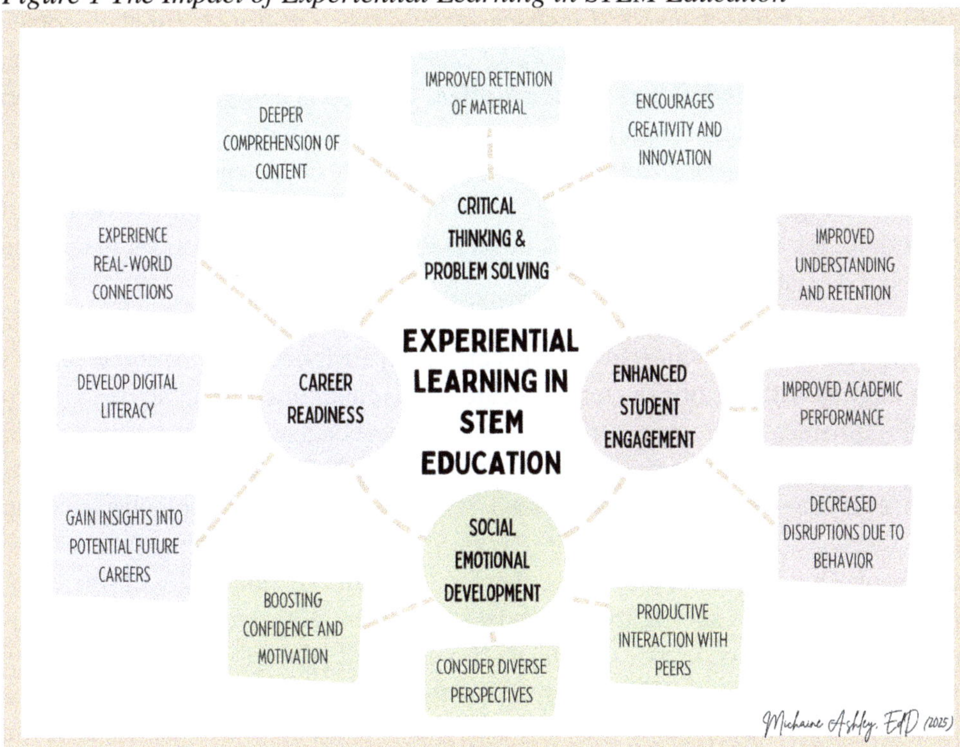

Why use Magic School AI?

This chapter will focus on the use of MagicSchool AI and how to utilize the AI driven "Magic Tools" to foster experiential learning in K-12 STEM classrooms. MagicSchool AI is an innovative AI-powered platform that is revolutionizing the implementation of experiential learning in K-12 STEM education. By leveraging advanced AI technologies, MagicSchool AI assists educators in creating dynamic, project-based learning experiences that cater to individual student needs. The platform's AI-driven tools facilitate the creation of personalized lesson plans, assessments, and interactive activities that align with curriculum standards while promoting hands-on engagement.

What sets MagicSchool AI apart is its unique approach to AI model selection. Rather than relying on a single large language model (LLM), at the time this chapter was written MagicSchool AI is utilizing a combination of multiple LLMs, including OpenAI's GPT-3.5 and GPT-4, Anthropic's Claude models, and Google's Gemini models 7; as new AI models are released MagicSchool AI continues to change and update alongside them. This multi-model approach allows MagicSchool AI to select the most performant LLM for each specific task, ensuring optimal outcomes for various educational needs. For K-12 STEM teachers, this tailored approach is particularly impactful. The platform offers over 60 specialized tools designed specifically for educators that makes it easy for teachers who aren't proficient with AI to still access and utilize these tools for their own classrooms. These tools go beyond what generic LLMs can offer by focusing on STEM-specific content and methodologies that align with curriculum standards and best practices in science and math education.

One of the key STEM-focused features of MagicSchool AI is its ability to generate project-based learning (PBL) plans that apply PBL principles to create project plans aligned with specific content standards. This functionality enables teachers to design immersive learning experiences that connect academic content to real-world problems, boosting student interest and motivation in STEM fields regardless of grade level or specific content focus area. By integrating interdisciplinary learning and fostering critical thinking skills, MagicSchool AI helps students take a more active role in their learning process. Pairing the PBL creation tool with the other STEM-focused tools such as the 5E model lesson plan, 3D science assessment generator, science labs generator, and UDL choice board generator allows teachers to begin designing experiential learning opportunities by creating a PBL lesson outline then filling it in with specific activities and assessments that meet the needs of the students in their own classrooms rather than using generic curriculum materials.

Case studies on the transformative potential of MagicSchool AI in STEM education have found that the platform has been successfully implemented across 5,500+ school and district partnerships, reaching over 3 million educators and impacting 1 million students through teacher-guided AI interactions (Anthropic, 2025). This case study additionally reported that schools with high concentrations of MagicSchool users have reported improved state performance ratings, highlighting the platform's potential to enhance educational outcomes. The study also quoted one of their large school district partners as saying MagiSchool AI is the "single most powerful tool that's ever been launched in our district."

As MagicSchool AI continues to evolve, it promises to further revolutionize experiential learning in STEM education. The platform's existing commitment to privacy and responsible AI use, evidenced by its 93% privacy rating from Common Sense Media, ensures that it can be safely integrated into educational settings (Anthropic, 2025). By combining the power of AI with the principles of experiential learning, MagicSchool AI is paving the way for a future where students can explore complex topics, create ambitious projects, and produce professional-quality work while still in school, ultimately preparing them for the challenges of the real world.

In the following sections of this chapter, we will delve deeper into specific STEM-focused tools offered by MagicSchool AI called Magic Tools. We will explore how these Magic Tools can be effectively utilized to enhance various aspects of STEM education, from creating interactive science experiments to designing complex mathematical models. Additionally, we will discuss best practices for implementing these AI tools in the classroom, addressing potential challenges, and maximizing their benefits for both teachers and students.

BEGIN PLANNING WITH PROJECT-BASED LEARNING

Project-based learning, as a core form of experiential learning, immerses students in extended, hands-on projects that require critical thinking, collaboration, and the application of STEM concepts to real-world challenges (Rehman et al., 2024; Zhang & Ma, 2023). Studies consistently show that PBL enhances student motivation, retention, and higher-order skills, particularly when supported by AI-driven adaptive feedback and resources (Gunawan et al., 2021; Kavitha & Joshith, 2024). MagicSchool AI's Project-Based Learning (PBL) Generator is a powerful tool designed to help educators create comprehensive, standards-aligned PBL experiences for their students. This MagicTool streamlines the process of developing engaging projects that adhere to the core principles of project-based learning while ensuring alignment with STEM content standards. Teachers have the ability to select which specific content standards they want their lesson built upon; state-specific content standards such as TEKS (Texas Essential Knowledge and Skills) or national science content standards such as NGSS (Next Generation Science Standards).

To use the PBL Generator, educators begin by accessing the tool through the MagicSchool AI platform. They are then prompted to input key information about their desired project, including the desired grade level, project topic or title, content standards to align to, and any additional details they wish to incorporate. The key to utilizing the PBL Generator effectively is to provide specific details on the project description and desired outcomes that you hope to see as the lesson is taught; the more specific you are, the better the product generated will be.

Before adding desired information, try clicking the "exemplar" button at the top of the PBL Generator page. This auto-generates examples of what information should be included in the required input boxes as well as providing an exemplar PBL lesson based on NGSS standards. Scroll down to see the exemplar as well as further probing questions that prompt the AI to provide more information and further fill in the outline that it generated. This helps teachers more effectively utilize the MagicTool to create their own PBL lesson plan. Unfortunately, the ability to prompt the AI for further information is a feature that is only offered on the premium plans and requires teachers to pay a fee to utilize. In later sections, this chapter will show you how to utilize other tools to fill in the lesson plan generated without paying for the premium features.

Once the necessary information is provided, the PBL Generator leverages its AI capabilities to create a comprehensive project overview plan. The tool's adherence to PBL principles ensures that the generated projects are immersive, inquiry-based, and focused on real-world problem-solving, encouraging students to explore, question, and collaborate throughout the learning process. The generated PBL lesson plan typically includes:

- Overview of key components(i.e. the driving question or challenge)
- Connection to real-world context
- Information on in-depth inquiry
- Opportunity for student voice and choice
- Student reflection piece
- Opportunities for collaboration
- Interdisciplinary connections
- Assessment ideas
- Specific standards the lesson is aligned to.

The PBL outline serves as a robust foundation for teachers to build upon but it does not give exact lesson items, assignments, timeline, or assessment questions. The PBL outline provides a structured framework that covers essential elements of project-based learning while allowing for customization based on specific classroom needs. Teachers can then review the AI-generated plan, making adjustments and refinements as necessary to tailor the project to their students' needs and their teaching style. One of the key advantages of using the PBL Generator is its ability to save teachers significant time in the planning process. By automating the initial stages of project development, educators can focus more on fine-tuning the details and preparing for implementation.

Science Sample Project: The Water Cycle

To illustrate the practical application of MagicTools in STEM education, this chapter will focus on one specific science topic and grade level: 6th-8th grade Science, the water cycle. By exploring this topic through various MagicTools, we will demonstrate how educators can create a comprehensive, engaging, and standards-aligned learning experience. The water cycle serves as an ideal sample project, as it encompasses multiple aspects of Earth science, allows for hands-on experimentation, is taught in various forms at all levels (i.e. elementary, middle, and high school), and relates directly to students' everyday experiences.

Throughout this chapter, we will use the water cycle as a central theme to showcase how different MagicTools can be employed to generate lesson plans, create interactive activities, design assessments, and develop project-based learning experiences. This approach will not only provide concrete examples of MagicTool usage but also illustrate how the various AI-powered resources can be integrated to create a cohesive and immersive learning journey for students. By focusing on this specific topic, educators will gain insights into how they can adapt and apply these tools to other STEM subjects, enhancing their teaching practices and fostering experiential learning in their classrooms.

PBL Generator & The Water Cycle

When inputting prompts into the PBL generator teachers begin by specifying the grade level; this chapter's comprehensive example will use 6th grade. Next, educators should input the specific content standards they want to address. For this chapter, we will utilize national Next Generation Science Standards (NGSS) rather than any state-specific standards.

For the water cycle, relevant NGSS standards include:

- MS-ESS2-4: Develop a model to describe the cycling of water through Earth's systems driven by energy from the sun and the force of gravity.
- MS-PS1-4: Develop a model that predicts and describes changes in particle motion, temperature, and state of a pure substance when thermal energy is added or removed

These standards should be entered into the PBL Generator to ensure alignment with curriculum requirements.

In the project description field, teachers should provide a brief overview of their desired topic (i.e. the water cycle). Include terms that are specific to the standards selected such as evaporation, precipitation, condensation, accumulation, force of gravity, thermal energy, particle motion, and pure substance. Additionally, teachers should specify desired project outcomes, such as creating a physical model of the water cycle or designing a presentation that explains how water moves through different states of matter. After inputting this information, the PBL generator will use its AI capabilities to create a project plan outline. Teachers can then review and refine this AI-generated plan, adding their own insights or adjusting elements to better suit their classroom needs. Do not hesitate to revise or add to the prompts when using any of the AI tools discussed in this chapter; remember, the better the prompts, the better the output generated. Once the MagicTool has generated an output, there will be an option at the top of the page to "edit prompt" that will allow teachers to revise and make changes as desired.

Figure 2 Inputting prompts into the PBL Generator

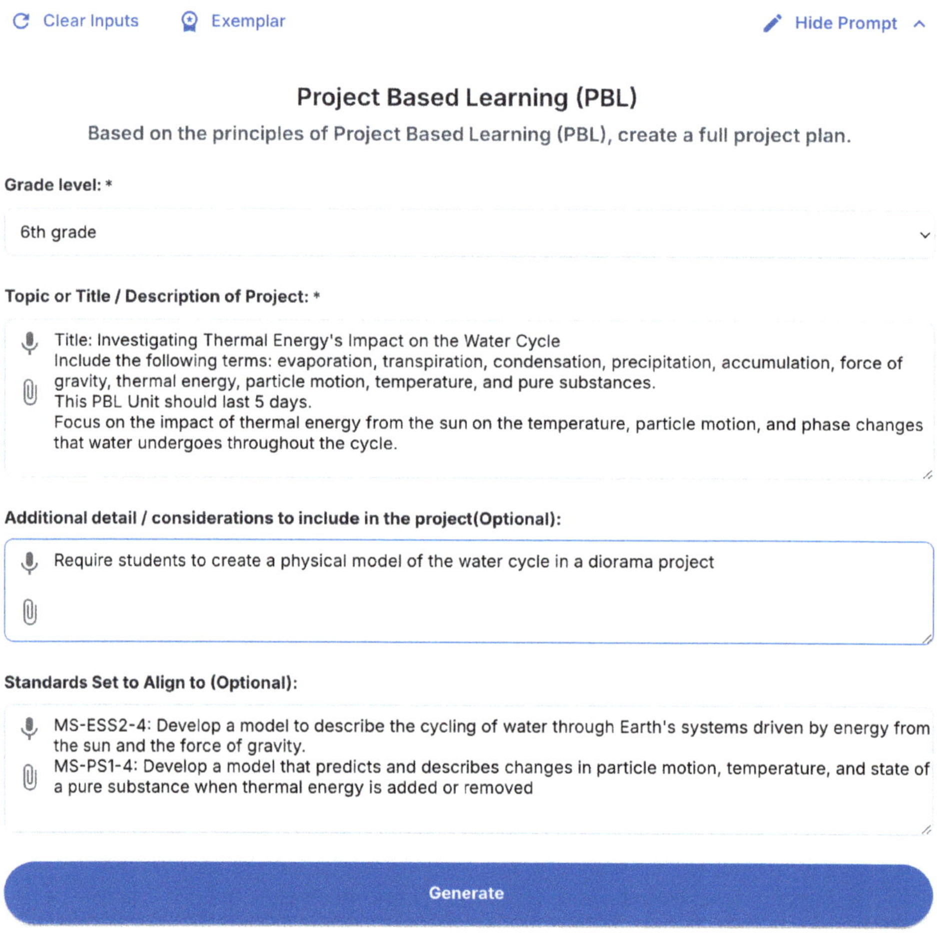

While the PBL Generator provides a solid foundation for project-based learning experiences, educators utilizing the free version of MagicSchool AI can further enhance these projects by utilizing other STEM-focused tools available within the MagicSchool AI platform. These additional tools, which will be explored in greater detail later in this chapter, can help flush out specific aspects of the PBL outline and allow teachers to feel confident in the PLB unit they have created. For instance, the Lesson Plan Generator can be used to develop detailed daily plans within the larger project framework, while the Science Labs Generator can create engaging hands-on activities that align with the project's learning objectives. By combining these various tools, educators can create rich, multifaceted STEM learning experiences that engage students and promote deep understanding of content standards.

DEVELOPING 5E MODEL LESSONS WITH MAGICSCHOOL AI

The 5E instructional model is a widely-used framework in science education that promotes inquiry-based learning and active student engagement (Bahadir & Dikmen, 2022; Cakir, 2017; Iscan & Seyhan, 2021). Developed by the Biological Sciences Curriculum Study (BSCS), the model consists of five phases: Engage, Explore, Explain, Elaborate, and Evaluate (Bybee, 2015). Each phase serves a specific purpose in the learning process, guiding students from initial engagement with a topic to a deeper understanding and application of concepts.

Implementing the 5E model in a K-12 classroom begins with the Engage phase, where teachers capture students' attention and stimulate their curiosity about the topic. This might involve presenting a puzzling phenomenon, asking thought-provoking questions, or demonstrating an intriguing experiment. The Explore phase follows, allowing students to investigate the concept through hands-on activities, experiments, or research. During this phase, teachers act as facilitators, providing guidance and resources while encouraging students to make observations and form hypotheses. In the Explain phase, students articulate their understanding of the concept, while teachers introduce formal terms and clarify any misconceptions.

Digital design tools can be incorporated throughout these phases to enhance both teaching and learning. For example, during the Explain phase, students can use Canva to create infographics or visual summaries that communicate their understanding of key concepts. In the Elaborate phase, Canva enables students to design project posters, digital reports, or presentations as they apply their knowledge to new situations or problems, deepening their learning and providing opportunities for creativity. Finally, in the Evaluate phase, teachers can assess student comprehension and skills through a variety of methods, including Canva-created presentations, digital portfolios, or collaborative projects, allowing students to demonstrate their mastery in visually engaging ways.

Figure 3 The 5E Inquiry Model in STEM

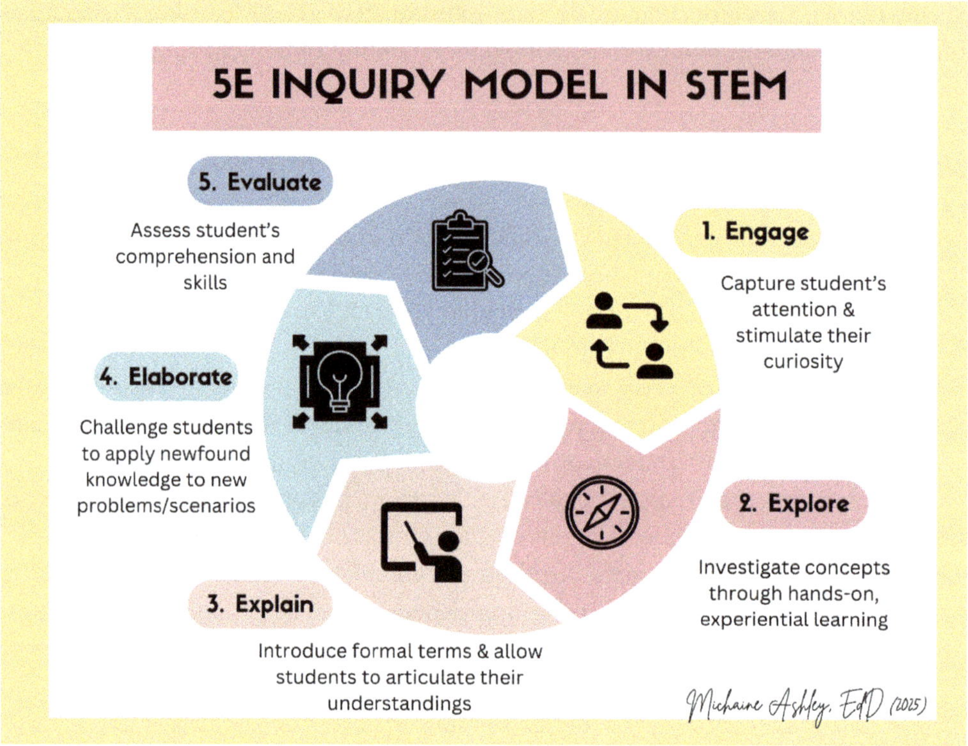

Bloom's Taxonomy & the 5E Model

The 5E instructional model aligns closely with Bloom's Taxonomy and promotes higher-order thinking skills in K-12 students (Cakir, 2017; Kaya & Yildirim, 2022). As learners progress through the five phases (i.e. Engage, Explore, Explain, Elaborate, and Evaluate), they naturally move up the cognitive levels of Bloom's Taxonomy. The initial Engage phase often activates lower-order thinking skills like remembering and understanding as students connect to prior knowledge. However, as students move through the Explore and Explain phases, they begin to apply and analyze information, transitioning to higher-order thinking. The Elaborate phase encourages students to synthesize and create, while the Evaluate phase promotes critical evaluation skills. The 5E model's structure inherently supports the progression from basic recall to complex problem-solving and creativity, making it an effective tool for developing critical thinking skills in K-12 classrooms (Sotakova & Ganajova, 2023).

The integration of the 5E model and Bloom's Taxonomy offers significant benefits for K-12 STEM students by providing a comprehensive framework for developing higher-order thinking skills and promoting active, inquiry-based, experiential learning (Tegegne & Kelkay, 2023). This integrated approach enhances student engagement and deepens understanding of STEM concepts by encouraging students to apply, analyze, evaluate, and create rather than simply memorize information. For example, during the Explore phase, students might apply and analyze concepts by creating their own model ecosystem and conduct an experiment using thermal energy to observe the 4 distinct stages of the water cycle. In the Elaborate phase, students can create a song or rap about the stages of the water cycle and how thermal energy from the sun impacted each stage. This alignment ensures that STEM instruction not only covers content but also develops critical thinking, problem-solving, and metacognitive skills essential for success in STEM fields. The integration of these frameworks allows educators to design more effective assessments that target various cognitive levels, providing a more comprehensive evaluation of student learning and guiding instructional decisions (Bahadir & Dikmen, 2022; Cakir, 2017; Sotakova & Ganajova, 2023).

Figure 4 Bloom's Taxonomy and the 5E Model

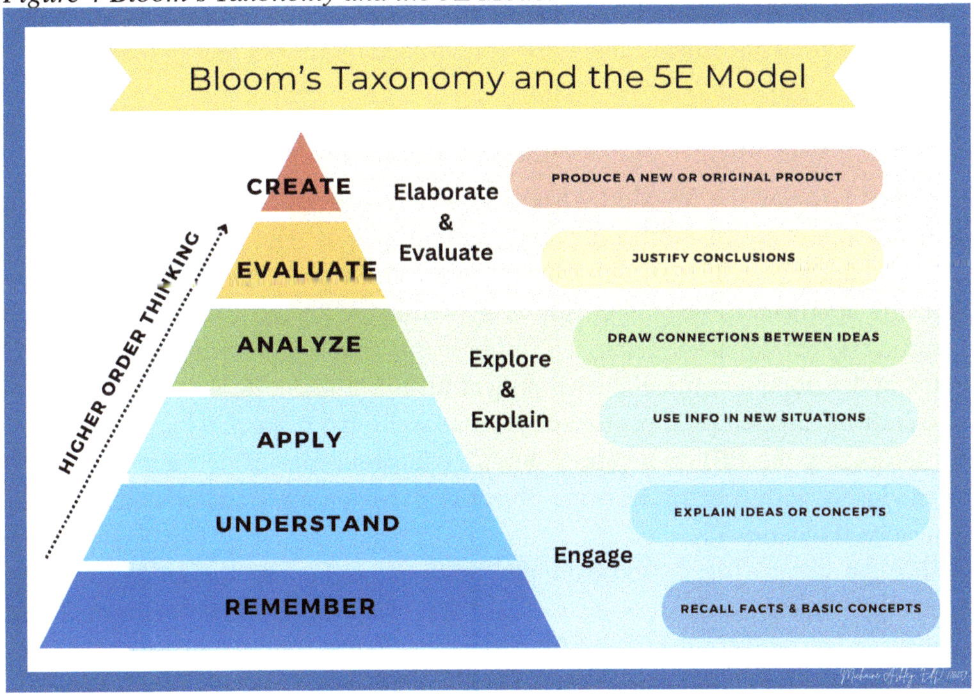

Utilizing the 5E Model MagicTool

MagicSchool's 5E Model Science Lesson Plan Generator has emerged as a powerful tool for educators seeking to implement the 5E instructional model effectively. Building off of the framework created by the PBL Generator, teachers begin by inputting basic information such as the subject, grade level, and learning objectives, to quickly obtain a structured lesson plan that follows the 5E framework, complete with suggested activities and assessments for each phase. The key to utilizing this tool effectively is to provide the AI with specific prompts that you obtained from the PBL generator and build from there. If the 5E model generated doesn't provide enough details or isn't what you were expecting, don't hesitate to edit the prompt to add more detail and specific expectations; remember that the majority of scientific advancements of today came from the process of multiple experimental trial and errors.

When using the 5E Model MagicTool teachers can expect for the AI to generate a list of objectives, a basic materials list for any experiments proposed, and a bulleted list of ideas for activities and experiments to utilize in each stage of the 5E model. While this tool does not provide specific lesson documents, it does provide a detailed outline of each of the 5 stages with specific activities and lesson elements for the K-12 teacher to build upon. Utilizing the 5E lesson plan generated with this MagicTool, teachers will then be able to utilize the Science Labs generator, Choice Boards generator, Worksheet generator, and 3D science assessment generator to create the lesson documents and activities outlined by the 5E Model MagicTool.

The 5E Model and The Water Cycle

When utilizing the 5E Model MagicTool, it is crucial to provide detailed and specific prompts to maximize the quality of the output. The precision and clarity of the input directly influence the effectiveness of the generated lesson plans. One strategic approach to achieving this is by starting with the PBL (Project-Based Learning) generator as we discussed earlier in this chapter. This initial step not only helps in developing comprehensive project ideas but also offers valuable insights into crafting targeted prompts for subsequent use in more specialized MagicTools. By leveraging the PBL generator's output, educators can refine their prompts to align closely with specific learning objectives, curriculum standards, and desired educational outcomes.

For the water cycle lesson example, teachers begin with the grade level and specific topic, standards, or objectives that they want the lesson to focus on. These inputs can be simple or very complex depending on the desired outcome of the lesson. Consider adding more information in the "additional customization" section to specify exactly what should be included in the lesson model (i.e. a choice board activity, how many hands on activities are desired, and the final assessment product model creation). In the final section, teachers should specify what specific content standards that the AI should align to; this chapter utilizes NGSS national standards.

Figure 5 Inputting Prompts into the 5E Model Lesson Plan Generator

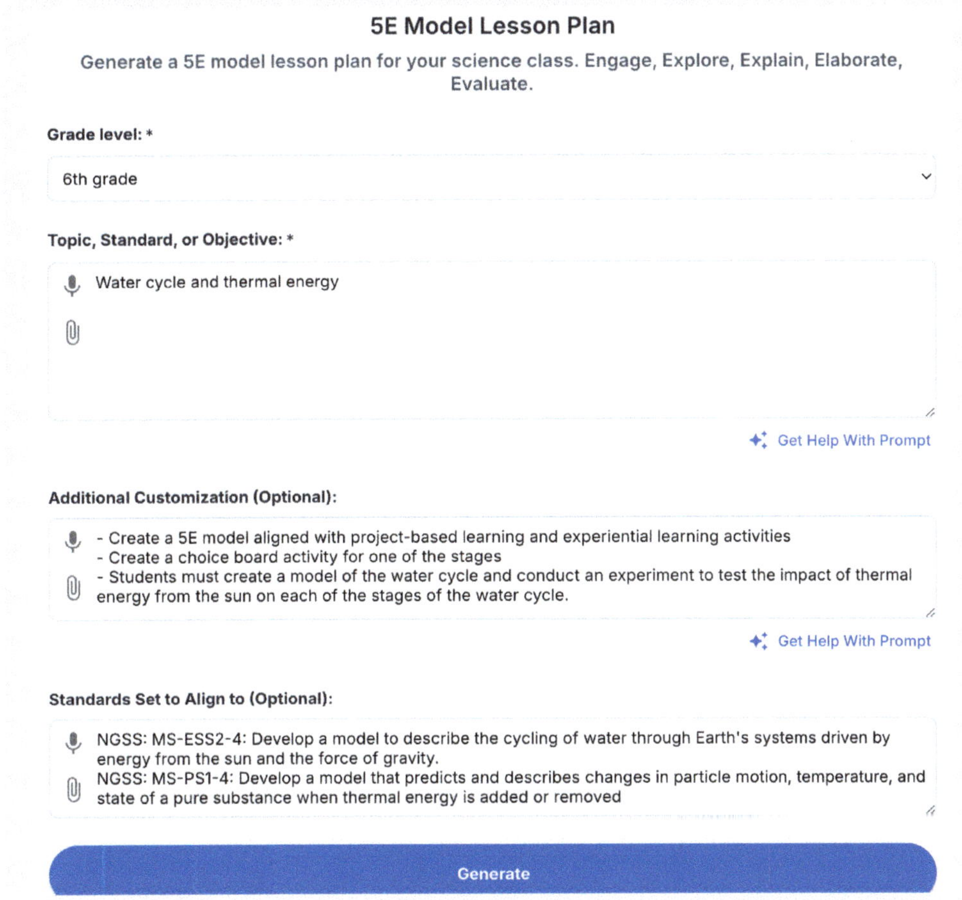

Upon inputting the required information, the AI generates a comprehensive 5E model lesson plan outline that includes a detailed, bulleted list of ideas and resources for each stage of the instructional sequence: Engage, Explore, Explain, Elaborate, and Evaluate. If a teacher specifies a particular number of desired activities, the AI will tailor the lesson plan to include that exact number of activities; ensuring alignment with the teacher's preferences. This feature is particularly advantageous for educators, as it significantly reduces the time spent on lesson design and brainstorming by providing concrete examples to incorporate into each phase of the 5E model.

Teachers can then review the generated lesson plan, select the ideas that best align with their teaching objectives and classroom needs, and easily integrate these elements into more specialized tools that will be discussed later in this chapter. These tools include the Science Labs generator, Choice Board Generator, Worksheet generator, 3D Science Assessments generator, and the Rubric generator. By leveraging these tools, educators can further refine and enhance their lesson plans, creating a cohesive and engaging educational experience that meets specific learning outcomes and assessment criteria. This streamlined process allows teachers to focus on refining their instructional strategies rather than starting lesson planning from scratch, thereby optimizing their time and resources while ensuring high-quality educational content.

Figure 6 Sample 5E Lesson Plan Generated by MagicSchool AI

5E Lesson Plan Model

Engage

- Begin with a question: "What happens to a puddle of water on a hot day?"
- Show a short video of the water cycle and discuss students' prior knowledge and experiences with water in their environment.
- Introduce the concept of thermal energy and its relationship to the water cycle.

Explore

- **Activity 1: Water Cycle Model Creation**
  - In groups, students will create a model of the water cycle using clear plastic containers, water, and small rocks or soil.
  - They will label each part (evaporation, condensation, precipitation, collection) and discuss the process within their groups.
- **Activity 2: Experiment on Thermal Energy**
  - Students will set up their models in a sunny location or under a heat lamp.
  - They will place ice cubes in one container to observe the effects of cooling on the water cycle.
  - Students will record the temperature of the water and observe the changes over time, focusing on evaporation and condensation.

Explain

- Facilitate a class discussion about the observations made during the experiments.
- Introduce key vocabulary terms such as evaporation, condensation, precipitation, and thermal energy.
- Explain the science behind each stage of the water cycle and how thermal energy affects these processes.

Elaborate

- **Choice Board Activity**
  - Students will choose one of the following options to extend their learning:

1. Create a poster explaining one stage of the water cycle and its importance.
2. Write a short story from the perspective of a water droplet traveling through the water cycle.
3. Design a simple experiment to test thermal energy's effect on evaporation (e.g., comparing covered vs. uncovered containers).
4. Create a digital presentation using a tool like Google Slides to share findings with the class.

Evaluate

- Students will present their models and findings from the experiments.
- Assess students on their participation, understanding of the water cycle, and their ability to connect thermal energy to the stages of the water cycle.
- Use a rubric to evaluate the choice board activity based on creativity, understanding of the concept, and presentation skills.

Conclusion

- Summarize the importance of the water cycle and the role of thermal energy.
- Encourage students to think about how these concepts apply to their everyday lives and the environment.

The benefits of using AI-generated 5E lesson plans are numerous for both teachers and students. For educators, it significantly reduces planning time, allowing them to focus more on personalization and delivery of instruction. The AI-generated plans often include innovative ideas and resources that teachers might not have considered, enriching the learning experience. For students, consistently structured lessons following the 5E model can lead to improved engagement, deeper understanding of scientific concepts, and enhanced critical thinking skills.

However, it's important to note that while AI tools like MagicSchool's MagicTools can provide a solid foundation, teachers should review and adapt the generated plans to suit their specific classroom needs and student demographics. The AI-generated content serves as a starting point, which educators can then refine based on their expertise and knowledge of their students. This combination of AI efficiency and human insight can lead to highly effective, engaging science lessons that truly embody the spirit of the 5E instructional model.

AI-ASSISTED SCIENCE LAB CREATION

Designing effective science labs for K-12 education poses several challenges, including limited resources, inadequate space, and the need for safety protocols. Traditional lab experiences often fall short of providing engaging, hands-on learning opportunities due to constraints such as outdated equipment, insufficient storage, and inadequate teacher training in lab management. This is especially true in elementary schools where the majority of teachers hold generalist certifications and did not receive the same level of specialty lab management training that teachers with STEM-specific degrees received. Despite the lack of lab-specific instructional training, ensuring student safety while conducting experiments is a vital part of designing engaging lessons that center around hands-on learning in a lab-style setting. However, this requires careful planning and adherence to safety guidelines which can be especially challenging for teachers who do not have a background in a STEM specialized fields.

MagicSchool AI offers a solution to these challenges by providing tools that can generate innovative lab ideas and procedures. The Science Lab Generator allows educators to create engaging, standards-aligned, hands-on laboratory activities tailored to specific topics and learning objectives. This MagicTool simplifies the process of designing meaningful science experiments, ensuring they are relevant and directly applicable to the topics being taught. By leveraging AI, teachers can access a wide range of lab ideas, reducing the time spent on brainstorming and planning while enhancing student engagement and curriculum alignment.

Teachers can also input specific constraints, such as a shortage of supplies or inadequate space, into the MagicTool Lab generator and the AI will adapt the lab design to accommodate these limitations. This feature is particularly beneficial for educators working in resource-constrained environments, as it allows them to create effective and engaging lab experiences despite logistical challenges. By specifying these constraints, the AI can suggest alternative materials or procedures that are readily available or require minimal space, ensuring that the lab remains feasible and safe for students. Additionally, the AI can provide suggestions for repurposing existing materials or leveraging digital tools to simulate lab experiences when physical resources are limited, further enhancing the flexibility and accessibility of the generated lab plans.

Safety considerations are a critical aspect of science lab design. Ensuring that students and teachers are aware of potential hazards and take necessary precautions is essential for preventing accidents. Traditional safety protocols involve teaching and posting science safety rules, providing proper personal protective equipment (PPE) such as goggles and lab aprons, and conducting regular inspections of the lab environment. AI can play a crucial role in enhancing safety by identifying potential risks and suggesting mitigation strategies.

When generating a lab with materials or chemicals that are hazardous, prompt the AI to reference the Materials Safety Data Sheet (MSDS), include specific instructions for wearing PPE, and discuss emergency procedures. Figure 7 provides an example from a high school chemistry lab investigating pH differences between a variety of household and laboratory substances. For this type of lab, the safety considerations are especially vital in ensuring that students are safe while simultaneously engaging in important experiential learning.

Figure 7 Example Chemistry lab demonstrating the importance of safety instructions

Science Lab: Testing pH of Various Substances

Grade Level: 10th Grade
Subject: Chemistry
Lab Duration: 1 hour

Objectives

- Understand and apply the concept of pH.
- Measure the pH of various household and laboratory substances.
- Differentiate between acidic, neutral, and basic substances.
- Compare strong and weak acids and bases.

Materials

- pH paper or electronic pH meter
- Distilled water
- Household substances: lemon juice, vinegar, baking soda solution, dish soap
- Laboratory chemicals: hydrochloric acid (HCl), potassium hydroxide (KOH)
- Beakers or small containers
- Safety goggles
- Gloves
- Lab aprons
- MSDS sheets for all chemicals

Pre-Lab Safety Instructions

1. **Personal Protective Equipment (PPE)**: Wear safety goggles, gloves, and lab aprons at all times.
2. **Handling Chemicals**: Always handle hydrochloric acid and potassium hydroxide with care. Refer to the MSDS sheets for each chemical to understand the hazards and first aid measures.
3. **Work Area**: Ensure that your work area is clean and organized. Avoid any food or drinks in the lab.
4. **Emergency Procedures**: Know the location of the emergency shower, eyewash station, and first aid kit. In case of chemical contact with skin or eyes, rinse immediately with plenty of water and seek assistance.

The integration of AI in lab safety assessment offers several benefits, particularly for newer teachers or those without a science background. AI systems can evaluate historical data to identify patterns that may lead to unsafe conditions, providing insights that human observers might miss. This proactive approach allows teachers to be aware of potential risks before conducting the lab and enables them to respond to safety hazards in real time. This is especially valuable for educators who may not have extensive experience with science labs, as it helps them prepare for and prevent safety issues from occurring. By leveraging AI's analytical capabilities, teachers can gain a deeper understanding of potential hazards, even if they are not familiar with them from personal experience. This awareness empowers them to take necessary precautions, ensuring a safer learning environment for their students and reducing the risk of accidents.

Science Lab Generator & The Water Cycle

When designing science lab activities with the support of AI tools such as the Science Lab Generator, it is essential that educators carefully craft their prompts to ensure both instructional rigor and student safety. One effective strategy is to draw on prompts generated from project-based learning (PBL) and the 5E model generators, while explicitly including elements of the scientific method. This approach ensures that the AI-generated lab activities are aligned with key principles of scientific inquiry, such as hypothesis formation, experimentation, and data analysis. By embedding these elements in their prompts, teachers can help students develop critical thinking skills and a deeper understanding of scientific processes, moving beyond rote memorization to authentic inquiry.

Figure 8 provides a practical example of this process. In the figure, you can see how specific keywords and activities-such as "hypothesis," "experiment," and "data analysis"-are incorporated into the prompt input for the Science Lab Generator. These terms guide the AI to produce lab activities that reflect the structure and logic of the scientific method. However, upon closer examination of Figure 8, it becomes evident that while the scientific method is well represented, there is a notable absence of explicit safety-related prompts. For instance, keywords like "PPE," "safety procedures," or "emergency protocols" are missing from the prompt area. This omission can result in lab plans that do not adequately address essential safety considerations, potentially putting students at risk.

To address this gap, educators should refine their prompts to include both scientific inquiry and safety requirements. For example, instead of simply asking for a lab plan on thermal energy in the water cycle, a more comprehensive prompt might be: "Generate a lab plan on thermal energy in the water cycle that includes the scientific method and detailed safety procedures for handling heat lamps and avoiding spills." By specifying these requirements, teachers can ensure that the resulting lab plan is not only educationally robust but also safe for all students. This practice is especially valuable for newer teachers or those less familiar with laboratory safety, as it helps them comply with school and district standards and fosters a culture of responsible scientific practice.

Figure 8 Inputting Prompts into the Science Labs Generator

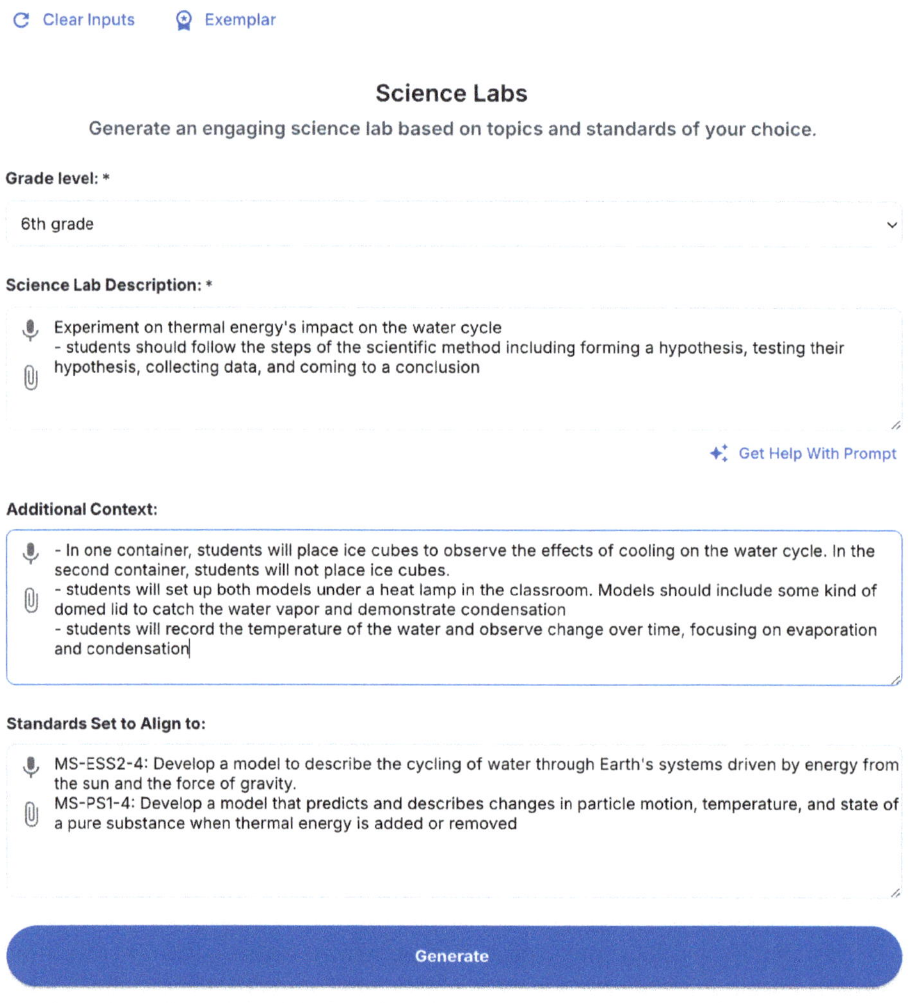

Finally, while AI can greatly enhance the efficiency and quality of lab planning, it is crucial for educators to review all AI-generated content for accuracy and safety before implementation. Teachers should verify that suggested experiments and procedures align with curriculum standards and are appropriate for their specific classroom environment. For example, if a lab station is set up near an electrical outlet, prompts should include precautions to prevent water spills near the outlet. By combining AI's capabilities with thoughtful human oversight, educators can create engaging, safe, and effective science labs that meet the needs of modern STEM education.

CREATING SCIENCE CHOICE BOARDS WITH AI

Choice boards are a versatile instructional tool that has gained popularity in STEM education for their ability to personalize learning and boost student engagement. These assignments present students with a variety of activities related to a specific topic or skill; allowing them to choose tasks that align with their interests, learning styles, and proficiency levels. By providing autonomy over their learning process, choice boards empower students to take ownership of their education, fostering a sense of responsibility and motivation. This approach not only enhances student engagement but also promotes a deeper connection to the subject matter, as students are more likely to be invested in activities they have chosen themselves.

The benefits of choice boards in STEM education are multifaceted. They cater to diverse learning styles (i.e. visual, auditory, and kinesthetic) ensuring that every student has an opportunity to excel, regardless of their strengths or challenges. Additionally, choice boards promote creativity and personal expression, as students can select activities that allow them to showcase their skills and interests in meaningful ways. By offering a range of options, choice boards also help teachers meet the unique needs of individual students; making them an effective tool for inclusive learning environments. This flexibility is particularly valuable in STEM subjects, where abstract concepts can often be daunting and the use of hands-on activities can make complex ideas more accessible.

MagicSchool AI's Choice Board Generator leverages AI to create diverse and engaging choice boards for STEM educators. This MagicTool allows teachers to generate customized boards that cater to specific learning objectives and student needs. By inputting the information already generated in the PBL project outline and 5E Lesson model, teachers will easily be able to provide specific prompts that will ensure the choice board generated matches the rest of the lesson they are designing. The efficiency and customization of this MagicTool enables teachers to focus more on teaching and less on planning potential choice elements for the board, allowing them to provide more personalized support to their students.

One of the key advantages of using MagicSchool AI's Choice Board Generator is its ability to personalize learning experiences. Teachers can create boards that offer different levels of complexity, formats, and assessment options, to ensure that each student can engage with the material in a way that suits their abilities and interests. This personalization is crucial for differentiation as it allows teachers to meet the diverse needs of their students within a single assignment. Teachers can easily generate multiple versions of the same assignment in tiers based on reading level (i.e., below grade level, at grade level, above grade level) to increase accessibility and differentiation for their students without reducing or removing requirements. By providing options that cater to various learning styles and strengths, choice boards help ensure that all students are challenged and supported appropriately.

Choice Boards & The Water Cycle

Implementing choice boards in STEM classrooms can be straightforward and effective. Teachers can use these boards for various purposes, such as independent work, review activities, or formative assessments. By allowing students to choose which activities they want to complete, teachers can encourage autonomy and creativity while ensuring that students meet specific learning objectives. This flexibility also allows educators to integrate choice boards seamlessly into existing curricula, enhancing the overall educational experience without requiring significant changes to their teaching practices.

When using the prompts from the PBL and 5E lesson generator to input into the Choice Board Generator, the first step involves specifying any particular activities or tasks that teachers want to include in the choice board. This might involve selecting specific STEM projects, experiments, or presentations that align with the learning objectives derived from the PBL and 5E models. By explicitly stating these activities, teachers can ensure that the AI-generated choice board includes relevant and meaningful options that support the broader educational goals of the lesson.

Another crucial aspect is determining the number of choices to include on the board. A typical setup is a 3x3 grid, offering students nine different activities to choose from. This structure provides a balanced range of options without overwhelming students while still allowing them to select tasks that align with their interests and learning styles. Teachers should input this preference directly into the prompts used to ensure that the AI produces a board with the desired number of choices. Specifying the learning objectives for the choice board assignment is another essential component. Educators should clearly define what skills or knowledge they want students to master by completing the activities on the board, ensuring that the AI-generated options align with these objectives. Figure 9 demonstrates an example of how to incorporate these prompts with the ones generated in the PBL and 5E Lesson to create a list of assignments and descriptions to include in a 3x3 choice board.

Figure 9 Inputting Prompts into the Choice Board Generator

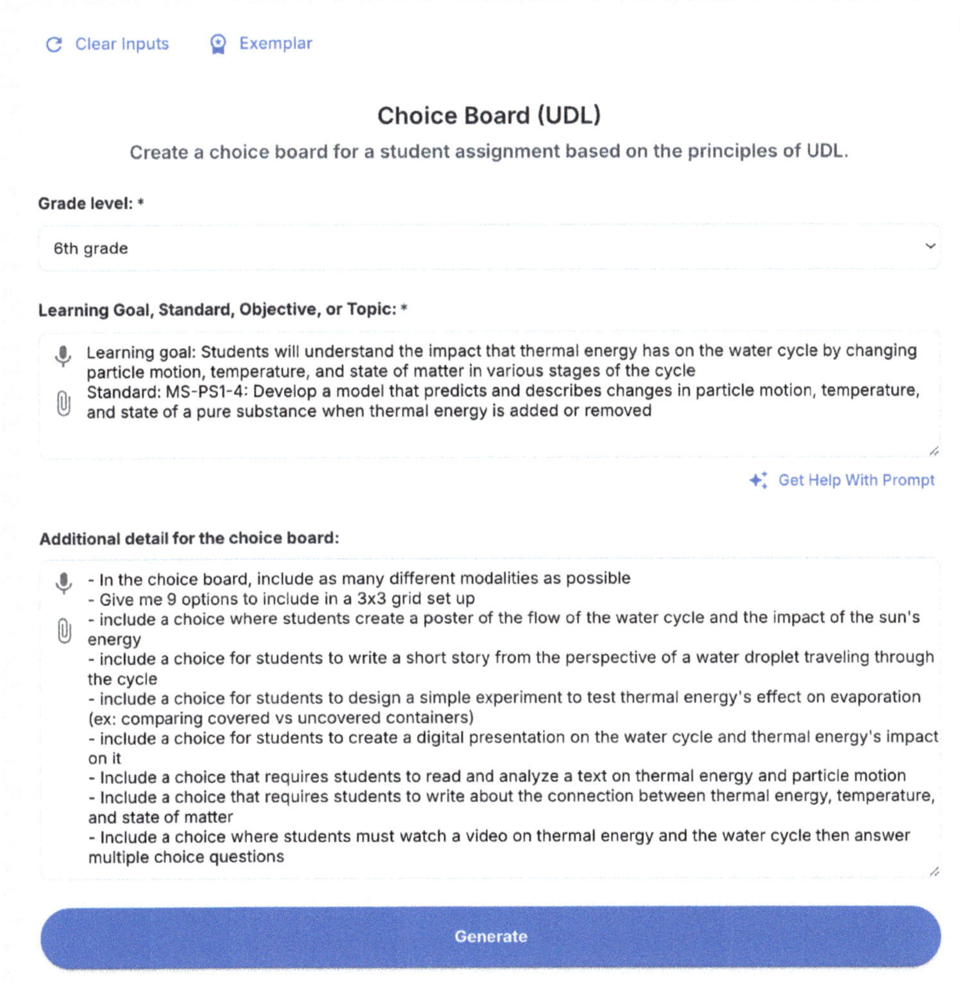

Editing and Formatting the Choice Board

The choice board generated by the AI tool will typically be presented in a table format with assignment titles in one column and detailed descriptions in another, as illustrated in Figure 10. If any of the generated assignments do not meet the teacher's criteria or align with their envisioned classroom activities, educators can utilize the "edit prompt" feature located at the top of the page. This allows them to revisit and refine the original prompts, removing or modifying items as needed. Once satisfied with the assignments, teachers will need to organize the information into a 3x3 grid format, or other grid size desired, which can be easily created using tools like Microsoft Word or Google Docs. Alternatively, educators can leverage platforms like Canva, which offers free access to K-12 educators and provides pre-formatted templates, to enhance the visual appeal of the choice board.

Choice boards can be structured to accommodate various completion methods, each offering unique incentives and challenges for students. The “Tic-Tac-Toe” approach requires students to complete assignments in a row (horizontally, vertically, or diagonally) which fosters a sense of strategy and accomplishment. Another option is the “Blackout” method, where students complete the entire board to earn additional incentives or bragging rights; providing a comprehensive learning experience by completing all of the different modalities included. The “Scatter” method offers more flexibility, allowing students to select any three assignments from the board, which can be particularly beneficial for students who prefer a more personalized learning path. To ensure clarity and consistency, it is essential to include clear instructions at the top of the choice board document. These directions should specify which completion method students are expected to follow, along with any additional guidelines or expectations. By providing this structure, educators can ensure that students understand the requirements and can navigate the choice board effectively.

Figure 10 Example Choice Board for the Water Cycle

Choice Board: Understanding Thermal Energy and the Water Cycle

Assignment Title	Assignment Description
Water Cycle Poster	Create a poster illustrating the water cycle and how the sun's energy impacts it.
Water Droplet Story	Write a short story from the perspective of a water droplet traveling through the water cycle.
Thermal Energy Experiment	Design a simple experiment to test how thermal energy affects evaporation (e.g., comparing covered vs uncovered containers).
Digital Presentation	Create a digital presentation explaining the water cycle and the impact of thermal energy on it.
Text Analysis	Read and analyze a text about thermal energy and particle motion, summarizing key points.
Connection Writing	Write an explanation about the relationship between thermal energy, temperature, and state of matter.
Video Analysis	Watch a video on thermal energy and the water cycle, then answer multiple-choice questions based on it.
Model Creation	Build a 3D model demonstrating the states of matter in the water cycle and how thermal energy changes them.
Group Discussion	Participate in a group discussion about how thermal energy affects weather patterns and the water cycle.

To further enhance personalized learning through choice boards, teachers can leverage digital design tools like Canva to create visually appealing and highly accessible learning resources. Canva offers a wide range of customizable templates, including popular formats such as 3x3 grids, which enable educators to organize and present choice board options clearly and attractively. By inputting content generated by the Choice Board Generator into these preformatted templates, teachers can tailor the visual layout to align precisely with their instructional goals and the diverse needs of their students. This thoughtful design not only improves the usability of choice boards but also helps students easily navigate and select from differentiated activities that match their abilities and interests. Furthermore, Canva's intuitive interface allows teachers to quickly modify and update choice boards, fostering flexibility and responsiveness in lesson planning. Integrating Canva into the creation of choice boards thus combines the power of AI-driven personalization with engaging visual design, enhancing both teacher efficiency and student motivation.

By modeling the use of Canva in designing choice boards, teachers not only create accessible resources but also introduce students to digital design tools they can use for their own learning products. Teachers can further boost student engagement in their choice boards by encouraging students to design personalized project artifacts (i.e. posters, infographics, or presentations) that showcase their unique understanding and creativity in Canva. This not only allows students to demonstrate mastery in diverse and engaging ways but also supports differentiated expressions aligned with their learning preferences. Teachers can provide Canva templates tailored to different complexity levels or scaffolding needs, making it easier for all students to participate meaningfully while maintaining rigorous standards. This combination of AI-driven personalization and creative digital design aligns with broader educational goals of promoting equity, inclusivity, and making STEM education more accessible and engaging for a wide range of learners.

As AI continues to evolve, the potential for choice boards to enhance STEM education will only grow. The flexibility and customization offered by AI-generated choice boards make them an invaluable tool for educators seeking to enhance student engagement and autonomy in STEM education. However, teachers must be mindful of how to balance student autonomy with the need for guidance and support, particularly for students who may struggle with self-directed learning. By leveraging platforms like Canva to create visually appealing boards and structuring the assignments to align with specific learning objectives, teachers can create engaging and effective learning experiences that cater to diverse student needs and preferences. This integration of technology and pedagogy holds significant promise for transforming STEM education, making it more inclusive, interactive, and aligned with the needs of the 21st-century learner.

AI-GENERATED WORKSHEETS AND PRACTICE PROBLEMS

AI-generated worksheets and practice problems have become a valuable resource in STEM education by offering teachers a way to create customized, standards-aligned materials efficiently. Platforms like MagicSchool AI and Monsha provide tools that can generate worksheets tailored to specific topics and learning objectives that align with state-specific and national standards (NGSS). This alignment ensures that the generated content supports curriculum requirements, making it easier for educators to integrate these materials into their lesson plans.

One of the key advantages of AI-generated worksheets is their ability to support adaptive learning. By analyzing student performance and learning data, teachers can utilize AI tools to create personalized content that adjusts to individual students' needs and provide more challenging or supportive materials as needed. This adaptive approach helps ensure that students are consistently engaged and challenged, regardless of their skill level or learning pace. Teachers can utilize AI to generate practice problems that gradually increase in difficulty as students demonstrate mastery of specific skills; this method fosters continuous learning and improvement without increasing teacher's time spent creating assignments.

In addition to supporting adaptive learning, AI-generated worksheets offer significant time savings for educators. Traditional worksheet creation involves researching topics, writing questions, and formatting documents, which can be time-consuming and tedious. AI tools automate this process, allowing teachers to generate comprehensive worksheets in seconds. This efficiency enables educators to focus more on teaching and less on administrative tasks; further enhancing their ability to provide personalized support and feedback to students.

The integration of AI-generated worksheets into existing educational frameworks, such as the 5E model and project-based learning, further enhances their effectiveness. By aligning AI-generated content with these instructional models, educators can create cohesive learning experiences that combine hands-on activities, real-world applications, and personalized practice opportunities. This approach not only supports curriculum standards but also fosters deeper student engagement and understanding of STEM concepts.

Worksheets & The Water Cycle

To effectively integrate AI-generated worksheets into K-12 STEM classrooms, educators can leverage prompts from both the PBL and 5E model generators to ensure alignment with curriculum standards and pedagogical goals. After creating the PBL lesson outline on the water cycle and refining it through the 5E model's phases (e.g., "Explore" experiments on evaporation or "Elaborate" activities analyzing climate impacts), teachers can input these structured prompts into a worksheets generator. By explicitly stating the content standards and specific 5E-aligned activities, the AI can generate questions that reinforce the lesson's objectives, such as understanding the impact of thermal energy from the sun on the phase changes and particle motion in the water cycle. This approach ensures worksheets are not isolated tasks but cohesive extensions of hands-on learning experiences, bridging project-based inquiry with formative assessment.

When configuring the worksheets generator, educators should specify the number of questions (e.g., 10–15 items for a 30-minute activity) and modalities that align with the lesson's cognitive demands. For example, multiple-choice and true/false questions can assess baseline knowledge retention after the "Engage" phase, while open-ended prompts and modeling/drawing tasks, such as sketching the water cycle or describing real-world examples of precipitation, support higher-order thinking in the "Explain" and "Elaborate" stages. Including varied modalities caters to diverse learners: visual learners benefit from labeling diagrams, kinesthetic learners from interactive simulations, and analytical thinkers from data-driven questions. Teachers might also reference prior outputs, such as the PBL project's driving question ("How does thermal energy from the sun affect the movement and changes in water throughout the water cycle?") to design scenario-based problems that apply concepts to authentic contexts.

Learning objectives should directly inform worksheet design, ensuring questions target mastery of specific skills. If the 5E lesson on the water cycle aims for students to "analyze the role of solar energy in driving hydrological processes," the worksheet might include a mix of question types:

- Fill-in-the-blank: Reviewing vocabulary words and definitions
- Multiple-choice: Identifying the sun's role in changes of state of matter
- Open-ended: Making connections between various parts of the water cycle and presence of thermal energy/lack of thermal energy
- Modelling: Completing a diagram of the water cycle or draw how temperature affects cloud formation

By aligning these elements with the PBL project's milestones (e.g., a student-created diorama of the water cycle) and the 5E's "Evaluate" phase, worksheets become dynamic tools for reinforcing concepts and assessing progress. For instance, after students present their PBL dioramas, a worksheet could include reflective questions comparing their models to real-world problems such as run off or acid rain, thus connecting iterative learning to critical analysis. Remember that the more specific the prompt input, the better the worksheet created. If the initial worksheet created does not meet expectations or target the specific content standards or skills desired, teachers can click the "edit prompt" button at the top of the page and return to add or change the prompts until the worksheet meets the needs of their students.

Figure 11 Inputting Prompts into the Worksheet Generator

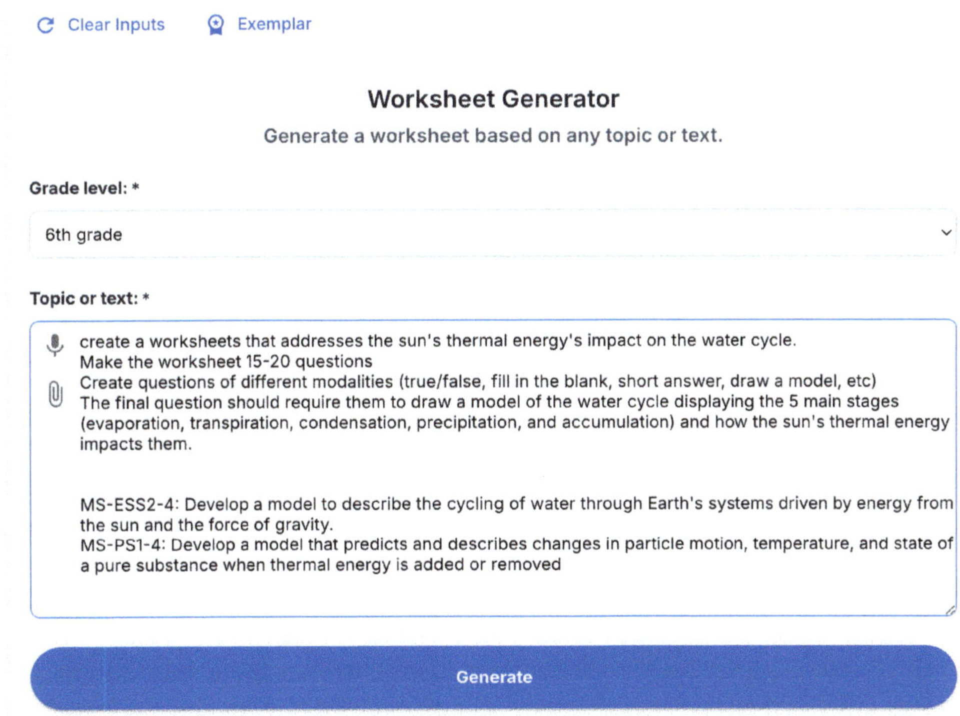

The strategic timing of worksheet integration enhances lesson coherence. During the 5E's "Explore" phase, a pre-lab worksheet might scaffold hypothesis development, while post-activity questions in "Explain" could guide data interpretation. In the water cycle PBL unit, teachers might deploy a worksheet after the "Elaborate" phase to evaluate interdisciplinary connections (e.g., math integration through rainfall data calculations, art integration through diorama creation, language art integration through research and presentations). By embedding AI-generated worksheets into this framework, educators streamline differentiation, adjusting question difficulty or modalities for diverse learners, while maintaining rigor. This method not only reinforces standards-aligned content but also cultivates metacognitive skills as students articulate their learning journey from hands-on exploration (PBL) to structured reflection (worksheets).

ASSESSMENTS, RUBRICS, AND GRADING

The integration of artificial intelligence into K-12 STEM education is rapidly transforming assessment practices, grading efficiency, and the development of rubrics. AI-powered assessment tools can streamline grading by providing timely, consistent, and personalized feedback to students, thus supporting teachers in managing large volumes of student work (Chen et al., 2021; Fu & Weng, 2024). Recent research demonstrates that AI-based platforms not only automate scoring for multiple-choice and short-answer questions but are increasingly capable of evaluating open-ended responses, offering nuanced insights into student understanding (Baker et al., 2023). These systems can also identify patterns in student errors, enabling teachers to adjust instruction responsively and target specific learning gaps (Stanja et al., 2022).

Despite these advantages, the effectiveness and fairness of AI-driven assessment tools depend on rigorous validation and ongoing teacher involvement. Studies emphasize the need for professional development to ensure educators can interpret and act on AI-generated data appropriately, as well as to mitigate potential biases inherent in automated systems (Baker et al., 2023; Frontline Research & Learning Institute, 2024). Additionally, teachers' preferences regarding AI-generated rubrics further highlight the importance of human expertise in the assessment process. While educators appreciate the efficiency of AI in generating initial rubric drafts and grading criteria, they consistently report a preference for customizing these tools to align with their instructional goals, subject matter, and student needs (Antonenko & Abromowitz, 2022; Keppler et al., 2024). Professional development that empowers teachers to co-design and refine AI-generated rubrics is critical for ensuring that assessment remains authentic, meaningful, and contextually relevant.

When thoughtfully integrated and paired with teacher expertise, AI tools can help educators create more comprehensive and meaningful assessments that capture the complexity of student learning. Building on this foundation, the 3D Science Assessment Generator exemplifies how AI can operationalize these principles by producing assessments grounded in the three-dimensional framework of scientific practices, crosscutting concepts, and disciplinary core ideas. This tool moves beyond traditional assessment formats to provide educators with innovative ways to evaluate deeper scientific understanding in alignment with the Next Generation Science Standards (NGSS).

3D Science Assessment Generator

The Three-Dimensional(3D) Science Assessment Generator tool produces assessments that evaluate students across three dimensions: scientific practices, crosscutting concepts, and disciplinary core ideas. This approach moves beyond traditional assessment methods, which often fail to capture the complexities of scientific thinking, towards a more comprehensive evaluation of students' scientific understanding (Furtak, 2023; Penuel et al., 2020). However, this specific MagicTool only utilizes the NGSS standards due to its alignment with the three dimensions. While this is a beneficial approach, teachers should be mindful to ensure the output aligns to the specific state standards desired by inputting specific prompts and key words.

The integration of the 3D Science Assessment Generator with the PBL generator and the 5E lesson generator enhances its effectiveness in STEM education by allowing teachers to create a comprehensive and cohesive learning experience for their students (Hardcastle et al., 2021; Herrmann-Abell et al., 2023; Herrmann-Abell & DeBoer, 2022) . As previously discussed, educators begin with the PBL generator to create their project outline, which provides a framework for the entire unit. This project-based approach aligns with the principles of experiential learning, allowing students to engage with real-world problems and develop critical thinking skills. The PBL outline serves as the foundation upon which the other elements of the unit can be built, ensuring that all components are working towards the same learning objectives.

Next, educators employ the 5E model generator to structure the learning experience, breaking down the project into the five phases: Engage, Explore, Explain, Elaborate, and Evaluate. This provides a systematic approach to inquiry-based learning, guiding students through the process of scientific discovery. Within each phase of the 5E model, educators can utilize the Science Lab, Choice Board, and Worksheet generators to fill in the detailed elements of the PBL unit. As discussed earlier in this Chapter, the Science Lab generator can be used to create hands-on experiments for the Explore phase, while the Choice Board generator can provide options for students to demonstrate their understanding in the Elaborate phase.

The 3D Science Assessment Generator can then be utilized at various stages of this process to create assessments that align with the project's objectives and the 5E model's phases. This integration ensures that assessments are not isolated tasks but integral components of a cohesive learning experience. For instance, formative assessments can be generated for the Explain phase to check students' understanding of key concepts, while summative assessments can be created for the Evaluate phase to measure overall learning outcomes. However, the types of assessments utilized will vary by the types of activities created for each stage of the 5E model. By aligning these assessments with the NGSS standards and the three dimensions of science learning (scientific practices, crosscutting concepts, and disciplinary core ideas), educators can ensure that students are developing a comprehensive understanding of STEM concepts and skills throughout the entire PBL unit

When inputting prompts into the 3D Assessment generator, teachers will select which stimulus type they prefer the AI to generate: data table, text written in scientific article style, grade-level appropriate text, or recommendation for the stimulus (see Figure 12). Additionally, similar to the other MagicTools already discussed in this chapter, the 3D assessment generator requires teachers to input the grade level, number of desired questions, and content standards to address. It is important to note that the 3D assessment generator does not incorporate state content standards due to its focus on the NGSS dimensions: disciplinary core ideas, crosscutting concepts, and scientific practices.

Figure 12 Inputting Prompts into the 3D Science Assessments Generator

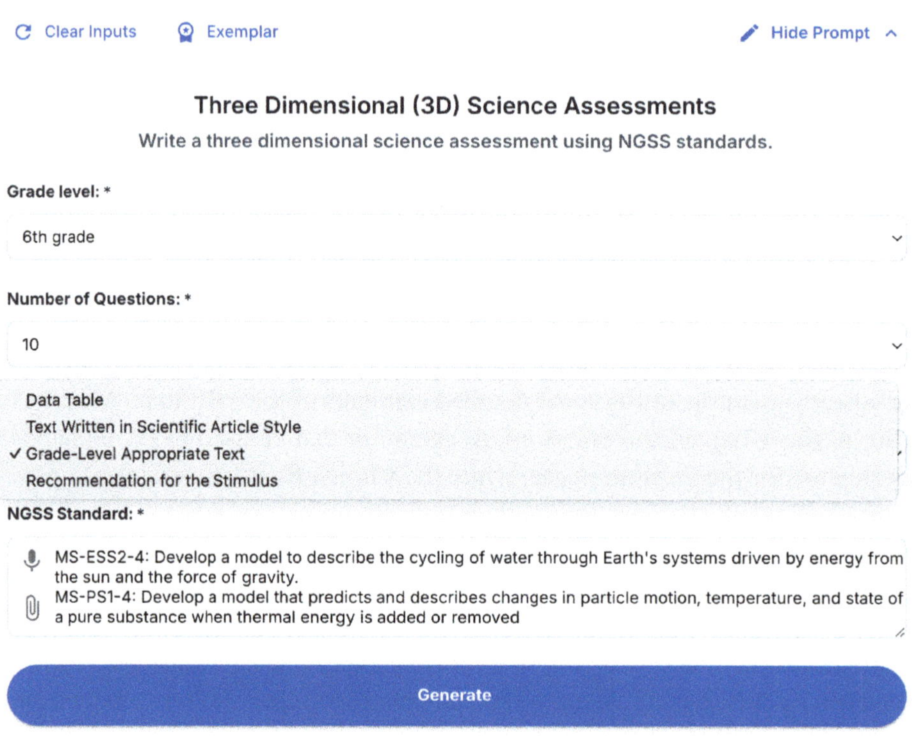

The assessments generated will vary greatly depending on the stimulus type selected. The data table stimulus will create a data table with quantitative information for students to analyze and interpret. This table may include numerical data on various topics, such as population statistics, scientific measurements, or species indicators. The data presented will be organized in rows and columns, allowing students to compare and analyze different variables or categories.

Beneath the table, a question set will be generated to drive students to analyze and interpret the data. These questions may ask students to identify trends, calculate percentages or averages, make comparisons between different data points, or draw conclusions based on the information provided. The number of questions in the set will be determined by the number specified in the original prompt, allowing teachers to customize the assessment's length and complexity to suit their instructional needs and student abilities.

Figure 13 Sample Assessment: Data Table Stimulus

Phenomenon: The Water Cycle in a Temperate Forest Ecosystem

Stimulus:

Data Table: Water Cycle Components in a Temperate Forest

Component	Amount (Liters per Day)	Description
Evaporation	150	Water turning into vapor from forest surfaces
Transpiration	200	Water released by plants into the atmosphere
Precipitation	350	Water falling as rain or snow
Runoff	100	Water flowing over the land into rivers
Infiltration	150	Water soaking into the soil

Question Set:

1. **What process is responsible for water turning into vapor from the forest surfaces?**
2. **How much water, in liters per day, is released by plants into the atmosphere through transpiration?**
3. **Which component of the water cycle has the highest amount of water movement in this temperate forest ecosystem?**
4. **Explain how the process of infiltration contributes to the water cycle in this ecosystem.**
5. **Calculate the total amount of water entering the atmosphere daily through evaporation and transpiration.**
6. **Describe the role of precipitation in the water cycle as observed in this temperate forest.**
7. **If the amount of precipitation increased by 50 liters per day, what would be the new total for precipitation?**
8. **What is the difference in the amount of water between runoff and infiltration?**
9. **Predict how a decrease in sunlight would affect the evaporation process in this ecosystem.**
10. **Discuss the importance of gravity in the movement of water in the runoff process.**

The other three stimuli types produced by the assessment generator vary significantly based on the grade level and standards selected, offering tailored options to meet specific educational goals. In this chapter's focus on the water cycle, the "recommendation for the stimulus" generated an assignment where students were asked to create a model of the water cycle. This task included labeling the role of the sun and thermal energy in driving water movement, as well as creating a close-up breakdown of the states of matter involved in various parts of the cycle. This type of stimulus encourages students to apply their understanding creatively while aligning with NGSS standards, such as MS-ESS2-4, which emphasizes modeling Earth's systems and understanding energy and matter flows.

The other two text-based stimuli provide students with paragraphs to read and interpret, followed by a set of questions designed to assess comprehension and analytical skills. These stimuli are particularly useful for integrating literacy into STEM education, as they require students to extract key information from informational texts and apply it to scientific concepts. For example, a text-based stimulus might describe how evaporation rates change under different environmental conditions, prompting students to answer questions about cause-and-effect relationships or compare data points presented in the text. The number of questions included in these sets is determined by the parameters specified in the original prompt, allowing educators to customize assessments to match their instructional needs.

By combining these different types of stimuli—modeling tasks, recommendation assignments, and text-based questions—educators can create comprehensive assessments that address multiple dimensions of learning. Modeling tasks encourage hands-on application and critical thinking, while text-based stimuli develop reading comprehension and data interpretation skills. Together, these tools ensure that assessments are not only aligned with state or national standards but also engage students in diverse ways, fostering a deeper understanding of scientific concepts like the water cycle example utilized throughout this chapter.

Figure 14 Sample Assessment: Recommendation for Stimuli

Phenomenon: The Role of the Sun and Gravity in the Water Cycle and Changes in State of Water

Stimulus:

Recommendation for the Stimulus:

Create a diagram that illustrates the water cycle, showing the processes of evaporation, condensation, precipitation, and collection. Label the roles of the sun in providing energy for evaporation and gravity in pulling water down during precipitation. Include a side panel showing a close-up of water particles in different states (solid, liquid, gas) and how they change with the addition or removal of thermal energy.

Question Set:

1. **Describe how the sun contributes to the process of evaporation in the water cycle.**
2. **Explain the role of gravity in the process of precipitation.**
3. **What happens to the motion of water particles when water changes from a liquid to a gas?**
4. **How does the removal of thermal energy affect the state of water particles?**
5. **Identify the process during which water vapor cools down and changes back into liquid water.**
6. **What is the effect of adding thermal energy to ice? Describe the change in state.**
7. **Describe how water collects in rivers, lakes, and oceans in the water cycle.**
8. **What is condensation, and what role does it play in the water cycle?**
9. **How does the sun's energy affect the temperature of water in the ocean?**
10. **Predict what would happen to the water cycle if there were no sun.**

Note to Educators: Please review the questions and answers for accuracy and alignment with your curriculum standards before using them in your classroom.

Copy Edit Export Read Aloud More

Multiple Choice Quiz/Assessment Generator

In addition to the 3D Science Assessments Generator, MagicSchool offers a Multiple Choice Quiz/Assessment Generator designed to create traditional multiple-choice tests aligned with state standards. Unlike the Three-Dimensional Science Assessment Generator, which focuses specifically on NGSS standards, this tool offers broader flexibility for educators across various subjects and grade levels. The Multiple Choice Assessment Generator allows teachers to input text, specify grade levels, and select the number of questions desired, quickly producing ready-to-use assessments that can be exported to platforms like Word Docs or Google Forms. While this MagicTool only generates multiple choice questions, teachers can prompt the AI to include true or false questions and use their own expertise to edit some of the questions generated into different formats (i.e. drop box, fill in the blank, short answer) when creating the assessment document to provide to students.

While the Three-Dimensional Science Assessment Generator emphasizes the integration of scientific practices, crosscutting concepts, and disciplinary core ideas as defined by NGSS, the Multiple Choice Quiz/Assessment Generator provides a more conventional approach to assessment. It focuses primarily on content knowledge and can be used across multiple subjects, not just science. This tool is particularly useful for educators who need to create quick, standards-aligned assessments for formative or summative purposes, without the need for the more complex, scenario-based questions typical of three-dimensional assessments. However, it's important to note that while this tool offers efficiency and ease of use, it may not provide the same depth of assessment in terms of scientific practices and crosscutting concepts as the Three-Dimensional Science Assessment Generator.

To create a comprehensive assessment that leverages the strengths of both the Multiple Choice Quiz/Assessment Generator and the 3D Science Assessment Generator, educators can adopt a hybrid approach. This method combines traditional content knowledge evaluation with the assessment of scientific practices and crosscutting concepts. The assessment could begin with multiple-choice questions generated by the Quiz/Assessment Generator to efficiently cover state standards and basic content knowledge. These questions can serve as a foundation for understanding students' grasp of key concepts. Following this, the assessment can incorporate more complex, scenario-based questions from the 3D Science Assessment Generator that align with NGSS standards, encourage higher order thinking skills, and evaluate students' ability to apply scientific practices and make connections across disciplines. This hybrid assessment allows for a balance between efficiency and depth, providing a more holistic view of students' scientific understanding and skills. By utilizing both tools, educators can create assessments that not only measure content knowledge but also assess students' ability to engage in scientific thinking and apply their understanding to real-world scenarios.

Alternate approaches to Lesson Design

The 3D Science Assessment and Multiple Choice Assessment Generators offer educators two powerful approaches that leverage the integration of PBL and the 5E model to enhance the effectiveness of AI-generated assessments as a whole. The first approach involves designing assessments after creating a PBL unit structured around the 5E model, ensuring that evaluations align with the hands-on activities and learning experiences already developed. The second approach adopts a backward design methodology, starting with desired learning outcomes and using the assessment generators to create summative assessments that drive the development of the entire unit. Both methods emphasize the importance of aligning assessments with state content standards and the Next Generation Science Standards (NGSS) dimensions: disciplinary core ideas, crosscutting concepts, and scientific practices.

1. Post-Lesson Alignment with PBL and 5E Units

This approach involves designing assessments after creating a PBL unit structured around the 5E model. Educators first use the Magic Tools discussed earlier in this chapter to develop the unit outline, science labs, choice boards, and other worksheets and activities. Once the unit is structured, the Assessment Generators align evaluations with the state content standards and NGSS dimensions (disciplinary core ideas, crosscutting concepts, and scientific practices) already embedded in the lesson. For example, after students build a watershed model (PBL activity), the generator can produce assessments that evaluate their ability to analyze human impacts on the water cycle (disciplinary core idea), identify cause-effect relationships (crosscutting concept), and interpret data (scientific practice). This method ensures assessments reinforce the learning trajectory of the unit while maintaining fidelity to state and national science content standards.

2. Backward Design Starting with Assessments

Alternatively, educators can adopt a backward design approach by first defining desired learning outcomes and using the Assessment Generators to create summative assessments. For instance, a teacher might start with an NGSS performance expectation like MS-ESS2-4: "Develop a model to describe the cycling of water through Earth's systems" and generate a rubric-driven task requiring students to design a 3D watershed model. From there, the PBL and 5E tools are used to scaffold lessons backward; designing "Explain" phase worksheets on evaporation or "Evaluate" phase reflections to ensure students meet the predefined criteria. This method aligns with research emphasizing the importance of starting with "desired results" to ensure assessments drive instruction and measure mastery of integrated skills

Designing Rubrics

The development of rubrics for project grading is a crucial aspect of assessment, particularly for non-traditional assignments like projects and presentations that are an integral part of PBL (Andrade & Brookhart, 2019; Panadero & Jonsson, 2013; Reynders et al., 2020). The Rubric Generator MagicTool offers educators a powerful resource for creating customized, high-quality rubrics with minimal effort. To use this tool, teachers can select a grade level, describe their standard or objective, title their assignment, and add a description and point scale. The generator then produces a comprehensive rubric, structured in a table format, that can be further tailored to meet specific needs. This feature is distinctive because many AI-generated rubrics are not initially created in a table format, making it challenging to convert them into a table-based rubric that students can easily access. This streamlined process not only saves time but also ensures that rubrics are carefully aligned with learning objectives and standards while also maintaining the desired number of points and categories, providing a consistent and structured framework for assessment.

Well-designed rubrics enable teachers to assess various aspects of student work objectively. In PBL and 5E projects, these may include content knowledge, critical thinking, creativity, communication skills, and teamwork. By breaking down these components into specific criteria, rubrics help teachers evaluate complex assignments more systematically and fairly (Diana et al., 2021; Reynders et al., 2020; Siew & Ambo, 2021). This approach ensures that all aspects of a project are considered, from the initial research and planning stages to the final presentation or product.

The use of rubrics in PBL and 5E projects also supports student learning by providing clear guidance throughout the project process (Brookhart & Chen, 2014; Panadero & Jonsson, 2013). When students have access to the rubric from the beginning of a project, they can better understand the expectations and use it as a roadmap for their work. This transparency helps students self-assess their progress, make improvements, and take ownership of their learning. Additionally, rubrics facilitate more targeted and constructive feedback, allowing teachers to highlight specific strengths and areas for improvement in a student's work.

Rubrics in PBL and 5E projects can be designed to align with specific learning standards and objectives. This alignment ensures that project assessments are not only comprehensive but also directly tied to curriculum goals. By incorporating standards into rubrics, teachers can demonstrate how project-based work meets or exceeds traditional academic expectations, bridging the gap between innovative teaching methods and standardized assessment requirements (Brookhart & Chen, 2014; Karakaya & Yilmaz, 2022; Siew & Ambo, 2021).

AI-enabled Grading

Although not a MagicSchool AI feature, recent advancements in artificial intelligence have led to the development of AI-enabled scoring systems for three-dimensional constructed-response assessments in science education. These innovative tools have demonstrated potential in delivering prompt and impartial feedback, enhancing the assessment process for both educators and students. This technology can be particularly beneficial when integrated with the PBL and 5E models, as it allows for consistent evaluation of complex, multi-faceted projects that students develop over time. By providing immediate feedback, students can make real-time adjustments and improvements throughout their project development, fostering a more dynamic and iterative learning process. The consistency of AI grading tools ensures fair evaluation across multiple projects and students, reducing potential bias and maintaining equitable assessment practices.

These systems can also personalize learning by analyzing student performance data to identify areas requiring additional support or challenge, enabling more targeted instruction. AI grading's efficiency in handling routine assessment tasks allows teachers to focus on complex, subjective elements of student work and provide individualized guidance. The multi-modal assessment capabilities of AI tools align well with the diverse outputs often produced in PBL and 5E learning environments, evaluating various forms of student work including written assignments, presentations, and multimedia projects. Additionally, AI grading systems can be programmed to assess work against specific learning standards, ensuring curriculum alignment while still allowing for creativity and exploration. The scaffolding feature of AI grading tools offers more detailed guidance for struggling students and gradually reduces support as students demonstrate mastery. These combined benefits enhance the effectiveness of PBL and 5E models by providing ongoing, data-driven support for both teachers and students throughout the learning process

However, despite the potential benefits of AI-assisted grading, many educators remain hesitant to fully embrace these tools for assessment purposes. This reluctance stems from various concerns, including the accuracy and reliability of AI-generated rubrics and grades. Teachers often worry about the AI's ability to capture nuanced aspects of student work, particularly in subjects that require complex reasoning or creativity. Additionally, there are apprehensions about the AI's capacity to provide constructive feedback that aligns with individual teaching styles and classroom contexts. Some educators also express ethical concerns regarding the use of AI in high-stakes assessments such as state testing, fearing potential biases or unfair evaluations. Furthermore, the lack of transparency in AI decision-making processes can make it difficult for teachers to explain or justify grades to students and parents. As a result, many teachers prefer to maintain control over the rubric creation and grading processes, viewing these tasks as integral to their professional judgment and pedagogical approach.

This chapter does not delve any further into AI-enabled grading, but it is an emerging technology that educators may consider as it continues to transform and improve. AI grading tools have the potential to transform the assessment process by offering efficiency, consistency, and personalized feedback, making them a promising area for future exploration in education as AI continues to evolve.

ETHICAL CONSIDERATIONS AND BEST PRACTICES

The integration of AI tools like MagicSchool AI into education introduces critical ethical considerations that educators and institutions must address to ensure responsible use. First, addressing potential biases in AI-generated content is paramount. AI systems trained on historical data may inadvertently perpetuate societal biases, such as gender or racial stereotypes, which can influence student assessments, lesson content, or project suggestions (Baker & Hawn, 2021; Boateng & Boateng, 2025). Although biases in AI-generated content may be less pronounced in Science compared to English Language Arts and Reading (ELAR) or Social Studies, it remains a significant concern that educators should address (Boateng & Boateng, 2025). For example, an AI-generated science quiz might overrepresent male scientists in its examples, reinforcing harmful stereotypes. To mitigate this, educators should audit AI outputs for fairness and pair AI tools with human oversight to flag and correct biased content (Baker & Hawn, 2021; Chinta et al., 2024). Schools can also adopt AI systems with built-in bias-detection algorithms and prioritize tools that transparently disclose their data sources and validation processes (Feng et al., 2024; Fu & Weng, 2024).

Second, maintaining the teacher's role in the AI-enhanced classroom remains essential. While AI can streamline administrative tasks and generate resources, it cannot replace the nuanced judgment, pedagogical expertise, and adaptability of human educators (Feng et al., 2024; Fu & Weng, 2024). Teachers must remain the primary decision-makers in curriculum design, student interaction, and ethical oversight. AI-generated assignments should be reviewed and adjusted by teachers to align with classroom context and individual student needs. Professional development programs can empower educators to use AI as a collaborative tool, such as refining lesson plans or automating grading, while preserving their role in fostering critical thinking, emotional support, and real-time adaptability (Feng et al., 2024). This balance ensures AI enhances, rather than diminishes, the human elements of teaching.

Data privacy and security concerns represent another critical challenge. AI tools often require access to sensitive student data, including academic performance, behavioral patterns, and demographic information, raising risks of breaches or misuse (Feng et al., 2024). For example, third-party AI platforms might use student data for commercial purposes without consent, violating privacy laws like FERPA or COPPA. Best practices include implementing strict data governance policies, such as encrypting student information, anonymizing datasets, and vetting AI tools for compliance with privacy regulations (e.g., ensuring data is not used to train public models) (Feng et al., 2024). Schools should also empower families with transparent opt-in/opt-out choices and provide clear explanations of how AI tools collect and protect data.

MagicSchool AI was chosen for this chapter due to its robust privacy and security measures in addition to the many science-specific MagicTools. The platform has implemented comprehensive safeguards to protect the confidentiality, accessibility, and integrity of user data. MagicSchool AI's commitment to data protection is evidenced by its 93% Privacy Rating from Common Sense Media, placing it at the forefront of AI tools in terms of privacy practices (MagicSchool AI, 2025). This dedication to data security has contributed to MagicSchool AI's widespread adoption by educators and school districts throughout the United States. The platform's emphasis on responsible AI use in education, coupled with its alignment with key privacy regulations such as FERPA and COPPA, has established it as a trusted resource in the K-12 educational technology landscape.

To navigate these ethical challenges, a proactive approach is vital. Educators should advocate for AI systems designed with "principled assessment" frameworks that prioritize equity, transparency, and accountability (Feng et al., 2024). By combining rigorous oversight, ongoing training, and community collaboration, schools can harness AI's potential while safeguarding the integrity of education and the trust of all stakeholders (Baker & Hawn, 2021; Feng et al., 2024).

FUTURE DIRECTIONS AND CONCLUSION

The integration of artificial intelligence into K-12 STEM education marks a transformative moment for both teaching and learning. As explored throughout this chapter, AI-powered platforms such as MagicSchool AI, when thoughtfully combined with digital design tools like Canva, offer educators powerful means to create more engaging, effective, and inclusive learning environments. These technologies not only streamline lesson planning and resource creation, thereby lightening teachers' mental load, but also fundamentally expand the possibilities for experiential, student centered learning.

By leveraging AI to generate scenario-based activities, interactive simulations, and authentic assessments, educators can bridge the gap between theory and practice. This synergy between AI and experiential learning empowers students to actively engage with STEM concepts through hands-on inquiry and real-world problem-solving-fostering deeper understanding, critical thinking, and sustained engagement. The ability to personalize learning experiences and adapt instruction to meet diverse student needs ensures that all learners have the opportunity to thrive.

Visual design platforms like Canva further amplify these benefits by enabling teachers to transform AI-generated content into visually compelling, accessible materials. Students, too, can use these tools to creatively communicate their understanding of complex STEM ideas, supporting both knowledge retention and the development of essential 21st-century skills. The integration of AI-driven personalization with dynamic visual design not only enhances motivation and inclusivity but also makes STEM learning more meaningful and relevant.

Looking ahead, emerging trends such as virtual and augmented reality, adaptive learning systems, and an increased emphasis on computational thinking and coding are poised to further reshape STEM education. These advancements promise to make abstract concepts more tangible and support individualized learning trajectories, preparing students for the demands of a rapidly evolving world. However, as we embrace the promise of AI, it is essential to recognize that technology should augment, not replace, the irreplaceable role of human teachers. The most effective learning environments will continue to rely on educators' expertise in fostering critical thinking, creativity, and collaborative skills. Responsible implementation of AI requires clear policies, ongoing professional development, and a steadfast commitment to equity, privacy, and ethical use.

In summary, the thoughtful integration of AI and experiential learning practices offers a pathway to more personalized, engaging, and effective STEM education. By harnessing these tools while upholding the core values of the teaching profession, educators can help shape a future where every student is empowered to succeed in a dynamic and interconnected world.

REFERENCES

Akcan, A. T., Yıldırım, B., Karataş, A. R., & Yılmaz, M. (2023). Teachers' views on the effect of STEM education on the labor market. *Frontiers in Psychology*, *14*, 1184730. Advance online publication. DOI: 10.3389/fpsyg.2023.1184730 PMID: 37377702

Akhmetova, A. I., Sovetkanova, D. M., Komekbayeva, L. K., Abdrakhmanov, A. E., Yessenuly, D., & Serikova, O. S. (2025). A systematic review of artificial intelligence in high school STEM education research. *Eurasia Journal of Mathematics, Science and Technology Education*, *21*(4), em2623. Advance online publication. DOI: 10.29333/ejmste/16222

Ally, M. (2019). Competency Profile of the digital and online teacher in future Education. *International Review of Research in Open and Distance Learning*, *20*(2). Advance online publication. DOI: 10.19173/irrodl.v20i2.4206

Andrade, H. L., & Brookhart, S. M. (2019). Classroom assessment as the co-regulation of learning. *Assessment in Education: Principles, Policy & Practice*, *27*(4), 350–372. DOI: 10.1080/0969594X.2019.1571992

Antonenko, P., & Abramowitz, B. (2022). In-service teachers' (mis)conceptions of artificial intelligence in K-12 science education. *Journal of Research on Technology in Education*, *55*(1), 64–78. DOI: 10.1080/15391523.2022.2119450

Antropic. (2025). MagicSchool transforms K-12 education for 3 million educators and their students with Claude. Anthropic. https://www.anthropic.com/customers/magicschool

Azzam, A., & Charles, T. (2025). K-12 STEM Teachers' Experiences with Artificial Intelligence. *TEM Journal*, 463–468. https://doi.org/DOI: 10.18421/tem141-41

Bahadir, F., & Dikmen, M. (2022) The Effect of 5E Learning Model on Students' Academic Achievement: A Meta-analysis Study. *İstanbul Aydın Üniversitesi Sosyal Bilimler Dergisi, 14(4),* 532-552.

Baker, R. S., & Hawn, A. (2021). Algorithmic bias in education. *International Journal of Artificial Intelligence in Education*, *32*(4), 1052–1092. DOI: 10.1007/s40593-021-00285-9

Barsoum, S. S., Elnagar, M. S., & Awad, B. M. (2022). The Effectiveness of Using a Cognitive Style-based Chatbot in Developing Science Concepts and Critical Thinking Skills among Preparatory School Pupils. *European Scientific Journal*, *18*(22), 52. DOI: 10.19044/esj.2022.v18n22p52

Bell, S. (2010). Project-Based Learning for the 21st Century: Skills for the Future. *The Clearing House: A Journal of Educational Strategies, Issues and Ideas*, *83*(2), 39–43. DOI: 10.1080/00098650903505415

Boateng, N. O., & Boateng, N. B. (2025). Algorithmic bias in educational systems: Examining the impact of AI-driven decision making in modern education. *World Journal of Advanced Research and Reviews*, *25*(1), 2012–2017. DOI: 10.30574/wjarr.2025.25.1.0253

Braaten, E., & Farnsworth, K. (2024). Educators' perspectives on generative AI in K-12: Informing AI in education guidance. *Friday Institute for Educational Innovation, North Carolina State University*. https://fi.ncsu.edu/resource-library/perspectives-ai-in-k12/

Brookhart, S. M., & Chen, F. (2014). The quality and effectiveness of descriptive rubrics. *Educational Review*, *67*(3), 343–368. DOI: 10.1080/00131911.2014.929565

Bybee, R. W. (2013). *The case for STEM education: Challenges and opportunities*. NSTA Press.

Bybee, R. W. (2015). *The BSCS 5E Instructional Model: Creating Teachable Moments* (1st ed.). National Science Teachers Association.

Cakır, N. K. (2017). Effect of 5E learning model on academic achievement, attitude and science process skills: Meta-Analysis Study. *Journal of Education and Training Studies*, *5*(11), 157. DOI: 10.11114/jets.v5i11.2649

Cao, W., Wang, Q., Sbeih, A., & Shibly, F. (2020). Artificial intelligence based efficient smart learning framework for education platform. *Inteligencia Artificial*, *23*(66). Advance online publication. DOI: 10.4114/intartif.vol23iss66pp112-123

Chen, L., Chen, P., & Lin, Z. (2020). Artificial Intelligence in Education: A review. *IEEE Access : Practical Innovations, Open Solutions*, *8*, 75264–75278. DOI: 10.1109/ACCESS.2020.2988510

Chinta, S. V., Wang, Z., Yin, Z., Hoang, N., Gonzalez, M., Quy, T. L., & Zhang, W. (2024). FairAIED: Navigating fairness, bias, and ethics in educational AI applications. *arXiv (Cornell University)*. https://doi.org//arxiv.2407.18745DOI: 10.48550

Chiu, M., Hwang, G., Hsia, L., & Shyu, F. (2022). Artificial intelligence-supported art education: A deep learning-based system for promoting university students' artwork appreciation and painting outcomes. *Interactive Learning Environments*, *32*(3), 824–842. DOI: 10.1080/10494820.2022.2100426

Damioli, G., Van Roy, V., & Vertesy, D. (2021). The impact of artificial intelligence on labor productivity. *Eurasian Economic Review, 11*(1), 1–25. DOI: 10.1007/s40821-020-00172-8

Darling-Hammond, L., Flook, L., Cook-Harvey, C., Barron, B., & Osher, D. (2019). Implications for educational practice of the science of learning and development. *Applied Developmental Science, 24*(2), 97–140. DOI: 10.1080/10888691.2018.1537791

Demszky, D., Liu, J., Hill, H. C., Jurafsky, D., & Piech, C. (2023). Can automated feedback improve teachers' uptake of student ideas? Evidence from a randomized controlled trial in a Large-Scale online course. *Educational Evaluation and Policy Analysis, 46*(3), 483–505. DOI: 10.3102/01623737231169270

Diana, N. (1882). Yohannes, & Sukma, Y. (2021). The effectiveness of implementing project-based learning (PjBL) model in STEM education: A literature review. *Journal of Physics: Conference Series*, (1), 12146. DOI: 10.1088/1742-6596/1882/1/012146

Freeman, S., Eddy, S. L., McDonough, M., Smith, M. K., Okoroafor, N., Jordt, H., & Wenderoth, M. P. (2014). Active learning increases student performance in science, engineering, and mathematics. *Proceedings of the National Academy of Sciences of the United States of America, 111*(23), 8410–8415. DOI: 10.1073/pnas.1319030111 PMID: 24821756

Frontline Research & Learning Institute. (2024). *Empowering K-12 Districts: Navigating AI Adoption for Enhanced Educational Efficiency and Effectiveness | Frontline Research & Learning Institute*. https://www.frontlineinstitute.com/reports/what-is-artificial-intelligence-ai-in-education/

Fu, Y., & Weng, Z. (2024). Navigating the Ethical Terrain of AI in Education: A Systematic Review on Framing responsible Human-Centered AI Practices. *Computers and Education Artificial Intelligence, 100306*, 100306. Advance online publication. DOI: 10.1016/j.caeai.2024.100306

Furtak, E. M. (2023). *Formative Assessment for 3D Science Learning: Supporting Ambitious and Equitable Instruction*. Teachers College Press.

Gunawan, K. D. H., Liliasari, L., Kaniawati, I., & Setiawan, W. (2021). Implementation of Competency Enhancement Program for science teachers assisted by artificial Intelligence in designing HOTS-based integrated science learning. *Jurnal Penelitian Dan Pembelajaran IPA*, 7(1), 55. DOI: 10.30870/jppi.v7i1.8655

Hannan, B., & Eynon, R. (2025). Widening the Digital Divide: The mediating role of Intelligent Tutoring Systems in the relationship between rurality, socioeducational advantage, and mathematics learning outcomes. *Computers & Education, 233*, 105312. DOI: 10.1016/j.compedu.2025.105312

Hardcastle, J. M., Herrmann-Abell, C. F., & DeBoer, G. E. (2021). Validating a Claim-Evidence-Science Idea-Reasoning (CESR) framework for use in NGSS assessment tasks [Conference presentation]. *NARST Virtual Annual Conference, Online.* https://files.eric.ed.gov/fulltext/ED612227.pdf

Herrmann-Abell, C. F., & DeBoer, G. E. (2022). Using Rasch measurement to develop 3D assessment tasks to measure students' understanding of energy. *Journal of Research in Science Teaching, 59*(9), 1543–1568. DOI: 10.1002/tea.21798

Herrmann-Abell, C. F., Hardcastle, J., & DeBoer, G. E. (2023). Exploring the comparability of multiple-choice and constructed-response versions of scenario-based assessment tasks. *Journal of Research in Science Teaching, 60*(1), 3–27. DOI: 10.1002/tea.21829

Hmelo-Silver, C. E. (2004). Problem-Based Learning: What and How Do Students Learn? *Educational Psychology Review, 16*(3), 235–266. DOI: 10.1023/B:EDPR.0000034022.16470.f3

Hmelo-Silver, C. E., & Barrows, H. S. (2006). Goals and strategies of a problem-based learning facilitator. *The Interdisciplinary Journal of Problem-Based Learning, 1*(1), 21–39. DOI: 10.7771/1541-5015.1004

Holicza, B., & Kiss, A. (2023). Predicting and comparing students' online and offline academic performance using machine learning algorithms. *Behavioral Sciences (Basel, Switzerland), 13*(4), 289. DOI: 10.3390/bs13040289 PMID: 37102803

Huang, L. (2023). Ethics of Artificial intelligence in Education: Student privacy and data protection. *Science Insights Education Frontiers, 16*(2), 2577–2587. DOI: 10.15354/sief.23.re202

Işcan, Y. V. V., & Seyhan, H. G. (2021). The Effect of the 5E Learning Model Supported with Material Ensuring Conceptual Change on Science Achievement: The Example of "Heat and Temperature.". *Mimbar Sekolah Dasar, 8*(3), 250–280. DOI: 10.53400/mimbar-sd.v8i3.33044

Jiao, P., Ouyang, F., Zhang, Q., & Alavi, A. H. (2022). Artificial intelligence-enabled prediction model of student academic performance in online engineering education. *Artificial Intelligence Review, 55*(8), 6321–6344. DOI: 10.1007/s10462-022-10155-y

Johnson, D. W., Johnson, R. T., & Smith, K. A. (2014). Cooperative Learning: Improving University Instruction by Basing Practice on Validated Theory. *Journal on Excellence in College Teaching*, *25*(3–4), 85.

Karaci, A., Akyuz, H. I., & Bilgici, G. (2018). Effects of web-based intelligent tutoring systems on academic achievement and retention. In *International Journal of Computer Applications* (Vol. 181, Issue 16, pp. 35–36). https://files.eric.ed.gov/fulltext/ED588768.pdf

Karakaya, F., & Yılmaz, M. (2022). Teachers views on assessment and evaluation methods in STEM education: A science course example. *Journal of Pedagogical Research*. DOI: 10.33902/JPR.202213526

Karan, E., & Brown, L. (2022). Enhancing Students' Problem-solving Skills through Project-based Learning. *Journal of Problem Based Learning in Higher Education, 10*(1).

Kavitha, K., & Joshith, V. P. (2024). Pedagogical incorporation of artificial intelligence in K-12 science education: A decadal bibliometric mapping and systematic literature review (2013-2023). *Journal of Pedagogical Research*. DOI: 10.33902/JPR.202429218

Keppler, S., Sinchaisri, W., & Snyder, C. (2024). Backwards Planning with Generative AI: Case Study Evidence from US K12 Teachers. SSRN *Electronic Journal*. DOI: 10.2139/ssrn.4924786

Kim, M. S. (2019). Developing a competency taxonomy for teacher design knowledge in technology-enhanced learning environments: A literature review. *Research and Practice in Technology Enhanced Learning*, *14*(1), 18. Advance online publication. DOI: 10.1186/s41039-019-0113-4

Koh, E., & Doroudi, S. (2023). Learning, teaching, and assessment with generative artificial intelligence: Towards a plateau of productivity. *Learning Research and Practice*, *9*(2), 109–116. DOI: 10.1080/23735082.2023.2264086

Kolb, D. A. (2015). *Experiential learning: Experience as the source of learning and development* (2nd ed.). Pearson Education.

Kotsis, K. T. (2024). Significance of experiments in inquiry-based science teaching. *European Journal of Education and Pedagogy*, *5*(2), 86–92. DOI: 10.24018/ejedu.2024.5.2.815

Li, K. C., & Wong, B. T. (2023). Artificial intelligence in personalised learning: A bibliometric analysis. *Interactive Technology and Smart Education*, *20*(3), 422–445. DOI: 10.1108/ITSE-01-2023-0007

Li, L., Chen, C. P., Wang, L., Liang, K., & Bao, W. (2023). Exploring Artificial Intelligence in Smart Education: Real-Time Classroom Behavior Analysis with Embedded Devices. *Sustainability (Basel)*, *15*(10), 7940. DOI: 10.3390/su15107940

MagicSchool AI. (2025). Privacy & Security. *Anthropic*. https://www.magicschool.ai/privacy

Martin, F., Zhuang, M., & Schaefer, D. (2023). Systematic review of research on artificial intelligence in K-12 education (2017–2022). *Computers and Education Artificial Intelligence*, *6*, 100195. DOI: 10.1016/j.caeai.2023.100195

Murtaza, M., Ahmed, Y., Shamsi, J. A., Sherwani, F., & Usman, M. (2022). AI-Based Personalized E-Learning Systems: Issues, challenges, and solutions. *IEEE Access : Practical Innovations, Open Solutions*, *10*, 81323–81342. DOI: 10.1109/ACCESS.2022.3193938

National Research Council. (2012). *A Framework for K-12 Science Education: Practices, Crosscutting Concepts, and Core Ideas*. National Academies Press.

National Science Board, National Science Foundation. (2024). U.S. STEM workforce: Size, growth, and employment (NSB-2024-5). *National Center for Science and Engineering Statistics*. https://ncses.nsf.gov/pubs/nsb20245/u-s-stem-workforce-size-growth-and-employment

Nja, C. O., Idiege, K. J., Uwe, U. E., Meremikwu, A. N., Ekon, E. E., Erim, C. M., Ukah, J. U., Eyo, E. O., Anari, M. I., & Cornelius-Ukpepi, B. U. (2023). Adoption of artificial intelligence in science teaching: From the vantage point of the African science teachers. *Smart Learning Environments*, *10*(1), 42. Advance online publication. DOI: 10.1186/s40561-023-00261-x

Panadero, E., & Jonsson, A. (2013). The use of scoring rubrics for formative assessment purposes revisited: A review. *Educational Research Review*, *9*, 129–144. DOI: 10.1016/j.edurev.2013.01.002

Pane, J. F., Griffin, B. A., McCaffrey, D. F., & Karam, R. (2013). Effectiveness of Cognitive Tutor Algebra I at scale. *Educational Evaluation and Policy Analysis*, *36*(2), 127–144. DOI: 10.3102/0162373713507480

Patiño, A., Ramírez-Montoya, M. S., & Buenestado-Fernández, M. (2023). Active learning and education 4.0 for complex thinking training: Analysis of two case studies in open education. *Smart Learning Environments*, *10*(1), 8. Advance online publication. DOI: 10.1186/s40561-023-00229-x

Penuel, W. R., Van Horne, K., & Bell, P. (2020). Steps to Designing Three-Dimensional Assessments that Connect to Students' Interests, Experiences, and Identities. *STEM Teaching Tools Practice Brief #29*. https://STEMteachingtools.org/link/2900

Pimthong, P., & Williams, J. (2018). Preservice teachers' understanding of STEM education. *Kasetsart Journal of Social Sciences*. Advance online publication. DOI: 10.1016/j.kjss.2018.07.017

Prince, M. (2004). Does active learning work? A review of the research. *Journal of Engineering Education*, *93*(3), 223–231. DOI: 10.1002/j.2168-9830.2004.tb00809.x

Qu, J., Zhao, Y., & Xie, Y. (2022). Artificial intelligence leads the reform of education models. *Systems Research and Behavioral Science*, *39*(3), 581–588. DOI: 10.1002/sres.2864

Rehman, N., Huang, X., Mahmood, A., AlGerafi, M. M., & Javed, S. (2024b). Project-Based learning as a catalyst for 21st-Century skills and student engagement in the math classroom. *Heliyon*, *10*(23), e39988. DOI: 10.1016/j.heliyon.2024.e39988 PMID: 39660178

Reynders, G., Lantz, J., Ruder, S. M., Stanford, C. L., & Cole, R. S. (2020). Rubrics to assess critical thinking and information processing in undergraduate STEM courses. *International Journal of STEM Education*, *7*(1), 9. Advance online publication. DOI: 10.1186/s40594-020-00208-5

Robins, A., Hunt, T., Robertson, D., & Carter, R. (2022). Amazon Alexa Skills as a Novel Modality for In-service Professional Micro-Development (WIP). *Association for Computing Machinery*, *284–288*, 284–288. Advance online publication. DOI: 10.1145/3491140.3528314

Rui, Z., & Badarch, T. (2022). Research on Applications of Artificial Intelligence in Education. *American Journal of Computer Science and Technology*, *5*(2), 72. DOI: 10.11648/j.ajcst.20220502.17

Sahota, N. (2023). *Precision Education: How K-12 schools are embracing AI*. Forbes. https://www.forbes.com/sites/neilsahota/2023/12/15/precision-education-how-k-12-schools-are-embracing-ai/

Salinas-Navarro, D. E., Vilalta-Perdomo, E., Michel-Villarreal, R., & Montesinos, L. (2024). Designing experiential learning activities with generative artificial intelligence tools for authentic assessment. *Interactive Technology and Smart Education*, *21*(4), 708–734. DOI: 10.1108/ITSE-12-2023-0236

Siew, N. M., & Ambo, T. (2021). Assessing creativity in elementary science project-based learning using rubrics. *Journal of Baltic Science Education, 20*(1), 120–134. DOI: 10.33225/jbse/21.20.120

Slavin, N. (2022). The datafication of education: Surveillance, privacy, and power. *Surveillance & Society, 20*(1), 85–102.

Sotáková, I., & Ganajová, M. (2023). The effect of the 5E instructional model on students' cognitive processes and their attitudes towards chemistry as a subject. *Eurasia Journal of Mathematics, Science and Technology Education, 19*(9), em2317. DOI: 10.29333/ejmste/13469

Stanja, J., Gritz, W., Krugel, J., Hoppe, A., & Dannemann, S. (2022). Formative assessment strategies for students' conceptions—The potential of learning analytics. *British Journal of Educational Technology, 54*(1), 58–75. DOI: 10.1111/bjet.13288

Sun, Y., & Yan, Z. (2025). Factors influencing teachers' technology adoption in technology-rich classrooms: Model development and test. *Educational Technology Research and Development*. Advance online publication. DOI: 10.1007/s11423-025-10454-5

Tapalova, O., & Zhiyenbayeva, N. (2022). Artificial Intelligence in Education: AIEd for Personalised Learning Pathways. *Electronic Journal of e-Learning, 20*(5), 639–653. DOI: 10.34190/ejel.20.5.2597

Tegegne, T. A., & Kelkay, A. D. (2023). Comparative study of using 5E learning cycle and the traditional teaching method in chemistry to improve student understanding of water concept: The case of primary school. *Cogent Education, 10*(1), 2199634. Advance online publication. DOI: 10.1080/2331186X.2023.2199634

Topsakal, İ., Yalçın, S. A., & Çakır, Z. (2022). The effect of problem-based STEM education on the students' critical thinking tendencies and their perceptions for problem solving skills. *Science Education International, 33*(2), 136–145. DOI: 10.33828/sei.v33.i2.1

Vesin, B., Mangaroska, K., & Giannakos, M. (2018). Learning in smart environments: User-centered design and analytics of an adaptive learning system. *Smart Learning Environments, 5*(1), 24. Advance online publication. DOI: 10.1186/s40561-018-0071-0

Wu, S., & Yang, K. (2022). The effectiveness of teacher support for students' learning of artificial intelligence popular science activities. *Frontiers in Psychology, 13*, 868623. Advance online publication. DOI: 10.3389/fpsyg.2022.868623 PMID: 35719487

Xu, W., & Ouyang, F. (2022). The application of AI technologies in STEM education: A systematic review from 2011 to 2021. *International Journal of STEM Education*, *9*(1), 59. Advance online publication. DOI: 10.1186/s40594-022-00377-5

Yılmaz, Ö. (2024). Personalised learning and artificial intelligence in science education: Current state and future perspectives. *Educational Technology Quarterly*, *2024*(3), 255–274. DOI: 10.55056/etq.744

Zhang, L., & Ma, Y. (2023). A study of the impact of project-based learning on student learning effects: A meta-analysis study. *Frontiers in Psychology*, *14*, 1202728. Advance online publication. DOI: 10.3389/fpsyg.2023.1202728 PMID: 37564309

Chapter 4
Enlightening Educators: Unlocking the Benefits of AI in Faculty Development

Tami Butler Morton
https://orcid.org/0009-0005-9191-4645
East Texas A&M University, Allen, USA

ABSTRACT

This chapter aims to familiarize teacher educators and college of education professors with generative artificial intelligence (AI). As the final instructors that pre-service teachers encounter before they enter the classroom, it is crucial for teacher educators to grasp the technology that their students will need to master in order to support them effectively. According to Shata and Hartley, while education professors tend to hold positive views on artificial intelligence, student perceptions are considerably more skeptical, despite the numerous advantages AI offers in streamlining and enhancing teacher preparation processes. This chapter will outline innovative strategies that provide compelling arguments for integrating AI into lesson development, ensuring alignment with state standards while fostering engaging content strategies and effective resource curation.

INTRODUCTION

According to a post on Reddit (r/ChatGPT, 2023, May 19), an agriculture and natural science professor at Texas A&M University-Commerce (now known as East Texas A&M University) failed his entire class of seniors who were preparing to graduate because he claimed that all students had used Chat GPT on their final exam. This shocked the entire university, including all faculty, staff, and students. Ultimately, the professor could not fail the students primarily because he could not

DOI: 10.4018/979-8-3373-1122-7.ch004

prove that all students used an AI tool. As a Curriculum and Instruction Professor, this shocked me because I had not realized the power of artificial intelligence (AI) and its widespread use in higher education, nor did I realize how many people regularly utilized AI.

After learning about this case, I became interested in exploring tools like ChatGPT and other generative AI (GenAI) applications. The university was making a point of learning more, too, and administrators quickly provided professional development for faculty and staff in artificial intelligence. The university also established an artificial intelligence task force comprising of faculty members. This task force provided resources and additional professional development at the university and created a university-wide statement for all faculty to use in their syllabi. The established statement reminds university students that their professors understand how AI works and will provide instructions and guidelines when using AI in any way. This accepting approach to artificial intelligence, which has been used at the university level if it is done legally and ethically, and where students are transparent about its use, was a very innovative way of thinking that I needed to adopt to utilize these technological tools. Despite the skepticism I (and many other faculty members) have about AI, it has demonstrated the ability to enhance instructional practices and increase educational effectiveness.

Artificial Intelligence (AI) is a set of technologies that enable computers to perform various advanced functions, including seeing images and understanding and translating spoken and written language (Google Cloud, n.d.). It is also capable of analyzing data at a rapid rate. AI is also able to make recommendations for all topic areas. AI is a field of science concerned with building computers that can learn and reason, typically requiring human intelligence. According to Google Cloud (n.d.) "AI is a broad field that encompasses many different disciplines, including computer science, data analytics and statistics, hardware and software engineering, linguistics, neuroscience, and even philosophy and psychology" (Artificial Intelligence Defined, para 2). This innovative field has also been applied in higher education, and AI has provided many benefits to educational settings.

Despite the benefits that generative artificial intelligence provides in higher education, a tremendous number of teacher educators and college of education professors find that it is a very complex field and needs to be studied further. Many educators are skeptical about using AI in education (Reza et al., 2023; Stano, 2024). Educators are concerned that AI may replace human instruction and hinder the development of critical thinking skills (McGehee, 2024). Educators also believe that students use AI for academic dishonesty, including cheating and plagiarism (McGehee, 2024). While it is understandable for educators to have reservations about using AI in educational settings, perceptions of both faculty and students at universities have been analyzed, revealing that faculty members are more positive than students about the use of AI (Barrett & Pack, 2023). Faculty understand that it is their responsibility to prepare students for a future that requires preparation for a society powered by AI (Chiu, 2024). However, the only "holdouts" as far as faculty are those who do not feel comfortable with technology. Bower et al. (2024) find that faculty attitudes and comfort levels with AI are mixed, despite their awareness that artificial intelligence can have a significant impact on higher education. Hence, the purpose of this chapter is to provide faculty with information about generative AI, which may have previously avoided it due to its technological aspects (Shata & Hartley, 2025). Faculty need to establish a sense of trust with generative AI to feel more comfortable with incorporating it within their classroom preparation and design.

AI BENEFITS TO EDUCATORS

All faculty members feel more comfortable using AI when they have been provided with the necessary professional development to adapt the relevant tools. Faculty want to understand how to obtain instructional guidance (Kim et al., 2022), including lesson plans. It is also essential that faculty understand strategies that will keep their students engaged (Zhang & Aslan, 2021). Lastly, instructors are also interested in the various ways they can curate literature on specific topics (Digital Learning Institute). The guarantee of all three of these elements will bring forth a positive comfort level for faculty members who have been hesitant in utilizing AI.

Instructional Design

In higher education, teacher educators and college of education faculty members typically have an opportunity to work with upper-level undergraduate students preparing to teach K-12, who typically participate in a teacher preparation program that includes coursework designed to equip them for future classroom environments. These students or pre-service teachers are the most appropriate audience when deciding whether to use AI in instructional practices. The pre-service teachers are preparing to become in-service teachers of children from an AI world. As previously mentioned, while faculty members are more accepting of this technology, many students are not. This is problematic in teacher preparation programs because research shows that the integration of digital technologies is greatly influenced by the teachers' perspectives (Liu & Wang, 2024). Hence, preservice teachers' perspectives and ideas often mirror those of the professors who trained them (Karata & Yüce, 2024). Professors and faculty in teacher preparation programs must stay current with digital technologies and the benefits they offer students. Instructors must reassure pre-service teachers that knowledge of AI will be transformational for their future students.

AI Integration in Education

Since AI offers a technological benefit in all classrooms for various reasons, most of the emphasis has been placed on math, science, and STEM fields. E-Learning faculty began incorporating AI around 2011, followed by special education in 2012 and math in 2013 (Xu & Ouyang, 2024). See Figure 1.

Figure 1. The application of AI technologies in STEM education: a systematic review from 2011 to 2021

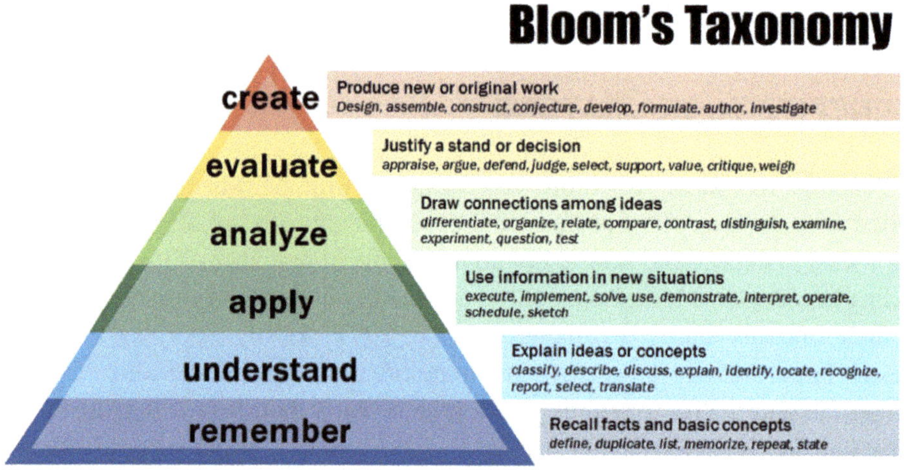

AI has benefited various education students, including those from diverse curricular areas. Generative AI and its numerous applicable tools have been recognized for not only educational purposes in various regions, but also for their ability to foster critical thinking. Critical thinking is one of the many characteristics necessary in today's world, particularly for professionals and working adults. Teacher educators and College of Education faculty make it a goal to prepare students, pre-service teachers, on how to engage in critical thinking, as well as how to foster this way of thinking for future students they will have.

One of the first approaches that many faculty members are providing instruction on is Bloom's taxonomy. Bloom's taxonomy is a framework that shares the stages and hierarchy of cognitive learning, which is very helpful when preparing teachers. Bloom's Taxonomy is named after its author, Benjamin Bloom, and it was used by educators in the 1950s and 1960s (Armstong et al., 2001). Therefore, it was easy for education faculty to see the connection of teaching and AI when Bloom's Taxonomy was considered in Patricia Armstrong's (2024) revision, facilitating an easy transition to using AI. Refer to Figure 2 for an illustration of the integration.

Figure 2. The Role of AI and Bloom's Taxonomy in Teaching

Figure 1.1

The application of AI technologies in STEM education: a systematic review from 2011 to 2021

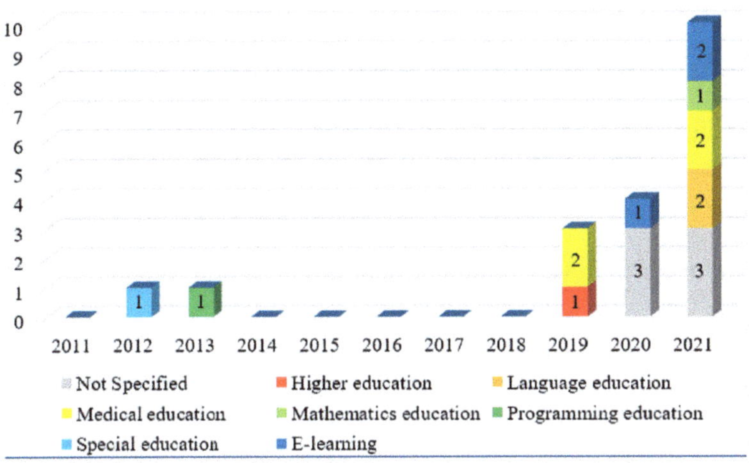

Armstrong, 2024, (n.p.)

As illustrated in this graphic, when using AI terminology, learners can adapt to various situations to match different levels of understanding and creation.

Lesson Planning

Many AI-driven innovations are utilized that cater to all the levels of the revised taxonomy discussed above. Lesson planning is one of the avenues that educators can use that falls under Create, because educators are asked to design new original instruction plans catered to classes. Teachers must use their gained knowledge of pedagogy to input prompts and receive tailored suggestions. Both ChatPro.ai and MagicSchool.ai are effective AI tools to use when lesson planning. Once the inputs are submitted, AI can create a lesson plan in seconds using an easy-to-understand template. While the creation is impressive in action, the person inputting the prompts must have educational background and knowledge of pedagogy to request the most effective lesson plan. See Table 1 for necessary inputs.

Table 1. Lesson Plan Inputs

Input Category	Details	Purpose
Learning Objectives	Specific knowledge of the skills students should achieve	To guide lesson content and assessment criteria
Prior Knowledge	What the current students already know relative to the topic	To build on existing knowledge and avoid redundancy
Learning Styles	Preferences (visual, auditory, kinesthetic)	To engage students effectively through diverse methods
Interests	Topics the current students find engaging	To enhance motivation and relevance to the lesson plan
Assessment Preferences	Methods that the current students feel comfortable with (quizzes, tests)	To align assessments with student comfort and capability.

This table provides a graphic organizer highlighting five necessary areas when creating a lesson plan, though the details and purpose are general. For example, when a teacher inputs a learning objective, it encompasses not only the specific knowledge and skills students should achieve, but also the broader learning outcomes that result from their acquisition. The teacher must also be aware of state and district objectives that must be met at specific grade levels. While the use of AI in creating lesson plans is impressive, it is not done without specialized human knowledge.

Lesson Plan Example

Here is an example of a lesson plan for a 3rd-grade class learning about forces and motion in a science class. This lesson plan was created using MagicSchool.ai, an AI tool for educators. The initial prompts asked for the grade-level topic that would be covered (force and motion) and any additional comments, where it was noted that this topic would be introduced with this lesson plan. The template also requested that the state standards be covered, and I intentionally specified TEKS without providing any specific identifiers. Refer to the following for the lesson plan that has been created:

Lesson Plan Example: Understanding Force and Motion

LEARNING OBJECTIVE

Students will be able to explain the concept of force and motion and describe how they affect objects in their environment.

ASSESSMENTS

Students will complete a hands-on activity where they will demonstrate force by using different objects to move a toy car. They will also complete a worksheet matching vocabulary words to their definitions.

KEY POINTS

- **Force**: A push or pull on an object that can cause it to move or change its motion.
- **Motion**: The change in position of an object over time.
- **Friction**: A force that opposes motion between two surfaces in contact.
- **Gravity**: A force that pulls objects toward each other, especially toward the Earth.
- **Acceleration**: The rate at which an object changes its velocity.

OPENING

- Begin with a demonstration using a toy car and a ramp to show how force can move an object.
- Ask students, "What do you think makes the car move?" to engage them in thinking about forces.
- Introduce the vocabulary words: force, motion, friction, gravity, and acceleration through a short interactive video.

INTRODUCTION TO NEW MATERIAL

- Explain the concepts of force and motion through real-life examples, such as pushing a swing or rolling a ball.
- Use visuals and diagrams to illustrate how different forces affect motion.
- Discuss common misconceptions, such as the belief that heavier objects always fall faster than lighter ones; clarify that gravity affects all objects equally.

GUIDED PRACTICE

- Pair students and provide them with toy cars, ramps, and weights.
- Ask them to experiment with different weights and angles of ramps to see how force affects motion.
- Scaffold questioning: Start by asking, "What happens when you push the car?" then progress to "How does adding weight change how far the car goes?"
- Monitor student performance by circulating the room and providing feedback as they conduct their experiments.

INDEPENDENT PRACTICE

- Each student will complete a worksheet that includes definitions of key vocabulary, illustrations of forces, and a short explanation of how they applied the concept of force in their experiment.
- Set expectations for quiet work time and remind students to show their thought process in their explanations.

CLOSING

- Have a quick class discussion where students share one thing they learned about force and motion.
- Ask students to illustrate their favorite example of force affecting motion on a whiteboard.

EXTENSION ACTIVITY

- For students who finish early, provide materials to create their own simple machine (like a lever or pulley) and explain how it uses force to make work easier.

HOMEWORK

- Assign students to observe a real-world example of force and motion in their own homes or neighborhoods. They will write a short paragraph describing what they observed and how force played a role.

STANDARDS ALIGNED

- TEKS 3.5(A): Explore and illustrate how forces cause changes in motion.
- TEKS 3.5(B): Investigate and identify the effects of friction and gravity on motion.

(MagicSchool.AI, 2025)

The lesson plan noted above is a skillful outcome due to the speed at which it was created, based on a few minor inputs, and the additional information added (i.e., key points, opening, closing, extension activity, and homework) based on the many lesson plan examples that AI had located with this focus.

Student Engagement Practices

In addition to instructional design, AI has been developing student engagement activities for teaching and learning over the last thirty years (Zhang & Aslan, 2021). In addition to generating lesson plans, AI is also helpful in recommending creative student engagement practices to incorporate into lesson plans. Innovative teaching practices are ideal for sharing with preservice teachers to help them understand how to leverage AI in future classrooms, engage students effectively, and refine their teaching methodologies. Refer to Table 1.2 for a list of applications that support student engagement practices.

Student Engagement Applications

1. Kahoot!: This game-based learning platform uses AI to create quizzes and interactive activities that encourage student engagement. Preservice teachers can create their games or use existing ones. www.kahoot.com
2. Google Classroom: This platform enables teachers to create, distribute, and grade assignments while integrating Google's AI tools to provide personalized learning experiences for students.https://edu.google.com/workspace-for-education/products/classroom/
3. Socrative: This formative assessment tool utilizes AI to analyze student responses and provide real-time feedback, enabling preservice teachers to gauge their understanding and adjust their teaching accordingly. https://www.socrative.com/
4. Quizlet: An educational app that includes AI features to create flashcards, quizzes, and games for various subjects, helping preservice teachers to develop study materials easily. https://quizlet.com/
5. Canva for Education: This design tool provides templates and resources that preservice teachers can use to create visually appealing lesson plans, presentations, and student materials. https://www.canva.com/education/

6. AI-Powered Tutoring Systems: Tools like Carnegie Learning and DreamBox Learning offer personalized tutoring experiences that adapt to students' learning styles and paces, providing insights for preservice teachers on differentiating instruction.
7. Teaching with Technology (EdTech) Platforms: Websites like EdSurge or Education Week provide news and insights on the latest AI tools and trends in education, helping preservice teachers stay informed.
8. Literacy and Numeracy Apps: Programs like Reading Eggs and Prodigy provide adaptive learning pathways for students, allowing preservice teachers to incorporate technology that personalizes learning experiences.
9. Online Courses and Webinars: Platforms like Coursera, edX, or even specific webinars on educational technology offer courses that explore the use of AI in education, giving preservice teachers valuable knowledge and skills.

(Chat GPT, 2025 June 19).

Each of these sites provides information about enhancements for lessons and topics. Integrating AI tools for student engagement represents a transformative opportunity for preservice teachers to innovate their instructional strategies and elevate their lesson plan preparation practices. By utilizing platforms such as Kahoot! Google Classroom, and Socrative, future educators can not only streamline their lesson preparation but also foster a dynamic learning environment that adapts to the diverse needs of their students. Furthermore, resources like Quizlet and Canva for Education empower preservice teachers to create interactive, visually appealing materials that enrich the educational experience. As they embrace these cutting-edge technologies, preservice teachers are better equipped to meet the challenges of modern education and inspire their students to learn effectively and enthusiastically. Ultimately, by leveraging the capabilities of AI, they can craft a future where education is personalized, engaging, and more accessible than ever before, paving the way for a new generation of innovative thinkers and lifelong learners.

BUILDING A SOLID FOUNDATION WITH AI

In addition to providing AI support for lesson plans and enhancements to make instruction more engaging, AI can also help teacher educators build a solid reading foundation with undergraduate students before they even begin to understand lesson planning. Undergraduate reading courses in the teacher preparation programs emphasize building a solid reading foundation, which includes phonemic awareness, phonics, vocabulary, fluency, and reading comprehension (NRP, 2000). Each component is essential when providing instruction on reading in the primary grades

(K-3) when students are focused on learning to read when instructed to engage in phonological awareness, phonics, vocabulary, and fluency strategies. Once students transition into upper elementary grades, the emphasis shifts to reading for learning, which takes place across various curricular areas as students leverage their decoding skills. While preservice teachers are instructed on the meaning and purpose of each critical element, the practice has been primarily through monotonous worksheets. The use of AI, however, has expanded significantly, and apps are being developed to support early literacy, focusing primarily on skill development in reading and writing (Magallanez, 2025). In the blog post, Magallanez explains that the science of teaching reading movement has become extremely large "in the U.S. with eighteen states having passed science of reading laws since 2021 and 9 states with legislation" (2025, n.p.). Due to this, educational technology has begun to explore programs that incorporate voice commands, particularly for early learners and writing. See the tools listed below.

Literacy for K-12 Apps

Apps Description Reading Foundations

Amira Learning Speech-recognition that listens to readers read Fluency
Ello Speech-recognition that listens to readers read Fluency

Ready4Reading phoneme-level-analysis Phonemic Awareness

Payback Writing support and grading assistance Writing, vocabulary
DeepDives' iterative writing process helps with grammar Writing, Vocabulary and vocabulary
Pressto Brainstorming for writing at the elementary Writing

Each app noted in above provides students with personalized learning experiences that will complement the traditional teaching methods listed previously (Magallanez, 2025 May 15). Developing personalized learning experiences is particularly crucial for teachers working with diverse student populations.

SCAFFOLDING TECHNIQUES FOR DIVERSE LEARNERS

Scaffolding is another educational term that education faculty teach to pre-service teachers. Scaffolding, as named by Jerome Bruner (1986), is a practice in which a more knowledgeable adult introduces a new topic to a student in a modified manner.

This term coincided with the instruction of Lev Vygotsky, his teacher. Vygotsky (1978), a psychologist, is well known for his work with students who needed additional help. He found that when a more knowledgeable other was around, the students were much more confident and consequently correct. Each of these psychologists was a social constructivist, and the idea that social interaction is necessary for learning could not be a facet of artificial intelligence. However, technological advances made scaffolding possible for all students. While not all diverse learners necessarily require scaffolding or modified attention in their academics, researchers have recognized that diverse learners are more successful with instruction or pedagogy that aligns with their learning styles.

The education faculty recognizes that today's classrooms comprise students from diverse racial, cultural, ethnic, socioeconomic, and linguistic backgrounds. Each teacher is responsible for ensuring that all students are taught how to become good citizens and part of the U.S. workforce. So, it is a goal for all faculty to confirm that the pre-service teachers they are preparing recognize the uniqueness of their future students and are capable of teaching all. Fortunately, technology and AI have become a significant part of education, and educators and students have found numerous ways that AI is used to support diverse students.

In agreement, Song et.al. (2019) point out that "acknowledging the importance of AI literacy, governmental and non-governmental educational initiatives, and research centers around the world have begun developing curriculum guidelines for K-12 AI education (i.e., teaching AI as a subject matter)" (p. 2). Further, Scott et al. (2022) explain the Universal Design for Learning (UDL). UDL is an interdisciplinary educational framework that creates flexible and inclusive learning environments. UDL is the most well-known framework for teaching styles that would aid diverse students.

Universal Design for Learners and Universal Design for Transitional Learners

Faculty are confident that researchers and instructors have found that an effective online approach called the Universal Design for Learning (UDL) and Universal Design for Transitional Learners (UDT) (Scott et al, 2022). This framework provides pre-service teachers with a guideline to create more inclusive lesson plans. Pre-service and in-service teachers felt more comfortable using the UDL and UDT to create lesson plans and activities that are more accessible to a broader range of students, including those with disabilities, in general education classrooms. Both the UDL and UDT were based on three principles:

(a) multiple means of engagement, (b) multiple means of representation, and (c) multiple means of action and expression. Based on the principles of UDL, all educators must understand their students' strengths and needs to provide learning opportunities for all (Scott et al., 2022, n.p.).

AI AND CULTURALLY RELEVANT PEDAGOGY (CRP)

While the UDL and UDT frameworks have proven to be inclusive, they are not AI tools. Generative AI can help generate more lesson plans that incorporate inclusive instruction when specifically searching for Universal Design for Learning (UDL) (Pack, 2024). Pack (2024) notes that SchoolAI (SchoolAI.com) is one tool that helps students access information in various ways and allows teachers to customize AI chatbots for specific learning opportunities. While UDL and UDT frameworks are designed to provide equity and inclusivity in lesson plans, they do not offer support for culturally relevant pedagogy. The AI tools that incorporate culturally relevant pedagogy (CRP) support students from diverse racial and ethnic backgrounds who are outside the mainstream. CRP was developed by Gloria Ladson-Billings (1995) and centers around student backgrounds and cultures when determining practical learning approaches. Bennett & Royce (2024) explain, "This approach aims to engage students more effectively, foster their academic success, and affirm their cultural identity. It is not just about understanding a student's culture, but also actively integrating it to make learning more meaningful and empowering" (n.p.). This article explores how AI catalyzes culturally relevant pedagogy in science.

An example of how CRT is utilized in Generative AI is primarily through the prompts that are provided. An example that was explored involved using a recent experience; AI can assist in accessing and summarizing various community factors that affect their communities, much like the water crisis in Flint, Michigan. AI can also provide comprehensive insights into other communities dealing with damaging factors. AI can also help with differentiating instruction in science topics by

- Generating questions, rubrics, and resources for different grade levels
- Curate culturally relevant readings and books to help build background knowledge, and
- Gather culturally resonant examples in chemistry, biology, physics, or environmental science lessons.

(Bennett & Royce, 2024)

AI can assist with providing culturally relevant teaching in various curricular areas other than science. AI can support students with language translations, check students' engagement, and identify bias in school materials.

Resource Curation

Generative AI also serves as a tool for resource or content curation. Neelakandan (2019) explains that content curation involves gathering all the relevant information related to a particular topic, subject, or audience and presenting it in a way that allows learners to quickly and easily find what they want. AI can automate tasks like identifying relevant articles, synthesizing information, and generating new knowledge. The Digital Learning Institute blog (2022, November 21) explains, "In the digital age, AI is like a lighthouse in the overwhelming sea of information. It draws our attention to credible, relevant, and engaging learning resources." This tool is significant for faculty, who are required to provide current information in their fields of study. Resource curation is also beneficial for teacher educators, as it provides access to existing content. Content curation also allows faculty to work with students who can engage with relevant content that encourages them to build their curation skills and share their ideas, thereby moving the learning from simplistic content consumption (Digital Learning Institute, 2022, November 21). Refer to Table 1.4 for a list of apps that offer useful curation tools as identified by the editorial team at Bit.AI blog (2019).

Useful Curation Tools

- elink
- Bit.ai
- Flipboard
- Listly
- Paper.li
- Feedly
- Pocket
- Triberr
- Scoop it
- ContentGems
- DrumUp

A description of each of these is noted here: https://blog.bit.ai/best-content-curation-tools/

Educators Developing an Open Mind

When AI is being introduced to faculty, it must be emphasized that AI is not going to replace human teachers. AI is a tool designed to help support teachers, not replace them. School leaders need to provide teachers with professional development to ensure this is clear and understood. In the August 2023 issue of the National Association of Elementary School Principals (NAESP) there were five strategies recommended to bring forth success when incorporating AI in classrooms:

1. **Encourage Exploration:** It's critical that educators have a chance to experience the capabilities of AI tools. Giving them freedom to explore AI tools empowers them to gain first-hand experience using the technology and to think about how to integrate it into their work. Doing this will foster a culture where teachers feel safe to experiment, make mistakes, and learn from mistakes.
2. **Provide Training:** Educators need training to feel comfortable using new technology. Offering workshops or professional development courses on AI (along with follow-up activities and discussions or opportunities to collaborate with colleagues) can help teachers understand its capabilities and limitations.
3. **Spotlight Success:** Spotlight examples of AI that are already being used in your school. Encourage educators to share what they're trying and whether it's working or not. Encourage teachers to work together in their exploration of AI. Collaboration allows them to learn from each other's experiences and builds a supportive community for this new journey.
4. **Host Conversations:** Host conversations with educators about how schools can prepare students with the skills to thrive in an AI-infused world. Some topics of conversations are ethical AI use and digital citizenship, promoting computational thinking, collaboration and interdisciplinary learning, and integrating AI into the curriculum.
5. **Set the Right Conditions:** When it comes to using AI or any other technologies in your school, it is important to establish conditions for effective use. Clearly outline the school's policies on data privacy and ethical considerations when using AI, including those related to plagiarism and proper use of secondary sources. Teachers should know what's expected of them and the boundaries within which they should operate.

(NAESP, 2023, Section 3)

In addition to providing an opportunity for teachers to explore, have training, and being set with the correct conditions for effective use of AI, school leaders and trainers must also address concerns about bias, ethics, and data privacy.

In William's (2024) article, "The ethical implications of using generative chatbots in higher education," he points out that comprehensive measures should be used to address all issues related to data privacy, algorithmic bias, autonomy in learning, plagiarism, and academic integrity. Once this is examined more closely, educators and all stakeholders can better leverage the potential of chatbots to create more inclusive and ethically sound educational environments. Educators must develop a mindset of continuous learning and experimentation with AI. School leaders and teachers must embrace the challenges and engage in open dialogue. In addition Williams (2024) reminds teacher educators that, "The ethical implications of using generative chatbots in higher education, (Section 1)" highlights the need for comprehensive measures to address all issues related to data privacy, algorithmic bias, autonomy in learning, plagiarism, and academic integrity. Once this is examined more closely, educators and all stakeholders can better leverage the potential of chatbots to create more inclusive and ethically sound educational environments. Educators must develop a mindset of continuous learning and experimentation with AI. School leaders and teachers must embrace the challenges and engage in open dialogue.

CONCLUSION

In conclusion, the incorporation of Generative AI is a transformative technological tool that can assist faculty members in numerous ways. AI provides instructional guidance (for course content to pre-service teachers), student engagement practices, and resource curation practices. These three elements are critical for faculty members who are incorporating Generative AI for the first time, primarily because they provide the framework that is important to follow. Specifically, the College of Education faculty plays a crucial role in preparing pre-service teachers by sharing effective teaching strategies and relevant experiences. Their first-hand encounters with students serve as valuable models for aspiring educators. By staying informed about current policies and practices, teacher educators can better support emerging teachers in navigating the complexities of modern classrooms. Leveraging artificial intelligence allows them to introduce innovative approaches, such as individualized learning experiences, AI-powered tools, and collaborative projects. Moreover, incorporating simulations and data analysis fosters decision-making skills in pre-service teachers. By employing these strategies, teacher educators can have a profound impact on the next generation of teachers, equipping them with the necessary skills to succeed in their careers.

REFERENCES:

Anderson, L. W., Krathwohl, D. R., & Bloom, B. S. (2001). *A taxonomy for learning, teaching, and assessing : a revision of Bloom's taxonomy of educational objectives* Longman.

Armstrong, P. (2010). *Bloom's Taxonomy*. Vanderbilt University Center for Teaching. https://cft.vanderbilt.edu/guides-sub-pages/blooms-taxonomy

Barrett, A., & Pack, A. (2023). Not quite eye to A.I.: Student and teacher perspectives on the use of generative artificial intelligence in the writing process. *International Journal of Educational Technology in Higher Education, 20*(1), 59. Advance online publication. DOI: 10.1186/s41239-023-00427-0

Bennett, V., & Royce, C. A. (2024, Dec. 9). AI and Culturally Relevant Pedgogy: A Great pAIr. *NSTA: Chalkboards to AI.* https://www.nsta.org/blog/ai-and-culturally-relevant-pedagogy-great-pair#:~:text=By%20using%20AI%2Dpowered%20learning,their%20cultural%20and%20eductional%20needs

Bit.AI Editorial Team. (2019). *11 Best Content Curation Tools for Marketers!* Bit. AI Blog. https://blog.bit.ai/best-content-curation-tools/

Bower, M., Torrington, J., Lai, J. W. M., Petocz, P., & Alfano, M. (2024). How should we change teaching and assessment in response to increasingly powerful generative Artificial Intelligence? Outcomes of the ChatGPT teacher survey. *Education and Information Technologies*. Advance online publication. DOI: 10.1007/s10639-023-12405-0

Bruner, J. (1986). *Actual Minds, Possible Worlds*. Harvard University Press. DOI: 10.4159/9780674029019

ChatGPT Pro. (2025, June 19). *Student engagement practices*. ChatGPT Pro. https://chatpro.ai-pro.org/chat/new

Chiu, T. K. F. (2024). Future research recommendations for transforming higher education with generative AI Future research recommendations for transforming higher education with generative AI. *Computers and Education. Artificial Intelligence, 6*, 100197.

Digital Learning Institute. (2022, November 21). AI's transformative effect on curating digital learning content. https://www.digitallearninginstitute.com/blog/ai-transformative-effect-on-curating-content

Google Cloud. (n.d.). *What is artificial intelligence (AI)?* https://cloud.google.com/learn/what-is-artificial-intelligence?hl=en#common-types-of-artificial-neural-networks

Karata¸, F., & Yüce, E. (2024). AI and the future of teaching: Preservice teachers' reflections on the use of artificial intelligence in open and distributed learning. *International Review of Research in Open and Distance Learning*, *25*(3), 304–325. DOI: 10.19173/irrodl.v25i3.7785

Kim, J., Lee, H., & Cho, Y. H. (2022). Learning design to support student-AI collaboration: perspectives of leading teachers for AI in education. *Education and Information Technologies, 27*(5), 6069. http://dx.doi.org.proxy.tamuc.edu/10.1007/s10639-021-10831-6

Liu, G. L., & Wang, Y. (2024). Modeling EFL teachers' intention to integrate informal digital learning of English (IDLE) into the classroom using the theory of planned behavior. *System, 120*, 103193. DOI: 10.1016/j.system.2023.103193

Magallanez, M. (2025, May 15). AI Meets the Science of Reading and Writing Skill Development. CSTA Voice Blog. https://csteachers.org/ai-meets-the-science-of-reading-and-writing-skill-development/

MagicSchool AI. (2025). Understanding Force and motion lesson plan. MagicSchool AI. https://app.magicschool.ai/tools/lesson-plan-generator?thread=78103107

McGehee, N. (2024). *Breaking Barriers: A Meta-Analysis of Educator Acceptance of AI Technology in Education.* Michigan Virtual. https://michiganvirtual.org/research/publications/breaking-barriers-a-meta-analysis-of-educator-acceptance-of-ai-technology-in-education/

Neelakandan, N. (2019). The Impact of Content Curation in eLearning. https://elearningindustry.com/content-curation-impact-in-elearning#:~:text=Content%20curation%20in%20eLearning%20is,to%20get%20what%20they%20need

Pack, J. (2024, April 1). Using AI to Enhance Universal Design for Learning. *Edutopia* https://www.edutopia.org/article/using-ai-in-universal-design-for-learning/r/ChatGPT

Reza, H. M., Deng, C., Justin, J. K., Zhou, P., Kwon, Y. D., Ahmed Hosny, S. M., Tlili, A., Bassanelli, S., Bucchiarone, A., Gujar, S., Nacke, L. E., & Pan, H. (2023). *Exploring User Perspectives on ChatGPT: Applications*. Perceptions, and Implications for AI-Integrated Education.

Scott, L., Bruno, L., Gokita, T., & Thoma, C. A. (2022). Teacher candidates' abilities to develop universal design for learning and universal design for transition lesson plans. *International Journal of Inclusive Education*, *26*(4), 333–347. DOI: 10.1080/13603116.2019.1651910

Shata, A., & Hartley, K. (2025). Artificial intelligence and communication technologies in academia: Faculty perceptions and the adoption of generative AI. *International Journal of Educational Technology in Higher Education*, *22*(1), 14–22. DOI: 10.1186/s41239-025-00511-7

Song, Y., Weisberg, L. R., Zhang, S., Tian, X., Boyer, K. E., & Israel, M. (2024). A framework for inclusive AI learning design for diverse learners. *Computers and Education. Artificial Intelligence*, *6*, 100212-. https://doi.org/DOI: 10.1016/j.caeai.2024.100212

Staff, N. A. E. S. P. (2023, August 26). 5 Strategies for Success in Bringing AI to Schools. *NAESP National Association for Elementary School Principals Blog*. https://www.naesp.org/resource/5-strategies-for-success-in-bringing-ai-to-schools/

Stano, E. (2024). Attending to Bias, Accessibility, and Ethical Concerns in the Use of AI in Education. *EdTech Digest*. https://www.edtechdigest.com/2024/11/20/attending-to-bias-accessibility-and-ethical-concerns-in-the-use-of-ai-in-education/#:~:text=One%20of%20the%20most%20pressing,negative%20outcomes%20for%20marginalized%20groups

Vygotsky, L. S., & Cole, M. (1978). *Mind in society: the development of higher psychological processes*. Harvard University Press.

Williams, R. T. (2024). The ethical implications of using generative chatbots in higher education. *Frontiers in Education*, *8*, 1331607. DOI: 10.3389/feduc.2023.1331607

Xu, W., & Ouyang, F. (2022). The application of AI technologies in STEM education: A systematic review from 2011 to 2021. *International Journal of STEM Education*, *9*(1), 1–20. DOI: 10.1186/s40594-022-00377-5

Zhang, K., & Aslan, A. B. (2021). AI technologies for education: Recent research & Future directions. *Computers and Education: Artificial Intelligence*, *2*, 100025. DOI: 10.1016/j.caeai.2021.100025

Chapter 5
AI as a Collaborative Tool:
Redefining Educator Roles in Content Development

Shivnath Ghosh
https://orcid.org/0000-0001-7368-7139
Brainware University, Kolkata, India

Olivia Jana
Brainware University, Kolkata, India

ABSTRACT

Currently, artificial intelligence (AI) is also transforming education as an effective means of cooperation in content production. This chapter explores the nature of AI not as an augmentation but as a disruptor that is changing the profession of educators. This advancement is made possible by the AI in that it is able to automate routine duties such as learning analytics, construction of assessments, and content development. The chapter draws frameworks and resources that support instruction as it discusses practical implementation of artificial intelligence in the construction of learning resources. Such are interactive simulations that map abstract concepts, multimodal teaching aids that address different types of learners, and intelligent adaptive learning environments that offer learning tailored to the type of the learner profile. The use of intelligent assessment system provides immediate feedback and analysis, which can assist educators/teachers and learners to identify their proficiency and deficits.

DOI: 10.4018/979-8-3373-1122-7.ch005

1. LITERATURE REVIEW

Since its inception in computer-assisted instruction in the 1960s, artificial intelligence (AI) integration in education has experienced substantial development. By delivering pre-programmed lessons and fundamental interactive learning, these early systems, like PLATO (Programmed Logic for Automated Teaching Operations), laid the groundwork for the use of technology in education (Luckin & Esparrell, 2024). Developments by the 1980s and 1990s resulted in the creation of intelligent tutoring systems (ITS), which mimicked the direction of human instructors using rule-based algorithms. A preview of the possibilities of personalized education could be provided by these systems' ability to adjust to the demands of the pupils (TeachFlow.AI, 2024).

With the use of machine learning algorithms that can analyze large datasets and produce highly tailored learning routes for each learner, adaptive learning technologies emerged in the twenty-first century. With the advent of real-time feedback from AI platforms, students may now learn at their own speed and close knowledge gaps as they advance. This flexibility has been further increased by tools like learning management systems and virtual tutors, which have made education more student-centric (Ramirez & Fuentes Esparrell, 2024; Luckin & Esparrell, 2024).

Furthermore, immersive learning environments have been produced by the incorporation of augmented and virtual reality (AR/VR) into AI-driven teaching systems. Through simulations, these technologies give students the chance to investigate difficult ideas, promoting experiential learning that is impossible with conventional approaches. Additionally, AI remains a vital component of accessibility, supporting students with disabilities using technologies including adaptive interfaces, text-to-speech systems, and speech recognition (TeachFlow.AI, 2024).

This historical journey demonstrates AI's transformative potential in education, from its modest beginnings to its current role in creating inclusive, personalized, and interactive learning environments. As AI technology advances, its ability to satisfy a variety of student needs and optimize learning outcomes is expected to grow quickly.

The use of artificial intelligence (AI) in education has grown in popularity and has had a profound impact on learner engagement, material creation, and instructional methods. The part that follows examines relevant research to comprehend how AI is changing the roles of educators and encouraging teamwork in content creation.

Moreover, the integration of augmented and virtual reality (AR/VR) into AI-driven Immersive learning settings have been made possible by educational tools. Through simulations, these technologies give students the chance to investigate difficult ideas, promoting experiential learning that is impossible with conventional approaches. Additionally, AI remains a vital component of accessibility, supporting students with disabilities using technologies including adaptive interfaces, text-to-speech systems, and speech recognition (TeachFlow.AI, 2024).

From its humble origins to its current function in establishing inclusive, customized, and interactive learning environments, this historical journey highlights AI's transformative potential in education. It is anticipated that AI technology's capacity to meet a wide range of student needs and maximize educational outcomes will increase rapidly as it develops.

1.1 AI in Content Development and Pedagogy

There has been much discussion about AI's potential to automate curriculum design and content production. Repetitive chores like curriculum mapping, assessment design, and grading are made easier by AI-powered solutions, freeing up teachers to concentrate on more strategic and creative work. Holmes et al. (2019), for example, highlighted how AI facilitates individualized learning by adjusting materials to each learner's requirements, encouraging inclusion and involvement. In a similar vein, Luckin et al. (2016) introduced the idea of the "Intelligence Amplifier," in which AI collaborates with educators to help them create adaptable and multimodal learning materials.

1.2 Enhancing Learning Experiences Through AI

Numerous studies emphasize how AI-powered tools can be used to improve educational opportunities. It has been demonstrated that AI tools, such as intelligent tutoring systems (ITS), may adjust to the learning preferences of students and offer prompt feedback, enhancing performance and retention (VanLehn, 2011). Additionally, AI-enabled virtual worlds and interactive simulations have been found to be effective resources for conceptual learning in fields such as STEM (Anderson et al., 2014). Additionally, these resources help develop problem-solving and critical thinking abilities.

1.3 Ethical Challenges and Human Oversight

Even while AI has the potential to be revolutionary, ethical issues with algorithmic bias, data privacy, and fair access are still very important. In his discussion of algorithmic bias's effects on educational technology, Binns (2018) emphasized the importance of inclusivity and justice in AI design. In order to guarantee ethical compliance and compatibility with educational goals, Williamson et al. (2020) emphasized the significance of human monitoring in AI applications.

1.4 AI in Teacher Professional Development

In order to successfully integrate AI into education, teachers must be given the necessary tools. Continuous professional development (CPD) is crucial for preparing instructors for AI-driven tools, according to studies. Koper (2014) emphasized that in order to ensure that educators can fully utilize new technologies, training programs that concentrate on the pedagogical and technical components of AI applications are necessary.

1.5 Bridging Accessibility Gaps

In educational studies, the promise of AI to promote diversity and eliminate accessibility gaps has frequently come up. Learners with impairments can easily access content thanks to adaptive technologies like screen readers and speech-to-text apps (Seale, 2014). Furthermore, AI-powered platforms can support real-time help and language translation, fostering inclusivity on a worldwide scale.

2. INTRODUCTION TO AI IN EDUCATION

AI in education, therefore, as a new teaching and learning model, incorporates new technologies in learning such as machine learning, natural language processing, and data analyt-ics. Routes, content, interactions, and behavioral patterns are leveraged by AI software systems showing insights for learning and test results. This approach enhances student participation and academic performance because learning paths are adapted to the needs and preferences of individual learners based on their demands; learning is presented in multiple formats and rates, which allows addressing the needs of all learners with different learning abilities (Luckin & Esparrell, 2024; TeachFlow.AI, 2024).

AI is not limited to educational activities or close assignments only. AI technologies in many administrative areas include; scheduling, monitoring their attendance and even grading where the work is monotonous and repeated work is done substantially reducing the loads that teachers usually have to handle. Since this automation can apply a variety of online grading algorithms, teachers can spend more time with the students such as being more engaging and focusing on students (TeachFlow.AI, 2024, p. 43; Ramirez & Fuentes Esparrell, 2024, p. 23). In addition, AI is capable of identifying at-risk students in advance while the schools offer interventions and consequently, increase the chances of these students' retention (Luckin & Esparrell, 2024).

AI also makes learning diverse: students can use speech to text software, lingual translation, and adaptive interfaces designed for disabled learners. These resources afford skills for accommodating various demands that may be required of the teachers and make learning as favorable as possible. AI work in tandem to support not only issues of customization but also of access while tightly integrating micro and macro educational environments (Luckin & Esparrell, 2024; TeachFlow.AI, 2024).

2.1 Definition and Scope of AI in Education

The application of collaborative applications such as machine learning and natural language processing, computer vision and others in the teaching and learning process of students is referred to as artificial intelligence in education. Here, AI encompasses programs and technologies that support learning, which is malleable, the administration, which is to be contractualized, and instruction is to be personalized according to the learner's requirements as cited by Luckin et al. (2016). For instance, the recent trend that has developed is that AI-based outcome assessment and intelligent tutor systems (ITS) are being used to evaluate the performance of students and give the educators as well as the students a backed up information. Mainly all those concepts that advocate development of virtual assistants, learning games and predictive analytics enhancing the process of education fall under this broad category.

Besides the automation, the AI in education can also be applied in order to enhance the creativity, diversity, and participation. On the basis of the success a learner displays, AI- assisted platforms like adaptive learning systems allow differentiation in instructions through adjusting either the speed or the level of the content provided. Also, the implementing of such processes as attendance control as well as grading through the help of AI solutions helps to increase the overall administrative effectiveness and eliminate teachers' time waste on administrative tasks that are not directly related to their main work of teaching. As a phenomenon, AI advances in practice, enhancing learning's traditional approaches to teaching, and offering new opportunities for creative and collaborative learning environments.

2.2 Historical Evolution of AI Tools in Educational Contexts

Early intelligent tutoring systems (ITS) like SCHOLAR, which integrated natural language processing with the delivery of educational content, were introduced in the 1970s, marking the beginning of artificial intelligence (AI) in education (Carbonell, 1970). These methods prepared the way for the creation of AI-powered instruments that could modify educational materials and offer tailored feedback. Systems like AutoTutor, which improved engagement through conversational interfaces, were made possible by advances in processing power and algorithms in the 1990s and early 2000s (Graesser et al., 2005).

With the creation of multimodal learning platforms, virtual reality (VR) simulations, and predictive analytics, artificial intelligence (AI) in education has rapidly expanded in the twenty-first century. AI technologies have been incorporated into massive open online courses (MOOCs) to evaluate user behavior and modify the way content is delivered (Kop et al., 2011). Students can now engage in dynamic, AI-mediated environments that foster critical thinking and problem-solving skills thanks to the adoption of AI-driven technologies in collaborative learning contexts more recently (Luckin et al., 2016). This development highlights how AI has the ability to revolutionize education by consistently adjusting to the requirements of a wide range of students.

2.3 The Significance of AI as a Collaborative Tool

AI is a highly effective means to enhance collaboration in education that redistributes traditional roles effectively, creating an opportunity for teachers and learners to respond and cooperate better. By performing those monotonous tasks and functions such as grading, assessing, and administrative work, AI relieves instructors for more sophisticated tasks such as curriculum development, and training or coaching, et cetera (Holmes et al., 2019). Moreover, AI tools make cooperation easier as they create common platforms where students work with the content, complete simulations, and receive feedback at once. Besides enhancing the level of engagement, these tools bring further understanding of the content under study.

In the same way, cohort building is promoted by the utilization of chatbots and virtual assistants because of the communication gaps between the teachers and the students. These tools save teachers' mental load while ensuring that students get the help they need by providing instant directions and ideas (Chen et al., 2020). Aware of the enormous datasets it can analyze and provide insights for, AI enables cooperative decision-making across educators, administrators, and legislators to deliver more effective educative practices universally. To epitomize this reinterpretation of roles, it is shown how AI can increase human know-ledge and create a collaborative learning climate.

By promoting interactive environments, providing insights into learning processes, and bridging gaps between instructors and students, artificial intelligence (AI) serves as a collaborative tool. Platforms with AI capabilities can create dynamic student groups according to complimentary learning styles and skill sets, promoting cooperation and teamwork. Additionally, chatbots and virtual assistants simplify administrative and communication duties, freeing up teachers to concentrate on teaching. Additionally, AI fosters diversity by facilitating real-time translation to provide global learning opportunities and by offering resources for students with disabilities. The introduction of AI into education signifies a paradigm shift, turning conventional teaching strategies into creative, inclusive strategies that serve a diverse and international student body. Leveraging AI's full potential in education will require addressing ethical issues and guaranteeing fair access as technology develops.

3. CASE STUDY

3.1 Redefining Educator Roles in the AI Era

Title: Blending AI and Human Expertise: A High School's Journey Toward Modern Pedagogy

Overview

A Finnish high school started a revolutionary path by incorporating AI-powered resources into its curriculum. The program's main goal was to help instructors use technology to lessen their administrative workload and improve their capacity to mentor and facilitate. The curriculum placed a strong emphasis on striking a balance between human expertise and technology in order to enhance learning outcomes and create a more engaging learning environment.

Example Data

AI Integration Context: To deploy adaptive learning platforms like SmartLearn and EdWise AI, the school partnered with EdTech businesses. These tools made it possible to modify lesson plans in real time in response to data on student performance.

Global Alignment: Finland, renowned for its cutting-edge educational system, sets the standard for contemporary pedagogy and offers insights on scalability for applications around the world

Implementation

AI Tools

- Adaptive learning platforms offering tailored course modules for individual students.
- Automated grading systems capable of assessing essays, quizzes, and project work with detailed feedback.
- AI-assisted attendance trackers to streamline administrative processes.

Educator Training Program:

- Duration: A structured 6-month program.

- Content Focus: Training emphasized the effective use of AI tools for
- Designing lesson plans integrated with adaptive modules.
- Delivering real-time, personalized feedback.

Monitoring and analyzing student progress using AI dashboards.

Shift in Educator Roles:

With repetitive tasks such as grading and attendance tracking automated, teachers focused on:

- Crafting creative, project-based learning activities to promote problem-solving and innovation.
- Facilitating in-depth group discussions to enhance critical thinking skills.
- Providing targeted mentorship to students needing extra support, especially in core subjects like mathematics and science.

Outcomes

Student Engagement:. Personalized learning paths created by AI modules led to a 25% increase in student engagement (TeachFlow.AI, 2024), especially in STEM subjects where adaptive content aligned with varying skill levels.

Academic Performance:

The school observed a significant boost in STEM subject scores, with average performance improving by 20% over the academic year(Ramirez & Fuentes Esparrell, 2024). Adaptive AI modules ensured students mastered foundational concepts before advancing, reducing failure rates (Luckin & Esparrell, 2024). This case study demonstrates how automation might reinterpret teachers' duties as facilitators of creativity and critical thinking rather than task managers, underscoring the revolutionary potential of AI in education. AI frees up teachers to concentrate on improving student experiences and creating a more creative and individualized learning environment by reducing administrative duties. This well-rounded strategy of fusing AI and human knowledge is a scalable model for contemporary education, especially when it comes to preparing students for the ever-changing demands of the twenty-first century.

3.2 AI Applications in Content Development

Title: Building Personalized Learning Journeys: An AI-Powered University Initiative

Overview

This case study demonstrates how automation might reinterpret teachers' duties as facilitators of creativity and critical thinking rather than task managers, underscoring the revolutionary potential of AI in education. AI frees up teachers to concentrate on improving student experiences and creating a more creative and individualized learning environment by reducing administrative duties.

This well-rounded strategy of fusing AI and human knowledge is a scalable model for contemporary education, especially when it comes to preparing students for the ever-changing demands of the twenty-first century.

Example Data:

Serving more than 25,000 students with diverse learning requirements who were enrolled in fields like engineering, biosciences, social sciences, and humanities was the initiative's main goal (TeachFlow.AI, 2023).

Implementation

Content Creation with AI Tools:

To create dynamic and adaptive material, the institution used GPT-based AI technologies, such as OpenAI's GPT-4 and related language models. These resources were utilized to create a range of educational materials, including.

- Lecture materials tailored to individual learning levels.
- Quizzes customized to assess and address knowledge gaps in different student groups.
- Interactive multimedia presentations, such as video tutorials, that improved engagement and accessibility.

Teachers' preparation time was cut down by AI-generated content, freeing them up to concentrate on mentorship and classroom engagement. One instance was a history lecture that used AI-generated timeline simulations to give students learning important world historical events an interactive visual representation (Luckin & Esparrell, 2024).

Adaptive Learning Systems

AI-driven platforms created individualized learning routes by analyzing past performance data and student learning behavior using machine learning algorithms.

- AI tools identified areas of student strengths and weaknesses.
- Personalized recommendations were made to tailor quizzes, assignments, and resource-sharing platforms for each learner.

For example, AI-driven analysis in a social science course revealed that while some students had advanced knowledge of important political theories, others had trouble with them. AI recommended additional resources for pupils who were having difficulty while moving high-achieving students on to more difficult subjects based on these observations (Ramirez & Fuentes Esparrell, 2023).

Interactive Simulations

AI-powered virtual labs have become an essential tool, especially in domains where practical experimentation is essential, such as engineering and biosciences. Students who might not have direct access to real labs were able to conduct research safely and remotely thanks to these virtual labs.

- Example: Without the limitations of a physical lab, students were able to realistically alter variables and examine results using an engineering lab simulation on fluid dynamics.
- Example: In biosciences, a virtual AI-generated lab allowed students to explore DNA sequencing techniques remotely, minimizing laboratory resource dependency.

While guaranteeing accessibility for distant learners and people with physical limitations, these virtual experiments provided universities with an affordable option (TeachFlow.AI, 2023).

Outcomes

Time Efficiency for Educators:

Teachers' time spent creating course materials was cut by 40% as a result of the use of AI tools. AI eased formerly time-consuming operations including creating multimedia presentations, grading tests, and designing lectures (Luckin & Esparrell, 2024).

Enhanced Student Satisfaction:

According to a poll, the tailored and focused quality of the material helped 85% of students express better comprehension of the course ideas. According to students, AI's personalized learning pathways let them study ideas at their own speed (Ramirez & Fuentes Esparrell, 2023).

Increased Accessibility and Equity:

Students with disabilities, remote learners, and underrepresented groups now have greater access to high-quality learning resources because to AI-generated content and virtual learning tools.

Example: AI tools provided text-to-speech features and alternative explanations for students with learning disabilities, enhancing their ability to access course content.

Improved Academic Performance:

When pre- and post-implementation data were compared, it was found that students who used individualized AI-driven learning routes performed better on average, with greater academic achievements in the biosciences and engineering fields. This case study illustrates the revolutionary potential of AI applications in content creation, showing how they may offer scalable, accessible, and customized learning experiences for a range of student demographics. AI is changing traditional teaching roles and enhancing learning results by enabling interactive simulations, adaptable learning paths, and a reduction in administrative responsibilities. This project serves as an example of how educational institutions can use AI to strike a balance between pedagogical objectives and technical developments, ultimately making education more effective and inclusive for all students.

4. AUTOMATING ROUTINE EDUCATIONAL TASKS

In a way, artificial intelligence-based applications for designing and grading of ex-ams and quizzes are becoming new age tools of enhancing productivity, accuracy, and customised approaches to knowledge delivery. These tools help to reduce the burden that such procedures might put in educators and by doing so, afford them time to focus on more critical tasks such as designing of curricula and guidance or support of students. To that end, AI systems may generate different forms of assessments that guarantee every child grasps their lessons, gets adequately challenged, and supports their learning process. These adaptive tests pro-vide an individualized learning environment where change is enacted as students supply answers to questions.

AI has grown to the extent that it also analyzes and judges open-ended responses including essays in addition to multiple-choice answers grading. Machine learning approaches, for example, the AI algorithms analyz-ing the writings by utilizing the NLP methods, which check the syntactic quality of the essays, together with both, their logical structuring and complexity of the critical thinking involved. This ensures unbiased and standardization which can more often be a challenge when grading is done manually. Besides, the system feedback that is often faster than manual check can provide the student with detailed information on the performance outcomes and areas of specific progress (Zawacki-Richter et al 2019).

Expanded Example: In addition to identifying plagiarism, the AI included in Turnitin provides more comprehensive analyses of written tasks. To be precise, these materials provide students with utility feedback as the assessments comment on style and approach, correct grammatical mistakes, check originality, and format. For instance, Turnitin company offers students the "Revision Assistant" which offers feedback to students as they write their papers. Besides, the saving of teachers' time, this empowers students to take personal responsibility of their learning through receiving prompt feedback on how they are writing.

Further, there are usually batteries of statistics that teachers can easily sample from ExamSoft in a bid to understand students' performances usually based on a particular topic or questions. On the brighter side, when teaching is based on data, educators can identify areas that have many cases and change their strategies ap-propriately. For example, if 80 percent of pupils have low achievement on a regular basis on a certain idea, the teacher should supplement the affected concept in the next classroom teachings.

All in all, to choose and mark assessments with the help of AI means gaining such benefits as meaning-ful and precise evaluation of the tasks, as well as the options for individual approaches both for teachers and students; in addition, teachers obtain valuable data that can enhance the effectiveness of their practice. Such advancements are making a more flexible and improved form of an education system.

4.1 Learning Analytics: Insights Into Student Performance and Engagement

AI-powered solutions are transforming the design and marking of assessments by guaranteeing precision, consistency, and personalization while also giving teachers insightful information to improve the efficacy of their instruction. A more dynamic and adaptable educational system is being made possible by these developments.

Analyzing Student Performance and Engagement

The behavior of learners as it relates to their engagement with learning platforms, frequency, and duration of usage, and even participation levels in assignments and discussions can be identified by AI. It means that thanks to AI, one can monitor the level of engagement and help teachers to recognize any of the below-mentioned behaviors that indicate that some children might be disengaged Click the button below to start the free trial and test AI-powered Engagement detection for Yourself. Schedules can be set for some activities and AI systems will inform teachers when a learner barely spends time on a certain module or when a learner has not submitted assignments in time.

Predicting Student Outcomes

Based on trends in past data, AI is able to forecast future academic success in addition to monitoring engagement. AI models may, for example, evaluate a student's performance on past tests to forecast how well they might do on subsequent ones. Teachers can identify children who are at danger far in advance of final examinations or other high-stakes tests because to this predictive capabilities. By providing more resources or modifying their teaching strategies, early intervention enables teachers to keep kids from falling behind.

Personalized Learning and Tailored Interventions

A customized approach to schooling is also made possible by AI-driven learning analytics. AI is able to generate unique learning paths for every student based on performance data. For instance, AI can suggest additional materials like videos, tests, or tutoring sessions that concentrate on a particular subject if it determines that a student is having difficulty with it. Instead of using a one-size-fits-all teaching strategy, this individualized approach guarantees that students get the help they require to succeed.

Example of Platforms Using Learning Analytics

Blackboard and Edmodo: Basic performance indicators such as quiz results, students' engagement, and the completion rates of assignments also make an appearance on the dashboards that such platforms afford educators. This helps the teachers elicit fast results concerning the general performance of their pupils and identify those who may need extra assistance. For instance, if a teacher over-hears that a few of students are poor in a particular subject, what s- he or she can do is offer more re-sources or center the day's lesson around that subject in an effort to assist the children.

Coursera:, the California-based online learning platform, Coursera uses artificial intelligence (AI) to monitor students' in-volvement through aspects such as the amount of time spent viewing videos, engagement in quizzes and forums. Thus, employing the data of students' activities, AI of Coursera proposes the courses to follow according to students' previous activity and preferences. For example, the AI could suggest extra credit courses in related disciplines if the student scores well on a data science class. In the cases when a student demonstrates signs of learning loss, the platform can also inform about the re-engagement strategies, like sending some inspiring messages, or suggesting the lessons that the student didn't complete.

AI for Intervention and Feedback

AI is also capable of giving teachers and pupils immediate feedback. Instant feedback on their strengths and shortcomings enables students to modify their study techniques or, if needed, seek assistance. In contrast, teachers can use data to inform their decisions about how to adapt their teaching methods to better suit the requirements of their pupils. For instance, if an AI system determines that a set of students is having trouble understanding a certain idea, the instructor can devote more time to that subject and, depending on the analytics, may employ different teaching strategies (Siemens and Long, 2011).

Improving Educational Outcomes

It is this potential that the use of AI in learning analytics opens for the creation of a far more dynamic and reactive learning environment that actually makes AI learning analytics possible. AI systems help teachers to detect patterns, recognize potential issues in the course of the academic process, and find proper solutions due to constant data collection and data analysis. This has led to better learning results, increased retention rates, and improved student engagement leading to increase efficiency and openness of education. In conclusion, learning analytics based on AI help teachers provide beneficial, tangible insights for more appropriate decisions about instruction and learning. Providing improved student-focused interventions, these methods ensure each learner has his/her needs met while also helping teachers narrow their focus toward those students who the education system needs to benefit most.

Streamlining Administrative Tasks to Enhance Teaching Efficiency

AI can help teachers and other educational workers save their time and reduce the rate of administrative mistakes in their line of work. Chores such as scheduling, recording attendance, and working on records for the students are general-ly tedious and drain a lot of resources, which can be focused on instruction and, or engaging the learners. AI enhances efficiency by reducing errors in the administrative work and making them more systematic, and also by speeding up work by providing a few standardized methods.

Automating Attendance Tracking

Many traditional systems of attendance tracking require manual checking and may often be time consuming and riddled with errors. This procedure is automated by various AI solutions, and the frequently used techniques are the use of sensors, or facial recognition technology for tracking the presence of the students. For, instance teachers can use online learning platforms or applications such as Classcraft and Powerschool to track attendance based on check-ins and out students who are most likely to miss classes due to absenteeism can be easily identified through these methods since they identify patterns of absenteeism. It also may also be programmed to send parent or guarding notification in cases of Student absence from class meaning parents are closely involved in their children's education.

Scheduling and Resource Management

With help of analyzing preferences, needs for certain courses, and free rooms, AI may enhance the daily schedule for students and educators. Besides, it eliminated chances of disputes to arise over issues such as allocation of classrooms, materials and teachers' aides among others. For instance, AI systems can help in the creation of the schedules that consider workload, exam schedules, and children activities in an attempt to cope with the needs of every student in his or her learning. AI makes this procedure trouble-free and efficient for the employees and thus increases the overall organization of educational activities.

Managing Student Records

Data management is made easier by AI with data such as student's academic history, grades, and personal data. Instead, teachers can leverage AI solutions that collect and sort such data or put in records and updates manually. This reduces the likelihood of mistakes and also enhances the quality of data being used. For example, there are programs, for example, Powerschool, that allow teachers to input assignments and tests to the program and have the grade updated in real time at the same time. This enhances the fostered school openness and better communication within the school community since the parents, students, and administrators got the latest information.

Automated Reporting

For teachers, creating reports on conduct, attendance, and student development can take a lot of effort, particularly in big class sizes. Reports are automatically generated by AI systems, which gather information from various sources and combine it into formats that are simple to comprehend. For instance, Classcraft offers analytics and dashboards that show patterns in student performance, conduct, and involvement. By enabling prompt interventions, these reports assist teachers in determining which children are performing well and which may require more assistance.

Virtual Assistants for Routine Queries

Students can ask regular questions about class schedules, assignment due dates, and course material to virtual assistants like Ada or ChatGPT. These AI assistants save teachers time by communicating with pupils via voice or text-based interfaces and offering prompt answers to often asked queries. Without having to wait for a teacher's response, a student might, for instance, question the virtual assistant about the deadline for an assignment or seek clarification on course material. While teachers can concentrate on more intricate and individualized interactions, this guarantees that pupils receive timely support.

Enhancing Teacher-Student Interaction

Teachers can interact with students more deeply when AI technologies take care of administrative duties. Teachers can devote more of their time to coaching, mentoring, and helping individual students rather than to administrative tasks. For instance, teachers can prepare more involved courses, give feedback on projects, or have one-on-one conversations with students using the time AI saves. AI contributes to the creation of a more encouraging and stimulating learning environment by automating repetitive chores. (Viberg and others, 2018).

Data-Driven Decision Making

In the same way, AI system can accumulate administrative data for informational purposes that are helpful for decision making. For instance, AI can analyze truancy trends and define which of the students might need assistance and propose how to tackle the problem. This data driven strat-egy can help schools to identify oddities early when they can be dealt with before they get out of hand, or be associated with behavioral difficulties, achievement or attendance. These data can also be helpful for administrators in an effort to assign resource more effectively, organize teacher professional develop-ment, and conduct other school-wide campaigns that may address the needs of the learners.

In conclusion, AI greatly lessens the workload of teachers by automating administrative duties, freeing them up to concentrate on what really counts: teaching and learning processes, the behaviour of students as well as their learning progression. Besides time, precision, efficacy and flexibility of methods of administration are promoted by these tools creating more efficient educational system.

5. REDEFINING EDUCATOR ROLES IN THE AI ERA

In the age of artificial intelligence, educators are becoming more facilitators and strategists rather than just information producers. Teachers can concentrate on directing students' learning experiences by using AI tools to create lesson plans, tests, and instructional materials. Teachers increasingly take on the role of strategists, creating individualized learning paths, using AI to find knowledge gaps, and encouraging student participation. As a result of this shift, educators must learn how to evaluate AI-generated insights and adapt them to the various needs of their students.

5.1 Enhancing Mentorship, Critical Thinking, and Creativity Through AI Collaboration

AI tools can help teachers encourage students' creativity, critical thinking, and problem-solving skills. AI enables teachers to spend more time on mentoring and higher-order thinking abilities by automating routine chores. AI, for example, can offer analytical insights on student development, allowing professors to properly mentor students. Through experiential learning, AI-powered simulations and creative tools can also foster creativity and foster critical thinking.

5.2 Balancing Human Intuition with AI Precision

Human intuition is still essential for comprehending the subtleties of student emotions, motivations, and contextual circumstances, even though AI is excellent at data analysis, pattern recognition, and precision. To provide a comprehensive learning experience, educators must strike a balance between the objectivity of AI and their own empathy and judgment. For instance, whereas AI may detect a decline in a student's performance, only a teacher is able to determine whether environmental or personal reasons are to blame. A well-rounded approach to education is ensured by this fusion of human intuition with AI precision.

6. ETHICAL AND PRACTICAL CHALLENGES IN AI ADOPTION

6.1 Algorithmic Bias and Its Impact on Educational Equity

When AI systems generate results that consistently disadvantage particular groups—often as a result of biases in the data used to train these systems—this is known as algorithmic bias. Algorithmic bias in education can result in unfair grading schemes or unequal access to resources. For instance, biased training data may cause AI-based admissions algorithms to inadvertently favor students from particular demographic groupings. This makes already-existing gaps in educational opportunity worse. Diverse datasets, openness in AI development, and recurring audits of AI systems are necessary to address these biases (Doshi-Velez and Kortz 2017).

6.2 Data Privacy and Security Concerns

Large volumes of data are needed for AI system operation and training, which raises serious privacy and security issues. Sensitive student data, such as learning progress and personal information, is frequently gathered in the field of education.

This data may be misused or vulnerable to cyberattacks if strict security measures are not taken. Furthermore, improperly built AI systems may unintentionally reveal private data. Privacy protection laws such as FERPA and GDPR are difficult to apply to AI-powered learning systems (Mittelstadt et al., 2016).

6.3 Challenges in Equitable Access to AI Tools and Infrastructure

When AI is used in education, it frequently benefits institutions with greater funding, leaving impoverished schools and underserved populations behind. Access to AI solutions that could otherwise overcome educational gaps, such as personalized learning platforms, is restricted by these inequities. Lack of access to contemporary gadgets and high-speed internet also widens the gap, resulting in a "digital divide" driven by artificial intelligence. For AI to be adopted in education in a way that is inclusive, efforts must be made to lower costs and create equal infrastructure (West 2019).

6.4 The Importance of Maintaining Human Oversight in AI Applications

Despite their strength, AI systems are not perfect. They can make mistakes that have major repercussions in educational settings, misread data, or neglect to take special student requirements into consideration. By ensuring that AI functions as a tool rather than a decision-maker, human monitoring enables educators to step in when needed. Maintaining trust, accountability, and moral results in AI applications requires striking this balance.

7. UPSKILLING EDUCATORS FOR AI INTEGRATION

7.1 Professional Development Programs and AI Literacy for Educators

One of the preconditions for effective AI implementation is allowing teachers to use AI in their classrooms (Luckin et al., 2016). On the basis of the results obtained, it can be concluded that proficiency that includes an understanding of the principles of AI and the ability to identify the presence of ethical issues, as well as an understanding of the pedagogical effectiveness of AI and how it can be used, should be the focus of current professional development programs . Such steps, for example, AI seminars and certification programs can allow educators to integrate AI tools and applications such as automated grading systems, and learning management systems with some level of confidence (UNESCO, 2021). Assuming the technology environment continues to evolve, however, on-going professional development will ensure that instructors retain flexibility.

7.2 Strategies for Effective Collaboration Between Educators and AI Systems

There is therefore the need to invent strategies on how best to align educators with AI capabilities in order to produce synergy between the education system and AI systems as stipulated by Selwyn (2019). In order to ensure that AI tools are practically helpful in real classrooms, educators should be involved both in the development and in the evaluation of a tool. Computer aided co-teaching models can actually be very effective provided that teachers focus on the affective and behavioral aspects of teaching while AI solutions provide analytical data. For example, the teacher may give more intensive promptings through the ability to analyze students' performance data via AI (Holmes et al., 2019). Thus, the cooperative method enhances learner's performance and increases the teaching efficiency.

7.3 Case Studies of Successful AI Adoption in Teaching Workflows

The cases from practical application exemplify how AI is transforming education today. The likes of 'AI Classmate' assists the teachers in Singapore by offering customized feedback to the learners and performing the administrative tasks (Nguyen et al., 2021). In a similar way, Finland's AI National Program uses AI technologies in classrooms, so that teachers can plan and create individual learning environments for students with different needs (UNESCO, 2021). All these case studies point to the fact that for sustained use of AI, it needs to be aligned with particular learning objectives as well as the compulsory professional development of educators.

8. IMPLEMENTATION MODEL FOR EDUCATOR-AI COLLABORATION

This implementation paradigm offers a methodical way to guarantee that teachers and AI systems work together effectively, matching AI capabilities with educational objectives.

8.1 Define Objectives and Use Cases

- **Description:** Identify the specific educational challenges and goals where AI can provide value.
- **Steps:**

1. Conduct workshops with educators to outline areas of need (e.g., grading, personalized learning).
2. Define clear objectives for AI tools (e.g., enhancing learning outcomes, automating repetitive tasks).

- **Outcome:** A prioritized list of use cases for AI in the classroom.

8.2 Collaborative Development and Testing

- **Description:** Involve educators in the development lifecycle of AI tools to ensure relevance and usability.
- **Steps:**

3. Create focus groups of educators and developers to discuss feature requirements.
4. Implement pilot programs to test AI tools in real classrooms.
5. Gather educator feedback to refine AI systems for better classroom integration.

- **Outcome:** AI tools tailored to meet the practical needs of educators.

8.3 Implement Co-Teaching Models

- **Description:** Design workflows where AI and educators complement each other's strengths.
- **Steps:**

6. Use AI for data-driven insights, such as performance tracking and predictive analytics.
7. Allow educators to focus on emotional intelligence, creativity, and personalized mentoring.
8. Establish protocols where AI suggests interventions, and teachers make final decisions.

- **Outcome:** A seamless co-teaching environment enhancing both teaching efficiency and learning outcomes.

8.4 Provide Ongoing Training for Educators

- **Description:** Build AI literacy among educators to increase confidence and competency in using AI tools.
- **Steps:**

9. Conduct regular professional development programs on AI fundamentals and applications.
10. Provide hands-on training sessions with AI tools to ensure comfort and familiarity.
11. Develop online resources and support channels for continuous learning.

- **Outcome:** Educators equipped to effectively collaborate with AI systems.

8.5 Monitor and Evaluate Impact

- **Description:** Establish a continuous feedback loop to assess the effectiveness of AI systems and identify areas for improvement.
- **Steps:**

12. Set measurable KPIs (e.g., improved student performance, reduced teacher workload).
13. Collect data from educators and students on AI tool performance and usability.
14. Periodically review and refine AI systems based on feedback and outcomes.

- **Outcome:** Sustained improvement in AI systems and educator satisfaction.

8.6 Ethical and Transparent Use

Description: Ensure ethical considerations and transparency in the deployment of AI systems.

Steps:

1. Communicate clearly how AI algorithms work and their limitations.
2. Protect student and teacher data privacy with robust security measures.
3. Involve stakeholders in creating guidelines for responsible AI use.
    - **Outcome:** Trust and accountability in the educator-AI partnership.

8.7 Visual Summary (Optional)

A flowchart or infographic can visually depict the above steps:

- **Input:** Define Objectives → Educator Workshops.
- **Development:** Collaborative Testing → Refinement.
- **Implementation:** Co-Teaching Models → Educator Training.
- **Feedback Loop:** Monitor Outcomes → Continuous Improvement.

This model ensures a collaborative approach where AI tools enhance teaching practices while educators maintain control over the learning process.

9. FUTURE IMPLICATIONS AND STRATEGIES FOR AI INTEGRATION

Envisioning a Balanced AI-Human Collaboration in Education: AI integration in education is a future in which technology augments not displaces human educators (Selwyn, 2019). When applied to grading and administrative tasks through transferring many routine jobs to AI, a symbiotic relationship enables educators to focus on one-on-one training. For instance, in the process of training teachers, they are able to incorporate specific measures for individual approaches by assisting an analysis of the specific needs of each learner (Luckin et al., 2016, pp.269). To establish this bal-alance, however, the public must learn about and embrace digital literacy in teachers and students so AI can become the useful friend, rather than the authoritarian taskmaster it might currently be portrayed as.

Bridging Global Gaps in Accessibility and Inclusivity Through AI: AI is capable of enhancing access to learning resources such that people with restriction in terms of class, wealth or location will not be restricted (Holmes et al., 2019). In translation systems that use artificial intelligence students with different linguistic backgrounds can retrieve educational information in their respective languages (Floridi & Cowls, 2019). Also, there are opportunities that AL can design the learning pathway for students with cognitive issues or in turn, translate text to voice in order to assist students with disabilities (Nguyen et al., 2021). With the help of AI, world education can be made absolutely equal with no prejudice, thus AI can help to make a connection to offer equal grounds for everyone.

Practical Recommendations for Policymakers

Educators and Technologists

AI is a complex and inclusive approach to realise its transformative potential fully in education (UNESCO, 2021). To do so, policymakers should fund the underlying digital infrastructure needed for AI adoption while also publicly declaring what kind of bias they will tolerate from AI systems. In order for teachers to effectively use the AI tools in teaching, there is a need for proprioceptive learning, and for technologists to focus on creating highly human-centred interfaces that are culturally appropriate (Luckin et al., 2016). With each other, these stakeholders can ensure that integration of AI serves learning achievements, enhances students' protection, and minimizes risks such as data protection compromises.

Preparing for the Future of AI-Driven Education Ecosystems

It is thus needed keen planning as intelligence educational ecosystems develop, given the rapid pace of advancement in technology (Selwyn 2019). Some of the ways that these institutions can foster innovation includes; incorporating AI literacy in the curriculum&s end users and supporting multidisciplinary research. Specific approaches for the development of AI solutions suggested include cooperation between the government, business, and academic institutions to address real problems facing education (UNESCO, 2021). In order to build trust in AI based systems some of the following ethical issues like responsibility in decision making should also be of paramount importance together with open-ness of the algorithms in use (Nguyen et al., 2021). It's, therefore, possible for stakeholders to build a strong, protective, progressive, and accessible education environment by using these strategies.

REFERENCES

Anderson, J. R., Corbett, A. T., Koedinger, K. R., & Pelletier, R. (2014). Cognitive tutors: Lessons learned. *Journal of the Learning Sciences*, *4*(2), 167–207. DOI: 10.1207/s15327809jls0402_2

Binns, R. (2018). Fairness in machine learning: Lessons from political philosophy. *Proceedings of the 2018 Conference on Fairness, Accountability, and Transparency*, 149-159.

Carbonell, J. R. (1970). AI in CAI: An Artificial Intelligence approach to computer-assisted instruction. *IEEE Transactions on Man-Machine Systems*, *11*(4), 190–202. DOI: 10.1109/TMMS.1970.299942

Chen, L., Chen, P., & Lin, Z. (2020). Artificial intelligence in education: A review. *IEEE Access : Practical Innovations, Open Solutions*, *8*, 75264–75278. DOI: 10.1109/ACCESS.2020.2988510

Doshi-Velez, F., & Kortz, M. (2017). Accountability of AI under the law: The role of explanation. *Harvard Law School Report.*

Floridi, L., Cowls, J., Beltrametti, M., Chatila, R., Chazerand, P., Dignum, V., Luetge, C., Madelin, R., Pagallo, U., Rossi, F., Schafer, B., Valcke, P., & Vayena, E. (2019). The Ethical Framework for a Good AI Society: Opportunities, Risks, Principles, and Recommendations. *Minds and Machines*, *29*(4), 689–707. DOI: 10.1007/s11023-018-9482-5 PMID: 30930541

Graesser, A. C., Chipman, P., Haynes, B. C., & Olney, A. (2005). AutoTutor: An intelligent tutoring system with mixed-initiative dialogue. *IEEE Transactions on Education*, *48*(4), 612–618. DOI: 10.1109/TE.2005.856149

Holmes, W., Bialik, M., & Fadel, C. (2019). *Artificial Intelligence in Education: Promises and Implications for Teaching and Learning*. Center for Curriculum Redesign.

Kallio, M., & Harju, P. (2023). *Technology-enhanced learning in Finland: A case study*. Finnish National Agency for Education.

Kop, R., Fournier, H., & Mak, J. S. F. (2011). A pedagogy of abundance or a pedagogy to support human beings? Participant support on massive open online courses. *International Review of Research in Open and Distance Learning*, *12*(7), 74–93. DOI: 10.19173/irrodl.v12i7.1041

Koper, R. (2014). Conditions for effective smart learning environments. *Smart Learning Environments, 1*(1), 5. DOI: 10.1186/s40561-014-0005-4

Luckin, R., & Esparrell, F. (2024). *Artificial intelligence in education: Adapting to individual needs*. Universitepark Press. Retrieved from ERIC Database.

Luckin, R., Holmes, W., Griffiths, M., & Forcier, L. B. (2016). *Intelligence Unleashed: An Argument for AI in Education*. Pearson Education.

Mittelstadt, B. D., Allo, P., Taddeo, M., Wachter, S., & Floridi, L. (2016). The ethics of algorithms: Mapping the debate. *Big Data & Society, 3*(2). Advance online publication. DOI: 10.1177/2053951716679679

Nguyen, H., Gardiner, E., & McGowan, J. (2021). AI Tools and Accessibility in Education: Enhancing Inclusivity. *Journal of Educational Technology, 18*(2), 45–62.

Obermeyer, Z., Powers, B., Vogeli, C., & Mullainathan, S. (2019). Dissecting racial bias in an algorithm used to manage the health of populations. *Science, 366*(6464), 447–453. DOI: 10.1126/science.aax2342 PMID: 31649194

OECD. (2023). *AI in education: A pathway to innovation*. OECD Education Working Paper Series.

Ramirez, R., & Fuentes Esparrell, F. (2023). *Multi-agent systems and adaptive learning environments*. Universitepark Press.

Seale, J. (2014). *E-learning and disability in higher education: Accessibility research and practice*. Routledge.

Selwyn, N. (2019). *Should Robots Replace Teachers? AI and the Future of Education*. Polity Press.

Siemens, G., & Long, P. (2011). Penetrating the fog: Analytics in learning and education. *EDUCAUSE Review, 46*(5), 30–32.

TeachFlow.AI. (2023). *The evolution of AI in education: Past, present, and future*. TeachFlow.AI.

UNESCO. (2021). *AI and Education: Guidance for Policy-Makers*. UNESCO Publishing.

Viberg, O., Hatakka, M., Bälter, O., & Mavroudi, A. (2018). The current landscape of learning analytics in higher education. *Computers in Human Behavior, 89*, 98–110. DOI: 10.1016/j.chb.2018.07.027

Wang, F., Fang, W., & Tang, Y. (2020). Human-AI collaboration in education: Strengthening outcomes through balance. *Journal of Educational Technology Research, 38*(4), 601–620.

West, D. M. (2019). *The Future of Work: Robots, AI, and Automation*. Brookings Institution Press.

Zawacki-Richter, O., Marín, V. I., Bond, M., & Gouverneur, F. (2019). Systematic review of research on artificial intelligence applications in higher education – where are the educators? *International Journal of Educational Technology in Higher Education, 16*(1), 1–27. DOI: 10.1186/s41239-019-0171-0

Chapter 6
AI in the Special Education Toolbox: Strategies, Tools, and Techniques for Teachers

Catherine S Howerter
https://orcid.org/0009-0004-1697-9361
Texas Woman's University, Denton, USA

Teresa Cardon
https://orcid.org/0000-0001-6684-0414
University of North Texas, Denton, USA

ABSTRACT

Special education teachers face challenges in addressing diverse student needs. This chapter explores how AI enhances both teacher efficiency and student outcomes. AI supports individualized lesson plans, behavioral management, and progress tracking, enabling tailored interventions. Assistive technologies like speech-to-text and adaptive learning platforms personalize instruction, while AI tools such as Magic School AI and Brisk Teaching provide real-time feedback and data-driven insights. This chapter will provide a variety of strategies, tools, and techniques for special education teachers. AI offers powerful tools to enhance efficiency and personalized learning in special education. Future advancements require ongoing teacher development and ethical considerations to ensure AI remains a supportive tool, empowering educators rather than replacing them.

DOI: 10.4018/979-8-3373-1122-7.ch006

INTRODUCTION

In ever changing academic environments, special education teachers face a unique and demanding set of responsibilities that require a diverse skill set, flexibility, and a deep commitment to their students' academic and personal growth. One of the most significant challenges special educators manage is meeting the diverse learning needs of their students (McKleskey, 2017). Special educators support students with a range of abilities and disabilities, including autism spectrum disorder (ASD), specific learning disabilities (SLD), emotional and behavioral disorders (EBD), and physical challenges. These students have varying ability levels, and their significantly different needs require educators to identify individual strengths, weaknesses, and preferred learning strategies, all while tailoring their instruction to accommodate the individual differences of their students (Cummings et al., 2008).

A core component of special education is the creation and implementation of individualized and differentiated instruction (Kaufman, 2018). Special educators are responsible for developing detailed, personalized curricula, using evidence-based practices, for each student's unique educational goals as outlined by their Individualized Education Plans (IEPs). Individualized instruction is flexible and adaptable, as students may progress at different rates, experience setbacks, or require differentiated instruction. In other words, special educators must regularly monitor each student's progress, assess their ongoing needs, and adjust lesson plans and instruction accordingly. This requires a significant amount of planning and organization to ensure that each child receives the appropriate level of support while still being challenged.

Managing challenging student behaviors is another critical skill that special educators need to develop (Kaufman, 2018). Many students in special education settings face difficulties with self-regulation, impulse control, and social interactions. These difficulties can lead to challenging behaviors that range from disruptions during class to more severe outbursts. Managing these behaviors requires a thorough understanding of behavioral contingencies and implementation of proactive strategies in the classroom all while fostering a positive and supportive learning environment (Hopman et al., 2018), can be emotionally draining, and takes a significant amount of time.

In fact, one of the biggest challenges special educators face is finding enough time. Managing the required administrative tasks, attending school meetings, communicating with caregivers, and supporting school partners all takes a significant amount of time and diverts time away from instructional time (Billingsley, 2004; Goldman et al., 2024). Special educators must juggle paperwork for IEP meetings, assessments, and communication with caregivers, all while ensuring they are providing direct instruction to their students.

Teacher workload has been described as unmanageable and a key factor contributing to stress and burnout among educators. Paperwork requirements are specifically noted as being "at the top of the list" for reasons why special educators leave the profession, contributing to unreasonable workload expectations (Carver-Thomas & Darling-Hammond, 2019). This workload, especially for special educators in self-contained settings, involves a disproportionate amount of time spent on non-teaching tasks, estimated to be up to 47% of their time (Zagona et al., 2022). These responsibilities extend beyond direct instruction and include essential duties like ongoing IEP management, including writing present levels, progress monitoring, and updating goals and progress, parent communication, lesson planning, adapting and modifying curriculum and materials to meet diverse student needs, and creating assessments. Innovative means and technologies are needed to alleviate some of these pressures and mitigate the struggles facing special educators.

Effective strategies and tools are essential for supporting their efforts in creating an optimal learning environment. Using AI can significantly reduce the time special educators spend creating resources from scratch (Goldman et al., 2024). One key need is for instructional tools that allow for the differentiation of instruction to meet the unique learning needs of students. Technology should play an increasingly important role in this regard, with assistive technologies such as speech-to-text software, audio books, and interactive apps helping students engage with material in ways that are more suited to their individual needs (Goldman et al., 2024; see Appendix). Additionally, data tracking tools enable teachers to monitor student progress in real-time, making it easier to identify areas of improvement or concern. By providing special educators with appropriate technology to support differentiated instruction and personalized learning, their ability to more effectively support their students and their educational communities can increase.

In addition to instructional tools, special educators could benefit from more efficient time management skills. By learning to engage with new assistive technologies, such as scheduling apps, generative language applications (e.g., ChatGPT), and integrative platforms (e.g., MagicSchool AI) and extensions (e.g., Brisk Teaching), special educators can minimize their time spent on administrative tasks and maximize their time educating students. With the right strategies and support systems in place, special educators will be better equipped to not only meet the needs of their students but also maintain their own well-being and effectiveness in the classroom.

THE PROMISE OF AI IN SPECIAL EDUCATION

Artificial Intelligence (AI) has the potential to significantly enhance both teacher efficiency and student outcomes by streamlining administrative tasks (Rakap, 2024) and providing personalized learning experiences (Ayeni et al., 2024). For special educators, AI tools can automate routine activities like progress tracking, documentation for IEPs, creating lesson plans, and generating emails and newsletters, allowing educators to dedicate more time to direct instruction and individualized student support. AI-powered platforms can also help identify specific learning patterns, enabling teachers to adjust strategies and lesson plans more efficiently to meet student's unique needs (see Appendix). With AI handling some time-consuming tasks, educators can spend more time on meaningful interactions and targeted support, leading to improved classroom dynamics and more effective instruction.

AI can also provide highly personalized learning experiences for adapting content and pacing based on each student's diverse abilities. Adaptive learning platforms powered by AI can provide immediate feedback and adjust lessons in real time, helping students to stay on track and learn at their own pace (Ayeni, Hamand, Chisom, Osawaru & Adewusi, 2024). AI can also help identify students who are at risk of falling behind, supporting response to intervention (RTI) and more tailored assistance in general education classrooms. In this way, AI has the potential to not only improve teaching efficiency but also foster more equitable and effective learning outcomes for all students.

While there are concerns with the encroachment of AI, used purposefully, AI has the potential to augment, rather than replace, special educators by acting as a powerful support tool enhancing their capabilities in the classroom. AI can streamline time-consuming tasks like grading, data collection, and progress monitoring, while allowing special educators' training and expertise to interpret results, make nuanced decisions, and provide interactive support to their students and their educational communities (see Appendix; Ayeni, Hamand, Chisom, Osawaru & Adewusi, 2024; Waterfield, Watson & Day, 2024). Special educators are essential for creating personalized learning environments, adapting strategies based on a student's individual needs, and building relationships with students, which are all elements that AI cannot replicate. Instead, AI can provide educators with more time and data-driven insights to fine-tune their instructional strategies, ensuring that students receive the most effective and individualized support.

UNDERSTANDING AI AND ITS APPLICATIONS IN SPECIAL EDUCATION

Theoretical Frameworks

Before we begin to understand AI and how it can support special education, it is important to understand key theoretical frameworks and models that support technology integration for students with disabilities (Adeshina, 2024; Edyburn, 2001). The Universal Design for Learning (UDL; CAST, 2018; Rose & Meyer, 2002) framework is an educational approach that aims to create inclusive and accessible learning environments for all students, recognizing that learners vary in many ways, including learning preferences and strengths. UDL guides educators in providing multiple means of representation, action and expression, and engagement to meet the needs of diverse learners, and while technology can be part of its implementation, UDL encompasses broader strategies and principles. Combining UDL with the SAMR framework (Substitution, Augmentation, Modification, Redefinition), which focuses on technology integration levels, leads to a new conceptual framework called the Inclusive Technology Integration Framework (ITIF; Adeshina, 2024). ITIF integrates technology effectively while transforming learning experiences to be more inclusive and accessible, emphasizing the dual goals of improving instruction through technology and ensuring equitable access for all students. It aims to create an environment where technology not only enhances instruction but also ensures accessibility and inclusivity, promoting accessibility, enhancing engagement, and promoting learner agency by catering to diverse needs and providing options for interaction and expression. Beyond these overarching frameworks, models specific to special education technology provide further support. The ABC Model (Lewis, 1993) suggests technology can *Augment* abilities and *Bypass* or *Compensate* for disabilities, highlighting its unique benefits for students with disabilities. The Human Activity Assistive Technology (HATT; Cook & Hussey, 2002) model examines how assistive technology interacts with the human, activity, and context to enhance performance. While not exhaustive, these frameworks and models provide a structured way to think about, organize, and implement technology to support the diverse needs of students with disabilities.

What Is AI?

Artificial Intelligence is a broad term that refers to computer systems designed to perform tasks that typically require human intelligence. These tasks include recognizing patterns, solving problems, making decisions, and even adapting to new information. AI systems can analyze large amounts of data quickly, learn from experience, and improve over time. There are various types of AI that can help with the aforementioned tasks: natural language processors, machine and adaptive learning components, and generative pre-trained transformers, including the commonly referenced ChatGPT (Goldman et al., 2024; ChatGPT, 2025). For special educators, AI offers powerful tools to enhance teaching and learning. AI-driven applications can provide personalized learning experiences, assist with speech recognition for students with communication challenges, and help analyze student progress through data-driven insights. Similarly, AI can help educators meet the diverse needs of students more effectively. As an example, portions of this explanation of AI were written via ChatGPT and took just under 15 seconds to generate, demonstrating one helpful aspect of AI to perform a task quickly (ChatGPT, 2025).

Types of AI Relevant to Special Education

Artificial Intelligence can be categorized into several different types, each offering unique benefits to special educators. One of the most commonly used types is machine learning, where AI systems analyze data and improve performance over time. For example, adaptive learning platforms (e.g., i-ready, Dreambox Learning, Edmark Reading Program; see Appendix) use machine learning to adjust instructional content based on a student's progress, providing personalized support for students with diverse learning needs. Similarly, predictive analytics can help educators identify early signs of learning difficulties, enabling timely interventions. Natural language processing (NLP) is another valuable AI tool that enhances speech-to-text and text-to-speech applications (see Appendix), making it easier for students with speech or writing impairments to communicate and engage with educational content. As indicated, special educators have numerous responsibilities that impact the amount of time they have for student instruction. AI-powered time management tools can help streamline these tasks and improve efficiency to allow teachers to focus more on student engagement and intervention (see Appendix).

Personalized Learning

Special educators are already using personalized learning AI tools for students who need a variety of support. Personalized learning tools help address challenges related to communication, literacy, and executive functioning. Some examples of personalized learning tools include text-to-speech and speech-to text, predictive text, and personalized writing assistants such as Grammarly.

Text-to-speech can assist students with reading difficulties, visual impairments, or attention challenges by converting written text into spoken words, thereby enabling multiple modalities students can engage with text (see Appendix; Ayeni,

Hamand, Chisom, Osawaru & Adewusi, 2024). Similarly, speech-to-text can assist students with writing difficulties, fine motor challenges, or executive functioning challenges by providing alternative paths to produce written work (Ayeni, Hamand, Chisom, Osawaru & Adewusi, 2024). Predictive text, also known as word prediction software, has been in use for many years and helps students by suggesting words and sentence structures to aid in the writing process (Waterfield, Watson & Day, 2024). Similarly, AI-based writing assistants can provide real-time grammar, spelling, and style suggestions to help students with writing or language difficulties (see Appendix). Writing assistants are also helpful for English Language Learners, students with attention concerns, or those with executive functioning challenges as it provides structure and real time writing support so students can focus on content and idea generation.

Personalized learning AI tools allow special educators to create more inclusive learning environments, enabling students to engage with content in ways that suit their individual needs. By integrating these technologies, teachers can enhance accessibility, independence, and academic success for students with disabilities.

AI for Differentiated Instruction

Differentiated instruction is essential to special education. AI can assist teachers with personalized instruction for individual students. It can help customize learning by adjusting content, pacing, and activities that are aligned with the student's strengths and areas of need. The purpose of differentiated instruction is to meet the needs of individual students (Tomlinson, 2000), which AI can assist with, while taking into account students' abilities, interests, and accommodations/modifications. Tools like Magic School AI, Diffit, and Brisk Teaching make it easy for special educators to meet the needs of individual students and tailor instruction (see Table 1; see Appendix). These three tools are free to teachers; however, they each have additional costs for added features

Table 1. Sample AI Tools for Differentiation

Tool/ Platform	Overview	Training
MagicSchool AI	80+ tools, assists teachers with lesson planning, assessments, IEPs, email communication.	Self-paced certification pathway, four levels of certification
Diffit	Adapts reading levels and creates differentiated materials for a variety of reading levels.	Self-paced course introduction course, digital badge
Brisk Teaching	Chrome extension tool that provides support for feedback, assessments, and creating differentiated curriculum	Professional Deck, Videos, and Webinars (live and recorded)

Magic School AI, was created by teachers to support classroom instruction, including but not limited to lesson planning, differentiation in the classroom, writing assessments, and Individualized Education Plans (IEPs; Magic School AI, 2025). Magic School AI can adjust the reading level of text, which means special educators can take a grade level text and re-level that text to meet a variety of reading levels. By tailoring content to students' abilities, Magic School AI helps ensure all learners, regardless of their starting point, can access the curriculum. Additionally, the platform offers tools to generate personalized assignments and quizzes, further enhancing individualized learning. MagicSchool AI also offers a self-paced, structured certification pathway that guides educators in using the platform effectively in their teaching practices. The four levels of certification allow teachers to earn badges and certificates. Of particular interest to special education teachers is the inclusion of tips for differentiation and accessibility features built into the platform.

Diffit, specifically focuses on differentiated instruction with tools that will vary the level of activities for a variety of learners. This website allows teachers to create materials based on a topic or theme, books, articles or YouTube links, text or PDF, and vocabulary lists (Diffit, 2025). Diffit will create leveled text, vocabulary, multiple choice questions, short answer and open-ended questions, and graphic organizers or worksheets. With its ability to generate multiple formats for the same content, Diffit helps teachers meet the diverse needs of students, from struggling readers to advanced learners, ensuring that all students engage with the material at an appropriate level. Diffit offers a self-paced course that provides a brief overview of the platform's features, and teachers can earn a digital badge upon completion.

Brisk Teaching is a Chrome extension that can create instructional materials, student interventions, support administrative tasks, and provide feedback (Brisk Teaching, 2025; table 2). Brisk Teaching uses AI to automate tasks such as grading and assessment analysis, allowing educators to spend more time on personalized instruction. The extension also helps with behavior management by offering data-driven interventions tailored to individual students' needs, which can be crucial for supporting students with behavioral challenges. With built-in templates for lesson plans and interventions, Brisk Teaching ensures that teachers are always prepared, helping them streamline administrative tasks so they can focus more on teaching. Brisk Teaching offers less structured professional development resources, including a slide deck, how-to videos, printables, and webinars (both live and recorded).

Table 2. Overview of Brisk Teaching Tools

Instructional Materials	Student Interventions	Administrative Tasks	Feedback
Decodable Texts Generator DOK Questions Guided Notes Generator Inquiry Worksheets Unit and Lesson Plan Generator Math Spiral Review Generator Math Word Problems Presentation Maker Progress Report Maker Rubric Maker SAT Practice Generator Science Lab Worksheet Maker Standards Unpacker	504 Plan Template Maker IEP Goal Generator MTSS Intervention Menu Creator	Email Generator College Recommendation Letter Generator Newsletter Generator	Feedback Insightful Tools Glow & Grow Feedback Generator Teacher Feedback Generator Targeted Feedback Generator

There are four elements of classroom instruction that teachers can differentiate: "(1) content--what the student needs to learn or how the student will get access to the information; (2) process--activities in which the student engages in order to make sense of or master the content; (3) products--culminating projects that ask the student to rehearse, apply, and extend what he or she has learned in a unit; and (4) learning environment--the way the classroom works and feels" (Tomlinson, 2000; pg 2). AI platforms can support teachers in addressing these aspects of differentiation by offering tools that help tailor content, adjust processes, enhance products, and create a more personalized learning environment. AI platforms such as MagicSchool AI, Brisk, and Diffit support teachers in addressing elements of differentiation. Magic School AI can generate scaffolded lesson plans and tiered assignments, helping to tailor content and create flexible learning pathways. Brisk allows teachers to modify existing materials, such as simplifying language or adding accommodations, making it easier to differentiate both content and process for diverse learners. Diffit excels in adapting reading materials to various Lexile levels and formats, giving teachers support in creating how students access and engage with texts. Together, these tools help create more inclusive, responsive, and personalized learning environments for students with and without disabilities.

When differentiating instruction, many special education teachers face challenges in providing grade-level content that aligns with each student's academic abilities. AI platforms can support teachers by adjusting the complexity of texts to better suit individual student needs. For example, a teacher can input a seventh-grade level text and have AI rephrase it to match the comprehension level of first grade (see Table 3).

Table 3. Sample AI Leveled Text Output: Anne Frank, The Diary of a Young Girl

AI Tool	Text Output
Original Text Seventh Grade Level	"Wednesday July 8, 1942 ...At three o'clock (Hello had left but was supposed to come back later), the doorbell rang. I didn't hear it, since I was out on the balcony, lazily reading in the sun. A little while later Margot appeared in the kitchen doorway looking very agitated. "Father has received a call-up notice from the SS," she whispered. "Mother has gone to see Mr. van Daan" (Mr. van Daan is Father's business partner and a good friend.) I was stunned. A call-up: everyone knows what that means. Visions of concentration camps and lonely cells raced through my head. How could we let Father go to such a fate? "Of course he's not going," declared Margot as we waited for Mother in the living room. "Mother's gone to Mr. van Daan to ask whether we can move to our hiding place tomorrow. The van Daans are going with us. There will be seven of us altogether." Silence. We couldn't speak. The thought of Father off visiting someone in the Jewish Hospital and completely unaware of what was happening, the long wait for Mother, the heat, the suspense – all this reduced us to silence." (Frank, 1989; pg. 19)
Brisk Teaching First Grade Level	One day, a girl and her sister were at home. It was a sunny day. The girl was reading outside. Then her sister came to her. She looked worried. She said, Dad got a bad letter. Mom went to talk to a friend. The girls were scared. They knew the letter meant something bad might happen to Dad. They didn't want him to go away. The sister said, Dad won't go. Mom is asking if we can move to a safe place tomorrow. Some friends will come too. There will be seven people. The girls were quiet. They couldn't talk. They were thinking about Dad. He was at the hospital and didn't know what was happening. They waited for Mom to come back. It was hot. They felt nervous. They just sat and didn't say anything.
Magic School AI First Grade Level	July 8, 1942 At three o'clock, the doorbell rang. I didn't hear it because I was outside on the balcony, reading a book in the sun. A little later, my sister Margot came into the kitchen looking very worried. "Dad got a letter from the SS," she whispered. "Mom went to see Mr. van Daan." (Mr. van Daan is Dad's friend and works with him.) I was shocked. A letter like that is very serious. I thought about scary places and being all alone. How could we let Dad go there? "Of course he's not going," Margot said as we waited for Mom in the living room. "Mom went to ask Mr. van Daan if we can move to our secret place tomorrow. The van Daans will come with us. There will be seven of us together." We were quiet. We couldn't say anything. I thought about Dad who was at the Jewish Hospital, not knowing what was happening. We waited for Mom, feeling hot and nervous. All of this made us silent.
Diffit First Grade Level	It was July 8th, 1942. Hello was gone, but he was coming back later. The doorbell rang, but I didn't hear it. I was outside on the balcony, reading in the sunshine. A little while later, Margot came into the kitchen. She looked worried. "Father got a letter from the SS," she whispered. "Mother went to see Mr. van Daan." Mr. van Daan is Father's friend and they work together. I was surprised. A letter from the SS means bad things. I thought about scary places called concentration camps. I didn't want Father to go there. "Father is not going," said Margot. We waited for Mother in the living room. "Mother went to Mr. van Daan to ask if we can go to our hiding place tomorrow. The van Daans are coming with us. There will be seven of us." We were quiet. We couldn't talk. Father was visiting someone at the hospital. He didn't know what was happening. We waited for Mother. It was hot and we were nervous. We were all quiet.

Teachers frequently use the Depth of Knowledge (DOK) framework to design questions to assess students' comprehension. Webb (2002) identified four levels of understanding content, known as the Depths of Knowledge (see Figure 1). These levels move from simpler (DOK 1) to more complex (DOK 4) questions. Special education students typically perform at DOK levels 1 or 2. Several AI platforms, such as MagicSchool AI and Brisk Teaching, can support teachers in creating DOK leveled questions. Teachers can enter a standard, topic, or book into the platform, and AI will generate suggested questions for each DOK level. Additionally, teachers can specify the grade level for the questions, enabling students performing below grade level to engage with DOK 1 and 2 questions, while still having the opportunity to tackle more challenging DOK 3 and 4 questions. (see Table 4).

Figure 1. Depths of Knowledge

Table 4. Sample AI DOK Questions: Anne Frank, The Diary of a Young Girl

DOK Output Based on Seventh Grade Level	**DOK Output Based on First Grade Level**
AI Tool: MagicSchool AI	
DOK Level 1: Recall & Reproduction	
● What is the full title of Anne Frank's diary? ● Who was Anne Frank and where was she born? ● List the main characters mentioned in Anne Frank's diary. ● Identify the time period during which Anne and her family went into hiding.	● Who was Anne Frank? ● What did Anne write in her diary? ● Can you name one thing that Anne liked to do? ● Where did Anne and her family hide?
DOK Level 2: Skills & Concepts	
● Summarize the reasons why Anne Frank and her family went into hiding. ● Compare the life of Anne Frank before going into hiding and during her time in the Secret Annex. ● Classify the different emotions Anne expresses in her diary entries. ● Estimate how long Anne Frank and her family stayed in hiding.	● How is Anne's life in hiding different from your life today? ● Can you list three important events that happened in Anne's diary? ● What are some feelings that Anne expressed in her diary? ● How would you compare Anne's life before hiding and during hiding?
DOK Level 3: Strategic Thinking	

continued on following page

Table 4. Continued

DOK Output Based on Seventh Grade Level	DOK Output Based on First Grade Level	
● Investigate how the events of World War II affected the lives of those in hiding with Anne Frank. ● Assess the significance of Anne Frank's diary in understanding the experiences of Jews during the Holocaust. ● Formulate a conclusion about how Anne's writing style reflects her personality and experiences. ● Construct a timeline of key events mentioned in Anne Frank's diary.	● Why do you think Anne kept a diary? What was important about it? ● How did Anne's thoughts change from the beginning to the end of her diary? ● If you were in Anne's place, what would you write about in your diary? ● What can we learn from Anne's experiences and feelings?	
DOK Level 4: Extended Thinking		
● Analyze the themes of hope and despair as presented in Anne Frank's diary. ● Critique the impact of Anne Frank's diary on modern society and its relevance today. ● Create a presentation that explores the historical context of Anne Frank's life and the Holocaust. ● Design a project that connects Anne Frank's experiences with current issues of discrimination and human rights.	● Imagine you are a character in Anne's diary. Write a diary entry about your day in hiding. ● Create a poster that shows what you think were Anne's biggest dreams and hopes. ● How would you help someone understand the importance of Anne's story today? ● Design a project that shows how you would spread awareness about Anne Frank's life and message.	
AI Tool: Brisk Teaching		
DOK Level 1: Recall & Reproduction		
● Who wrote "The Diary of a Young Girl"? ● In what year did Anne Frank begin writing her diary? ● Where did Anne Frank and her family hide during World War II? ● What was the name of the Secret Annex helper who gave Anne her diary? ● On what date was Anne Frank's last diary entry?	● Who was Anne Frank? ● What did Anne Frank write? ● Where did Anne Frank live? ● When did Anne Frank write her diary? ● What was the name of Anne's diary?	
DOK Level 2: Skills & Concepts		

continued on following page

Table 4. Continued

DOK Output Based on Seventh Grade Level	**DOK Output Based on First Grade Level**
● How did Anne's relationship with her mother change during their time in hiding? ● Compare and contrast Anne's personality at the beginning of the diary with her personality towards the end. ● Explain how Anne used writing as a coping mechanism during her time in hiding. ● Describe the challenges the Frank family faced while living in the Secret Annex. ● How did World War II affect Anne's daily life, based on her diary entries?	● How did Anne feel when she wrote in her diary? ● What did Anne write about in her diary? ● Why was Anne's diary important? ● How was Anne's life different from yours? ● What did Anne like to do for fun?
DOK Level 3: Strategic Thinking	
● Analyze how Anne's writing style evolves throughout the diary. What factors might have contributed to this change? ● How does Anne's diary challenge or support common perceptions about the Holocaust? ● What themes does Anne explore in her diary, and how do these themes relate to her experiences? ● How might Anne's diary be different if she had survived the war? What additional perspectives might she have included? ● Evaluate the historical significance of Anne Frank's diary. Why has it remained relevant for so many years?	● Why do you think Anne wrote in her diary? ● How do you think Anne's diary helps us learn about history? ● What can we learn from Anne's story? ● How might Anne's life be different if she lived today? ● What would you say to Anne if you could meet her?
DOK Level 4: Extended Thinking	
● If Anne Frank were alive today, how might she view current global issues? Support your answer with evidence from her diary. ● Compare Anne Frank's diary to other personal accounts of the Holocaust. How do they differ, and what common themes do they share? ● Discuss how Anne Frank's diary has influenced our understanding of the Holocaust and its impact on individuals. How might this understanding be different without her account? ● Analyze the ethical implications of publishing and reading Anne's private thoughts. How do we balance the historical importance of her diary with her right to privacy? ● How has Anne Frank's diary influenced literature, art, and media about the Holocaust? Provide specific examples and explain their significance.	● How can Anne's story help us be kind to others? ● What can we do to make sure everyone feels safe like Anne wanted? ● How can writing help us when we feel sad or scared? ● Why is it important to remember Anne's story? ● How can we make the world a better place like Anne hoped for?

Another way special education teachers can differentiate instruction is by designing and implementing choice board activities. This approach aligns with the principles of Universal Design for Learning (UDL), which emphasizes providing multiple means of engagement, representation, and expression (CAST, 2018). Choice boards are instructional tools that offer students a menu of activities to demonstrate their understanding, allowing them to select tasks based on their interests, learning styles, and ability levels (Tomlinson, 2001). AI tools can support the creation of these activities. For example, ChatGPT can help teachers quickly generate a range of activity ideas and support students by brainstorming responses, offering examples, or rephrasing prompts to meet individual needs (Holmes et al., 2022). Similarly, MagicSchool AI can generate templates and differentiated tasks aligned with state standards, including grade-level appropriate choice boards (see Table 5). These tools help streamline the planning process and make differentiation more accessible and effective for diverse learners.

Table 5. Magic School AI Sample Choice Boards: Anne Frank, The Diary of a Young Girl

Choice Board Output Based on Grade Level 7	
Prompt Input: Learning Goal, Standard, Objective, or Topic	Anne Frank, The Diary of a Young Girl
Assignment Title	Assignment Description
Character Analysis	Write a short paragraph about your favorite character and what makes them unique.
Diary Entry Reflection	Create a diary entry from the perspective of Anne Frank on a significant day.
Theme Exploration	Identify a central theme in the diary and explain its significance in a few sentences.
Artistic Representation	Draw or create a digital artwork that represents a scene from the diary.
Timeline Creation	Develop a timeline of key events mentioned in the diary.
Letter to Anne	Write a letter to Anne Frank offering her advice based on her experiences.
Group Discussion	Participate in a group discussion about the impact of the diary on history.
Book Review	Write a brief book review discussing what you liked or didn't like about the diary.
Vocabulary List	Create a list of important vocabulary words from the diary and define them.
Choice Board Output Based on Grade Level 1	
Assignment Title	Assignment Description
Draw a Scene	Illustrate your favorite scene from the diary.
Write a Letter	Write a letter to Anne about what you admire about her.
Character Collage	Create a collage of characters using magazine pictures.
Story Retelling	Retell your favorite part of the diary in your own words.
Create a Timeline	Make a timeline of important events in Anne's life.

continued on following page

Table 5. Continued

Choice Board Output Based on Grade Level 7	
Diary Entry	Write a diary entry as if you were Anne for a day.
Act It Out	Perform a short scene from the diary with your friends.
Poem About Courage	Write a short poem about courage inspired by Anne.
Map of Places	Draw a map showing important places in Anne's life.

Feedback and Adjustments

Many AI platforms can provide feedback on students' progress and understanding. AI will adapt to the needs of the student and provide feedback in a timely manner. AI can streamline the grading process by using natural language processing (NLP) to automatically assess written assignments. As discussed previously, an AI-powered grading tool can evaluate the content, structure, grammar, and relevance of a student's response to a prompt. AI tools can grade assignments based on rubrics and provide specific feedback, including instant feedback on spelling, sentence structure, writing clarity, and even assess the alignment of a response with targeted learning objectives. AI supported grading allows teachers to focus more on personalized feedback for students who need further assistance.

The Brisk Teaching Chrome extension tool assists teachers with providing specific feedback to students. This tool only works in Google Docs or Google Slides, which is a limitation to the tool. Brisk Teaching Provides four feedback styles:

1. Targeted (premium feature): Provides comments that align to rubric and state standards.
2. Glow & Grow: Provides areas of strength, growth, and prompting questions.
3. Rubric Criteria: Provides feedback based on criteria in a teacher provided rubric.
4. Next Steps: Gives suggestions for next steps and strategies to improve skills. (Brisk Teaching, 2025)

Using the ongoing example of *The Diary of Anne Frank*, the following student response was generated by ChatGPT in response to the selected prompt from the choice board: *Write a brief book review discussing what you liked or didn't like about the diary*. This is an example of using AI to generate sample assignments to support student work. The AI-generated response serves as a model to clarify expectations, scaffold instruction, and facilitate peer or self-assessment. The Anne Frank student response has been paired with feedback using the Brisk Teaching framework (see

Table 6) to demonstrate how Brisk Teaching can be used to support instructional planning and student growth. Brisk Teaching supports teacher feedback options by including areas for growth (i.e., grows), what the student is already doing well (i.e., glows), and potential topics for critical thinking (i.e., wondering). This approach aligns with Hattie and Timperley's (2007) findings on the power of feedback to enhance student learning when it is specific, timely, and focused on improvement. Applying this framework to AI-generated responses can help teachers practice giving targeted, meaningful feedback and plan more effectively for differentiated instruction. This method also supports equity by providing clear models for students who benefit from additional scaffolding, including multilingual learners and those with diverse learning needs. As Darling-Hammond et al. (2020) emphasize, scaffolding and responsive teaching strategies are essential for supporting whole child development and ensuring access to high-quality learning opportunities for all students.

Table 6. Brisk Teaching Assignment

ChatGPT student generated example	Assignment: Book Review – The Diary of Anne Frank Book Review: The Diary of Anne Frank is a powerful and moving book that shares the experiences of a young girl hiding from the Nazis during World War II. What I liked most about the diary was how honest and personal Anne's writing felt. It was interesting to read about her hopes, fears, and daily life while in hiding. Anne's courage and optimism, even in such difficult times, really stood out to me. However, sometimes the diary was a little hard to understand because Anne's emotions changed quickly, which made the story feel a bit confusing. Also, since it is a diary, it doesn't have a clear ending, which left me wanting to know more about what happened afterward. Overall, I think The Diary of Anne Frank is an important book that teaches us about history and the strength of the human spirit. I would recommend it to others because it helps us remember the impact of war on real people.
Brisk Teaching: Glow and Grow Feedback	Glow: • You've done an excellent job capturing the emotional core of Anne Frank's diary, highlighting her courage and optimism • Your review shows genuine empathy and understanding of the historical context • You effectively communicated the book's importance and why others should read it Grow: • Consider providing a specific example from the diary that illustrates Anne's courage or emotional journey • Work on developing a more structured review by discussing specific themes or key moments in the book • Try to explain more about why the changing emotions felt confusing to you Wondering: • Have you learned more about the historical context of World War II and the Holocaust after reading this book? • What made Anne's personal writing style so compelling to you? • How do you think reading this diary might help people understand the human impact of war?

continued on following page

Table 6. Continued

Brisk Teaching: Next Steps	Content and Analysis: Next Steps: • Expand on specific examples from the book that demonstrate Anne's courage and optimism • Provide more context about the historical significance of the diary • Consider researching what happened to Anne Frank after the diary to address the "unclear ending" you mentioned Critical Thinking: Next Steps: • Explore why Anne's changing emotions might be important to understanding her experience • Reflect more deeply on how the diary connects to broader themes of human resilience during difficult times • Try to analyze why Anne's writing style and emotional journey are significant, rather than just noting they were confusing Writing Style: Next Steps: • Use more specific language when describing your reactions (instead of general words like "interesting") • Include a quote from the book to support your observations • Work on creating a more structured review with a clear introduction and conclusion Personal Reflection: Next Steps: • Connect the book's themes to your own life experiences or current world events • Explain more about why you think this book is important for others to read • Consider the broader historical context of the Holocaust when discussing the book

Several AI platforms can provide automatic grading for multiple-choice and short-answer questions (e.g. GradeScope, Socrative, Quizlet). These often allow positive feedback to be given for incorrect answers, which teachers will need to monitor carefully. Typically, these platforms are limited in terms of grading written assignments. When using any AI tool that provides feedback on written work, educators should proceed with caution, as these tools can give inaccurate results. For example, praise can be provided for an incorrect answer.

AI FOR STREAMLINING ADMINISTRATIVE TASKS

Efficient Data Collection and Analysis

To further streamline administrative tasks, special educators can leverage AI to efficiently collect and analyze student data. Many websites and publishers are now incorporating AI-enabled assessment tools (e.g., Kahoot!, Quizziz) where student responses can automatically be scored and performance trends monitored over time.

AI can then further analyze student data by automating scoring, identifying learning and error patterns, and providing personalized insights. For example, Microsoft Insights or Google Classroom can analyze student performance over time, helping special educators identify strengths and weaknesses, and in turn identify areas for differentiated instruction. Adaptive learning programs, such as Lexia or DreamBox, adjust instruction based on real-time assessment data, ensuring students receive content at their appropriate skill level. Programs like DreamBox Learning use AI to adapt instruction moment-by-moment based on a student's responses and strategies, generating insights into conceptual understanding and informing intervention plans (DreamBox Learning, 2024). Using AI tools for assessment and data collection provides special educators insights into their students' learning needs and allows for the creation of more individualized learning experiences in a timely manner.

Addressing Challenges and Ethical Considerations for Special Education

One major challenge of using artificial intelligence (AI) in special education is the "digital divide", which refers to disparities in access to technology and digital resources (Moore, Vitale & Stawinoga, 2018). Many schools, particularly those in low-income or rural areas, may lack the necessary infrastructure, such as high-speed internet, updated devices, and AI-powered educational tools (see Table 7). Special educators who work in under-resourced schools may struggle to integrate AI effectively, leaving students with disabilities at a disadvantage compared to their peers in more resourced districts. Additionally, families of students with special needs may not have access to AI-driven assistive technologies at home, further widening the educational gap. Without equitable access to these resources, AI's potential to support personalized learning and accommodations remains limited.

An additional concern is the potential bias in AI systems, which can negatively impact diverse learners in special education (Whitaker et al., 2019; Khan, 2024). AI models are trained on vast datasets that may not always include sufficient representation of students with disabilities, leading to inaccurate or ineffective recommendations for personalized learning. For example, AI-driven speech recognition tools might struggle with students who have atypical speech patterns, while adaptive learning programs might misinterpret the needs of neurodiverse students. Bias in AI can also reinforce existing stereotypes about students with disabilities, resulting in automated decision-making that limits opportunities rather than expands them. Further bias in AI algorithms may exist for culturally diverse learners. Many AI-driven educational tools are trained on datasets that may not adequately represent students from diverse linguistic, cultural, and/or socioeconomic backgrounds (Whitaker et al., 2019; Khan, 2024). This can result in AI-generated recommendations that do not align with students lived experiences, learning styles, or language needs. For example, speech-to-text or language processing AI may struggle with non-standard dialects, multilingual learners, or culturally specific expressions, leading to inaccurate assessments or inappropriate instructional strategies. Additionally, AI-powered behavioral or performance monitoring tools may misinterpret culturally influenced behaviors as signs of noncompliance or learning difficulties, potentially reinforcing biases and mislabeling students. To address these challenges, special educators must critically evaluate AI tools, advocate for more inclusive data representation, and ensure that AI-driven decisions are supplemented with culturally responsive teaching practices.

Table 7. Technological Barriers Faced by Underserved Special Education Populations

Barrier	Description	Example	Implications for Special Education Students
Limited Internet Access	Inconsistent or no access to high-speed internet at home or in rural/low-income areas.	A student in a rural district cannot join virtual speech therapy sessions.	Missed services, reduced participation in remote learning, increased learning gaps.
Lack of Devices	Inadequate or no access to personal computers, tablets, or assistive tech devices.	A family shares one smartphone among four children.	Inability to access learning platforms or communication tools; hinders IEP implementation.
Inaccessible Technology Platforms	EdTech tools not designed with accessibility features (e.g., screen readers, captions).	A visually impaired student cannot navigate a learning app.	Exclusion from digital learning, limited independence, frustration, and disengagement.
Limited Tech Literacy (Students and Families)	Students or caregivers lack the skills to operate educational technology effectively.	A caregiver cannot help a student log into a virtual classroom.	Reduced support at home, student falls behind, miscommunication with school staff.
Language Barriers in Tech Tools	Educational platforms lack multilingual support for diverse families.	A Spanish-speaking parent cannot understand tech instructions.	Limits parental engagement, impairs understanding of IEP progress and school communication.
Lack of Training for Educators	Teachers may lack training in using technology with students who have disabilities.	A teacher doesn't know how to incorporate speech-to-text tools in lessons.	Inconsistent accommodations, reduced effectiveness of virtual learning supports.

continued on following page

Table 7. Continued

Barrier	Description	Example	Implications for Special Education Students
Cost of Assistive Technologies	High cost of specialized devices and software (e.g., AAC devices, screen readers).	A district cannot afford individualized communication devices.	Students miss out on essential tools that support learning and communication.
Inadequate IT Support	Schools may not have sufficient staff to troubleshoot or maintain technology.	A student's device breaks, but there's no tech support for repairs.	Long delays in access, interrupted instruction, IEP goals not met.

PRIVACY AND DATA SECURITY

When using AI tools in special education, safeguarding student data is crucial to protect privacy and remain in compliance with legal and ethical standards (Kahn, 2024). Special educators manage sensitive information, including individualized education plans (IEPs), medical records, and behavioral data, which must be securely stored and shared appropriately. AI-powered tools that collect and process student data should adhere to regulations like the Family Educational Rights and Privacy Act (FERPA, 1974) and the Individuals with Disabilities Education Improvement Act (IDEA, 2004) ensuring that data is only accessed by authorized individuals. Educators should work closely with their schools and districts to verify that AI tools have strong security measures, such as encryption, access controls, and anonymization of data. Additionally, they should educate themselves about data-sharing policies, ensuring that families understand how their child's information is being used and have the option to opt out.

Beyond security concerns, ethical considerations around AI data collection in special education require careful attention to issues of consent, transparency, and bias (Ayeni et al., 2024; Khan, 2024). Special educators must ensure that AI tools prioritize student well-being rather than simply tracking performance metrics. Ethical AI use involves obtaining informed consent from families, clearly explaining how data will be used, and ensuring that AI recommendations do not lead to discriminatory practices.

As AI becomes more accessible and even more platforms become available, it will grow as a continued support for special educators. While AI has the capability of drastically increasing efficiency for various tasks used every day by special educators, it is also important to remember that the special educator is the personal connection in the classroom that all students need as they navigate various learning challenges. AI generated content will not be able to tell you what your students like, or what they value on a day-to-day basis. The AI platforms that can support time management and assist with differentiated instruction will not be able to listen to your students' stories or offer support as they express frustration with a particular task. So while engaging with AI and embracing new tools that support our students, our classrooms, our schools, and our communities, it is important to remember that our personal connections with our students and our teams will always be one of the most powerful aspects of our profession.

CONCLUSION

Special education teachers face significant demands, including supporting diverse learning needs, providing individualized instruction, managing behaviors, and handling an often overwhelming amount of administrative paperwork. This heavy workload is often cited as reasons special educators leave the profession and contributes to stress and burnout. Artificial intelligence (AI) has emerged as a promising tool to potentially alleviate some of these pressures by streamlining administrative tasks such as progress tracking, documentation for IEPs, creating lesson plans, and generating emails and newsletters, and by enhancing instructional practices through personalized learning experiences and differentiated materials creation (Ayeni et al., 2024; Goldman et al., 2024). AI tools can support tasks like generating IEP snapshots, creating resources for parents and students, adjusting reading levels of texts, and developing components for progress monitoring. However, the implementation of AI in special education is not without challenges, including the digital divide, potential bias in AI systems, and critical concerns regarding data privacy and security, which must be carefully addressed to ensure equitable and ethical use (Whitaker et al., 2019; Khan, 2024). Ultimately, while AI can significantly augment the special education toolbox and enhance efficiency (Waterfield, Watson & Day, 2024), it is essential to remember that AI is intended to augment, rather than replace, the vital role of the special educator. The special educator's expertise, ability to interpret results and make nuanced decisions, build personal connections, understand individual student stories and values, and provide the essential human support and relationships that AI cannot replicate remain the most powerful aspects of the profession. Leveraging AI effectively requires balancing technological innovation with the indispensable human element that is at the heart of special education.

REFERENCES

Adeshina, A. E. (2024). From Theory to Practice: A Framework for Inclusive Technology Integration in Education. *International Journal of Instructional Technology and Educational Studies*, *5*(1), 1–6. DOI: 10.21608/ihites.2024.380764

Ayeni, O. O., Al Hamad, N. M., Chisom, O. N., Osawaru, B., & Adewusi, O. E. (2024). AI in education: A review of personalized learning and educational technology. *GSC Advanced Research and Reviews*, *18*(2), 261–271. DOI: 10.30574/gscarr.2024.18.2.0062

Billingsley, B. S. (2004). Promoting teacher quality and retention in special education. *Journal of Learning Disabilities*, *37*(5), 370–376. DOI: 10.1177/00222194040370050101 PMID: 15460345

Brisk Teaching. (2025). *The simple ai teaching assistant that works wherever you do.* https://www.briskteaching.com/

Carver-Thomas, D., & Darling-Hammond, L. (2019). The trouble with teacher turnover: How teacher attrition affects students and schools. *Education Policy Analysis Archives*, *27*(36), 36. DOI: 10.14507/epaa.27.3699

CAST. (2018). *Universal Design for Learning Guidelines version 2.2.* http://udlguidelines.cast.org

ChatGPT. (2025). OpenAI. https://chatgpt.com/

Cook, A. M., & Hussey, S. M. (2002). *Assistive technologies. Principles and practice.* Academic Press.

Cummings, K. D., Atkins, T., Allison, R., & Cole, C. (2008). Response to intervention; Investigating the new role of special educators. *Teaching Exceptional Children*, *40*(4), 24–31. DOI: 10.1177/004005990804000403

Darling-Hammond, L., Flook, L., Cook-Harvey, C., Barron, B., & Osher, D. (2020). Implications for educational practice of the science of learning and development. *Applied Developmental Science*, *24*(2), 97–140. DOI: 10.1080/10888691.2018.1537791

Diffit. (2025). *Learning resources for all.* https://web.diffit.me/

DreamBox Learning. (2024). *DreamBox Learning Math: Adaptive learning for student growth.*https://www.dreambox.com

Edyburn, D. L. (2001). Models, theories, and frameworks: Contributions to understanding special education technology. *Special Education Technology Practice, 4*(2), 16–24.

Family Educational Rights and Privacy Act (FERPA) of 1974, 20 U.S.C. § 1232g

Frank, A. (1989). *The diary of Anne Frank*. Longman.

Goldman, S. R., Taylor, J., Carreon, A., & Smith, S. J. (2024). Using AI to support special education teacher workload. *Journal of Special Education Technology, 39*(3), 434–447. DOI: 10.1177/01626434241257240

Hattie, J., & Timperley, H. (2007). The power of feedback. *Review of Educational Research, 77*(1), 81–112. DOI: 10.3102/003465430298487

Holmes, W., Bialik, M., & Fadel, C. (2022). *Artificial Intelligence in Education: Promises and Implications for Teaching and Learning*. Center for Curriculum Redesign.

Hopman, J. A., van Lier, P. A., van der Ende, J., Struiksma, C., Wubbels, T., Verhulst, F. C., Maras, A., Linda, D., Breeman, L. D., & Tick, N. T. (2018). Impact of the Good Behavior Game on special education teachers. *Teachers and Teaching, 24*(4), 350–368. DOI: 10.1080/13540602.2017.1379389

Individuals with Disabilities Education Improvement Act (IDEA), 20 U.S.C. § 1400 (2004).

Kauffman, J. M., Hallahan, D. P., Pullen, P. C., & Badar, J. (2018). *Special education: What it is and why we need it*. Routledge. DOI: 10.4324/9781315211831

Khan, W. N. (2024). Ethical Challenges of AI in Education: Balancing Innovation with Data Privacy. *Journal of AI in Education: Innovations, Opportunities, Challenges, and Future Directions, 1*(1), 1–13.

Lewis, R. B. (1993). *Special education technology: Classroom applications*. No Title.

Magic School AI. (2025). *Magic School AI*. https://www.magicschool.ai/

McLeskey, J. (2017). *High-leverage practices in special education*. Council for Exceptional Children, & Collaboration for Effective Educator Development, Accountability and Reform. Council for Exceptional Children: Arlington, VA.

Moore, R., Vitale, D., & Stawinoga, N. (2018). The digital divide and educational equity. Insights in Education and Work, 1-10.

Rakap, S. (2024). Chatting with GPT: Enhancing individualized education program goal development for novice special education teachers. *Journal of Special Education Technology, 39*(3), 339–348. DOI: 10.1177/01626434231211295

Rose, D. H., & Meyer, A. (2002). *Teaching Every Student in the Digital Age: Universal Design for Learning* (Alexandria, V. A., Ed.).

Tomlinson, C. A. (2000). *Differentiation of instruction in the elementary grades* (ED443572). ERIC. https://files.eric.ed.gov/fulltext/ED443572.pdf

Tomlinson, C. A. (2001). *How to Differentiate Instruction in Mixed-Ability Classrooms*. ASCD.

Waterfield, D. A., Watson, L., & Day, J. (2024). Applying artificial intelligence in special education: Exploring availability and functionality of AI platforms for special educators. *Journal of Special Education Technology, 39*(3), 448–454. DOI: 10.1177/01626434241257237

Webb, N. (2002). *Depth-of-knowledge: Levels for four content areas*. Wisconsin Center for Educational Research.

Whittaker, M., Alper, M., Bennett, C. L., Hendren, S., Kaziunas, L., Mills, M., Morris, M. R., Rankin, J., Rogers, E., Salas, M., & West, S. M. (2019). *Disability, bias, and AI*. AI Now Institute. https://ainowinstitute.org/wp-content/uploads/2023/04/disabilitybiasai-2019.pdf

Zagona, A. L., Kurth, J. A., Lockman Turner, E., Pace, J., Shogren, K., Lansey, K., Jameson, M., Burnette, K., Mansouri, M., Hicks, T., & Gerasimova, D. (2022). Ecobehavioral analysis of the experiences of students with complex support needs in different classroom types. *Research and Practice for Persons with Severe Disabilities : the Journal of TASH, 47*(4), 209–228. DOI: 10.1177/15407969221126496

APPENDIX

Educational AI Tools

1. **DreamBox Learning**: A math-focused adaptive learning platform that adjusts instruction in real-time based on a student's responses. It can be beneficial for students with learning disabilities, such as dyscalculia, by providing personalized scaffolding and multisensory learning experiences.
2. **Lexia Core5 Reading**: A literacy intervention program that adapts to individual students' skill levels, offering structured, research-based support for students with dyslexia and other reading difficulties. It provides immediate feedback and additional practice as needed.
3. **Kurzweil 3000**: An assistive technology platform with text-to-speech, speech-to-text, and other learning supports for students with dyslexia, ADHD, and other learning differences. It adjusts content presentation to match students' needs, enhancing comprehension and engagement.
4. **i-Ready**: A diagnostic and instructional platform that personalizes reading and math instruction. It helps educators create tailored learning paths for students with learning disabilities, ensuring they receive the right level of challenge and support.
5. **N2Y Unique Learning System**: Designed for students with complex learning needs, this platform provides differentiated, standards-based instruction with built-in supports, such as symbol-supported text and interactive activities for students with intellectual disabilities.
6. **Edmark Reading Program**: A structured, adaptive literacy program specifically designed for students with special needs, including those with autism and intellectual disabilities. It emphasizes repetition and errorless learning to build reading confidence.
7. **Khanmigo (by Khan Academy)**: AI tutor integrated with Khan Academy's platform for personalized help.
8. **Socratic (by Google)**: AI-powered homework helper that explains concepts using image and voice input.
9. **Quizlet AI**: AI generates quizzes and flashcards tailored to user content.
10. **Century Tech**: Adaptive learning platform that uses AI to tailor lessons to students' strengths and weaknesses

AI Tools for Differentiation in Special Education

1. **DreamBox Learning:** Adapts K-8 math lessons in real time to meet students needs. It supports math IEP goals, targeted interventions, and self-paced learning.
2. **Lexia Core5 / Lexia PowerUp: Creates** personalized reading instruction with embedded scaffolds in literacy for Pre-kindergarten to 12th grade.
3. **Classkick: Provides** interactive lessons and live feedback from a teacher or peer with visual, audio, and drawing options.
4. **Diffit:** Generates differentiated texts at multiple reading levels with built-in supports. It helps teachers present grade-level content in accessible formats for students with reading challenges or English learners.
5. **Brisk Teaching:** AI analyzes student work and generates "glows," "grows," and "wonderings." It will scaffold teacher feedback to guide student improvement and critical thinking.
6. **MagicSchool AI:**:Includes tools for IEP goal writing, differentiated lesson plans, leveled texts, and parent communication.
7. **Scribbr AI Paraphraser / Quillbot:** Simplifies or rephrases content to match student reading levels. It also helps students with writing challenges or who are learning English.
8. **Curipod:** Creates interactive lessons based on topic and grade level, and allows teachers to easily modify and adapt instruction for diverse learners.

Speech-to-Text Applications (Converts Spoken Language Into Written Text)

1. **Dragon NaturallySpeaking (Dragon Professional Individual)**: A powerful speech recognition software that allows users to dictate text and control their computer hands-free, beneficial for students with physical disabilities or dysgraphia.
2. **Google Voice Typing**: A free tool built into Google Docs that enables speech-to-text functionality, making it accessible for students who struggle with writing.
3. **Otter.ai**: An AI-powered transcription tool that converts speech into text in real time, useful for students who need note-taking assistance.
4. **Microsoft Dictate**: A speech recognition feature integrated into Microsoft Office applications, allowing students to dictate text instead of typing.
5. **Apple Dictation**: A built-in tool on macOS and iOS devices that allows users to dictate text in any app that accepts text input.
6. **Rev AI:** Offers both automatic and human-edited transcription services.
7. **IBM Watson Speech-to-Text:** Real-time transcription for educational applications.

8. **Speechmatics:** Accurate, multi-language speech recognition tool.
9. **Sonix:** AI-driven transcription service with speaker labeling and searchable transcripts.

Text-to-Speech Applications (Converts Written Text Into Spoken Language)

1. **Kurzweil 3000**: A robust assistive technology tool that reads text aloud, highlights words as they are spoken, and supports students with dyslexia, ADHD, and other learning disabilities.
2. **NaturalReader**: A text-to-speech application with multiple voice options, ideal for students who need assistance with reading comprehension.
3. **Read&Write by Texthelp**: A literacy support tool that provides text-to-speech, word prediction, and reading comprehension supports, beneficial for students with learning disabilities.
4. **Speech Central**: A text-to-speech app that reads webpages, documents, and books aloud, supporting students with visual impairments or reading challenges.
5. **Microsoft Immersive Reader**: A built-in accessibility tool in Microsoft products that reads text aloud and includes features like line focus and picture dictionaries for students with reading difficulties.
6. **Voice Dream Reader**: A mobile-friendly text-to-speech app that supports multiple file formats, making it an excellent tool for students with dyslexia or visual impairments.
7. **Amazon Polly**: Cloud-based TTS with lifelike voices for educational content.
8. **Microsoft Azure TTS**: AI speech service with neural voice generation for learning platforms.
9. **Balabolka:** Free TTS program that supports a variety of file formats and voices.
10. **iSpeech**: Offers high-quality TTS for web and mobile apps.

AI-Powered Scheduling and Task Management

1. **Google Calendar with AI Suggestion:** Uses AI to suggest the best times for meetings, reminders, and recurring tasks, helping special educators manage IEP meetings and lesson planning more effectively.
2. **Microsoft Outlook Calendar (Cortana Integration)**: Provides smart scheduling, email summarization, and automatic reminders to help educators keep track of deadlines and appointments.
3. **Motion**: An AI-powered task manager that automatically schedules to-do lists, lesson planning, and grading time into an educator's calendar based on priority.
4. **Clockwise:** AI calendar assistant that optimizes meeting times and focus time.

5. **Reclaim.ai:** Automatically schedules tasks around meetings and class schedules.
6. **Calendly:** Scheduling tool with smart availability and integration for parent-teacher meetings.
7. **SkedPal:** Combines calendar and to-do list with AI optimization.
8. **Trevor AI:** Smart task manager that syncs with calendars and prioritizes work.
9. **Vyte:** Group scheduling tool ideal for student projects and school meetings.

Automated IEP and Data Tracking Tools

1. **IEP & Special Education Management Software (e.g., Frontline Special Ed & Interventions, SpedTrack)**: AI-enhanced platforms that help manage IEP timelines, automate documentation, and generate progress reports.
2. **Otus**: A data-driven education platform that uses AI to organize student performance data, track accommodations, and support teachers in making informed instructional decisions.
3. **Scribely**: AI-powered document automation software that assists in creating, managing, and sharing IEP documents efficiently.
4. **ABLE AI**: Generates IEP goals, PLAAFPs, and accommodations based on student data.
5. **Sonday System + AI:** Structured literacy program incorporating AI progress tracking.
6. **IEPWriter (PennData):** Streamlines the IEP writing process with built-in compliance checks.
7. **NarrativeBuilder.ai:** Creates student narratives and summaries for IEP documentation.
8. **Learning Genie:** Collects data for IEP reporting and progress monitoring in early education.
9. **SpedTrack:** Comprehensive IEP management system that uses automation to reduce paperwork.
10. **EDPlan by Public Consulting Group**: Supports educators with IEP development, data tracking, and compliance.
11. **Bright IDEA** (by Vanderbilt University): AI-supported tool for improving IEP planning and implementation.

AI-Powered Notetaking and Transcription Tools

1. **Otter.ai**: Transcribes meetings and classroom discussions in real time, which can be useful for documenting IEP meetings and professional development sessions.

2. **Microsoft OneNote with AI**: Uses AI to organize notes, transcribe audio, and categorize information for easier retrieval and lesson planning.
3. **Notion AI**: A notetaking and project management tool that summarizes documents, generates task lists, and assists in organizing teaching materials.
4. **Fireflies.ai:** Transcribes meetings, calls, and lectures with searchable transcripts and automatic note summarization. Integrates with Zoom, Google Meet, and other platforms.
5. **Scribe AI**: Automatically records, transcribes, and organizes conversations or presentations, turning them into shareable documents with highlights and key points.
6. **Tactiq:** Chrome extension that captures live captions from Google Meet and turns them into transcribed notes with automatic tagging and summarization.
7. **Supernormal**: Chrome extension that captures live captions from Google Meet and turns them into transcribed notes with automatic tagging and summarization.
8. **Sonix.ai**: Offers high-accuracy, multi-language transcription with tools for editing, summarizing, and exporting notes. Ideal for academic research and interviews.

AI-Driven Behavior and Intervention Tracking

1. **ClassCharts**: Uses AI to track student behavior, helping special educators identify patterns and adjust interventions accordingly.
2. **LiveSchool**: An AI-powered behavior tracking system that records student progress, provides insights into classroom management, and automates reports.
3. **Aula**: An AI-driven communication and engagement platform that helps special educators streamline communication with students, parents, and support staff.
4. **ClassDojo**: Tracks positive and negative student behaviors and communicates with parents.
5. **Kickboard**: Monitors behavior data and connects it with school culture analytics.
6. **Hero K12**: Tracks student conduct, attendance, and rewards systems with AI insights.
7. **Bark for Schools**: Uses AI to monitor student communication for safety and behavior concerns.
8. **TeachBoost**: AI-enhanced observation and feedback platform that tracks behavior trends.
9. **Edulastic Insights**: Offers behavioral data analytics in combination with academic metrics.

Chapter 7
Smart Tools, Smarter Teachers:
Perspectives and Practices of AI in Literacy Planning for Pre-Service Teachers

Heather M. Huling
https://orcid.org/0009-0005-6468-3597
Georgia Southern University, Statesboro, USA

Kathleen Crawford
https://orcid.org/0000-0001-9176-0563
Georgia Southern University, Statesboro, USA

ABSTRACT

This chapter investigates the use of artificial intelligence (AI) tools in preservice teacher education, with a specific focus on Elementary English Language Arts (ELA). It explores how AI tools can be used to support preservice teachers (PSTs) to create effective lesson plans, develop engaging instructional resources, differentiate instruction, and promote active student participation. The chapter explores tools like ChatGPT, MagicSchool.ai, Brisk, Perplexity, Canva, Diffit, and Curipod and illustrates how they can be used responsibly and effectively, offering valuable insights for educators seeking to integrate AI into teacher preparation programs. The chapter concludes with an overview of PSTs' perspectives on AI, addressing perceived benefits, limitations, and ethical considerations in educational settings, as well as offering a glimpse into the next steps of AI in teacher education.

DOI: 10.4018/979-8-3373-1122-7.ch007

SETTING THE STAGE: AI'S PLACE IN TEACHER PREPARATION

Artificial Intelligence (AI) has shifted from a theoretical innovation to a practical tool that is reshaping the way teachers plan, instruct, and engage with students in today's classrooms. From adaptive learning platforms to AI-driven content generation, technology is shifting the ways in which teachers plan, teach, and assess student learning in the classroom (Kamalov et al., 2023). With AI-powered tools, educators can automate lesson planning, personalize instruction, and analyze student progress more efficiently than ever before. However, while AI offers numerous benefits, it should not serve as a substitute for the expertise, creativity, and professional judgment of educators. Instead, it should serve as a powerful support system, helping teachers engage students in new and innovative ways and more effectively manage their workload of more tedious tasks. When used thoughtfully and with a critical lens, AI has the potential to enhance both productivity and creativity, allowing educators to focus on building meaningful connections and relationships with their students, perhaps the most critical aspect of teaching.

For pre-service teachers (PSTs), understanding AI's impact on education is not just beneficial, it is essential. As future educators, they must be prepared to navigate classroom environments where technology is deeply embedded in instructional practices. There are numerous theoretical frameworks that support the integration of technology and instruction, and this chapter uses the Technological Pedagogical Content Knowledge (TPACK) framework which was developed to explain how teachers can effectively integrate technology into their teaching practices (Mishra & Koehler, 2006; Bautista et al., 2024; Tarisayia, 2024; Wang et al., 2024). Today's classrooms demand tech-savvy teachers who can apply AI's capabilities while maintaining a critical perspective on its limitations and ethical implications. It is not enough to simply use AI; educators must develop the ability to evaluate its outputs, refine its suggestions, and ensure that it aligns with best practices in teaching and learning. A thoughtful and intentional approach to AI integration will empower PSTs to make informed decisions about lesson design, student assessment, and classroom engagement, as supported by the TPACK framework.

As AI continues to evolve, teacher preparation programs must also adapt, ensuring that future educators are well-equipped to integrate these tools effectively and responsibly. This requires not only hands-on experience with AI-driven educational platforms but also opportunities for PSTs to reflect on the pedagogical and ethical considerations of AI use in the classroom under the guidance of their professors and mentor teachers. By emphasizing a balanced, research-informed approach to AI in education, teacher preparation programs can help prepare a generation of educators who are both innovative and intentional in their use of technology.

How Ai Is Reshaping Teacher Training

Teacher training programs are integrating AI at a steady pace to enhance the learning experience for PSTs (Zhang et al., 2023; Baustista et al., 2024). Staying up to date with technological advances is essential in preparing future educators to be prepared for the classroom. AI tools can be used in a multitude of ways to enrich the development of PSTs, and they can simulate classroom scenarios, provide instant feedback, and offer personalized learning paths (U.S. DOE, 2023). For example, AI-driven platforms can create virtual classrooms where PSTs practice teaching in a controlled environment, receiving feedback on their performance (Abrams, 2025). This approach not only improves teaching skills but also builds confidence in managing real classroom situations in a low-risk environment.

AI can also be used to help PSTs be better prepared for the daily responsibilities of teaching, including understanding content and standards, building lesson plans, generating content presentations, creating assessments, and managing paperwork such as composing emails and creating class newsletters. Generative AI can help maximize teacher productivity by assisting in the creation of these materials to make them user and reader-friendly, as well as visually appealing. By incorporating AI, teacher training becomes more interactive, efficient, and tailored to the needs of future educators (Sanusi et al., 2024), specifically in elementary literacy methods courses.

Zooming In: Ai In Elementary Ela Methods Courses

Elementary English Language Arts (ELA) methods courses are utilizing AI to assist in lesson planning, student assessment, and personalized instruction (Treve, 2024). AI tools are able to analyze student writing, provide feedback on grammar and style, and suggest improvements. Additionally, AI-powered reading programs can adapt to individual student reading levels, offering personalized reading materials, decodable texts, and comprehension activities. In order to better understand how these applications support pre-service teachers in developing effective teaching strategies and enhancing student learning outcomes, teacher educators must be purposeful in the exposure and application of the tools in their teacher preparation programs (Ayanwale et al., 2024a). To illustrate a specific example of how instructors teach pre-service to utilize AI efficiently and critically, the authors of this chapter describe two consecutive class sessions in their own undergraduate Language Arts Methods course in the following sections.

In these two class sessions, elementary education majors in a language arts methods course engaged in an in-depth exploration of artificial intelligence (AI) and its role in literacy instruction, particularly in the context of planning an interactive read-alouds. The two sessions aimed to introduce pre-service teachers to AI as a tool for lesson planning while guiding critical thinking about its limitations, ethical considerations, and potential for enhancing instructional practices.

Class Session 1: Introducing Ai In Read-Aloud Planning

The first session began with an introduction to AI and its growing presence in education. Students reflected on their prior knowledge and experiences with AI tools such as ChatGPT and discussed their perceptions, including excitement, skepticism, and ethical concerns. To provide a foundation for exploration, students watched a brief video on AI's capabilities and limitations before being introduced to MagicSchool.ai, an AI-powered platform designed specifically for teachers (Magicschool.ai, n.d.).

To demonstrate AI's versatility beyond the classroom, the authors modeled several practical, relevant examples using ChatGPT, such as generating recipes with grocery lists, creating travel itineraries for the local college town, composing fun social media posts, and drafting emails to professors. After seeing these examples in action, the PSTs were guided through the sign-up process for MagicSchool.ai. They were then given time to explore its various tools, identifying features they found useful, surprising, or potentially problematic. This hands-on experience allowed the PSTs to critically engage with AI and consider its implications for teaching and learning. The focus then shifted to AI's application in interactive read-alouds. The class examined an AI-generated lesson plan for the book *Dragons Love Tacos* (Rubin, 2012), a mentor text for the class, analyzing its strengths and weaknesses. Using a structured framework, each of the PSTs evaluated the lesson plan for content accuracy, developmental appropriateness, engagement strategies, and alignment with best practices in literacy instruction. The PSTs noted areas where the AI-generated plan offered useful starting points, such as generating discussion questions and interactive elements, but they also identified gaps, including inaccuracies, extraneous or unnecessary elements, a lack of depth in questioning, and missed opportunities for meaningful student interaction.

The first class session concluded with a discussion on ethical AI use in education, emphasizing the importance of transparency and responsible application. The pre-service teachers were reminded that while AI can serve as a valuable brainstorming tool, it should never replace their professional expertise as educators. They were encouraged to think critically about AI-generated outputs, refine them as needed, and always disclose AI assistance in their lesson planning or other assignments for school. At the end of class, the pre-service teachers reflected on their learning by responding to journal prompts that asked them to consider their evolving understanding of AI, identify any remaining questions, and explore potential applications of AI in their future classrooms. Specific prompts included: "How has your understanding of AI changed today?", "What questions do you still have about using AI in education?", and "How will you integrate AI into your teaching practices?".

Class Session 2: Applying AI to Create Read-Aloud Lesson Plans

The second class session built on the foundational knowledge from class session one, transitioning from analysis to hands-on application. The class began with a reflection activity where the PSTs revisited their experiences from the previous session, sharing insights about AI's potential and challenges. In small groups, the PSTs discussed questions, hesitations, or excitement about AI in education before transitioning into the day's main activity: generating and analyzing their own AI-assisted lesson plans.

Using MagicSchool.ai, students were tasked with creating an interactive read-aloud lesson plan for *The Secret Pizza Party* by Adam Rubin (Rubin, 2013), which was an unfamiliar text read aloud in class for the first time. Before reading, the authors instructed the PSTs to take notes and think like a teacher, considering how to get students excited about the book before reading, stopping points for a read aloud, potential questions to ask, and assessment ideas. The authors modeled the process of using MagicSchool.ai by entering specific prompts to guide the lesson plan tool in generating a structured lesson plan, including comprehension questions, interactive elements such as gestures and sound effects, and an assessment activity focused on sequencing events in the story. These outcomes were projected on a large screen in real-time, allowing the PSTs to observe the AI's process. Once the AI-generated plan was produced, they critically examined it individually using a graphic organizer, assessing aspects such as engagement, alignment with the text, question quality, developmental appropriateness, and overall coherence.

After their individual analyses, the PSTs engaged in peer discussions, comparing their AI-generated lesson plans and identifying common strengths and areas for improvement. This collaborative review process reinforced key takeaways from the previous session: while AI can generate useful ideas, human judgment remains essential in refining lesson plans to meet diverse student needs. The class also discussed broader implications, including AI's potential role in differentiation, its risks, such as perpetuating biases or generating superficial content, and strategies for integrating AI while maintaining high-quality literacy instruction. To conclude class session two, students documented their reflections in their interactive journals, capturing their key takeaways about AI's role in education.

These two class sessions provided PSTs with both theoretical knowledge and practical experience in using AI for literacy instruction. Through critical analysis and hands-on application, students gained a clearer understanding of AI's potential and limitations. The sessions emphasized that while AI can be a helpful tool in generating lesson plans, it cannot replace the humanistic and personal nature of teaching. Educators' expertise, creativity, and judgment are necessary to refine and personalize AI-generated content, ensuring that the final outputs meet the diverse needs of students and maintain high-quality instruction. Building on the insights gained from these two class sessions, the next section of this chapter explores the role of AI as a co-teacher in literacy lesson planning and instruction, highlighting how AI can support and enhance the teaching process.

AI AS A CO-TEACHER: LITERACY LESSON PLANNING & INSTRUCTION

AI-powered tools are significantly reshaping how educators design literacy lessons, moving toward a more data-driven, personalized, and effective approach. In elementary schools, these tools are invaluable in creating tailored reading and writing experiences that meet each student's unique needs. By automatically analyzing data on student performance, participation, and responses, AI uncovers patterns that might otherwise be overlooked. For instance, in a literacy classroom, if AI detects that a student is consistently struggling with decoding words or reading comprehension, it can suggest specific interventions. These could include modified texts with simplified vocabulary, scaffolding strategies like small group reading sessions, or interactive, multisensory phonics games to strengthen foundational literacy skills.

AI also meets the needs of advanced learners by recommending enrichment activities that push their abilities further. For example, if a student is excelling in their ability to summarize stories or make inferences, AI might suggest more challenging texts or comprehension tasks that focus on higher-order thinking, such as analyzing themes or predicting plot outcomes. By doing so, AI ensures that all students, whether struggling or advanced, are provided with appropriate resources to meet their developmental needs, enabling more inclusive literacy instruction.

In addition to supporting individual student needs, AI can also detect gaps in collective student knowledge across the classroom. If a significant portion of the class is having difficulty with identifying the main idea of a passage, AI has the capability to alert the teacher of this trend and recommend adjustments to future lessons. These could include providing additional practice with identifying key details using less complex passages, using graphic organizers to break down complex ideas, or integrating peer discussions to reinforce the concept. This adaptability helps teachers respond to the real-time needs of their students and adjust their teaching strategies to improve literacy outcomes for all learners.

Another benefit of AI in literacy lesson planning is its ability to save time. By automating repetitive tasks such as resource suggestions or assessment analysis, AI allows educators to focus more on meaningful, in-person interactions with students. Teachers can use the time saved to engage with students during independent reading activities, provide targeted writing feedback, and facilitate small-group discussions focused on literacy skills. In this way, AI enhances both instructional quality and teacher-student interaction, giving educators the flexibility to fine-tune lessons based on ongoing student needs.

AI is reinventing traditional lesson design in elementary literacy classrooms by offering a more tailored, efficient, and responsive approach to instruction. Whether it is through identifying individual reading challenges, recommending appropriate resources, or providing real-time feedback on student performance, AI equips teachers with tools to create more meaningful, effective literacy lessons that result in student growth, achievement, and engagement.

From Passive to Participatory: AI's Role in Student Engagement

AI technologies are significantly transforming traditional classrooms by shifting the focus from passive consumption of information to active, student-driven learning. In elementary literacy instruction, this restructuring is particularly impactful. Traditionally, young students often engage in reading and writing activities in a structured, teacher-directed manner. While this is essential, AI is enhancing these practices by introducing adaptive learning platforms, interactive simulations, and real-time feedback systems, all of which encourage students to become active participants in their own literacy development.

For instance, adaptive learning platforms powered by AI can assess individual student progress in reading fluency, comprehension, and phonics, adjusting content to meet their specific needs. If a student requires extra guidance and support with recognizing letter sounds or blending phonemes, the system can recommend more targeted exercises to strengthen these skills. Conversely, if a student is excelling in their understanding of story structure, AI can provide examples of more challenging texts or comprehension questions. This personalized approach helps students not only engage more deeply with the content but also provides a sense of ownership over their learning. In literacy, this translates into students who are more confident in approaching reading and writing tasks, knowing that their unique needs are being met instantly and authentically.

AI-supported real-time feedback systems are particularly valuable in elementary literacy classrooms. For example, as students read aloud, AI tools can offer immediate corrections on pronunciation or fluency, guiding them step by step through the process. This instantaneous feedback helps students improve their reading skills by providing constant reinforcement in a safe, judgment-free environment, whether it is correcting an error in word recognition or encouraging them to slow down for better comprehension. By receiving immediate responses to their efforts, students develop a growth mindset, seeing mistakes as learning opportunities rather than setbacks.

Interactive simulations can also enhance literacy instruction in elementary classrooms. AI-powered tools have the power to immerse young learners in virtual story worlds where they can interact with characters, manipulate objects related to the plot, or even take part in decision-making moments within a story. For example, students might read a story about a character overcoming challenges and then be asked to choose how the character should act in a similar situation, thus enhancing deeper comprehension and critical thinking. These simulations not only engage students in literacy learning but also allow them to experiment with storytelling techniques, vocabulary development, and narrative structure through interactive, hands-on experiences.

Ultimately, AI's role in elementary literacy education goes beyond just simply enhancing individual student engagement. It creates a classroom community where students are actively involved, excited, and growing academically and personally. Through personalized instruction, immediate feedback, immersive simulations, and gamified learning, AI helps form a more interactive and collaborative classroom experience, motivating students and giving them the tools to succeed in their literacy development. Building on this interactive classroom experience, the next section explores how AI-powered teaching resources can further bring lessons to life, refining and improving the way literacy instruction is delivered and experienced.

Bringing Lessons to Life: AI-Powered Teaching Resources

AI is transforming the classroom by providing teachers with innovative and interactive teaching resources that make learning more engaging and effective. In the context of literacy instruction, AI-powered tools such as virtual reality (VR) and augmented reality (AR) are particularly useful. These technologies allow students to immerse themselves in content, making abstract concepts more concrete and accessible. For example, in a literacy lesson, students could use AR to interact with elements of a story, such as animated characters or scenes from a text, bringing the narrative to life in a way that reading alone cannot achieve. This immersive experience can enhance comprehension and deepen students' connection to the material (Karataş & Yüce, 2024).

In addition to bringing stories and reading comprehension to life, VR and AR also support vocabulary acquisition and understanding of figurative language. Students can visualize and interact with new vocabulary words through contextual scenes, increasing retention and engagement. For example, if students are reading a book about the ocean, they might use VR to "dive" into an underwater world, giving them a rich, contextual understanding of terms like "coral reef," "currents," or "marine life." This approach not only enhances vocabulary knowledge but also helps students better understand the nuances of language across different contexts (Abdulayeva et al., 2025).

AI-powered resources like VR and AR can also be used to scaffold complex literacy tasks. For instance, students struggling with story structure can use interactive applications to break down a story's plot or analyze character development in real time. By visually mapping out a story's key elements or engaging with interactive character profiles, students can deepen their understanding of narrative structure and, in turn, improve their writing skills. Utilizing VR to assist in differentiation and inclusion continues to assist in building a supportive classroom where all learning needs are met (Carreon et al., 2023). These technologies provide alternate modes of learning and immediate feedback, which helps students develop their literacy skills through active participation and high engagement.

In addition to AI-powered resources, other AI tools have the ability to shift literary analysis by making it more interactive, inclusive, and engaging for students. Early literacy learners can benefit from AI tools designed to support phonics skills, where AI-driven platforms provide targeted activities that help students practice letter-sound correspondences, blend sounds, and segment words. These tools can adjust to individual progress, offering personalized phonics exercises based on each learner's current level. For more advanced learners, AI can guide students in analyzing texts and exploring themes, character motivations, or symbolism in an interactive manner. For example, an AI tool might help students identify key themes in a novel and present interactive activity that allow them to explore these themes through multimedia, such as video clips, infographics, or audio narrations. This deepens engagement with the text, helping students make connections between the story and their own experiences while also building critical thinking skills that are crucial for literacy development.

Ultimately, AI-powered teaching resources like VR and AR are improving literacy instruction by creating immersive, interactive environments that enhance comprehension, vocabulary development, and literary analysis. These technologies not only make learning more engaging but also help students connect more meaningfully with the content, resulting in a deeper understanding of the material (MacDowell et al., 2024). With AI, literacy education becomes an experience that extends beyond the page, allowing students to actively engage with and internalize what they learn. As AI continues to modernize literacy education into a more immersive experience, the following section will explore practical tools and strategies that future teachers can use to integrate AI effectively into their classrooms.

AI IN ACTION: A TOOLKIT FOR FUTURE TEACHERS

As AI continues to grow, teacher preparation programs will need to continue to stay ahead of the curve by being cognizant of the many AI applications out there geared toward education. Being knowledgeable in the variety of applications allows teacher educators to purposefully select and have pre-service teachers engage with AI tools that are focused on supporting student learning and increasing their own productivity (Ayanwale et al., 2024a). AI tools applicable to pre-service teachers include ones that can assist in creating detailed, effective lesson plans, analyzing data sets, as well as assisting in the creation of resources and materials for student use.

AI tools that support student learning and increase teacher productivity can help pre-service teachers generate detailed, aligned lesson plans that can be tweaked to meet the diverse learning needs of the classroom. These tools can be used to help create interactive, high-engagement lessons that promote deeper learning while also assisting in the creation of connected materials. AI tools have the power to create professional posters, visuals, videos, and presentations that aid in student understanding and engagement.

To provide more personalized learning experiences, AI tools can be used to analyze student data and differentiate the learning materials based on the trends in the data sets. These tools can also be used to offer tailored feedback based on those identified student needs, helping them to better grasp their strengths and areas of growth. To build on the feedback, AI tools can be used to create alternate learning experiences that better meet student needs, such as simplifying complex concepts, varying teaching methods, or using more AI-powered tools, like VR, to enhance learning.

The AI applications described below were selected based on their ability to assist in literacy planning and instruction and to increase teacher productivity. A brief description of each application, along with a detailed analysis of the specific tools that are most beneficial, provide valuable insights for educators. This will help both future and current educators, as well as teacher preparation programs, identify and explore tools that can improve their teaching practices and be shared with others.

ChatGPT: Your AI Teaching Assistant

ChatGPT, one of the most commonly used chatbots, is an AI tool used across disciplines and professions. In the field of education, elementary teachers can use ChatGPT in various areas of instruction, particularly in literacy education (OpenAI, 2023). Teachers are able to use this tool to assist with researching content, creating lesson plans that are tailored to various topics, and generating learning objectives across different grade levels, and classroom contexts. For example, if a teacher designs a phonics level for first graders and inputs the following prompt, "Design a phonics lesson on short vowels. Include a fun introduction, modeling, guided practice, and an assessment. Be sure to make the lesson interactive with a game that gets students up and moving and make the lesson revolve around an animal theme." The output then breaks the lesson plan into parts and includes a recommended script to follow along and specific examples to use such as, "Welcome, explorers! Today, we're on a safari to discover the sounds animals make—and the short vowel sounds hidden in their names!" and "A fat cat sat on a mat. (short a), The red hen met ten men. (short e), A big pig did a jig. (short i), A dog got on a log. (short o), A duck is stuck in the mud. (short u)". The lesson plan ideas provide teachers with time-saving resources, allowing them to devote more time on actual instruction.

In addition to automatically generating lesson plan ideas, ChatGPT has the ability to answer students' questions. During independent or small group work, older elementary students are able to use ChatGPT to clarify concepts, review vocabulary, or ask for help with assignments. For example, if a student is struggling with reading a passage because of complex vocabulary, the chatbot can support the student by breaking down difficult words using student-friendly definitions and examples. For example, a 5th grader may get to the word "evaporate" in a passage and ask the chatbot for a definition and real-world examples on a first grade level. ChatGPT then produces an output such as, "Evaporation is when water gets warm and turns into a gas called water vapor. It goes up into the art, even though we can't see it! Some examples are a puddle disappearing, wet clothes drying, or a damp sidewalk on a hot day". This immediate feedback helps students become more independent learners while at the same time allowing their teacher to offer support to other students.

Beyond supporting teachers and students in numerous ways, ChatGPT can also track individual student progress and whole class learning over time. Teachers can input the data in the textbox and ask the chatbot to create a table or graph to illustrate the patterns and trends. The chatbot can also recommend materials and strategies to support students in small and whole-group settings, ensuring that each child's learning needs are met based on the provided data. In turn, teachers can use the output generated to inform future instructional practices. For example, if a teacher notices that he has several students in his class who are struggling with comprehension skills, particularly with identifying the main idea of a passage, he can input the assessment data into ChatGPT, such as test scores, anecdotal notes, and observations from students teaching journals. The chatbot will then describe patterns in the data and offer specific suggestions for the teacher, such as using graphic organizers, games, and personalized texts based on students' interest. The teacher can then add a follow-up prompt to differentiate the levels of the text to meet each students' instructional needs.

Each of the example features of ChatGPT described above enables teachers to personalize learning experiences, enriching literacy development in meaningful, interactive, and engaging ways. The examples represent just a snippet of the possibilities of how ChatGPT can assist teachers with everyday tasks to save time on tasks that are typically time-consuming and to design the most effective, engaging learning experiences for students.

Magicschool.ai: Where Innovation Meets Education

Magicschool.ai, an AI tool designed specifically for teachers, by teachers. The creators of this application hold the belief that the various tools they offer save teachers "up to 10 hours per week" so they can dedicate more time to students and families, easing the pressures that lead to teacher burnout (Magicschool.ai, n.d.). Tools that are particularly beneficial for elementary literacy teachers are the Lesson Generator, Unit Plan Generator, Presentation Generator, Text Leveler, Text Summarizer, Rubric Generator, Choice Board, Writing Feedback, Decodable Texts, Standards Unpacker, and DOK Questions. Teachers also have the capability to use Raina, the chatbot who introduces herself in the following way: "Hello! My name is Raina, your AI instructional coach. You can ask any questions related to best practices in teaching or your work in a school building. Feel free to ask me for ideas for your classroom, research on best practices in pedagogy, behavior management strategies, or any general advice! The more specific your questions, the better my responses will be. How can I help you today?" Each feature is not only effective to use on its own, but they can be used in tandem with one another. For example, a teacher could prompt Raina to give some hands-on ideas for teaching comparing and contrasting stories. Raina will produce a list of ideas such as Venn diagram art, a drama comparison with puppets, or a story quilt. From there, teachers can use those ideas in the lesson plan generator for more specific details, including books to use, take their favorite ideas of assessments given to create a choice board for students, and finally use the rubric generator for each of the choice board options to assist with assessing projects. If some of the choice board options include a writing component, the teacher can also use the Writing Feedback tool to automatically generate narrative feedback for students.

Magicschool.ai also supports teachers in ways to differentiate instruction in their literacy practices. The platform can tailor the levels of reading materials by automatically producing advanced texts for high-achievers and less challenging texts, including texts that are easier to decode and incorporate more commonly used vocabulary words for those still developing their reading skills. For early readers, Magicschool.ai is able to generate decodable texts based on individual needs using the Decodable Texts tool. Here, teachers are prompted to enter an "Objective/

Pattern/Example Word" with over one hundred phonics patterns to choose from. To illustrate this, a first-grade teacher could select "sh, /sh/, wish, shed" and can choose "Shy Sam sees a fish. The fish is in the dish. Sam wishes for a big fish." Teachers can then use the "Read Aloud" option for students to listen to the audio of the produced text.

Not only can the tools listed above in the platform support and ease instructional practices, Magicschool.ai also allows teachers to conduct administrative tasks automatically. Teachers can generate emails to families, generate data sets, produce class newsletters, proofread texts, and create social media posts. Using these tools allows teachers to dedicate more time to instruction, and less time with time-consuming, behind the scenes tasks that can overconsume a teacher's school day and day-to-day operations of a classroom.

Magicschool.ai's suite of tools supports teachers in delivering customized, effective, and responsive literacy education to their students. Whether it is through generating engaging presentations, creating detailed rubrics, or providing immediate feedback, these tools help enhance the learning experience and improve student outcomes in literacy.

Brisk Teaching: Transforming Teaching with Seamless System Integration

Brisk Teaching (Brisk Labs Co, 2025), much like MagicSchool.ai, is an AI toolkit designed specifically for teachers. Brisk offers tools such as lesson planning, presentation generation, text leveling for differentiation, quiz creation, AI detection, student feedback, and student work examples. Since Brisk is a Google Chrome extension, it has the capability to work on multiple platforms without bouncing back and forth between websites and other AI tools. Brisk integrates seamlessly within existing systems like YouTube, Canva, Google Slides, Docs, Forms, and websites, as well as in Word and PDF documents which makes it easier to use than other sites with stand-alone functionalities.

Elementary teachers can use Brisk in numerous ways to enhance literacy teaching and learning. For example, teachers can generate personalized stories based on students' interests to make reading more relatable. From there, the teachers can differentiate the Lexile level of the reading to make it easier or more challenging for the readers. Quizzes can then be created to assess students' understanding of the stories, and if a teacher prefers to create more of a project-based assessment, Brisk can outline the project and generate an aligned rubric. Much like this, teachers can navigate to different websites such as National Geographic Kids (National Geographic Society, 2025) to find nonfiction passages and automatically change the readability levels in a Google Doc, followed by producing a quiz or project. This task can also be mirrored by showing educational YouTube videos, clicking the Brisk extension, and choosing "change reading level." Brisk transcribes the video's audio into a Google Doc, and teachers can then adjust the text by prompting it to make passages shorter or longer and revising the content to better align with their students' needs.

Brisk also instantly produces slideshows where it prompts teachers to describe the content, select the state standard, choose if they want to add images or not, identify the number of slides wanted, and then select an appropriate template design. To illustrate this, if a teacher wanted to create a slideshow on nonfiction text features, she could prompt it to: 1) create a slideshow on nonfiction text features such as table of contents, captions, diagrams, headings, glossaries for 4th graders and use pop culture references, 2) align the slideshow with (insert state standard), 3) add in relevant images with labels, 4) include 15 slides, and 5) use the 3rd template offered. From there, the slideshow automatically generates, and the teacher can make revisions to best meet her students' needs and interests.

Brisk also has the capability to offer narrative feedback to students on written work. For example, a teacher could assign the following writing assignment to her students: Your task is to write a nonfiction piece on a topic of your choice, like animals or historical events. Be sure to include at least five text features, such as headings, captions, or diagrams. You will also need to start with a strong introduction, provide accurate information in the body, and finish with a clear conclusion. Remember to use reliable sources for your research, and don't forget to check your work for any mistakes before submitting it. Once students submit their work in Google Classroom, the teacher can simply click the Brisk extension, attach the rubric, and select the "Give Feedback" option. The feedback option then offers "glows, grows, and wonderings" to the student. Additionally, the Brisk extension also gives teachers the option to "Inspect Writing" and will track the number of edits and pastes with timestamps to track possible AI assistance or other forms of plagiarism.

It is clear that Brisk Teaching streamlines instructional tasks by integrating into commonly used platforms, allowing teachers to easily create materials, differentiate instruction, and assess student learning. Brisk's ability to generate personalized content, automate feedback, and align with standards makes it a valuable tool for developing meaningful literacy instruction. By minimizing time spent on lesson planning and assessment, Brisk enables teachers to focus more time spent actively working with students and less time working on tedious tasks.

Perplexity: AI-Driven Inquiry and Research

Perplexity is an AI tool that distinguishes itself as the 'Swiss Army Knife' in generative AI (PerplexityAI, 2023). It is a free AI search engine that can answer questions, explore topics in-depth to build understanding, complete analysis of data or files, and create a library or storage system for resources found from searches. Perplexity offers two ways for users to explore topics, quick search and pro search. Quick search is the free search engine with unlimited searches per day on the free site. It provides quick, reliable information for the student, teacher, or user on a variety of topics or ideas. Pro search, however, is a deep dive into a specific topic or idea that can map out steps to solve problems, summarize multiple data resources or sets, and interpret code. Pro search is a valuable tool for students and teachers, as it assists in academic and professional research based on credible resources.

Perplexity is also used to enhance student learning in the classroom for teachers, as it can help to generate lesson ideas, craft questions to ask students, and recommend assessment ideas. This tool can take different text passages and change the reading level to meet the needs of diverse learners in the classroom. Teachers can then use these differentiated passages and prompt Perplexity to create corresponding questions to ask to check for comprehension in small reading groups. To support younger literacy development through phonics instruction, teachers can prompt the tool to generate a kindergarten level reading passage containing common consonant-vowel-consonant (CVC) words that relate to students' interests or other relatable connections. Prompting Perplexity further, teachers could then have the AI tool create learning centers, individual activities, or assessments based on the created passage.

When working with older students, teachers and students can use Perplexity to aid in the research process when learning new material. Teachers can use it to summarize abstract or complex topics for students into easily comprehensible passages or develop study guides for student use. Additionally, students can engage in research on varying topics, such as science or social studies integrated informational writing. Perplexity, when prompted correctly, can provide students with resources on their grade level along with a variety of cited resources.

Perplexity can also enhance student writing by assisting in organizing ideas, suggesting writing prompts, and providing grammar assistance. Students can also upload files or paste their writing into the application and ask for specific feedback to provide strengths and areas for improvement within the writing piece. For teachers, Perplexity can create student-friendly learning activities where students can explore and practice a variety of grammar and phonics skills.

Perplexity's tools can be used by both teachers and students to enhance literacy instruction and skills through its quick and deep-dive search engines. Teachers can maximize productivity by using the tool to assist in the planning and creation of lessons, resources, and materials. Students can engage with and feel supported in their literacy learning through the AI generated materials and the use of the search engine for research projects.

Canva: Designing the Future of Learning

Canva is an online design tool that has been helping users across many disciplines design visuals, presentations, and written materials. However, Canva also has an AI feature built into its website that connects users to the power of AI to assist in content creation (CanvaAI, n.d.). The AI-powered apps range from no-cost options to Pro options that require a paid subscription, and all can be used to assist users in creating enticing and informative content. When thinking of literacy instruction, Canva offers teachers and students the opportunity to embed AI-generated images, voiceovers, translations, and content creation.

Canva can help to create AI-generated visuals to enhance content for others. Teachers can embed images in their presentations to develop student understanding of literacy content when working with phonological and phonemic awareness. The AI-generated images can represent words for rhyming activities or sounds within words for phoneme activities. Students can also benefit from the AI generated image feature by prompting Canva to create images to match self-authored works in the classroom. These images can further develop their ideas and add meaning to their writing pieces.

To maximize teacher productivity, Canva assists in the creation of presentations to be used within lessons in the classroom. These professional presentations can be created with a variety of designs relatable to literacy content or the grade level of the students. Teachers are able to select the design that best suits their classroom, and Canva can generate the content to assist teachers in meeting the state standards. For example, teachers can prompt Canva to AI generate a presentation on identifying the main idea and supporting key details, and it will create a presentation that is accurately aligned with the standard along with visuals and text tailored to the appropriate grade level. The use of visuals and text helps to solidify student comprehension of the standard and allows for multiple learning needs to be met.

Another feature of Canva AI is to add voiceovers or voice translations into literacy presentations as an assistive technology feature. Teachers can create presentations or visuals and then add voiceovers to enhance understanding or elaborate on the text. This feature helps to engage auditory learners and provides additional support to students who may need help with reading. Additionally, Canva has the capability to create captions or translations as well within presentations. This allows all students within the literacy classroom to have equitable access to the content and feel inclusive in the learning environment.

Canva can also create resources or student materials to be used within the literacy classroom. Teachers can create study guides, infographics, and reading passages in varying text sizes to accommodate learning and differentiated needs in the classroom. This is especially helpful when focusing on vocabulary development in creating a visual for classroom use and an accompanying study guide to be kept by the students. For phonics, teachers can generate flashcards to be used within lessons that work on final e sounds that include the word and a connected image. Students can also use Canva to create their own images. For instance, students could list the internal and physical traits of a character within a text and then ask Canva to create a visual of their described character. This allows the student to showcase their understanding of this literacy standard in a unique way. These resources and student materials are crucial in building student understanding while maintaining engagement in the classroom.

With so many features that are AI-powered, Canva is able to assist both teachers and students within literacy classrooms to enhance instruction, assessment and engagement. AI-generated presentations, materials, and the inclusion of tools such as generated images, voice recordings, or translations create an inclusive and exciting learning environment in the classroom. Literacy instruction is improved through professional visuals and presentations, and learning is showcased through the AI-powered applications of visual and video creation. Canva AI is not only user-friendly but also offers a wide variety of tools that support literacy learning in the classroom.

Diffit: Differentiated Learning Made Simple

Diffit is an AI tool that is specifically designed with educators in mind to assist with creating highly functional and differentiated materials that can be utilized in the classroom (Diffit, n.d.a). Diffit has multiple search engine prompts, including an open-ended question option, uploading a file, book chapter, link to an article or YouTube video, text or PDF, or inputting a vocabulary list. From there, teachers or users can also specify the reading level and language to create a more desired output. Diffit can also assist teachers in generating full lesson plans, student resources and materials and samples or examples to be used in the lesson.

To support literacy instruction, Diffit offers teachers the opportunity to connect current curriculum resources or state standards with cited, effective materials for the classroom (Diffit, n.d.b). Then to further differentiate, teachers can select the grade level and language while also adding supporting images, leveled passages, or other translations of the materials. ELA teachers or teacher educators can use Diffit to assist in text analysis, differentiating readings, creating vocabulary or word work activities, engaging in critical thinking, and creating practice materials.

The ability to customize so many portions of content lends itself greatly to teachers as no classroom or student is the same. Early elementary teachers can use Diffit to create phonics lesson plans and instructional materials that assist students in developing an understanding of CVC words through multiple hands-on activities. Students can engage in small group instruction that is mapped out by Diffit to maximize student engagement and teacher productivity. Teachers can also utilize the enormous library of resources to create student-friendly materials that can be used to enhance instruction, organize ideas, provide a study tool, or be used as an assessment tool. Teachers can input their vocabulary lists into Diffit and have it create engaging lessons to teach and activities to reinforce vocabulary instruction. The resource materials can also be used to support or assess student learning in this area as well.

Undoubtedly, Drift has an edge over other AI tools in the area of differentiation. Not only can teachers differentiate the lessons by grade level and language, but they can also differentiate those materials by varying reading levels and accompanying support materials. Teachers are able to embed images to support visual learners, change the reading level of a passage to either support or challenge learners, and they are able to use a variety of student-ready activities that can be easily adaptable to their literacy content. Diffit lightens the workload of the teacher while creating a classroom that is inclusive of all learning needs.

Curipod: Sparking 100% Participation

Curipod is an AI tool that focuses on enhancing classroom participation and engagement for teachers in their classrooms (Curipod AS, 2025). This tool aids in sparking discussions through interactive prompts that capture student voices, it allows teachers to adjust lessons from a lesson bank to fit their classroom needs for standardized test preparation and also allows teachers to create their own lessons within the system and then AI enhances the lessons with additional interactive elements.

The interactive elements that Curipod provides to teachers and students maximize engagement and instructional time. Interactive elements such as polls, word clouds, open-response questions, and illustrations allow students to respond and showcase understanding in real-time through a variety of methods. The open AI system allows teachers to upload their personal lessons and find ways to embed these interactive activities so an ELA teacher can upload a reading comprehension passage, and Curipod can assist in creating interactive discussion activities that correspond with the uploaded reading passage and indicated grade level. The AI system will align specific interactive activities based on the teacher's input and create a presentation that feels engaging and game-like as students engage in deep discussions about the passage. These can include word clouds, open-response questions, or different types of graphic organizers.

Curipod can also be used as a form of formative assessment for teachers as well. Students can engage in these AI generated interactive activities to evaluate their understanding of literacy topics such as phonological awareness and phonics instruction. Teachers can use the interactive activities of polls or drawings to assess students' understanding of sounds and letters in an engaging, fun way for students. This deepens teachers' understanding of their students' strengths and areas for growth through these engagement activities.

Another way Curipod can assist teachers at all levels in literacy instruction is to use the AI Feedback tool to assist in identifying specific feedback to guide student growth in different writing types. Teachers can upload specific rubrics and select state standards for Curipod to analyze student work and provide personalized and actionable feedback to students in real-time. This feature maximizes teacher productivity and gives students specific feedback to work on to improve the quality of their writing based on the rubric criteria.

As teachers use lessons created or enhanced by Curipod in their classrooms with their students, the AI system will also measure student analytics to showcase engagement and accuracy within the lesson. This real time data assists teachers in understanding individual student progress but also in understanding which types of questions students can easily complete or which they are challenged by to ensure the validity of the questions being used. These analytics assist teachers greatly and maximize their productivity in the classroom to best meet the diverse needs of the students in the classroom.

Curipod offers teachers a unique opportunity to increase student participation and engagement with interactive activities embedded in presentations. Teachers can use the AI tool to generate lessons based on topics, grade levels, and testing criteria or upload their materials to generate these exciting presentations. Students will benefit from the lively discussions that stem from the use of these interactive activities as well as the varying opportunities to showcase their knowledge on literacy content. Teachers can maximize their productivity and differentiation by utilizing the AI-powered analytics and personalized feedback from Curipod to support diverse learning needs in the classroom. Overall, Curipod provides an AI experience that is beneficial to both teachers and students for literacy instruction.

Each of the AI tools described above allows teachers to easily address the everyday tasks of teachers in more efficient and personalized ways. Eliminating the tedious tasks teachers endure every day provides teachers the ability to allocate more time spent supporting students academically, socially, and emotionally. The advancement of adaptive learning tools and automated tutoring systems gives teachers the ability to differentiate instruction to the fullest potential. Since there is a growing trend of in-service teachers using AI in their classrooms, it is imperative that PSTs are well-prepared to effectively, appropriately, and critically use these technology tools in classrooms fo their own. Additionally, PSTs should be given explicit, ongoing instruction regarding which AI tools to use and when, including guidance on selecting tools based on the type of output desired. For example, choosing text generators for drafting lesson plans, image generators for visual aids, or data analysis tools for interpreting student assessment results. Teacher educators, in both content courses and in field-based courses, have the power to model the selection of individual tools to showcase which AI platforms work best for given desired outcomes while simultaneously thinking aloud a critical analysis of outputs. It is also critical for teacher educators to introduce the AI tools like the ones provided above to their PSTs across various contexts, grade levels and content areas. Teacher educators should not only introduce these tools but also provide continuous professional development or training to PSTs as AI continues to evolve and new tools are made available. Be embedding this learning throughout their preparation, PSTs can develop the critical habits of mind needed to adapt to future technology while maintain a student-centered, pedagogically sound approach. See Table 1 below for a snapshot of each of the AI tools and features delineated in the section above.

Table 1. Selected AI Tools and Features

AI Tools							
	ChatGPT	**Magic School. ai**	**Brisk**	**Perplexity**	**Canva**	**Diffit**	**Curipod**
Feature							
Lesson Planning	✓	✓	✓	✓		✓	✓
Differentiation	✓	✓	✓	✓		✓	✓
Content Research	✓	✓	✓	✓		✓	
Assessments & Rubrics	✓	✓	✓		✓	✓	✓
Real-time Feedback	✓	✓					✓
Multimedia & Visual Content		✓	✓		✓		✓

PREPARING PSTS FOR AN AI-ENHANCED CLASSROOM

Before pre-service teachers can use each of these AI tools effectively, they need a clear understanding of what AI is and how it is intended to be used. This includes recognizing the differences between machine learning, natural language processing, and generative AI. Teacher candidates should explore key AI concepts such as data training, algorithmic decision-making, and automation. Engaging in hands-on experiences with AI-powered educational tools can help demystify the technology and build confidence in its use. This section provides an overview of AI literacy, focusing on foundational knowledge, practical applications, and ethical considerations.

AI Literacy 101: Teaching Pre-service Educators to Think Critically

AI literacy is essential for pre-service teachers to effectively integrate AI into their teaching practice (Guan et al., 2025). In order to help pre-service teachers to become literate, teacher educators not only have to explain and show AI tools and their usage but also model how to critically analyze the outputs and how to ethically use AI tools. It is a multi-faceted approach to being considered as AI literate. Being able to understand the responsible use of AI in educational settings will create an ethical mindset in pre-service teachers as they navigate effective uses of AI in educational contexts. As AI-driven tools become more prevalent in classrooms, educators must understand not only how these technologies function but also their implications for teaching and learning (van der Berg & Plessis, 2023).

A crucial aspect of AI literacy for PSTs is the ability to critically evaluate AI-generated content. It is essential that future educators have the ability to assess the reliability, accuracy, bias, and appropriateness of AI outputs for student learning. This involves understanding the data AI systems rely on, recognizing biases, and ensuring the content aligns with effective and engaging pedagogical practices. Pre-service teachers should be trained to question how AI-generated content is created and how it fits into diverse classroom settings. Structured activities, such as comparing AI-generated lesson plans with human-created ones or evaluating AI-recommended strategies with best practices, assist future educators in developing a critical lens for AI use, as outlined previously in this chapter.

AI tools in education often present challenges such as bias, reliability issues, and a steep learning curve, contributing to pre-service teachers' hesitations and anxieties. Many future educators express concerns about AI's effectiveness in creating lesson plans or materials (Wang et al., 2024). To address these anxieties, teacher educators must guide pre-service teachers in critically evaluating AI outputs, particularly in detecting biases and inaccuracies. AI systems are only as unbiased as the data they are trained on, so understanding and recognizing these biases is crucial for ensuring the accuracy and fairness of AI-generated content. Additionally, AI-generated "hallucinations" can undermine the quality of instruction. Pre-service teachers must develop the skills to identify and correct these inaccuracies to ensure the content, materials, and instructional strategies used in their classrooms are reliable and accurate.

Ethical Considerations: Establishing Boundaries

The ethical implications of AI in education raise complex questions about fairness, privacy, and accountability. Teachers and pre-service educators must be prepared to address concerns related to data privacy, algorithmic bias, and AI's role in decision-making. For example, the use of student data by AI systems must comply with privacy regulations such as the Family Educational Rights and Privacy Act (FERPA) to ensure confidentiality. AI systems must be transparent and secure, and they must prioritize student safety with clear protocols for data handling and consent.

Algorithmic bias is another concern, as AI systems may unintentionally reinforce inequalities based on race, gender, socioeconomic status, or disability. Pre-service educators must be trained to assess AI tools for fairness and equity, ensuring that these technologies do not disproportionately affect any student group. Furthermore, AI's role in decision-making, such as grading or identifying at-risk students, should not replace professional judgment. Establishing ethical guidelines for AI use in educational settings is essential, and ongoing professional development for educators is necessary to navigate these challenges responsibly.

Clearly, AI can significantly enhance teaching and learning when used responsibly. By training pre-service teachers to critically evaluate AI outputs and consider ethical issues such as bias, privacy, and fairness, we can ensure that AI serves as a tool to support, rather than replace, the human connections central to effective education. To better understand how pre-service teachers perceive AI and its potential in the classroom, it is important to explore their perspectives on how these tools can be integrated into their future teaching practices.

PRE-SERVICE TEACHERS SPEAK: AI THROUGH THEIR EYES

As pre-service teachers (PSTs) begin their careers, they often perceive AI as a valuable tool for managing lesson planning and classroom challenges. Through their eyes, AI offers the ability to automate tasks, boost creativity, and support differentiated instruction, allowing them to focus on developing their teaching skills (Guan et al., 2025; MacDowell et al., 2024). This section explores the positive perceptions PSTs have of AI and how they believe it can help them build a strong foundation for their teaching practices.

The Perks: AI as a Timesaving, Creativity-Boosting Tool

As PSTs engage more with AI tools, they begin to see the benefits that come with their use. PSTs begin to understand the time-saving aspect of AI use as they explore how to use it within their everyday activities of lesson planning. PSTs find AI to be a time-saving tool that can help with idea generation, content understanding, and resource creation (Guan et al., 2025). Using AI to assist in generating ideas for lesson themes, activities, or assessments assists PSTs in having a variety of different activities within their classrooms to keep learning lively and exciting for their students. AI can also be used in resource creation for PSTs to maximize their time. The creation of presentations, student materials, and assessments is a benefit to PSTs using AI as it takes a time-consuming process and quickly streamlines it. PSTs can then review the created materials and make adjustments to best suit the needs of their classrooms and standards. PSTs can use these to assist in their understanding of content standards and ensure they are delivering accurate information to their students. AI can also assist in classroom management procedures, such as creating seating charts to free up time for teachers to engage in more critical thinking for their diverse classroom needs.

AI generated materials can also inspire creativity within teachers by providing alternate activities and ideas for lesson plans. Since AI-generated materials are pulled from multiple sources, teachers are able to be exposed to multiple ideas for one standard or topic instantly. This eliminates the time required to search through multiple websites or books for innovative ways to teach literacy content. AI can also generate specific visuals to match presentations or literacy content to enhance the meaning of the skill or text. These are incredibly timesaving for teachers as it often takes hours to create and manipulate an image to match perfectly with the text.

These AI generated materials can also be differentiated based on student needs. Teachers can prompt the AI application to change the grade levels, add images, or include text to voice when needed for materials. It can also create authentic, real-life examples to connect learning on a personal level and help students apply skills in real-world situations. AI can also generate real-world simulations through AR and VR to enhance PST learning in classroom settings when delivering literacy instruction. Differentiation and engaging in real-life scenarios are often challenging, and AI provides ways to alleviate the stressors and time constraints.

AI provides teachers, both in-service and pre-service, with the ability to promote creativity and maximize efficiency. AI assistance in creating materials, developing an understanding of content, and addressing differentiation assists teachers in several time consuming tasks that are required in their everyday lives in the classroom. Each is equally important but takes a considerable amount of time and brain power. AI allows teachers to ease the thought process behind this by creating materials that teachers can then critically analyze for accuracy, developmental appropriateness, and effectiveness in their classroom contexts.

The Challenges: Limitations of AI in Education

While AI has significant potential to enhance education by streamlining tasks, personalizing learning, and analyzing data, several concerns must be addressed. PSTs must understand that AI cannot replace the human interactions that are essential for teaching and learning, such as face-to-face communication, which develops both social-emotional and collaboration skills. It is important for PSTs to come to the realization that over-reliance on AI could limit their opportunities for critical thinking, discussion, and mentorship, diminishing relationships with their students. While AI tools can be powerful supports in lesson planning and instructional design, there is a risk that PSTs may become overly reliant on them, using AI-generated content without critically evaluating its accuracy or alignment with student needs. Overdependence on AI can also hinder the development of essential pedagogical decision-making skills and limit opportunities for creative, responsive teaching rooted in authentic classroom contexts. Additionally, some PSTs have concerns about AI's potential to automate the everyday functions of a classroom, which they believe could result in job displacement for educators.

Pre-service teachers have also raised concerns about the challenges related to bias, privacy, and accessibility. Many AI tools require reliable internet access, up-to-date devices, and digital literacy skills that may not be equally available to all PSTs or the students they serve. These disparities raise important questions about digital equity, as students in under-resourced schools may have limited exposure to or benefit from AI-enhanced instruction. Since AI systems use data from all parts of the internet, they can perpetuate societal biases if trained on biased data, leading to inequitable treatment of students. PSTs know that ensuring fairness in the outputs requires continuous monitoring and adjustments to prompts in the AI tools as well as a critical eye. Privacy concerns also arise for PSTs as AI tools collect and analyze student data, fueling the need for confidentiality to avoid unauthorized access or data breaches. Since confidentiality is a large part of the educational experience, this is a fear among PSTs (Karataş & Yüce, 2024).

PSTs must also be able to identify inaccuracies in outputs generated by various AI tools, often referred to as "hallucinations," to ensure high-quality, trustworthy instructional practices that are reliable and accurate. Ethical concerns, such as algorithmic bias, data privacy, and AI's role in decision-making, require PSTs to have a comprehensive understanding of clear guidelines and transparency to ensure their responsible and ethical use of AI tools and features in their future classrooms.

Another concern raised is that of necessary training and potential financial burdens associated with the AI tools. While most AI tools out there offer free versions, there are benefits to paying for upgraded or premium versions of the AI tools, such as enhanced tools or more accurate outputs with current information and news being searched. Pre-service and in-service teachers understand the strain of financial commitments and feeling the need to pay for upgraded accounts can be a challenge. Along with that is the need to complete additional trainings to better understand the free and paid tools within each AI tool as they are all vastly different in their interface. These trainings can range from online videos to watch to in-person trainings offered by professionals in school settings, all of which can be a challenge to schedule or afford depending on the training.

LOOKING AHEAD: THE FUTURE OF AI IN TEACHER EDUCATION

The future of AI in education holds exciting possibilities, with ongoing advancements that promise to reshape how teachers are trained and how instruction is delivered in classrooms (Kamalov et al., 2023; Karataş, F. & Yüce, 2024). One of the most promising trends is the continued development of AI for personalized learning. As AI systems become more sophisticated, they will be able to tailor lessons and resources to meet the unique needs, preferences, and learning styles of each student. This has the potential to enable teachers to provide highly individualized support, ensuring that every student receives the optimal level of challenge and assistance to succeed.

In addition to personalized learning, AI tools are also expected to significantly adapt and improve the feedback process in education. Real-time, actionable feedback powered by AI can help both students and teachers identify areas for improvement instantly. For example, AI tools could provide teachers with immediate insights into student performance during lessons, helping them adjust instruction in the moment to best address gaps in understanding. Similarly, students have the opportunity to receive instant feedback on assignments and assessments, allowing them to track their progress and make corrections before moving forward. This constant, real-time feedback loop could significantly enhance the learning experience and result in a more proactive, growth-oriented classroom environment.

Another exciting development lies in AI's potential to enhance data analytics in education. With the ability to analyze large volumes of data, AI has the ability to help educators gain deeper insights into student learning patterns and engagement levels and even predict academic outcomes. By identifying trends and patterns in student performance, AI can support teachers in making data-driven decisions about instructional practices, identify students who may need additional or adjusted assistance, and even predict future performance. This level of insight could empower teachers to be more proactive in their approach to teaching, ensuring that every student's unique needs are met.

In teacher preparation specifically related to literacy, AI, through AR and VR, has the potential to play a role in simulating classroom scenarios, allowing preservice teachers to experience a wide range of teaching challenges and student interactions in a risk-free environment overseen by their instructors. Advanced AI simulations have the power to replicate diverse classroom settings, from managing student behavior to responding to different literacy needs, giving future educators the opportunity to practice and refine their skills before stepping into a real classroom. As AI technology evolves, these advancements have the potential to make teacher preparation programs more flexible, personalized, and efficient while also equipping educators with the tools they need to provide the highest quality instruction in safe, online spaces.

NEXT STEPS: PREPARING FUTURE TEACHERS FOR AN AI-DRIVEN WORLD

As AI continues to become a driving force in technology, teacher preparation programs must continue to commit to exploring and learning more about the different applications and their uses within and across educational contexts. Doing so allows them to best equip pre-service teachers (PSTs) with the knowledge and skills that come with responsible use of AI in the classroom. A focus not only on practical uses but also critical analysis is key to ensuring PSTs are ethically using AI within their educational practices. Teacher preparation programs can utilize hands-on activities and insightful dialogue to prepare PSTs in this effective use of AI.

Through these hands-on activities, PSTs can learn how to critically analyze AI-generated content for accuracy, bias, developmental appropriateness, and effectiveness. These areas are key to ensuring the activities that are AI-generated are going to be successful in their respective classrooms. By teaching these critical analysis skills, PSTs will begin to build their knowledge of ethical and responsible uses of AI. Teacher preparation programs can engage in insightful dialogue that highlights data privacy and bias when prompting in AI applications, disclosure of AI use, and the overall purpose behind AI usage. Focusing on critical analysis and ethical uses gives PSTs a solid foundation to ensure the responsible use of AI to enhance their teaching abilities versus replacing them with AI applications.

As AI continues to evolve, teacher preparation programs must acknowledge these advancements and stay adaptable, ensuring they grow alongside emerging technologies. AI applications and uses are constantly changing and growing, and PSTs need to be aware of this fast-paced world. A constant update of information, applications, and uses will be key in keeping PSTs up to date on AI and its uses within educational contexts. In this ever-changing space, creating a culture of risk-free exploration and innovative uses of AI will be beneficial in helping PSTs navigate its place in the classroom. This further allows PSTs to see the truly game-changing role AI can play in the classroom through its efficiency and student engagement opportunities.

AI integration in the classroom is not a thing of the future; it is here and now. Pre-service teachers need to be prepared not only for how to use AI tools to maximize their time and efficiency but also for how to use them to create engaging, inclusive, and high-achieving lessons for their classrooms. Literacy education can greatly benefit from the lessons, resources, and feedback that the AI-powered tools listed in this chapter describe. By modeling and guiding our PSTs through their learning of these tools and discussing ethical implications (Ayanwale et al., 2024b), we are creating a generation of teachers who embrace what AI has to offer and preparing them to continue the journey of AI integration in their future classrooms.

CONCLUSION

As we conclude this chapter, it is clear that integrating AI into the planning and delivery of literacy lessons for young learners can both enhance and challenge the work of pre-service teachers. Just as Dr. Smith demonstrated in her Language Arts methods class, the process of planning a read-aloud lesson can be supported by AI tools that offer fresh perspectives and new ways to engage students. However, the real value comes not from relying on these tools entirely but from using them as collaborators in the creative process.

Dr. Smith's students began with hesitation, unsure of how to balance technology with their own teaching expertise. By the end of the session, they were energized, having discovered how AI could assist with brainstorming, lesson structuring, and differentiating instruction. But, as they learned, the use of AI was never the focal point, it was their own knowledge, creativity, and commitment to their students' literacy development that ultimately shaped their lessons.

In this way, technology can serve as a powerful ally in elementary literacy instruction, not as a replacement for the expertise and care that teachers bring to the classroom. By critically engaging with the tools at their disposal, pre-service teachers are able to build lessons that are engaging, responsive, and grounded in the needs of their diverse learners. The experience in Dr. Smith's classroom is a reminder that the blend of human expertise and technological support can lead to exciting innovations in literacy instruction, empowering future educators to make a lasting impact on their students' literacy journeys.

REFERENCES

Abdulayeva, A., Nazym, Z., Yerlan, A., & Farzana, B. (2025). Fostering AI literacy in pre-service physics teachers: Inputs from training and co-variables. *Frontiers in Education, 10*, 1505420. Advance online publication. DOI: 10.3389/feduc.2025.1505420

Abrams, Z. (2025). Classrooms are adapting to the use of artificial intelligence. *Monitor on Psychology, 56*(1). https://www.apa.org/monitor/2025/01/trends-classrooms-artificial-intelligence

Ayanwale, M. A., Adelana, O. P., Molefi, R. R., Adeeko, O., & Ishola, A. M. (2024b). Examining artificial intelligence literacy among pre-service teachers for future classrooms. *Computers and Education Open*, *6*, 100179. Advance online publication. DOI: 10.1016/j.caeo.2024.100179

Ayanwale, M. A., Frimpong, E. K., Opesemowo, O. A. G., & Sanusi, I. T. (2024a). Exploring factors that support pre-service teachers' engagement in learning artificial intelligence. *Journal for STEM Education Research*. Advance online publication. DOI: 10.1007/s41979-024-00121-4

Bautista, A., Estrada, C., Jaravata, A. M., Mangaser, L. M., Narag, F., Soquila, R., & Asuncion, R. J. (2024). Preservice teachers' readiness towards integrating AI-based tools in education: A TPACK approach. Educational Process. *International Journal (Toronto, Ont.)*, *13*(3), 40–68. DOI: 10.22521/edupij.2024.133.3

Brisk Labs Co. (2025). Brisk teaching [Large language model]. https://www.briskteaching.com/

Canva, A. I. (n.d.). Canva [Large language model]. https://www.canva.com/your-apps/ai-powered

Carreon, A., Criss, C., & Mosher, M. (2023). Classroom virtual reality for students with disabilities: A preliminary guide to available virtual content. *Journal of Special Education Technology*, *0*(0), 1–8. DOI: 10.1177/01626434231170593

Curipod, A. S. (2025). Curipod [Large language model]. https://curipod.com/

Diffit. (n.d.-a). Diffit for teachers [Large language model]. https://web.diffit.me/

Diffit. (n.d.-b). Diffit in the ELA classroom. https://docs.google.com/presentation/d/16a8ZTmea0AWCGnljjDTmnZrqMA5EAxHkvQfz6yjJM5Q/edit?slide=id.g2ee86109b2d_0_0#slide=id.g2ee86109b2d_0_0

Guan, L., Zhang, Y., & Gu, M. M. (2025). Pre-service teachers preparedness for AI-integrated education: An investigation from perceptions, capabilities, and teachers' identity changes, Computers and Education. *Artificial Intelligence*, *8*, 100341. Advance online publication. DOI: 10.1016/j.caeai.2024.100341

Kamalov, F., Santandreu Calonge, D., & Gurrib, I. (2023). New era of artificial intelligence in education: *Towards a Sustainable Multifaceted Revolution. Sustainability (Basel)*, *15*(16), 12451. DOI: 10.3390/su151612451

Karataş, F., & Yüce, E. (2024). AI and the future of teaching: Pre-service teachers' reflections on the use of artificial intelligence in open and distributed learning. *International Review of Research in Open and Distance Learning*, *25*(3), 304–325. DOI: 10.19173/irrodl.v25i3.7785

MacDowell, P., Moskalyk, K., Korchinski, K., & Morrison, D. (2024). Preparing educators to teach and create with generative artificial intelligence. *Canadian Journal of Learning and Technology*, *50*(4), 1–23. Advance online publication. DOI: 10.21432/cjlt28606

MagicSchool.ai. (n.d.). MagicSchool.ai [Large language model]. https://www.magicschool.ai

Mishra, P., & Koehler, M. J. (2006). Technological Pedagogical Content Knowledge: A Framework for Teacher Knowledge. *Teachers College Record, 108*(6), 1017-1054. (Original work published 2006)DOI: 10.1111/j.1467-9620.2006.00684.x

National Geographic Society. (2025). National geographic kids. https://kids.nationalgeographic.com/

Open, A. I. (2023). ChatGPT (Mar 14 edition) [Large language model]. https://chat.openai.com/chat

Perplexity, A. I. (2023). Perplexity [Large language model]. https://www.perplexity.ai

Rubin, A. (2012). *Dragons love tacos*. ENH Penguin Young Readers Group.

Rubin, A. (2013). *Secret pizza party*. Dial Books for Young Readers.

Sanusi, I. T., Ayanwale, M. A., & Tolorunleke, A. E. (2024). Investigating pre-service teachers' artificial intelligence perception from the perspective of planned behavior theory. *Computers and Education: Artificial Intelligence*, *6*, 100202. Advance online publication. DOI: 10.1016/j.caeai.2024.100202

Tarisayia, K. S. (2024). A theoretical framework for interrogating the integration of artificial intelligence in education. *Research on Education and Media, 16*(1), 38-44. DOI: 10.2478/rem-2024-0006

Treve, M. (2024). Integrating Artificial Intelligence in Education: Impacts on Student Learning and Innovation. *International Journal of Vocational Education and Training Research, 10*(2), 61–69. DOI: 10.11648/j.ijvetr.20241002.14

U.S. Department of Education, Office of Educational Technology. (2023). *Artificial intelligence and future of teaching and learning: Insights and recommendations.* Author.

Wang, K., Ruan, Q., Zhang, X., Fu, C., & Duan, B. (2024). Pre-service teachers' genAI anxiety, technology self-efficacy, and TPACK: Their structural relations with behavioral intention to design genAI-assisted teaching. *Behavioral Sciences (Basel, Switzerland), 14*(5), 373. DOI: 10.3390/bs14050373 PMID: 38785864

Zhang, C., Schießl, J., Plößl, L., Hofmann, L., & Gläser-Zikuda, M. (2023). Acceptance of artificial intelligence among pre-service teachers: A multigroup analysis. *International Journal of Educational Technology in Higher Education, 20*(1), 49. DOI: 10.1186/s41239-023-00420-7

KEY TERMS AND DEFINITIONS

Brisk: AI tool that assists educators in automating tasks in classrooms with single system integration.

Canva (AI): AI tool that creates innovative, appealing materials like presentations, videos, and handouts.

ChatGPT: AI chatbot that provides tailored outputs based on prompts from users.

Curipod: AI tool that creates interactive presentations for use in the classroom.

Diffit: AI tool that assists educators in differentiating content and materials.

Generative AI: Computer systems designed to perform tasks that typically require human intelligence.

Magicschool.ai: AI tool that assists educators in the creation of materials and tools that ease teachers' workloads.

Perplexity: AI tool that ensures current and comprehensive research with cited sources.

Productivity: Efficient use of time to accomplish tasks.

PSTs: Pre-service teachers enrolled in an initial certification program.

Chapter 8
Empowering Learner Autonomy for Developing Writing Skills Through AI-Enhanced Reflective Journals

Sena Könez
https://orcid.org/0009-0005-3939-6350
Turkish National Defense University, Istanbul, Turkey

Selami Aydin
https://orcid.org/0000-0003-1614-874X
Istanbul Medeniyet University, Turkey

ABSTRACT

This study aims to investigate the impact of traditional versus reflective journals, enhanced with artificial intelligence (AI), on developing learner autonomy in writing skills among EFL learners. Following a quasi-experimental design, the data collection involved 36 college students in an English preparatory program. A demographic information questionnaire and the Learner Autonomy Scale (LAS) were used to collect the data. While the control group kept traditional reflective journals after each writing task, the experimental group wrote AI-assisted reflective journals using AI chatbot software for five weeks. The findings revealed that traditional reflective journaling had a negligible impact on students' autonomy. However, the implementation of AI-enhanced reflective journals showed a noticeable change in students' self-evaluation skills.

DOI: 10.4018/979-8-3373-1122-7.ch008

INTRODUCTION

Writing has an essential place in English as a foreign language (EFL) teaching and learning since it serves as a versatile and indispensable tool, crucial for facilitating global communication (Marlina & Giri, 2014), conveying diverse messages (Celce-Murcia, 2001), and supporting various objectives, including professional, academic, and social contexts (Cook, 2014). Improving writing skills is correlated with overall language development (Hyland, 2003), as it supports the development of other skills, such as listening, speaking, and reading (Javed et al., 2013). Regarding the development of writing skills, learner autonomy plays a significant role. It enables learners to develop personalized learning strategies that they can adapt to align with their specific needs and interests (Dam, 1995). It can also boost learners' motivation and eagerness for learning by allowing them to make decisions about their language proficiency (Littlejohn, 1985), as notably developing abilities such as self-discipline and responsibility can enhance their efficacy as productive learners when writing. Regarding the fostering of learner autonomy, reflective journal writing is essential. For instance, keeping a reflective journal provides an opportunity to foster learner autonomy by encouraging learners to take charge of their learning paths independently (Çakıcı, 2015). It is a useful tool that helps learners engage in reflective thinking as they assess their thoughts, activities, and experiences (Kim & Park, 2019). The use of AI-supported reflective tools in developing EFL writing skills may offer a range of opportunities that can benefit both learners and instructors. These tools can provide instant feedback as well as individual guidance on how to use certain words or phrases correctly in a sentence; hence, they are helpful in developing students' writing skills (Okonkwo, 2011). Moreover, they can increase student participation throughout their time in class by providing an all-inclusive and dynamic writing platform (Sharma & Sharma, 2022), which retains learners' interest and boosts their motivation for writing.

While developing learner autonomy can help learners improve their writing skills, several potential issues must be addressed. To begin with, learners may encounter challenges when they lack the ability to make independent decisions. Moreover, their autonomy is unlikely to develop without learners' desire to take responsibility for their education (Borg & Al-Busaidi, 2012). According to Yildiz and Yucedal (2020), the absence of motivation and interest is another factor that hinders the development of learner autonomy. Considering that developing learner autonomy relies on the presence of motivation in learners, without motivation, learners are likely to experience failure in their efforts to become autonomous. Another key issue is that some learners may lack the confidence to engage in more active learning, which can lead to a passive and dependent learning style. Considering the aforementioned problems, AI-enhanced reflective journals may provide possible effective solutions to them. First, such reflective journaling can help minimize problems associated with learners' limited knowledge of reflective writing, as it provides clear directions and leads that make it easier for them to engage in reflective practice (Okonkwo, 2011). In addition, the journals would cater to different learning styles and provide individualized assistance to each learner, tailored to their specific needs, making it more accessible to a wider range of students (Zheng et al., 2019). Finally, utilizing artificial intelligence (AI) in reflective writing can effectively address the challenges related to motivation and interest, as it enhances learner engagement and satisfaction throughout the process (Pardo et al., 2019). However, the impact of AI-enhanced reflective journals on learner autonomy within the scope of writing skills among EFL learners remains an unanswered question within the research context, as evident in the research synthesis presented below. Before presenting the results of previous studies, a theoretical framework should also be drawn.

THEORETICAL BACKGROUND

Writing development in the EFL context involves cognitive, affective, and metacognitive features (Hyland, 2003). Effective writing instruction goes beyond technical proficiency, enabling students to take an active role in self-assessment and personal growth. Two associated concepts, reflection and learner autonomy, play critical roles in this context. This chapter conceptualizes writing development as a process facilitated by students' ability to reflect on their experiences and take ownership of their learning processes, with AI acting as a facilitating tool.

Various definitions and approaches to specific terms and concepts require explanation within the context of the current study. According to Zamel (1982), *writing* can be defined as a cognitive activity in which learners self-reflect and explore multiple interpretations to convey their intended meanings. Holec (1981) proposes a definition of *learner autonomy* in a report to the Council of Europe, which has since become mostly agreed upon and frequently referenced: "the ability to take charge of one's learning". According to Dewey (1933), *reflection* is the deliberate and comprehensive examination of a thought or presumed knowledge, considering the supporting evidence and the potential outcomes it may lead to. Russel and Norvig (2010) refer to *AI* as the ability of machines to show human-like thinking and rational actions.

Writing development in EFL is a complex process that involves linguistic competence, cognitive strategies, and sociocultural awareness (Hyland, 2003). It is unique compared to native language writing because it requires learners to confront more challenges regarding language structure, vocabulary use, and audience expectations (Grabe & Kaplan, 1996). Earlier cognitive models, such as the Process Approach

(Zamel, 1982), assumed that writing is a recursive process involving planning, drafting, revising, and editing. This perspective views writing as a problem-solving activity that is enhanced by metacognitive regulation, a skill that directly relates to the development of learner autonomy. While students self-monitor and adjust their writing processes, they assume greater responsibility for their learning, laying the foundation for autonomous behavior. Sociocultural theory (Vygotsky, 1978) broadened the understanding of EFL writing by emphasizing the role of social interaction and mediated learning. Not only does improvement in writing occur through individual practice, but it is also contended that it can occur through cooperative conversation, peer negotiation, and engagement with cultural tools. Reflection, at this point, serves as a mediator between internalized knowledge and social learning. Reflective activities, such as journaling, self-reflection, and critical reflection on feedback, enable learners to evaluate their progress, make informed decisions, and adjust their strategies, thereby encouraging both writing proficiency and learner independence (Kim & Park, 2019). Writing development, therefore, is not an isolated skill acquisition process but an evolving practice nurtured through reflective, autonomous learning. In EFL contexts, where writing presents unique linguistic and cognitive challenges, fostering this interconnection is particularly crucial for empowering learners to become independent and self-aware writers.

Several different theories have shaped writing instruction. Hodges (2017) identifies four primary theories that are fundamental to writing instruction. These theories include the Cognitive Process Theory, the Sociocultural Theory, the Social Cognitive and Self-Efficacy Theory, and the Ecological Theory. *The Cognitive Process Theory* suggests that writing requires cognitive processes such as generating ideas, preparation, structuring, and creatively composing. It underlies the understanding of writing as a recursive, cognitively demanding process that can be enhanced through regular reflection and feedback. When learners reflect on these processes and evaluate their writing, they build a deeper understanding of their own strategies and areas for improvement, enhancing both writing proficiency and autonomous learning. For example, students can use brainstorming techniques, outlines, and multiple drafts to progressively refine their essays, embodying the recursive nature of cognitive writing processes. The second theory, introduced by Vygotsky (1978), is the Sociocultural Theory of writing, which emphasizes the significance of motivational, affective, and social factors as key elements of the writing process (Hodges, 2017). In classroom practice, this is evident when students engage in peer review, group writing, or collaborative editing workshops, thereby acquiring knowledge through social interaction and dialogue. The concept of social cognitive and self-efficacy theory in the context of writing is related to the interaction between mental, behavioral, personal, and external factors that influence motivation and actions (Bandura, 1993). For example, teachers can gradually assign more challenging writing tasks to help students develop a sense of self-efficacy in their ability to self-regulate and improve their writing skills. According to Cooper (1986), *the Ecological Theory* proposes that the idea of "an ecology of writing" extends far beyond the close surroundings of a single writer. Practically, this might involve persuading students to write texts for a real audience, such as posting readers on personal blogs, thereby helping create an understanding that writing exists within rich and dynamic social networks. Together, these perspectives highlight that writing development is deeply intertwined with learners' cognitive regulation, social engagement, and self-evaluative abilities, which appear to be closely linked to learner autonomy —a crucial factor in writing development.

Learner autonomy has its foundations in several prominent educational theories, including Constructivism, Critical Theory, Humanism, and Experiential Learning Theory. In the first theory, *Constructivism* can be defined as the concept that learners actively build knowledge for themselves (Hein, 1991). It views learners as active agents constructing their knowledge, implying that autonomy is necessary for sustained writing development. This could involve letting students choose subjects for writing on their own, which can make the learning process self-constructed around their interests and knowledge level. The second one is *Critical Theory, a theoretical framework within the humanities and language studies, which* suggests that the learning process includes active involvement within the social environment. In practice, learners can be encouraged to write critical essays analyzing societal issues to enhance language skill development and critical consciousness. Another theoretical framework regarding learner autonomy is *Humanism*, which asserts that learning is a pursuit aimed at uncovering personal significance from within, highlighting the importance of autonomy in writing education. Students can maintain reflective diaries or journals to write about their feelings, aspirations, and problems they encounter while learning English, promoting autonomy in them. Last, *the Experiential Learning Theory* describes the learning process as "the mechanisms by which knowledge is constructed via the transformation of experience" (Kolb, 1984). In practice, students would perform a reflection following a writing task, analyze how they dealt with the writing process, and identify which portion of their strategies worked well or should be reexamined for their next writing task pieces in an experiential learning cycle. This theory provides the foundation for understanding how learners transform their writing experiences into knowledge through structured reflection. Consequently, building learner autonomy is closely tied to reflective practices, enabling learners to critically analyze their thinking and learning behaviors.

Several educational theories have underscored the role of reflection in enhancing learner autonomy. Three main theoretical frameworks form the basis of reflective practice, and these frameworks were developed by some of the most prominent researchers in the field: Dewey (1933), Kolb (1984), and Boud et al. (1985). Dewey (1933) views reflection as a rationalized process. He argues that reflecting on our experiences can help us make sense of things that are confusing or difficult to understand. For instance, students can be asked to write a brief reflection on their experiences after completing some writing task, explaining what problems they faced and how they were solved. Kolb (1984) examines the components of reflection and uses them to develop the learning cycle framework. The *Experiential Learning Theory* has four phases: concrete experience, reflective observation of the new experience, abstract conceptualization, and active experimentation. In a writing class, students might complete an essay (experience), reflect on what worked (observation), develop hypotheses regarding successful writing techniques (conceptualization), and apply these strategies to the next assignment (experimentation). According to Boud et al. (1985), the emotional context of reflection is overlooked by both Dewey's and Kolb's theories. Emotions may shape how learners recall events and situations and can be interpreted differently under the influence of strong emotions. Teachers may work this out by asking students to reflect on what they have learned and how they felt about the writing process, thus merging emotion with learning. These theories suggest that reflective practices are not merely cognitive exercises but holistic engagements that foster autonomy. Thus, reflection is not an ancillary activity but a core mechanism that links learner autonomy to writing development.

Emerging technologies, particularly AI, offer promising new pathways for enhancing reflection and autonomy in writing instruction. To thoroughly understand the influence of AI on language learning, two major frameworks must be examined: Activity Theory and the Technology Acceptance Model. *The Activity Theory* emerged based on Vygotsky's (1978) triangle model of subject, object, and tools regarding psychological development and was further developed by Engeström (1987). It explores the interaction between subjects and objects facilitated by tools and frames the use of AI as a mediational tool that shapes learners' interaction with writing tasks and reflective processes. AI applications act as mediational tools that enable learners to interact with their writing tasks more reflectively and autonomously. In practice, AI tools like ChatGPT serve as tools that shape how students approach writing tasks, providing them with support. Another widely recognized framework is *the Technology Acceptance Model,* which posits that user acceptance of technology is determined by perceived usefulness and ease of use, which in turn influence behavioral intentions towards using the technology (Davis, 1989). This theory informs attention to learners' perceptions of the usefulness and ease of AI tools, which influence their engagement with reflective writing activities. When user-friendly AI tools provide meaningful and personalized feedback, they can motivate learners to engage more actively in reflective writing practices, thereby fostering greater learner autonomy and enhancing writing development. For example, if students find an AI writing assistant easy to navigate and helpful for improving their essays, they are more likely to use it consistently and integrate it into their learning practices.

This chapter is grounded in an integrated theoretical framework that sees reflection, learner autonomy, and writing development as mutually reinforcing processes. Reflective practices may cultivate learners' awareness of their cognitive and emotional learning strategies, which in turn strengthens their autonomy. Greater autonomy can enable learners to take more deliberate and informed control of their writing practices, leading to deeper engagement and improved writing performance. In sum, the theoretical framework underpinning this chapter establishes a dynamic relationship among reflection, learner autonomy, and writing development, with AI tools serving as potential catalysts for enhancing these processes. By fostering deeper reflection, encouraging greater autonomy, and supporting more effective writing development, AI-enhanced reflective journals present a promising pedagogical innovation for EFL contexts.

PREVIOUS RESEARCH

Recent studies highlight the integration of direct instruction with room for reflective practice and autonomous learning. Reflective journaling, in this context, can provide learners with the tools to critically reflect on their writing processes, set specific goals, and track their progress over time. EFL learners, through the development of reflection and autonomy, may not only improve their writing abilities but also develop the self-regulatory skills necessary for lifelong language learning. Hence, fostering reflective practices and facilitating learner autonomy can be considered critical teaching practices to facilitate extensive writing development in EFL settings.

Research shows that platforms providing automated feedback and AI-based reflective tools are effective instruments for enhancing learner autonomy in engaging with writing activities. Cheng et al. (2016) investigated the impact of automated feedback on the development of reflective ability in Chinese EFL students, as reflected in their diary entries. Initially, diary entries and essays were collected from 138 Chinese undergraduates who studied English for three months. The students were divided into an experimental group (n = 82) and a control group (n = 56). The experimental group obtained automatic feedback on their reflective diaries. It was observed that the experimental group exhibited noticeable improvement in their reflectivity, whereas the control group showed no such development. In addition, learners who were more adept at analyzing reflective diaries tended to score higher grades on essays than those who did less well with this aspect. The study revealed that automated feedback could enhance students' reflective skills, and this was associated with a positive relationship to essay writing proficiency. Similarly, Cheng

(2017)employed a mixed-methods design that included reflective diaries, surveys, and interviews to investigate the impact of online automated feedback on students' diary entries in a 13-week EFL course at the college level. One hundred thirty-eight undergraduate students participated in this survey, comprising 82 students in the experimental group and 56 in the control group, which is the same sample as Cheng's (2016) study. Additionally, both sets of participants received similar training on reflective writing from the same instructor. However, the experimental group had the opportunity to use the web-based ePortfolio platform_to create online analytic feedback on their second and third reflective diaries, whereas the control group did not. The experimental group showed a notable improvement in scores throughout the reflective diaries. The data primarily confirmed the importance of online automated feedback for written reflection. Han and Sari (2022) used a quasi-experimental research design to investigate the effects of automated feedback on students' writing assessments and correctness. Data was gathered from a sample of 75 Turkish EFL students at a university. The experimental group was subjected to a combination of automated and teacher feedback, whereas the control group got feedback solely from an instructor. Data was gathered via both quantitative and qualitative methods, including pre-test/post-test writing activities, Criterion evaluation reports, and student reflections. The findings indicated that those who got both automated teacher feedback and complete teacher feedback had comparable progress in their writing grades. Nevertheless, the integration of automated teacher feedback proved to be more effective than receiving complete teacher feedback in reducing students' grammatical mistakes. The outcomes of the responses presented some clues on the automatic writing evaluation in EFL writing classes. Malik et al. (2023) aimed to explore students' opinions on the use of AI in creating academic essays. This study included 245 undergraduate students from 25 different universities in the Central and Eastern regions of Indonesia. The objective was to collect information using a Google form that would help reveal students' attitudes towards integrating AI technologies into their academic essay writing processes. According to the findings, students showed a positive reaction towards AI-powered tools for writing essays, as they recognized their strengths in areas such as grammar correction and essay organization. However, some students expressed concerns about possible outcomes related to creativity and critical thinking.

OVERVIEW OF THE CURRENT STUDY

With the recent developments in AI technologies, particularly the growing popularity of using them to enhance productive skills, there has been a significant increase in demand for AI applications in EFL education. Since the integration of

AI applications such as ChatGPT can be viewed as an innovative concept, there has been relatively limited research on these applications. While most earlier studies focused on improving writing skills or developing strategies for learner autonomy, a noticeable gap exists in the use of AI applications in writing practice, particularly in promoting learner autonomy through reflective journaling. Additionally, it is worth noting that no such research has been conducted within the Turkish EFL context. With these concerns in mind, the current study investigates how AI technology can be utilized to enhance writing skills and enrich the learning experiences of EFL learners. It also highlights the potential of AI-supported reflective journals to promote learner autonomy and evaluates the contribution of this method to the development of reflective writing. Therefore, this study aims to answer the following research questions:

1. Does the use of traditional reflective journals contribute to developing learner autonomy in writing skills among EFL learners?
2. Does the use of AI-enhanced reflective journals contribute to developing learner autonomy in writing skills among EFL learners?
3. Is there a difference between the use of traditional and AI-enhanced reflective journals regarding developing learner autonomy in writing skills among EFL learners?

METHOD

Research Design

This study primarily examines the impact of AI-enhanced reflective journals on learner autonomy in EFL writing. Thus, it is designed based on research conducted with specific participants and settings to address a particular real-life issue. The study employs an analytical approach, breaking down data into components and linking them to create a comprehensive understanding of the current concept of learner autonomy. There is a deductive purpose in investigating whether using AI-enhanced reflective journals in EFL classes is efficient in promoting learner autonomy, as this type of reflective journaling has several advantages in developing EFL writing skills. Furthermore, since the current study will focus on examining the results of specific and controlled procedures provided to subjects, the research design can be regarded as experimental, in which the outcomes of these procedures administered to participants are typically divided into groups (Selinger & Shohamy, 1989). Moreover, it employs a particular kind of experimental design, a quasi-experimental design, in which the experimental and control groups are selected from pre-established groups, such as classes or settings, rather than participants being randomly allocated to groups (Creswell, 2014).

Participants

The study involved 36 students enrolled in the English preparatory program at the School of Foreign Languages of a foundation university in Turkey. All participants were native speakers of Turkish and EFL learners at the intermediate (B1) level, as defined by the Common European Framework of Reference (CEFR) standards. Male participants comprised 17 of the participants (47.22%), while there were 19 female participants (52.78%). The mean age of the participants was 18.83 years, with ages ranging from 18 to 21. Regarding the departments of the participants, 18 participants (50%) were from the Faculty of Health Sciences, and the other half were from the Faculty of Engineering. Eighteen participants were from the Physiotherapy and Rehabilitation Department (50%), 16 participants were from Software Engineering (44.4%), and 2 of them were from Industrial Engineering (5.6%). Students whose department courses are in English take the English proficiency exam before starting their education at the preparatory school. If they get under 60 points out of 100, they must follow a comprehensive English language curriculum in which all classes are conducted in English after taking the placement exam. Their placement in classes is based on the levels suggested by their achievement results in the exam before starting the first module. They receive a total of 23 hours of English instruction over the course of one week. The core curriculum is derived from a coursebook selected by the department and covers all aspects of language proficiency, including vocabulary, grammar, listening, reading, writing, and speaking. Additionally, students were provided with writing guides that they were expected to follow throughout class time. Due to their availability, two classes that had already been present were selected for the research using convenience sampling. Furthermore, a focus group study was conducted to explore some underlying reasons behind the observed results. Six participants from each group were chosen at random for a 30-minute session held separately. The participants were evenly divided by gender, half male and half female. The participants' ages ranged from 18 to 20 years, with an average age of 18.75 years.

Tools

A background questionnaire and the Learner Autonomy Scale (LAS), developed by Orakcı and Gelişli (2017), were used to collect data for the research. Additionally, a focus group interview was conducted with 12 participants from both groups. The background questionnaire was used to collect demographic data, such as the participants' ages, genders, departments, and proficiency levels in English. The LAS, a validated instrument specifically designed to measure learner autonomy, consisted of a five-point Likert Scale with 14 items, and participants were asked to respond based on their autonomy in English language learning. A scale was used for each statement to demonstrate the degree of agreement, ranging from one to five as follows: 1 = strongly disagree, 2 = disagree, 3 = neutral, 4 = agree, and 5 = strongly agree. The items in the LAS were tested for construct validity and reliability through exploratory and confirmatory factor analyses, with certain items being reverse-coded to capture nuances in responses related to learner autonomy. A high score on the LAS indicated a greater degree of learner autonomy, while a low score suggested a lower level of autonomy. Regarding validity and reliability, the percentage of variance explained by the scale was 74%, indicating a high level of reliability, as evidenced by its reliability coefficient of .97. Therefore, it is a reliable and valid instrument for measuring learners' autonomy in writing English. Last, a focus group interview involving 12 participants—six participants from each group—was conducted as part of the study. To capture genuine and unrestrained opinions, participants from the control and experimental groups were interviewed separately, with each session lasting around 30 minutes. The interview consisted of eight questions designed to explore participants' views on reflective writing and autonomous learning. The researcher carefully recorded each participant's responses during these face-to-face interview sessions. All personal information concerning the participants was anonymized and kept confidential.

Procedure

The foundation university at which the research was intended to be carried out was notified to request confirmation following the ethical committee acceptance. Next, the participants were informed regarding the objective, significance, and process. Additionally, it was emphasized that participation in the study was voluntary and that all responses would be kept confidential. The participants were further assured that the research would be conducted anonymously and that the data collected would be used exclusively for scientific purposes. Participants' permission was requested by adding a special segment that asked for their consent at the start of the Google Forms survey, which they could view through Microsoft Teams.

The study took place during the Spring Semester of the 2023-2024 Academic Year. Initially, the control and experimental groups were selected at random from two previously formed sections. Then, the participants in both groups completed the pre-test. Subsequently, they participated in various tasks that involved writing paragraphs. The control group kept traditional reflective journals after each writing task, whereas the experimental group wrote AI-assisted reflective journals using the AI chatbot ChatGPT. In the end, both groups completed the post-test.

Following the post-tests, a focus group interview was conducted with 12 participants, including 6 participants from each group. The face-to-face interviews lasted for a total of 60 minutes. Despite following the same syllabus and studying parallel subjects and concepts from the matching materials, the two classes were taught by different teachers, as required by school policies. Therefore, measures were taken to ensure that all participants were provided with identical directions, activities, and learning resources throughout the treatment phase. Any biased remarks or prompting inquiries were avoided to eliminate the risk of potential influence. In the control group, participants kept traditional reflective journals after completing five writing practices, whereas the participants in the experimental group wrote AI-assisted reflective journals after completing the same writing exercises using the chatbot. Each group then wrote their journals on a piece of paper in their native language. The participants were instructed to write in Turkish while keeping their journals, as it would be easier for them to reflect on themselves, especially given their English level. To meet the research objectives, it was ensured that the participants in the experimental group were familiar with signing up and logging in to their ChatGPT accounts, and they were also explicitly guided on providing appropriate prompts to obtain assistance from the chatbot for writing a reflective journal. Before writing each week's journals, specific prompts were given to the AI tool. In the first step, that week's writing task and focus were shared with the tool. (Today, I learned how to write a comparison and contrast paragraph and wrote one comparing different education systems.) Then, the purpose and expectations were stated so that the AI tool could guide participants in writing reflective journals, enabling them to thoroughly reflect on their writing process and improve their writing skills. (Now provide guidance for me to write a reflective journal that allows me to revisit and reflect on the paragraph writing process and the result so that I can understand what I have achieved and what I need to achieve to improve my skills.)

Pre-Test Administration

The background questionnaire added to the LAS was provided before treatment to gather demographic information regarding the participants' departments, genders, and ages. Following the administration of the LAS, participants were required to select the most suitable option for themselves, which lasted around ten minutes. Their responses were to be based on 14 items that assessed their learner autonomy. The survey was administered in Turkish, which was consistent with the original study; therefore, it was convenient for the participants to comprehend all the items and provide an appropriate response. In addition, the instructors offered assistance and clarifications to prevent any misconceptions and ambiguity.

The Practice Phase

The writing exercises were shared as supplementary materials, and all participating students were required to compose paragraphs of between 200 and 250 words on specific IELTS subjects. They had a basic understanding of paragraph structure throughout their writing lessons, as they were taught different kinds of paragraphs, including academic, narrative, cause-and-effect, and comparison-and-contrast paragraphs. Several paragraph samples were examined in their writing booklets, and they completed various exercises designed to enhance their comprehension of content, organization, grammar, vocabulary, unity, and coherence. The practice phase lasted for five weeks, during which all participants in both the control and experimental groups followed the same tasks and procedures, as outlined in Table 1. Throughout this period, the participants participated in discussions, composed paragraphs, and received weekly instructions and feedback.

Table 1. The weekly writing tasks

Weeks	Writing Task	Focus	Procedure
Week 1	Writing an academic paragraph about a special person	How to practice the format, sentence structure and organization	Analyzing the sample paragraphs Brainstorm Outlining Writing Instructor feedback
Week 2	Writing a narrative paragraph about a memorable moment	How to identify and use time-order signals in narratives	
Week 3	Writing an academic paragraph about a favorite sport or hobby	How to identify parts of a paragraph and use transition signals	
Week 4	Writing a cause-and-effect paragraph about an asocial issue	How to use transition signals and organize causes and effects	
Week 5	Writing a comparison and contrast paragraph about two different education systems	How to identify and organize similarities and differences using appropriate transition signals	

Post-Test Administration

In the final phase, the LAS, which measures participants' autonomy level in writing English, was completed by the participants again so that any differences in their autonomy in writing after the treatment could be detected.

Data Analysis

The data collected were analyzed using IBM SPSS Statistics 29.0 software. Initial calculations were performed to determine the highest and lowest ages of the participants as well as the mean values. The participation rates and proportions by department and gender were subsequently computed. After that, the reliability coefficients were calculated using Cronbach's alpha, and the Varimax rotation was applied for factor analysis to present the overall variance values for both the pre-test and the post-test. The reliability coefficients were 0.70 for the pre-tests and 0.75 for the post-tests, as shown in Table 2. The variance percentages were 72.32 for the pre-tests and 71.44 for the post-tests, indicating satisfactory reliability and validity.

Table 2. Reliability coefficient and % of the variance of the pre-tests and post-tests

Tests	Reliability Coefficient (Cronbach's Alpha)	% of the Variance
Pre-tests	.70	72.32
Post-tests	.75	71.44

To ensure consistency across all scale items and accurately reflect the intended measurement outcomes, reverse coding was applied to items 9 and 14, aligning them with the overall measurement direction of the scale. This process involved inverting the response scale for these questions so that higher scores on these items correspond appropriately with the increased levels of the measured construct, thus maintaining consistency across all items. In addition, non-parametric tests were utilized to assess and compare the data, as the participant size did not allow for the assumption of a normal distribution. Initially, the Wilcoxon test was applied to assess if significant differences existed in learner autonomy levels between the pre-tests and post-tests within the control group. This analysis was similarly performed for the experimental group to evaluate differences resulting from the intervention. Subsequently, the Mann-Whitney U test was employed to identify any disparities in learner autonomy between the control and experimental groups.

Additionally, a focus group interview was conducted to thoroughly examine the resulting data. The interview consisted of eight questions and was conducted face-to-face with 12 participants, six from each group, lasting a total of 60 minutes. Responses from each participant were meticulously recorded and later analyzed using narrative analysis, which allowed for an in-depth exploration of the participants' stories and experiences (Riessman, 2008). The aim was to thoroughly examine views and identify distinctions between the control and experimental groups. To ensure the reliability of the findings, member checking was employed, whereby participants reviewed the interpreted data to verify accuracy and resonance with their experiences (Lincoln & Guba, 1985). Confidentiality was maintained throughout the process, with all personal information of the participants being anonymized.

RESULTS

The Effects of Traditional Reflective Journals on Learner Autonomy in Writing Skills

The Wilcoxon test was performed to assess the effects of traditional reflective journals on the learner autonomy of participants. The findings are presented in Table 3, which compares pre-test and post-test responses through paired analysis of each survey item related to learner autonomy within the control group. As indicated in the table, only one item reached the predefined significance level of .05. The first item on the scale, which measures learners' inclination to select the most appropriate activity for learning English, showed a significance level of .05. This indicates a heightened propensity among learners to choose the best-suited activity for enhancing their English skills. The notable difference between the pre-tests and post-tests suggests an increased preference for selecting the most appropriate learning activity after the intervention, with a mean rank of 5.63.

Table 3. The Wilcoxon Test for the control group (n=18)

Item	Ranks	N	Mean Rank	Sum of Ranks	Asymp. Sig. (2-tailed)
1. I would like to choose the most suitable activity to help me learn English.	Negative Ranks	8[a]	5.00	10.00	.05
	Positive Ranks	2[b]	5.63	45.00	
	Ties	8[c]			

The Effects of AI-Enhanced Reflective Journals on Learner Autonomy in Writing Skills

The Wilcoxon test was administered to the experimental group to assess the effects of AI-enhanced reflective journals on participants' learner autonomy. The results, shown in Table 4, are based on the paired comparison of each item in the pre-tests and post-tests within the experimental group. According to the table, two items demonstrated significant correlations, with their significance levels at or below the designated threshold of .05. The first item, which assessed the participants' capacity to self-evaluate their English work, was recorded at .05, indicating a marked increase in their tendency towards autonomous learning. Learners notably engaged more in evaluating their work in the writing process than previously, achieving a higher mean rank of 6.83. Additionally, the other item, which addressed concerns about learning English without teacher explanation, had a significance level of 0.02, with a mean rank of 8.50 for positive ranks, learners reported feeling more independent in their learning.

Table 4. The Wilcoxon Test for the experimental group (n=18)

Items	Ranks	N	Mean Rank	Sum of Ranks	Asymp. Sig. (2-tailed)
12. I can evaluate my work in English on my own.	Negative Ranks	3[ah]	5.50	8.50	.05
	Positive Ranks	9[ai]	6.83	57.50	
	Ties	6[aj]			
14. If the teacher does not explain something in English, I don't feel afraid that I will not be able to learn it.	Negative Ranks	10[an]	5.75	8.50	.02
	Positive Ranks	1[ao]	8.50	57.50	
	Ties	7[ap]			

Comparison of the Effects of Traditional and AI-Enhanced Reflective Journals on Learner Autonomy in Writing Skills

Table 5 presents the mean ranks, total ranks, and significance values from the initial tests of the groups. The findings show that the control group had a mean rank of 17.17, while the experimental group had a mean rank of 19.83. However, the pre-test scores between the two groups did not show a significant difference, with a significance value of .44, which is much higher than the designated significance level.

Table 5. Pre-test scores for the control and experimental groups (Mann-Whitney U Test)

	Groups	Mean Rank	Sum of Ranks	Asymp. Sig. (2-tailed)
Pre-test	Control Group	17.17	309.00	.44
	Experimental Group	19.83	357.00	

Table 6 presents the only item in which a significant difference was observed, specifically concerning participants' ability to identify their strengths in learning English. The control group had a mean rank of 15.03, whereas the experimental group had a higher mean rank of 21.97. The significance value recorded was .03, which is below the predetermined significance level, a notable difference between the groups regarding this item.

Table 6. The Mann-Whitney U Test for the pre-tests of the control and experimental groups

Item	Group	N	Mean Rank	Sum of Ranks	Asymp. Sig. (2-tailed)
6. I can identify my strengths when learning English.	Control Group	18	15.03	270.50	.03
	Experimental Group	18	21.97	395.50	

Table 7 displays the mean rank, sum of ranks, and significance value from the post-tests of the control and experimental groups. The results indicated a mean rank of 15.75 for the control group and 21.25 for the experimental group. Despite the mean rank values, the significance value of .11 suggests that there was no meaningful difference in the post-test scores between the two groups.

Table 7. Post-test scores for the control and experimental groups (Mann-Whitney U Test)

	Group	N	Mean Rank	Sum of Ranks	Asymp. Sig. (2-tailed)
Post-test	Control Group	18	15.75	283.50	.11
	Experimental Group	18	21.25	382.50	

Table 8 displays the results for three items that showed significant correlations between the control and experimental groups in the post-tests. For the item related learners' openness to consultation while learning English, the mean ranks were 15.33 for the control group and 21.67 for the experimental group, suggesting a meaningful difference with a significance value of .04. The analysis of the item on identifying weaknesses in learning English showed mean ranks of 14.83 for the control and 22.17 for the experimental, indicating a considerable difference with a significance value of .02. Finally, the item regarding the recognition of strengths in learning English recorded mean ranks of 15.03 for the control and 21.97 for the experimental, with a significance value of .03, confirming a notable difference between the two groups.

Table 8. The Mann-Whitney U Test for the post-tests of the control and experimental Groups

Items	Group	N	Mean Rank	Sum of Ranks	Asymp. Sig. (2-tailed)
3. I would like to be consulted while learning English.	Control Group	18	15.33	276.00	.04
	Experimental Group	18	21.67	390.00	
5. I can identify my weaknesses when learning English.	Control Group	18	14.83	267.00	.02
	Experimental Group	18	22.17	399.00	
6. I can identify my strengths when learning English.	Control Group	18	15.03	270.50	.03
	Experimental Group	18	21.97	395.50	

CONCLUSIONS AND DISCUSSION

Several conclusions can be drawn from the findings of the data gathered and analyzed. First, Turkish EFL learners appear to display a certain level of writing autonomy both before and after the implementation, with the participants experiencing only slight increases after the intervention. Second, keeping traditional reflective journals does not significantly influence learners' autonomy in writing skills. It is observed that this type of journal results in only minor increases in learners' autonomy, with a positive shift in their preference for choosing the most suitable activity to help them learn English. However, more items exhibited considerable differences in the use of AI-enhanced reflective journals. The self-evaluation abilities of the learners showed a noticeable change, which could be attributed to the structured feedback provided by AI, which might help learners identify specific strengths and weaknesses in their writing more clearly than traditional journals. In contrast to the traditional reflective journal's set of questions, the AI tool provided participants with diverse reflective questions tailored to each week's writing task by asking for the definition of the paragraph, thereby providing personalized and on-point feedback. The guidance provided by the tool was shaped by that week's task and participants' individual needs and expectations, but there were some basic directions the AI tool provided for participants to write their reflective journals. To focus on the writing process, it asked questions about the challenges, strategies, and what is learned during the writing process. It asked questions on plans and strategies to follow for future writing sessions. When participants interacted with the tool after writing their paragraphs and recorded their journals accordingly, this immediacy allowed them to engage with their writing while it was still cognitively fresh, thereby increasing their motivation to revise and reflect on their work. Considering participants' writing development, improved organization and coherence were observed in their paragraphs after the intervention. The structure of academic paragraphs became more logical and cohesive, partly due to the improved use of discourse markers. They also exhibited a more consistent ability to support ideas and present arguments, suggesting growth in critical thinking. In addition, there is a substantial shift in learners' feeling afraid of not being able to learn something without the teacher's explanation, which could be related to the reflective nature of the journaling process, possibly enhanced by AI's immediate feedback mechanism, which reassures students of their understanding and encourages them to tackle linguistic challenges independently. Lastly, compared to traditional reflective journals, AI-enhanced reflective journals appear to positively influence learners' preference for being consulted during the learning process. This type of journal also helps learners identify their weaknesses more effectively and better aids learners in recognizing their strengths. To sum up, although the adoption of AI-enhanced reflective journals in EFL writing presents certain advantages, it does not markedly elevate all levels of learner autonomy.

The insights from the focus group interview, conducted with six randomly chosen participants from each group, suggest that certain variables may influence the observed results. The interview questions included how keeping a reflective journal affected the participants' structure and organization of their paragraphs, as well as how it guided them to evaluate and critique their own paragraph writing, and to understand their own learning habits and preferences during this process. Participants who kept traditional reflective journals report that writing in a reflective journal provides them with a structured and organized routine that makes their learning process more consistent. However, some of them also note that this procedure is time-consuming and that teacher feedback is sufficient to improve their paragraph writing. On the other hand, those who kept AI-enhanced reflective journals state that AI-enhanced journal writing helps them understand their learning habits or preferences, which can be a result of the finding that the questions in these journals are personalized and addressed to individual needs and tendencies; although some of the participants also mention that AI sometimes becomes repetitive in its prompt patterns. To this end, it can be suggested that there is a nuanced distinction between the two types of feedback. Within this scope, it can be noted that while teacher feedback contributes to a sense of structure and routine, it is sometimes perceived as sufficient on its own. On the other hand, AI-generated feedback, through its personalized and adaptive prompts, appears to foster greater learner self-awareness and metacognitive engagement. Nevertheless, it should be noted that some participants are aware of the limitations, specifically the repetitive patterns in AI prompts, as they highlight a potential drawback in its dynamic responsiveness compared to teacher feedback.

The aforementioned theoretical frameworks directly informed the design and delivery of the current study. Kolb's (1984) Experiential Learning Theory informed the use of reflective journals to transform learners' writing experience into deeper knowledge through guided reflection augmented by AI feedback. Social Cognitive and Self-Efficacy Theory (Bandura, 1993) underpinned the focus on developing students' self-assessment abilities and reducing their dependence on teacher explanations, both of which were measured in the pre-test and post-tests for the investigation. Additionally, Activity Theory (Engeström, 1987) provided the conceptual foundation for applying AI as a tool of mediation within learning activities, while the Technology Acceptance Model (Davis, 1989) focused on the role of students' attitudes towards AI tools in terms of their impact on engagement and agency. Finally, the Cognitive Process Theory (Flower & Hayes, 1981) underpinned the view of writing as a reflective, recursive process of cognition, justifying the emphasis on iterative writing tasks combined with reflective journaling.

Pedagogical Implications

The conclusions of this study and prior research provide several pedagogical implications about the influence of AI-enhanced reflective journals on the autonomy of EFL learners. The conclusions indicate that AI-enhanced reflective journals have a limited impact on developing learner autonomy. This stands in contrast to various studies that have explored the impact of AI-enhanced reflective journals on learner autonomy in EFL writing courses and found that these tools substantially enhance the autonomy of EFL learners (Wei, 2023; Abdalkader, 2023; Yan, 2023; Han & Sari, 2022; Malik et al., 2023). In other words, these studies demonstrate that AI-enhanced reflective journals contribute to increased autonomy in writing among EFL learners. However, the current study reveals that the application of AI-enhanced reflective journals alone does not significantly increase learner autonomy. Differences in the broad impact of AI tools may stem from variations in how AI tools are implemented (Wei, 2023). The reason may be the features of more integrated or advanced AI, or the instructional context might have been more conducive to exploiting AI's potential, leading to significant improvements not observed in the current study. The diverse results can be ascribed to variations in the participant groups and educational contexts (Abdalkader, 2023). Research conducted in diverse cultural or educational settings, such as high schools versus colleges or across different countries, can impact how learners engage with and benefit from AI tools, thereby altering the overall reported efficacy of these tools. Yan (2023) and Han and Sari (2022) report more conclusive positive results, potentially attributed to their particular research methodologies, such as qualitative approaches that capture intricate user experiences or the integration of automated and human feedback. In addition, Malik et al. (2023) emphasize enhancements in domains such as grammar and essay organization, whereas the present study primarily examines the motivational and confidence factors related to autonomy. It is also worth noting that though the difference between keeping traditional and AI-enhanced reflective journals is insignificant, the latter has continued to improve certain aspects of learner autonomy. Introspection is one key area where AI can help improve crucial skills, as it fosters self-assessment and is necessary for enhancing writing proficiency, according to studies pointed out in this paper and ongoing research. The current study supports literature suggesting that AI tools are more effective in enhancing writing skills when aligned with specific learning goals (Wei, 2023; Cheng et al., 2016). These gains may not necessarily be achieved when applied to broader aspects of autonomy in general, but they are expected to be strongly advantageous in specific areas where such specificity is important. The results of this study support the findings of Nagata et al. (2020) and Agustini (2023), who also observe improvements in specific writing abilities through the use of comparable AI techniques, which provide instant feedback and personalized prompts. Such a system can help in building task-specific learning activities that foster self-reflection, thereby honing targeted competencies. Related research provided deeper insight into how AI could be applied to enhance reflection in students' diaries, based on its assistance system that promotes deeper analytical skills in eflective writing (Cheng, 2017). Structured feedback benefits learners as it makes them evaluate their work independently, leading to self-improvement (Cheng et al., 2016). Thus, using AI-enhanced reflective journals would serve as an additional tool for enhancing learner autonomy in EFL writing. These observed alignments and misalignments can provide a better grasp of the variables influencing the impacts of AI on learner autonomy and writing skills. By comparing the outcomes of the current study with those of previous studies, detailed insights into the effectiveness of AI-enhanced tools in EFL learning can be drawn, which will be further discussed in the next section.

Practical Recommendations

Based on the findings on the utilization of AI-enhanced reflective journals in EFL writing, specific recommendations can be provided to students, teachers, curriculum developers, and policymakers. To begin with, students should set aside time to consider what they have done well and which areas they would improve after receiving feedback from the AI tool and backed-up sources. They should spend time consistently after every writing task with at least one AI-generated feedback. After all, it would be important to write a brief "reflection note," quickly highlighting two things they did well and one thing they needed help with in the AI tool feedback. For instance, after writing an essay, students could quickly view AI suggestions and enter them into a journal, focusing on how to apply them to their next task. Further extending their self-awareness and skills in writing could be aided by maintaining a "feedback tracking log," or "feedback incorporation log," as some people refer to it, which tracks changes based on suggestions from the AI model. Through reflection, learners could cultivate metacognitive awareness, identify their strengths and weaknesses, and become better equipped to navigate the challenges of writing development. In essence, it gives these learners greater responsibility for their learning, enabling them to make independent decisions and interact constructively with the writing process. In addition, teachers should utilize AI tools that provide them with immediate, tailored responses to enhance the effectiveness of these tools in schools, thereby increasing student motivation and engagement. They should also be motivated to employ a blend of AI-driven critical writing and traditional methods in their teaching, such as hybrid methods. In terms of professional growth, teachers should receive continuous training on the proficient integration of AI tools to enhance their skills in incorporating AI tools into their teaching methods. They should integrate AI reflections into their training. For instance, after a writing activity, students should reflect on the work in journals, specifically highlighting the points of AI feedback they used to develop their final draft. Teachers may want to experiment with setting up reflection workshops assisted by AI, where students would, with the help of tools like ChatGPT, review drafts and discuss together how the AI feedback was helpful to them. Professional development should enable teachers to learn how to use AI tools and to design reflective prompts that lead to deep thinking perspectives ("What did you notice about your writing that you hadn't seen before using the AI feedback?"). They can encourage learners' autonomy by asking them to analyze their own writing experiences, articulate any difficulties they encounter, and set additional objectives to work on. Hybrid models that combine traditional teacher comments with AI suggestions can prove to be much more useful. The practical aspects of AI technologies require coverage through training, methods for integrating them into the curriculum, and approaches for controlling and assessing their impact on education. When it comes to curriculum developers, they should adapt AI components to correspond with the desired learning objectives. This means, for instance, that where the objective of a syllabus is to improve critical writing skills, AI should provide comments that engage learners in critical thinking while they compose texts. Through customization, the features of the AI system should be aligned with particular educational goals. Learners' educational and cultural backgrounds are important considerations to make while developing a curriculum that integrates AI tools. The AI teaching resources can be more personalized, efficient, and helpful to the learners if the developers are sensitive enough, thus making them better at enhancing their autonomy inside a classroom situation. Fulfilling these goals is impossible without understanding what learners from specific groups require and how AI solutions can be tailored to better suit them. Curriculum developers should design reflection activities with enhanced AI purposely integrated into learning objectives. For example, they could design writing modules with an AI feedback-review stage built into each major assignment, including a final reflection journal task. AI will need to encourage students to engage in higher-order thinking through prompts that analyze, deepen, or revise their arguments while also correcting grammar and punctuation in courses that aim to develop critical writing skills. In addition, AI activities can be customized to suit cultural and educational contexts and, most importantly, include prompt examples with culturally relevant writing inputs on AI-driven platforms. Finally, policymakers should create support systems for the efficient use of AI in teaching and provide technical support to teachers. This entails organizing training courses and ensuring that both tutors and learners have sufficient resources for effective AI tool applications. It is also necessary for them to ensure that institutions employ adaptive strategies in integrating AI-based instruments that can be customized for various educational settings. Policymakers should establish robust support systems to facilitate the effective integration of AI tools into educational practice. This includes organizing compulsory training for teachers in the effective use of AI tools and reflective facilitation, ensuring equal access to AI tools across different schools within the country, and establishing evaluation frameworks to monitor the impact of AI-enhanced learning on writing and autonomy among students. AI solution developers also need to promote adaptive AI applications that can be tailored to local educational standards and the individual needs of students.

Limitations and Recommendations for Further Research

The current study has several limitations. The study employed a quasi-experimental design due to certain factors in schools that prevented the random assignment of participants. Furthermore, the data collection of the present study was limited to a single control group and a single experimental group, employing two instruments. Additionally, this study involves only 36 participants enrolled in an English preparatory program at a Turkish institution, which may limit the generalizability of the findings to other locations and educational settings. The duration was only five weeks; therefore, a longer period might have revealed different outcomes. Another constraint to mention is that the study results are derived from a single AI software, potentially failing to accurately represent the effects of other AI tools.

This study provides a basis for future research directions. First, employing qualitative approaches and various data collection technologies can lead to deeper insights into how various factors, such as perspectives, cognitive processes, experiences, and individual choices, interact with learner autonomy. Second, further research might investigate the association between learner autonomy and writing proficiency in EFL contexts by incorporating a wider range of writing tasks and activities. Third, conducting future studies in diverse educational settings and among various demographic groups, such as those with different genders, ages, language competencies, and technological proficiencies, can contribute to a more comprehensive understanding of the topic. Last, it is advisable to conduct studies with larger sample sizes and longer durations to enhance the effectiveness of the findings and enable more accurate generalizations.

REFERENCES

Abdalkader, S. M. A. (2023). *The impact of using artificial intelligence on enhancing EFL language fluency and self-regulation for the preparatory stage students in distinguished governmental language schools.* PhD thesis. Ain Shams University.

Agustini, N. P. O. (2023). Examining the role of ChatGPT as a learning tool in promoting students' English language learning autonomy relevant to Kurikulum Merdeka Belajar. *EDUKASIA: Jurnal Pendidikan Dan Pembelajaran, 4*(2), 921–934. DOI: 10.62775/edukasia.v4i2.373

Bandura, A. (1993). Perceived self-efficacy in cognitive development and functioning. *Educational Psychologist, 28*(2), 117–148. DOI: 10.1207/s15326985ep2802_3

Borg, S., & Al-Busaidi, S. (2012). Teachers' beliefs and practices regarding learner autonomy. *ELT Journal, 66*(3), 283–292. DOI: 10.1093/elt/ccr065

Boud, D., Keogh, R., & Walker, D. (1985). *Reflection: Turning experience into learning*. Kogan Page.

Çakıcı, D. (2015). Autonomy in language teaching and learning process. *İnönü Üniversitesi Eğitim Fakültesi Dergisi, 16*(1), 31–42.

Celce-Murcia, M. (2001). Language teaching approaches: An overview. *Teaching English as a Second or Foreign Language, 2*(1), 3–10.

Cheng, G. (2017). The impact of online automated feedback on students' reflective journal writing in an EFL course. *The Internet and Higher Education, 34*, 18–27. DOI: 10.1016/j.iheduc.2017.04.002

Cheng, G., Law, E., & Wong, T.-L. (2016). Investigating effects of automated feedback on EFL students' reflective learning skills. *2016 IEEE International Conference on Teaching, Assessment, and Learning for Engineering*, 226–230. DOI: 10.1109/TALE.2016.7851798

Cook, V. (2014). How do people learn to write in a second language? In *Key topics in second language education* (pp. 73–88). MM Textbooks. DOI: 10.2307/jj.26931996.9

Cooper, M. M. (1986). The ecology of writing. *College English, 48*(4), 364–375. DOI: 10.58680/ce198611607

Creswell, J. W. (2014). Research design: Qualitative, quantitative and mixed methods approaches. *Sage (Atlanta, Ga.).*

Dam, L. (1995). *Learner autonomy: From theory to classroom practice*. Authentik Language Learning Resources.

Davis, F. D. (1989). Perceived usefulness, perceived ease of use and user acceptance of information technology. *Management Information Systems Quarterly, 13*(3), 319–339. DOI: 10.2307/249008

Dewey, J. (1933). *How we think: A restatement of the relation of reflective thinking to the educative process*. D.C. Heath & Co Publishers.

Engeström, Y. (1987). *Learning by expanding: An activity-theoretical approach to developmental research*. Orienta-Kosultit Oy.

Grabe, W., & Kaplan, R. B. (1996). *Theory and practice of writing*. Pearson Education Limited.

Han, T., & Sari, E. (2022). An investigation on the use of automated feedback in Turkish EFL students' writing classes. *Computer Assisted Language Learning*, 1–24. DOI: 10.1080/09588221.2022.2067179

Hein, G. E. (1991). *Constructivist learning theory*. Institute for Learning.

Hodges, T. S. (2017). Theoretically speaking: An examination of four theories and how they support writing in the classroom. *The Clearing House: A Journal of Educational Strategies, Issues and Ideas, 90*(4), 139–146. DOI: 10.1080/00098655.2017.1326228

Holec, H. (1981). *Autonomy and foreign language learning*. Pergamon.

Hyland, K. (2003). *Second language writing*. Cambridge University Press. DOI: 10.1017/CBO9780511667251

Javed, M., Juan, W. X., & Nazli, S. (2013). A study of students' assessment in writing skills of the English language. *International Journal of Instruction, 6*(2), 129–144.

Kim, Y.-S. G., & Park, S.-H. (2019). Unpacking pathways using the direct and indirect effects model of writing (DIEW) and the contributions of higher-order cognitive skills to writing. *Reading and Writing, 32*(5), 1319–1343. DOI: 10.1007/s11145-018-9913-y

Kolb, D. A. (1984). *Experiential learning: Experience as the source of learning and development*. Prentice-Hall.

Lincoln, Y. S., & Guba, E. G. (1985). Naturalistic inquiry. *Sage (Atlanta, Ga.).*

Littlejohn, A. (1985). Learner choice in language study. *ELT Journal, 39*(4), 253–261. DOI: 10.1093/elt/39.4.253

Malik, A. R., Pratiwi, Y., Andajani, K., Numertayasa, I. W., Suharti, S., Darwis, A., & Marzuki, . (2023). Exploring artificial intelligence in academic essay: Higher education student's perspective. *International Journal of Educational Research Open*, *5*, 1–11. DOI: 10.1016/j.ijedro.2023.100296

Marlina, R., & Giri, R. A. (2014). *The pedagogy of English as an international language: Perspectives from scholars, teachers, and students*. Springer., DOI: 10.1007/978-3-319-06127-6

Okonkwo, U. (2011). Computer assisted language learning (CALL) software: Evaluation of its influence in a language learning process. *UJAH: Unizik Journal of Arts and Humanities*, *12*(1), 76–89. DOI: 10.4314/ujah.v12i1.4

Orakcı, Ş., & Gelişli, Y. (2017). Learner autonomy scale: A scale development study. *Malaysian Online Journal of Educational Sciences*, *5*(4), 25–35.

Pardo, A., Jovanovic, J., Dawson, S., Gašević, D., & Mirriahi, N. (2019). Using learning analytics to scale the provision of personalised feedback. *British Journal of Educational Technology*, *50*(1), 128–138. DOI: 10.1111/bjet.12592

Riessman, C. K. (2008). Narrative methods for the human sciences. *Sage (Atlanta, Ga.)*.

Russel, S. J., & Norvig, P. (2010). *Artificial intelligence: A modern approach*. Pearson Education.

Seliger, H. W., & Shohamy, E. (1989). *Second language research methods*. Oxford University Press.

Sharma, R. C., & Sharma, Y. (2022). Augmenting learning through virtual reality applications in education. *Tenth Pan-Commonwealth Forum on Open Learning*, 1–6. DOI: 10.56059/pcf10.7986

Vygotsky, L. (1978). *Mind in society: The development of higher mental processes*. Harvard University Press.

Wei, L. (2023). Artificial intelligence in language instruction: Impact on English learning achievement, L2 motivation, and self-regulated learning. *Frontiers in Psychology*, *14*, 1–14. DOI: 10.3389/fpsyg.2023.1261955 PMID: 38023040

Yan, D. (2023). Impact of ChatGPT on learners in a L2 writing practicum: An exploratory investigation. *Education and Information Technologies*, *28*(11), 1–25. DOI: 10.1007/s10639-023-11742-4 PMID: 37361815

Yildiz, Y., & Yucedal, H. M. (2020). Learner autonomy: A central theme in language learning. International. *Journal of Social Sciences and Educational Studies*, *7*(3), 208–212. DOI: 10.23918/ijsses.v7i3p208

Zamel, V. (1982). Writing: The process of discovering meaning. *TESOL Quarterly*, *16*(2), 195–209. DOI: 10.2307/3586792

Zheng, W., Cheng, H., Yu, J. X., Zou, L., & Zhao, K. (2019). Interactive natural language question answering over knowledge graphs. *Information Sciences*, *481*, 141–159. DOI: 10.1016/j.ins.2018.12.032

Chapter 9
AI-Guided Professional Development:
A Vygotskian Approach for Teachers in Multilingual Classrooms

Luis J Hernandez-Ledezma
https://orcid.org/0009-0004-5848-1473
Enabling Learning LLC, Lavon, USA

Uvaldina Janecek
https://orcid.org/0009-0000-5375-5245
Independent Researcher, Corsicana, USA

ABSTRACT

This chapter presents a Vygotskian approach to AI-guided professional development through the case study of Verónica, an AI-powered virtual tutor designed to support preservice and in-service teachers in multilingual classrooms. By integrating constructivist and constructionist learning principles, the model emphasizes personalized, continuous support rooted in sociocultural theory and responsive AI design. The chapter outlines how prompt engineering, fine-tuning, and custom embeddings improve Verónica's context awareness and educational effectiveness. It also explores the hybrid training model that combines face-to-face workshops, online modules, and AI interaction to enhance teacher preparation, promote equity, and empower educators with culturally relevant tools for bilingual and ESL instruction.

DOI: 10.4018/979-8-3373-1122-7.ch009

UNDERSTANDING THE COMPLEX LANDSCAPE OF MULTILINGUAL EDUCATION

Based on our collective experiences as bilingual classroom teachers, we have witnessed firsthand the unique challenges educators in multilingual settings face. These challenges extend well beyond the standard hurdles of teaching and create a complex landscape that requires specialized support.

One of the most daunting challenges we encountered during our early teaching careers was implementing effective differentiation in classrooms where students possessed varying levels of language proficiency. Unlike monolingual classrooms, bilingual settings require teachers to simultaneously address content understanding while supporting language acquisition across multiple proficiency levels. During our experiences teaching in dual-language programs, we had students ranging from newcomers with minimal English proficiency to fully bilingual children fluent in both Spanish and English. Each morning, we would review our lesson plans, questioning whether we had adequately addressed the needs of all our students. Were we challenging our bilingual students sufficiently while not overwhelming our newcomers? Were we providing the right scaffolds for intermediate language learners to access grade-level content?

We vividly remember teaching science units on objectives like the ones related to ecosystems where some students could comfortably engage with complex ecological concepts in both languages, while others struggled to understand basic vocabulary even in their native language. Creating materials that honored both content objectives and language development goals felt like preparing for two separate classes, which is a constant, comprehensive, and exhausting process.

This reality translates into what effectively amounts to double the planning workload compared to monolingual instruction. Our approach typically involved first identifying core content objectives, then determining appropriate language allocation, followed by developing differentiated approaches for various proficiency levels in each language. This multi-layered process extended our workdays by several hours, contributing to professional burnout. Even routine tasks became complex endeavors. Creating anchor charts meant producing parallel versions in both languages while maintaining content consistency, and selecting appropriate texts required finding materials in both languages that addressed the same concepts but weren't mere translations, a difficult challenge given the limited bilingual resources available to most teachers. Unsurprisingly, statewide data show that bilingual and ESL teachers leave the profession at about 18% per year (six points higher than the overall teacher attrition rate) underscoring how this workload fuels staffing instability in multilingual programs (Carver-Thomas & Darling-Hammond, 2022).

Challenges in Addressing Language Proficiency Variations

The reality of language proficiency variations within a single classroom creates instructional puzzles that even experienced teachers find challenging. Beyond the obvious spoken language differences, we quickly learned that reading comprehension, writing abilities, and academic language development varied dramatically among our students. One particularly challenging aspect was supporting cross-linguistic transfer or helping students apply knowledge from their first language to their second. Some students showed remarkable ability to transfer literacy skills from Spanish to English, while others compartmentalized their languages, struggling to make connections between them. This required us to develop strategies that explicitly highlighted these connections, which weren't aspects our teacher preparation programs had thoroughly addressed at the time.

Additionally, we discovered that language proficiency wasn't static; it fluctuated based on content area, emotional state, and even time of day. A student who appeared fluent during a social studies discussion might struggle significantly during mathematics instruction, where specialized academic vocabulary created additional barriers. These shifting proficiency levels required constant assessment and adjustment of instruction.

The Role of Cultural Responsiveness in Multilingual Classrooms

Deeply intertwined with language considerations is the critical importance of cultural responsiveness. Our classrooms represented diverse cultural backgrounds, primarily Mexican, Central American, and Mexican-American, each with distinct histories, values, and educational experiences. Making content culturally relevant wasn't simply about celebrating holidays or incorporating surface-level cultural references, but it required a deep understanding of how culture shapes learning styles, communication patterns, and educational expectations.

We learned this lesson powerfully when teaching units on family traditions. What we intended as engaging, personal assignments sometimes revealed significant tensions for students whose families had recently immigrated under difficult circumstances. Some were reluctant to share details about family members who remained in their home countries, while others struggled to reconcile differences between their home culture and American school culture. These experiences taught us that cultural responsiveness demands more than good intentions, it requires ongoing education, community engagement, and a willingness to adapt curriculum and instruction to honor students' cultural identities while building bridges to new cultural contexts.

This aspect of teaching was perhaps the least addressed in our formal education, yet it proved fundamental to creating successful learning environments.

Navigating State Certification Standards (TEKS and TELPAS)

The technical demands of navigating state standards add another layer of complexity for bilingual and ESL educators. In Texas, where we taught, this meant aligning instruction with the Texas Essential Knowledge and Skills (TEKS) while simultaneously addressing the language development needs outlined in the Texas English Language Proficiency Assessment System (TELPAS).

The TEKS provided content guidelines, but implementing them in a bilingual context required significant adaptation. For instance, teaching the same writing standard in both English and Spanish necessitated understanding not just linguistic differences but also rhetorical and stylistic variations between languages. A well-constructed paragraph follows different patterns in English than in Spanish, a nuance rarely addressed in standard curriculum materials.

Meanwhile, TELPAS requirements meant consistently documenting and supporting language development across listening, speaking, reading, and writing domains. This documentation process alone consumed hours that could have been spent on instructional planning, creating a tension between compliance and quality teaching that many new teachers struggle to reconcile.

Federal Accountability and Its Impact (ESSA)

Federal mandates under Every Student Succeeds Act (ESSA) created additional pressure, particularly around testing and accountability for English learners. Our schools, like many serving large populations of emergent bilinguals, faced intense scrutiny regarding standardized test performance and language development benchmarks.

This accountability framework often failed to account for the complexity of language acquisition or the varied starting points of multilingual learners. We frequently found ourselves explaining to administrators why newcomer students couldn't reasonably be expected to perform at grade level on standardized assessments administered in English after just months in the country. These conversations highlighted a fundamental disconnect between policy expectations and classroom realities.

The pressure to produce rapid results, particularly visible improvements in standardized test scores, created significant stress and sometimes led to instructional decisions that prioritized test preparation over deeper language development and content understanding. This tension between authentic learning and accountability measures represents one of the most challenging aspects of multilingual education.

Complexities of Assessment in Bilingual Education

Assessment in bilingual classrooms introduces further complexities and workload. Beyond the standard assessments required for all teachers, we needed to conduct regular language proficiency evaluations, monitor cross-linguistic transfer, and document language development across multiple domains. These additional assessment responsibilities required not only extra time but specialized knowledge about language acquisition and biliteracy development. Understanding whether a student's difficulty stemmed from content comprehension challenges, language proficiency limitations, or transfer issues between languages demanded sophisticated diagnostic skills that many new teachers haven't fully developed.

Furthermore, communicating these complex assessment results to parents, some of whom had limited experience with the American educational system, required careful consideration of both language choice and cultural sensitivity. Parent-teacher conferences often took twice as long as those in monolingual classrooms, as we explained progress in both languages and across both content and language development dimensions.

Ongoing Need for Targeted Professional Development

The specialized nature of bilingual education necessitates continuous professional growth beyond what's required of mainstream teachers. During our early years, we found ourselves simultaneously learning new district initiatives, general pedagogical approaches, and bilingual-specific methodologies. This professional development often occurred after school or on weekends, further extending already demanding schedules. While our monolingual colleagues might attend a workshop on guided reading, we needed to understand how guided reading works differently in each language and how to build bridges between languages during literacy instruction.

Many district-provided professional development sessions failed to address the specific needs of bilingual educators, focusing instead on generic approaches that required significant adaptation for multilingual contexts. This meant that much of our professional learning occurred through informal networks, personal research, and trial-and-error, an inefficient and often frustrating process that highlighted the need for more targeted support systems for bilingual educators.

While some aspects of professional development occur in collaborative settings (such as attending workshops or engaging in learning communities) much of the daily work of planning and adapting instruction, particularly for bilingual educators, happens in relative isolation. For many new teachers, especially those entering multilingual classrooms without a robust support system, this can result in a sense of professional solitude and uncertainty. We, too, experienced this reality firsthand in our early years, navigating complex linguistic and cultural challenges with limited guidance. Over time, however, this initial isolation gave way to opportunities for mentorship, reflection, and growth, highlighting the critical role that supportive networks and accessible guidance play in teacher development.

THE TRANSFORMATIVE POWER OF MENTORSHIP AND SUPPORT

Many of us enter bilingual education with vibrant visions of our classrooms, students seamlessly transitioning between languages, engaging deeply with content in both languages, and classroom environments celebrating cultural diversity. Yet for most new bilingual and ESL teachers, the reality quickly proves dramatically different.

Those first weeks in our own classrooms reveal a universal pattern: the overwhelming demands of managing basic procedures, addressing widely varying language needs, and navigating administrative requirements leave little room for the thoughtful bilingual instruction we imagined. Sometimes we might find ourselves making on-the-spot decisions about language allocation based on time constraints and available materials rather than pedagogical principles.

Nearly every bilingual educator can recall those sobering moments that highlight the gap between aspiration and reality. After hours of preparing carefully differentiated materials with visual supports, and scaffolding in both languages, unexpected schedule changes or classroom management challenges force us to abandon these resources. The disconnect between our preparation and classroom realities can feel overwhelming. Additionally, the sense of isolation is perhaps the most pervasive challenge facing new bilingual educators. Despite working alongside other teachers, the specific complexities of balancing content instruction across two languages while supporting diverse proficiency levels create challenges that monolingual colleagues often cannot fully understand.

Resource limitations intensify this isolation. School professional libraries typically contain shelves of materials for mainstream instruction but minimal resources for bilingual contexts. When we raise questions about adapting school initiatives for multilingual learners, responses like "use your judgment" or "do what works for your students" may be well-intentioned but ultimately reinforce the sense that we are navigating uncharted territory alone.

Perhaps most disconcerting is the persistent uncertainty about whether our instructional approaches effectively meet students' needs. Without clear models or consistent feedback specific to bilingual instruction, we question fundamental decisions: Are we allowing sufficient time for primary language development? Are we inadvertently privileging one language? Are we appropriately addressing cross-linguistic differences in our instruction?

Commercial "bilingual" materials, sometimes consisting of direct translations that ignore cultural and linguistic nuances, compound this uncertainty. Creating appropriate resources requires time and expertise that new teachers are still developing, resulting in constant compromise, using imperfect materials while attempting to compensate for their limitations.

The Power of Experienced Mentors

For those fortunate enough to find them, experienced colleagues can transform this challenging landscape. In our careers, we've witnessed how access to veteran bilingual educators who recognize these struggles and proactively reach out can fundamentally change a teacher's trajectory. These mentors provide immediate practical support through classroom observations, sharing of resources, and modeling of effective strategies. But perhaps more importantly, they normalize the challenges, sharing their own stories and assuring new teachers that what they're experiencing isn't a sign of inadequacy but rather the normal process of becoming a bilingual educator. They help replace self-doubt with a growth mindset, reframing challenges as opportunities to develop specialized skills.

These "More Knowledgeable Others," as Vygotsky would describe them, offer more than just information (Vygotsky et al., 1979). They provide scaffolded guidance within new teachers' zones of proximal development, helping bridge the gap between current practices and potential growth. They demonstrate what's possible, share practical resources, and provide emotional support that humanizes the professional development process.

Our collective experiences with both the challenges of bilingual teaching and the transformative impact of effective mentorship inspired our collaboration. We kept returning to a central question: How might we replicate the invaluable guidance of experienced mentors in a way that would be continuously accessible to all teachers, regardless of their school environment or the availability of veteran bilingual educators? This question became especially important as we transitioned to teacher preparation roles ourselves. We recognized that even the most comprehensive preparation programs face inherent constraints that limit their ability to provide the ongoing, context-specific support that new teachers need, especially during those critical first years when they're simultaneously developing classroom management skills, instructional techniques, and cultural competence.

THE ARTIFICIAL INTELLIGENCE REVOLUTION

The introduction of large language models (LLMs) in 2022 (such as ChatGPT) presented an unprecedented opportunity for innovation in education. LLMs are a type of artificial intelligence (AI) system trained on vast amounts of text data to generate human-like responses in natural language. While they are a subset of AI, they have become some of the most visible and widely used examples of it. The release of ChatGPT marked a watershed moment, showcasing how AI could engage in seemingly conversational, context-aware dialogue with users (Kasneci et al., 2023; OpenAI, 2023; Rudolph et al., 2023). At that moment we realized that this new generation of AI had evolved to a point where it could meaningfully enhance teacher preparation and support in ways that had previously been unimaginable. A large-scale systematic review of 164 empirical studies conducted between 2015 and 2024 shows that AI-mediated professional development most consistently boosts teachers' reflective practice, differentiated-instruction skills, and data-driven decision-making, while privacy, algorithmic bias, and infrastructure gaps remain the main barriers to adoption (Tan et al., 2024). These findings reinforce the need for human-guided, equity-minded AI design such as the approach we followed with Verónica.

A particularly transformative development was the release of Application Programming Interfaces (APIs) for large language models. APIs are not exclusive to artificial intelligence, they are widely used in software development as connection points that enable different systems or services to communicate with one another. Whether connecting to a weather service, payment gateway, or language model, APIs allow developers to integrate external functionalities into their own tools and platforms (Ikumapayi, 2023). However, the introduction of APIs for generative AI models marked a pivotal moment, especially for those of us working at the intersection of education and technology. For the first time, we could embed the advanced capabilities of tools like ChatGPT into custom applications built specifically for multilingual learning environments. This unlocked new possibilities for reimagining teacher support, not through generic automation, but through dynamic, responsive, and context-aware systems designed to enhance the educational experience.

With access to APIs and the flexibility to build tools around LLMs like ChatGPT, we saw an opportunity to create something that could address the persistent gaps in mentorship and guidance faced by bilingual and ESL educators. That's when we asked ourselves: What if we could create an AI-powered mentor, one that embodied the expertise of veteran bilingual educators, was available 24/7, never grew tired or impatient, and could provide individualized support precisely when educators needed it most? This idea led to our development of Verónica, an AI-powered virtual tutor specifically designed to support educators in multilingual settings.

Calibrated to understand the unique challenges of bilingual and ESL education, Verónica functions as a Vygotskian "More Knowledgeable Other," providing scaffolded support that helps teachers bridge the gap between their current practices and their potential for growth. Unlike static resources or occasional workshops, Verónica provides immediate, contextually relevant guidance at the precise moment a teacher faces a challenging situation, whether that's planning differentiated instruction for students with varying language proficiency levels, developing culturally responsive approaches to teaching specific content, or troubleshooting classroom management issues unique to multilingual settings.

This approach doesn't aim to replace human mentorship but rather to complement and extend it, ensuring that no teacher faces the challenges of multilingual education without support. In the spirit of Vygotsky's sociocultural theory, Verónica serves as an additional voice in the professional community surrounding each educator, one that is consistently available when human colleagues might not be (Enabling Learning LLC, 2024b, 2024a; Vygotsky et al., 1979).

As educational contexts grow increasingly diverse and the demands on bilingual and ESL educators become more complex, innovations like Verónica offer a promising pathway toward more comprehensive and accessible professional development ecosystems. By democratizing access to high-quality support, we can help ensure that all teachers, and ultimately all multilingual students, have the opportunity to thrive.

THE GENESIS OF VERÓNICA: A DIGITAL MORE KNOWLEDGEABLE OTHER

The conceptualization of Verónica emerged from our combined experiences in bilingual education and educational technology. Drawing from our backgrounds in bilingual classroom teaching and higher education, we envisioned a tool that would address specific challenges we had witnessed repeatedly: isolation, overwhelm, and the difficulty of applying theoretical knowledge in dynamic classroom contexts. From the outset, our design principles centered on creating a system that would be:

- Continuously accessible: Available whenever teachers required support, whether during late-night lesson planning sessions, weekend preparation, or moments of uncertainty during the school day.
- Contextually responsive: Understanding the specific contexts of bilingual and ESL education, including state standards, certification requirements, lan-

guage acquisition processes, and cultural considerations relevant to diverse student populations.

- Pedagogically sound: Aligning with established best practices in bilingual education, ESL instruction, and teacher development.
- Adaptively supportive: Adjusting support levels based on educators' career stages, providing comprehensive guidance for novices while offering nuanced suggestions for experienced educators.
- Practically oriented: Helping teachers translate theory into practice through concrete strategies and applications relevant to their specific teaching contexts.

Our partnership became the foundation of Verónica's development. Mr. Hernandez brought his background in AI systems and educational technology implementation, while Dr. Janecek contributed her extensive knowledge of bilingual education practices, classroom management strategies, and instructional methodologies. Together, we embodied what we've always believed: *that effective educational technology must be anchored in sound pedagogy and real classroom experiences*. We maintained a human-centered approach throughout, ensuring the technology served genuine educational needs rather than forcing educators to adapt to technological constraints.

We envisioned Verónica supporting pre-service and in-service teachers through several key functions, serving as a:

- Teacher certification preparation assistant
- Lesson planning partner offering differentiation and scaffolding suggestions
- Reflective coach engaging teachers in analysis of their instructional decisions
- Cultural and linguistic resource providing insights for responsive teaching

Throughout this conceptualization, Vygotsky's framework provided a theoretical foundation. While Verónica cannot yet automatically measure a teacher's Zone of Proximal Development through initial interactions, the system embodies the MKO principle by being consistently present and responsive to teachers' expressed needs. The ZPD concept guided our design of interaction patterns that allow teachers to self-select the level of support they require. When a teacher requests assistance, Verónica provides information in an accessible format while offering opportunities to explore concepts at greater depth (Burner & Svendsen, 2020; Villamizar Castrillón, 2017; Vygotsky et al., 1979). For instance, a teacher might begin with a basic question about differentiation strategies and, through continued dialogue, receive increasingly sophisticated guidance as their understanding evolves. This approach allows teachers to progress at their own pace, with the system adapting the complexity of materials and instructions based on the specific questions asked rather than through automatic assessment of capabilities.

The Unique Strengths of AI as a Mentorship Tool

Artificial intelligence offers unique capabilities that address many limitations of traditional support systems (Lin et al., 2023; Otto et al., 2023; Ouyang & Jiao, 2021). While nothing can replace human mentorship's richness, Verónica was conceived as a digital embodiment of the "More Knowledgeable Other" concept, complementing and extending human mentors' reach rather than replacing them. Recent survey research with 245 K-12 educators found that while 79% believe AI tools can enhance continuous learning, only 38% currently experience measurable skill gains, underscoring the importance of scaffolded, mentor-style systems that translate potential into practice (Shezad et al., 2025). This approach offers several distinctive advantages that traditional professional development cannot match:

- Equity through scalability: Verónica can engage with thousands of educators concurrently, ensuring that teachers in under-resourced settings receive the same quality of support as those in more privileged environments, helping address systemic inequities in professional development access.
- Critical moment accessibility: An AI assistant that can provide specific guidance at 10:00 PM on a Sunday represents a fundamental shift in how support is accessed, addressing those crucial planning moments when human mentors are unavailable.
- Multidimensional expertise integration: By drawing on extensive knowledge bases covering language acquisition theories, pedagogical practices, cultural contexts, and state standards, Verónica can synthesize information and provide guidance that connects these domains in ways individual mentors might not consistently achieve. Tammets and Ley's (2023) conceptual model for AI-supported teacher learning argues that effective systems must surface teachers' "professional vision" by making noticing and decision processes visible, an idea operationalized in Verónica's transcript-based reflection prompts

This complementary relationship between human judgment and AI support represents a promising direction for educational applications. A growing ecosystem of specialized AI tools illustrates what targeted, data-rich feedback can look like in practice. For example, TeachFX harnesses automatic-speech-recognition technology to give teachers quantitative reports on talk time, wait time, and question complexity, helping them connect discourse patterns to student engagement (TeachFX, 2024). Video-analysis platforms such as Edthena apply computer-vision and natural-language-processing algorithms to tag key instructional moments, prompting teachers to annotate, reflect, and share evidence with mentors, an approach linked to measurable gains in questioning and feedback strategies during induction programs (Martin & Sun, 2022). Together with tools like GoReact, which overlays time-stamped AI comments on micro-teaching videos to support rapid-cycle practice (Williams & Fowler, 2023), these platforms show how narrowly focused analytics can strengthen specific dimensions of pedagogy. Verónica builds on this momentum by weaving multiple strands (lesson design, language scaffolding, and cultural responsiveness) into a single conversational interface tailored to multilingual contexts. By handling information-intensive aspects of professional support, AI frees human mentors to focus on what benefits most from human interaction: building relationships, modeling complex decision-making, providing emotional support, and helping teachers develop a strong sense of professional identity grounded in reflection, experience, and shared values (Lin et al., 2023; Otto et al., 2023; Ouyang & Jiao, 2021; Vassileva, 2008).

Our vision for future development includes more sophisticated adaptive support that better approximates how human mentors intuitively gauge and respond to a learner's developmental readiness, but the current implementation already provides valuable scaffolding that respects teacher agency while promoting professional growth.

The Essential Human Element in AI-Enhanced Teacher Development

Our conviction that effective educational technology must be grounded in human expertise led to our collaboration. While one of us (Mr. Hernandez) brought technical knowledge of AI systems, Dr. Janecek provided the crucial educational expertise needed to ensure Verónica would truly address the complex realities of multilingual classrooms.

This human-centered approach to development distinguishes Verónica from generic AI applications. Dr. Janecek's decades of experience in bilingual classrooms and teacher education informed every aspect of the system's design, from the content knowledge base to the instructional strategies recommended, ensuring that technology served sound pedagogical goals rather than operating from abstract algorithms disconnected from educational realities. The importance of this human expertise cannot be overstated. An AI system is only as good as the knowledge and values embedded within it (Inkpen et al., 2023; Otto et al., 2023; Retzlaff et al., 2024). By centering the development process around experienced educators' insights, we ensured that Verónica would reflect not just theoretical principles, but practical wisdom gained through years of successful classroom practice.

This collaborative work exemplifies our fundamental belief that the future of educational technology lies not in replacing human expertise but in amplifying it, creating tools that extend the reach of experienced educators' knowledge while maintaining the human judgment, ethical awareness, and contextual understanding that technology alone cannot provide.

Our development of Verónica focused on creating a system that could genuinely enhance teacher preparation and support for multilingual education. We believe strongly that this approach can be replicated and adapted by other teacher preparation programs to address their unique contexts, state requirements, and local needs.

BUILDING VERÓNICA'S KNOWLEDGE

To create an AI assistant truly capable of supporting bilingual and ESL educators, we began by developing a specialized knowledge base, which we call Verónica's "smart library." This smart library is a curated collection of expert-reviewed materials drawn from our real-world work in bilingual education, and it serves as the foundation for everything Verónica knows and can do. This library includes:

- Certification preparation resources aligned with Texas bilingual and ESL competencies
- Professional development materials from workshops on sheltered instruction and culturally responsive teaching
- University-level coursework, including assignments and instructor feedback
- Lesson plans, classroom activities, and differentiation strategies
- Authentic case studies from bilingual classrooms

We stored this information in a vector database, a type of storage system that uses numerical representations (called vectors) to encode the meaning of each document. This allows Verónica to understand the conceptual relationships between ideas, rather than relying only on keyword matching.

For example, when a teacher asks about strategies for "*newcomer students*," Verónica can find and connect information about "*primary language support*," "*visual scaffolding*," and "*comprehensible input*," even if those exact phrases weren't used in the question. This process is powered by a technology known as embeddings.

Understanding Embeddings: Making Connections Between Ideas

Embeddings are a way to translate text into mathematical form so that an AI system can "understand" the relationships between different concepts. In simple terms, it's like creating a map of ideas where related terms are placed close together. This means that even if a teacher uses informal or varied terminology, Verónica can still respond with accurate and relevant information drawn from the smart library.

For instance, even if a user asks, "*How do I help a newcomer in science class?*", Verónica knows to link that to concepts like scaffolding, dual language support, and TEKS-aligned science strategies. Embeddings help Verónica "see" how different pieces of information relate, which is especially helpful in multilingual education, where terminology often overlaps across languages and instructional models.

Fine-Tuning: Teaching the AI How to Talk Like a Bilingual Expert

Once we had built this library and created embeddings to help Verónica navigate it, we took an additional step: fine-tuning the language model. Fine-tuning is like giving the AI extra training using real examples from the field, so it doesn't just know what to say, it learns how to say it like an experienced bilingual educator.

We formatted our materials as realistic teacher conversations, pairing common questions with expert responses. This helped the AI learn the tone, depth, and instructional approach needed to guide teachers effectively. Unlike the general ChatGPT model, which draws on broad Internet data, our fine-tuned model reflects the specific language, scenarios, and pedagogical thinking used in bilingual and ESL contexts. By combining this fine-tuning with the smart library and embeddings, Verónica became more than a question-answering tool, it became a responsive, knowledgeable mentor.

How It All Comes Together: Retrieval-Augmented Generation (RAG)

To ensure that Verónica delivers responses that are both accurate and grounded in best practices, we implemented a method called Retrieval-Augmented Generation (RAG). This means that when a teacher asks a question, the system first retrieves the most relevant information from the smart library (via the vector database and embeddings) and then generates a natural-language response using the fine-tuned language model. This approach delivers several key benefits:

- Ensures that responses are aligned with research-based practices and state standards
- Provides clear, classroom-ready guidance tailored to bilingual and ESL educators
- Cites specific resources, terms, and instructional strategies used in real teacher training

Human Expertise and Continuous Improvement Loop

While the technical approaches created powerful capabilities, the most crucial aspect of Verónica's development was the human expertise that guided every step. Dr. Janecek's extensive classroom and teacher education experience was integral, serving as the "pedagogical conscience" of the project and ensuring that every aspect reflected the nuanced realities of multilingual classrooms. This human-centered approach manifested through:

- Expert content curation and selection
- Development of authentic teaching scenarios
- Systematic evaluation of responses for pedagogical soundness
- Insistence on maintaining human values throughout development

From its inception, we conceptualized Verónica as an evolving system rather than a static product. This commitment ensures the system remains relevant, effective, and aligned with current best practices in bilingual and ESL education. Our improvement process encompasses several interconnected approaches. We systematically collect feedback from diverse users through surveys, and interaction analysis. This feedback helps us understand how the system performs across different contexts and user needs.

We maintain active engagement with current research and policy changes, regularly updating our knowledge base to reflect emerging understandings. When Texas updated its English Language Proficiency Standards, for example, we systematically revised all related content to ensure Verónica's guidance remained aligned with current and future requirements taking effect in the 2026-2027 school year.

By analyzing interaction patterns, we identify specific improvement opportunities. We examine common questions that required frequent clarification, revealing content areas needing expansion or refinement. Early feedback from pre-service teachers, for instance, showed they wanted more grade-specific examples of differentiation strategies. In response, we expanded our knowledge base with concrete, contextual examples that significantly improved implementation success.

PRACTICAL APPLICATIONS OF VERÓNICA FOR PRE-SERVICE TEACHERS

A recent case-based professional-development study with seven middle-school science teachers showed that working through AI-annotated classroom cases raised participants' AI literacy across all four Zhao et al. (2022) domains (conceptual understanding, tool fluency, ethical awareness, and integration strategies) and prompted immediate classroom experimentation (Ding et al., 2024). We mapped Verónica's scenario chatbots to that same case-learning sequence (problem presentation, AI-guided reflection, and human-facilitated debrief) so that the system can drive comparable literacy gains at scale.

Verónica is not simply another general-purpose chatbot, it is a thoughtfully engineered educational system integrated into comprehensive online preparation courses for bilingual and ESL teacher certification. What sets Verónica apart is its deliberate instructional design, which combines advanced AI technologies, carefully calibrated interaction strategies, a specialized knowledge base, and structured scenario-based learning activities.

These online courses incorporate multiple interconnected AI-enhanced components, all of which operate within a shared framework grounded in a curated vector database and empowered by Retrieval-Augmented Generation (RAG). This foundational structure ensures that every activity is consistent, context-aware, and pedagogically aligned. Each AI-powered activity or interaction is built on several tightly integrated components that work together to ensure accuracy, relevance, and educational effectiveness:

- Prompt Engineering: This is the process of designing the instructions or questions we give to the AI to shape how it responds. Prompts are more than simple questions, they are crafted carefully to reflect authentic classroom language, anticipate how teachers think and ask for help, and guide the AI to respond with the appropriate tone, format, and detail. In Verónica's case, prompts are written by bilingual education experts to ensure the system generates responses aligned with real classroom needs, teaching standards, and culturally responsive pedagogy.
- Retrieval-Augmented Generation (RAG): Large language models like ChatGPT can sometimes generate responses based on their general training, which may be outdated or inaccurate for specific instructional contexts. RAG is a technique that solves this problem by allowing the AI to search a custom database (in this case, our vector database of expert-reviewed bilingual and ESL teaching materials) before generating a response. This ensures the system is always grounded in the most relevant and accurate information. Think

of RAG as the AI doing its "research" before speaking, using our curated library instead of relying on memory alone.

- Temperature Control: This setting affects how creative or cautious the AI is in its responses. A low temperature means the AI stays close to the facts and the content it retrieves, making it ideal for situations where accuracy and consistency are key (like writing a standards-aligned lesson plan). A higher temperature allows the AI to explore ideas more freely, making it useful for brainstorming or storytelling. By adjusting this setting based on the instructional goal, we can control how "safe" or "creative" the AI's output should be. This helps reduce the chances of AI hallucinations, or responses that sound correct but are actually inaccurate or misleading.

Together, these three elements (expert prompt engineering, precise retrieval of information through RAG, and purposeful temperature settings) form a layered instructional design framework that helps Verónica deliver trustworthy, accurate, and meaningful support tailored to educators' specific needs.

AI-Enhanced Instructional Components in Practice

The system that forms Verónica is not a single chatbot, but a comprehensive instructional ecosystem composed of several integrated components, each designed for a specific type of educational interaction. Together, these components exemplify how a unified AI framework, which is built on expert-designed prompts, a specialized vector database, and Retrieval-Augmented Generation (RAG), operates across multiple tools to deliver customized, accurate, and pedagogically sound support. It is this orchestration of features and functionalities that makes Verónica a truly effective AI-powered mentor for bilingual and ESL educators. These capabilities come to life through two primary components of the Verónica system: specialized chatbots tailored to distinct instructional needs and AI-powered instructional forms that dynamically generate context-specific resources.

- Specialized Chatbots: Each chatbot is designed around a specific instructional goal or certification area (e.g., sheltered instruction, assessment, language development). These bots use targeted prompts and draw from the shared vector database via RAG to provide accurate, responsive, and pedagogically grounded guidance.
- AI-Powered Instructional Forms: These forms allow users to select key instructional variables (such as grade level, content objectives, or language proficiency) through dropdowns, checkboxes, and sliders. Once submitted, the

system activates tailored prompts that generate highly relevant materials like lesson plans, differentiation strategies, or linguistic supports.

These components are highly adaptable and can be customized to support different instructional goals and program requirements. Specialized chatbots, for example, can simulate mentor-like conversations that begin with open-ended questions, respond dynamically to user input, and guide reflection or discussion aligned with specific bilingual education competencies. One chatbot might focus on scenario-based decision-making for newcomer support, while another could coach pre-service teachers through the principles of sheltered instruction, offering real-time feedback and clarification.

AI-powered instructional forms, on the other hand, generate personalized materials based on selected instructional variables. These tools are especially useful for lesson planning, language scaffolding, and differentiation. They can be tailored not only to meet the expectations of certification courses but also to align with district-specific instructional models or multilingual student populations. Examples of AI-powered forms include:

- ExCEL Method Form: Teachers select grade level, TEKS-aligned (Texas Essential Knowledge and Skills) content objectives, and language needs (e.g., English, Spanish, Vietnamese). Verónica then generates a full lesson plan using the ExCEL (Explain, Create, Elaborate) instructional model, tailored to the selected parameters.
- Language Scaffolding Form: Based on Texas English Language Proficiency Assessment System (TELPAS) proficiency levels and academic goals, this form produces targeted supports such as vocabulary previews, sentence stems, and structured language development activities.
- Cultural Connection Generator: Links academic content to culturally relevant themes or contexts, increasing engagement and linguistic relevance for specific student groups.
- Differentiated Reading Passage Creator: Produces versions of academic texts adapted to various language proficiency levels, maintaining content integrity while adjusting linguistic complexity.

Using Scenario-Based Learning Activities With AI Feedback

In our online preparation courses pre-service teachers engage with realistic classroom scenarios designed to assess and develop key competencies required for certification. These interactive online activities integrate videos, texts, and interactive chatbot dialogues that elicit teacher responses. Upon receiving responses, Verónica uses precisely engineered prompts and RAG methods to deliver immediate, personalized, and pedagogically grounded feedback.

The Bilingual Homework Hotline (BHH)

The Bilingual Homework Hotline (BHH) represents one of Verónica's most impactful applications, extending beyond certification preparation into authentic practical experience for pre-service teachers. This collaborative initiative between two universities and a school district creates a symbiotic relationship that benefits both pre-service teachers and K-12 emergent bilingual students while complementing existing teacher preparation coursework.

The BHH operates as a virtual tutoring service where pre-service teachers enrolled in bilingual and ESL certification programs volunteer to assist K-12 students with homework challenges via Zoom sessions. These students, predominantly emergent bilinguals from the partner school district, receive personalized academic support while the pre-service teachers gain invaluable real-world experience applying their theoretical knowledge in authentic instructional contexts.

We were invited to join this project while working at one of the participating universities. While the hotline was initially established as a service-learning opportunity designed to enhance teacher preparation through authentic tutoring experiences, we quickly saw that this context offered a powerful opportunity to integrate AI-driven support aligned with the bilingual and ESL pedagogical model we had been developing through Verónica. Although the system in this project does not use the name "Verónica," it is built upon the same foundational knowledge base and instructional design. In this case, the AI takes on a new persona, a small robot icon embedded in the interface used by pre-service teachers to access tutoring session links and related information. In addition to providing access to those logistical elements, the interface also features that same robot as a specialized chatbot, powered by the same foundations as Verónica: a large language model and a retrieval-augmented generation (RAG) system, designed with carefully crafted prompts to provide accurate, pedagogically grounded responses in real time.

These online tutoring sessions often present unexpected challenges that test the limits of pre-service teachers' current knowledge and skills. A fifth-grader might struggle with mathematics terminology that the pre-service teacher doesn't know how to explain in Spanish; a middle schooler might need help with science concepts the tutor hasn't encountered since their own K-12 education; or a recently arrived student might speak a language variation unfamiliar to the tutor.

To address these challenges, we adapted Verónica's underlying model to create a specialized Bilingual Homework Hotline (BHH) chatbot designed explicitly to provide real-time, targeted support to pre-service teachers during their tutoring sessions. Utilizing the robust knowledge base and advanced AI architecture, this chatbot delivers contextually relevant assistance, empowering pre-service teachers to confidently guide emergent bilingual students effectively.

The BHH chatbot serves multiple essential functions during tutoring sessions. It helps make the problem or question understandable by briefly explaining the significance of the concept within the subject area. It suggests straightforward explanations using real-world connections, visuals, or analogies, and highlights common misconceptions students might encounter. For example, a pre-service teacher working with a fourth-grader on fractions might ask, “How can I explain equivalent fractions to a fourth-grader who is still developing academic English?” The chatbot provides grade-appropriate explanations, recommends visual models, and points out relevant cognates to support the student's understanding. Then it provides step-by-step problem-solving support and guides the pre-service teachers through the process of facilitating the student's problem-solving skills by suggesting thoughtful questions the pre-service teacher can use to prompt student reasoning, rather than directly giving answers.

When tutors encounter specific domain vocabulary, they might request support by asking, “What's the appropriate Spanish terminology for discussing the water cycle with a third-grader?” The chatbot then offers precise translations and contextual examples, aiding the teacher in maintaining academic rigor in the student's first language.

The chatbot can also help with adapting to students' language needs by simplifying explanations to ensure clarity for emergent bilingual students, recommending the use of visuals, gestures, or tangible, real-world examples and highlighting helpful cognates between English and the student's primary language. For instance, if a tutor faces challenges explaining geometric shapes, they might ask, “Can you suggest culturally relevant examples of geometric shapes that would resonate with a student from Guatemala?” The chatbot then suggests culturally relevant examples that make mathematical concepts more accessible and engaging.

The chatbot responses include suggestions to encourage active learning by prompting tutors to ask students to explain concepts in their own words and providing additional practice ideas, such as mnemonics, sentence frames, or hands-on activities, to reinforce learning. When a student has difficulty understanding cause-and-effect relationships in a reading passage, pre-service teachers might ask the chatbot, “What visuals or graphic organizers could support a sixth-grader's comprehension of cause and effect?” The chatbot responds with specific recommendations, including bilingual examples, visual aids, and step-by-step guidance for implementation, directly addressing the student's linguistic and academic needs.

The multilingual capabilities of the BHH chatbot have proven especially valuable in addressing unexpected language-related challenges. While most tutors are proficient in English and Spanish, they occasionally encounter students who speak other languages or regional variations that complicate communication. The chatbot helps bridge these gaps by offering translations, insights into linguistic patterns, cultural contexts, and communication strategies, thus enabling more effective tutoring despite linguistic diversity.

Just like any other system where we integrate Verónica, our implementation leverages advanced large language models, structured specifically to apply best practices for emergent bilingual learners. Rather than simply generating answers, the chatbot mirrors the pedagogical thinking process of skilled bilingual educators by considering factors such as grade level, language proficiency, and prior knowledge. For example, if a pre-service teacher seeks help explaining a fifth-grade mathematics word problem on fractions to a newcomer, the chatbot provides mathematical explanations alongside suggestions for activating prior knowledge, connecting to familiar contexts, building academic vocabulary in both languages, and offering visual supports. This comprehensive approach supports pre-service teachers in developing the pedagogical reasoning needed to make complex content accessible while fostering language development.

Integrating the BHH chatbot into tutoring sessions transforms these interactions into valuable learning laboratories. Pre-service teachers acquire practical skills with immediate, contextually relevant support, complementing traditional teacher preparation programs. Rather than feeling overwhelmed by unfamiliar academic or linguistic challenges, pre-service teachers can access targeted guidance that builds their competence, reduces anxiety, and accelerates their professional growth.

Ultimately, the BHH chatbot demonstrates how AI tools can meaningfully enhance teacher preparation programs by facilitating authentic teaching experiences, enabling pre-service teachers to apply theoretical knowledge effectively, and fostering the adaptive expertise essential for teaching in multilingual classrooms. Just as importantly, the emergent bilingual students receiving support through the Bilingual Homework Hotline also benefit from this technology-enhanced model, gaining access to academic assistance that is more responsive, linguistically appropriate, and instructionally sound. In this way, all participants in the project, from tutors to students, experience the value of thoughtful, purpose-driven integration of AI in education.

EXTENDING AI SUPPORT TO IN-SERVICE TEACHERS

To better support in-service teachers, we've expanded Verónica's capabilities through a hybrid professional development model that blends in-person workshops with ongoing digital support. This approach addresses a well-known limitation in traditional professional learning: the difficulty of sustaining new strategies once teachers return to their classrooms. Even the most engaging workshops often fall short without consistent follow-up, leaving educators without the support they need to implement change effectively (Erdem Coşgun & Savaş, 2024; Rizk et al., 2024; Zhang et al., 2022).

In our model, the professional development journey begins with face-to-face workshops centered on bilingual instruction, especially in complex subjects like STEM, where academic language and content intersect in challenging ways. During these sessions, Verónica functions as a co-facilitator, offering immediate, context-aware guidance as teachers plan collaboratively. Participants don't just listen, they engage in applying concepts to their own classroom situations with support from both human experts and the AI system.

But what truly sets this model apart is what happens after the workshop ends. Instead of leaving with static handouts, teachers continue to access Verónica as they implement new approaches. They can revisit workshop materials, explore resources, and ask specific follow-up questions when real-world application raises new challenges. This transforms professional learning from a one-time event into an ongoing process, available whenever teachers are planning or reflecting.

One of Verónica's most appreciated features is its ability to support personalized instructional planning. Using interactive tools, teachers can generate classroom-ready resources tailored to their students' needs, language profiles, and cultural backgrounds. For instance, when planning a science lesson, a teacher can select relevant parameters (grade level, language program model, and student demographics) and receive a customized instructional package that includes lesson sequences, academic vocabulary, scaffolds, and cultural connections. These are not generic templates but highly contextualized materials designed to meet teachers where they are.

Beyond simply generating or suggesting lesson plans, Verónica acts as a collaborative partner. Teachers can ask for revisions, request additional supports, or adapt strategies based on their expertise. The system respects teacher autonomy while offering insight and suggestions that reflect the complexity of multilingual classrooms.

Accessibility has also been enhanced through natural language voice interaction. Teachers can speak to Verónica as they would to a colleague, whether during a planning period or while preparing materials. This voice interface supports both English and Spanish, allowing bilingual educators to express themselves naturally and fluidly. Teachers often use this feature to ask about content explanations, check pronunciation of academic terms, explore cross-linguistic connections, or seek culturally relevant strategies. The system maintains understanding even during code-switching, making it a rare tool that aligns with how bilingual educators actually communicate.

The system's support is especially impactful for first-year teachers, who often face the steepest learning curves. Navigating classroom management, instructional planning, and the added complexity of language support can feel overwhelming. New teachers may hesitate to ask questions repeatedly for fear of appearing unprepared, but Verónica offers a private, judgment-free space to seek guidance. It provides resources on topics ranging from bilingual planning and communication with families to assessment practices and strategies for teacher well-being.

For school districts, Verónica offers a scalable way to extend support to new teachers without adding strain to existing human resources. It doesn't replace mentors, but it fills critical gaps, providing on-demand assistance that complements limited mentoring time and builds a strong foundation for long-term success. By offering responsive, relevant, and affirming guidance, Verónica is helping create a more sustainable path for teachers working in linguistically diverse classrooms.

Looking Ahead: AI-Augmented Professional Learning Communities

Recent research underscores how Professional Learning Communities (PLCs) can magnify the impact of digital professional development. A 2024 scan of 37 U.S. districts documented early pilots in which chatbots quietly curate resources and keep PLC conversations moving, provided that privacy safeguards are explicit (Krall et al., 2024). Likewise, a large-scale study involving more than 16,000 STEM teachers found that regular PLC participation is the key factor that turns online PD into tangible classroom technology integration (Liu et al., 2024). Guided by these findings, our next development cycle will add a modest "micro-PLC" layer to our existing WordPress site: when several teachers raise similar questions, the platform will invite them to a shared discussion page, suggest Verónica-curated readings, and email a brief weekly digest of the thread. Dialogue and decisions will remain firmly in teachers' hands; the AI's role is simply to connect colleagues working on similar challenges and to lighten the note-taking load.

Challenges, Limitations, and Ethics

The enthusiasm surrounding AI-mediated PD must be tempered by a candid look at persistent risks. Large-scale reviews highlight three pressure points: *data privacy*, as instructional chat logs can expose student information; *algorithmic bias*, where dominant-culture language norms may shape feedback; and the *digital divide*, which still limits bandwidth-heavy tools in rural districts (Smith & Chen, 2024; Zawacki-Richter et al., 2019). Throughout Verónica's build we addressed these issues through encrypted log storage, quarterly bias-audit prompts, and "low-spec" design that runs on entry-level Chromebooks. Even so, strong district data-governance policies, teacher agency in choosing AI suggestions, and ongoing equity reviews remain non-negotiable guardrails as the system scales.

USING AI IN TEACHER EDUCATION: OPPORTUNITIES AND CONSIDERATIONS

The integration of artificial intelligence into teacher preparation and professional development presents a timely opportunity to enhance the ways educators are supported, particularly in complex and evolving fields like multilingual education. Our experience with Verónica demonstrates how emerging technology can enrich existing preparation efforts and offer new possibilities that were previously difficult to achieve at scale.

While early feedback (collected through post-session surveys, brief pre-/post-quizzes, and chat-log reviews) tells us teachers find Verónica useful, we also recognize the need for a more systematic understanding of its impact. To that end, we plan to organize future study around Guskey's five-level professional-development model. The pulse-checks we already gather address Levels 1 and 2 (teacher reaction and learning). In partnership with a university teacher-preparation program, we will explore teacher-focused indicators for the remaining levels, for example, how often AI-supported lesson ideas are implemented (Level 3), whether certification-exam pass rates improve (Level 4), and whether program-completion or first-year retention numbers rise over time (Level 5). No formal research has begun; this simply outlines the structure we intend to follow once IRB approvals and institutional agreements are in place.

Our goal with this work is not to replace or critique current teacher-preparation models, but to introduce tools that can complement and strengthen them. We believe that embracing emerging technologies, already influencing nearly every aspect of society worldwide, is essential. Educators must be equipped not only to understand these tools but to use them purposefully to empower their own growth and, ultimately, their students' success. One of the most promising aspects of AI integration is the flexibility it provides. Verónica has been designed with adaptability in mind, capable of delivering custom activities, interactive forms, and conversational tools that can be tailored to meet the unique requirements of different school districts, certification programs, or instructional goals. Whether it's scenario-based coaching, bilingual planning tools, or on-demand support for classroom implementation, the system can evolve to support local needs without imposing a rigid framework.

A key advantage of this approach is the expansion of access to high-quality, personalized support. In many parts of the country, educators (particularly those in rural or under-resourced areas) face limited access to professional development aligned with their instructional context. AI-powered systems like Verónica offer a way to deliver consistent, responsive support regardless of geography or time constraints. Teachers can engage in meaningful learning when it aligns with their planning schedules or classroom demands, not just during formal training sessions.

Rather than offering one-size-fits-all resources, the system helps translate theoretical principles into practical strategies that reflect each teacher's grade level, student population, and language program model. For educators navigating the complexities of multilingual classrooms, this connection between theory and practice can be particularly helpful. AI systems can act as a bridge, delivering real-time suggestions and resources grounded in best practices, while always deferring to the professional judgment of the teacher.

This work also reinforces the idea that AI is most valuable when it complements human expertise. Teaching is a profoundly human endeavor, built on relationships, professional intuition, and contextual decision-making. Verónica is designed not to replace these qualities, but to enhance them, serving as a thinking partner that helps teachers explore options, reflect on decisions, and access research-backed guidance at their own pace. Importantly, we have trained Verónica to consistently encourage teachers to seek support from more experienced colleagues within their schools, districts, or professional networks. From the beginning, we have emphasized that one of the most powerful ways to grow as an educator is by building connections with seasoned professionals and learning from their lived experience in the classroom.

To ensure this kind of meaningful integration, thoughtful implementation becomes essential. AI systems like Verónica must be developed with careful attention to pedagogical integrity, ethical considerations, and the diverse realities of teaching contexts. Human oversight plays a critical role, not only during initial development, but also in maintaining high standards of content quality, cultural responsiveness, and alignment with evolving educational practices. At the same time, protecting data privacy and maintaining transparency are fundamental to building trust and fostering authentic engagement with these tools. As AI continues to evolve through real-world use, ongoing evaluation and feedback are key to refining its effectiveness and keeping the system aligned with the goals and values of the educators it serves.

Ultimately, we see AI not as a solution in itself, but as a valuable addition to the broader ecosystem of teacher support. Used thoughtfully, these tools can expand what's possible, offering new ways to practice, reflect, and grow as educators. They can help close gaps in access, offer just-in-time support, and create more responsive preparation experiences. Most importantly, they allow educators to engage with emerging technologies in ways that strengthen, not diminish, their expertise and impact in the classroom.

By embracing this opportunity, we not only support the evolving needs of teacher preparation but also empower educators to confidently navigate and lead in a rapidly changing educational landscape.

A HUMAN-CENTERED VISION FOR AI IN TEACHER PREPARATION

Throughout this chapter, we have shared the evolution and practical application of Verónica, an AI-powered virtual tutor intentionally designed to complement and enhance teacher preparation for multilingual classrooms. This work is grounded in the belief that artificial intelligence, when developed thoughtfully and applied responsibly, can become a powerful tool for supporting educators without replacing the human relationships, professional judgment, and cultural understanding that define effective teaching.

By drawing from Vygotsky's concept of the "More Knowledgeable Other," we explored how AI can offer scaffolded support that aligns with teachers' zones of proximal development. Verónica was developed not just to deliver information, but to serve as a dynamic thinking partner that helps teachers translate theory into practice in real time. From pre-service preparation to in-service professional growth, the system offers sustained, individualized guidance that adapts to the user's context, goals, and needs.

Importantly, Verónica's development was never about replacing teacher preparation programs or mentorship structures, but about enhancing them. We have consistently trained the system to encourage teachers to seek out and build relationships with more experienced professionals in their schools and communities. In fact, we believe the most effective growth happens when teachers use AI not in isolation, but as part of a broader, human-centered network of professional learning and support. Verónica extends that network by being available when mentors aren't, by prompting reflection, and by offering relevant, research-based strategies aligned with standards like the TEKS and TELPAS.

The examples we've shared (from lesson planning support to speaking practice, from differentiated instruction to just-in-time tutoring assistance) illustrate how AI can help address persistent challenges in multilingual education. By integrating content knowledge, cultural responsiveness, and linguistic development into a cohesive system, Verónica supports teachers as they navigate the realities of diverse classrooms and prepares them for certification success and sustained effectiveness.

Our long-term vision extends beyond one system or tool. We see this work as part of a broader movement to rethink how we support teachers, especially those working with emergent bilingual students. With the increasing presence of generative AI across sectors, education must actively engage with these technologies, not only to respond to change but to shape it. If we want to ensure that AI tools serve human learning, equity, and ethical practice, educators must be at the forefront of development, evaluation, and implementation.

That's why Verónica was designed with flexibility at its core. Whether it's used in certification preparation, during professional development workshops, or in real-time classroom problem solving, the system can be adapted to align with local needs, district models, and state expectations. This adaptability is not just a technical feature—it reflects our fundamental commitment to honoring the diversity of educational contexts and the autonomy of teachers and institutions.

Looking ahead, we envision even more immersive and collaborative experiences: adaptive simulations that respond to teacher choices, co-teaching practice environments, and deeper integration with multimodal analysis tools like video-based reflection and real-time instructional feedback. These innovations will continue to build on our central commitment: to create tools that empower teachers—not by replacing human insight, but by amplifying it. Ultimately, our work with Verónica reflects a broader imperative. As AI becomes increasingly embedded in every aspect of our lives, educators must learn how to use and shape these tools with intentionality. Teacher preparation programs are uniquely positioned to lead this effort, not only by incorporating AI as a subject of study, but by modeling how it can be used ethically, creatively, and effectively in service of real learning.

We hope this chapter serves as both a blueprint and an invitation. The blueprint outlines how AI can be applied to support educators in linguistically and culturally diverse classrooms. The invitation is to all teacher educators, researchers, district leaders, and instructional designers: join us in continuing to explore, question, and build tools that reflect the best of what education can be, human-centered, equitable, and responsive to the real challenges teachers and students face. The success of this work will not be measured by technological innovation alone, but by how effectively it helps teachers support multilingual learners in developing the knowledge and language skills they need to thrive. If we stay grounded in that purpose, AI can become a meaningful partner in strengthening teaching and learning across a wide range of classrooms and communities.

REFERENCES

Burner, T., & Svendsen, B. (2020). A Vygotskian perspective on teacher professional development. *Education, 141*(1), 24–32.

Carver-Thomas, D., & Darling-Hammond, L. (2022). *Teacher turnover and the teacher shortage: Why teachers leave and why it matters*. Learning Policy Institute.

Ding, A.-C. E., Shi, L., Yang, H., & Choi, I. (2024). Enhancing teacher AI literacy and integration through different types of cases in teacher professional development. *Computers and Education Open*, *6*, 100178. Advance online publication. DOI: 10.1016/j.caeo.2024.100178

Enabling Learning, L. L. C. (2024a, March 15). *Enhancing AI interactions in teacher education*. Enabling Learning LLC. https://www.enablinglearning.com/enhancing-ai-interactions-in-teacher-education/

Enabling Learning, L. L. C. (2024b, January 8). *Veronica*. Enabling Learning LLC. https://www.enablinglearning.com/veronica/

Erdem Coşgun, G., & Savaş, P. (2024). Enhancing teaching skills of in-service English teachers through online professional development. *Journal of Learning and Teaching in Digital Age*, *9*(1), 58–72. DOI: 10.53850/joltida.1248625

Guskey, T. R. (2002). Does it make a difference? Evaluating professional development. *Educational Leadership*, *59*(6), 45–51.

Holmes, W., Bialik, M., & Fadel, C. (2019). *Artificial intelligence in education: Promises and implications for teaching and learning*. Center for Curriculum Redesign.

Ikumapayi, N. A. (2023). Automated front-end code generation using OpenAI: Empowering web development efficiency. SSRN *Electronic Journal*. DOI: 10.2139/ssrn.4590704

Inkpen, K., Chappidi, S., Mallari, K., Nushi, B., Ramesh, D., Michelucci, P., Mandava, V., Vepřek, L. H., & Quinn, G. (2023). Advancing human-AI complementarity: The impact of user expertise and algorithmic tuning on joint decision making. *ACM Transactions on Computer-Human Interaction*, *30*(5), 74. Advance online publication. DOI: 10.1145/3534561

Kasneci, E., Sessler, K., Küchemann, S., Bannert, M., Dementieva, D., Fischer, F., Gasser, U., Groh, G., Günnemann, S., Hüllermeier, E., Krusche, S., Kutyniok, G., Michaeli, T., Nerdel, C., Pfeffer, J., Poquet, O., Sailer, M., Schmidt, A., Seidel, T., & Kasneci, G. (2023). ChatGPT for good? On opportunities and challenges of large language models for education. *Learning and Individual Differences*, *103*, 102274. Advance online publication. DOI: 10.1016/j.lindif.2023.102274

Krall, B., Fagan, C., Schwartz, N., & Boguslav, A. (2024, May). *AI in professional learning: Navigating opportunities and challenges for educators* [Report]. Annenberg Institute at Brown University.

Lin, C. C., Huang, A. Y. Q., & Lu, O. H. T. (2023). Artificial intelligence in intelligent tutoring systems toward sustainable education: A systematic review. *Smart Learning Environments*, *10*(1), 41. Advance online publication. DOI: 10.1186/s40561-023-00260-y

Liu, J., Aziku, M., Qiang, F., & Zhang, B. (2024). Leveraging professional learning communities in linking digital professional development and instructional integration: Evidence from 16,072 STEM teachers. *International Journal of STEM Education*, *11*(1), 56. Advance online publication. DOI: 10.1186/s40594-024-00513-3

Martin, M., & Sun, J. (2022). AI-augmented video reflection and its impact on novice teachers' questioning strategies. *Teacher Education Quarterly*, *49*(2), 67–90.

Open, A. I. (2023, November 30). *ChatGPT: Optimizing language models for dialogue*. OpenAI Blog. https://openai.com/blog/chatgpt

Open, A. I. (2024a). *Embeddings – OpenAI API*. OpenAI. https://platform.openai.com/docs/guides/embeddings

Open, A. I. (2024b). *Fine-tuning – OpenAI API*. OpenAI. https://platform.openai.com/docs/guides/fine-tuning

Otto, F., Kling, N., Schumann, C.-A., & Tittmann, C. (2023). Conceptual approach to an AI-based adaptive study support system for individualized higher education. *International Journal of Advanced Corporate Learning*, *16*(2), 78–89. DOI: 10.3991/ijac.v16i2.35699

Ouyang, F., & Jiao, P. (2021). Artificial intelligence in education: The three paradigms. *Computers and Education: Artificial Intelligence*, *2*, 100020. Advance online publication. DOI: 10.1016/j.caeai.2021.100020

Retzlaff, C. O., Das, S., Wayllace, C., Mousavi, P., Afshari, M., Yang, T., Saranti, A., Angerschmid, A., Taylor, M. E., & Holzinger, A. (2024). Human-in-the-loop reinforcement learning: A survey and position on requirements, challenges, and opportunities. *Journal of Artificial Intelligence Research, 79*, 349–415. DOI: 10.1613/jair.1.15348

Rizk, N., Taylor, S., & Taylor, N. (2024). Remote classroom modelling: A professional development model for in-service generalist primary teachers of science. *Australian Educational Researcher, 51*(1), 287–309. DOI: 10.1007/s13384-022-00594-5 PMID: 36568710

Rudolph, J., Tan, S., & Tan, S. (2023). War of the chatbots: Bard, Bing Chat, ChatGPT, Ernie and beyond: The new AI gold rush and its impact on higher education. *Journal of Applied Learning and Teaching, 6*(1), 364–389. DOI: 10.37074/jalt.2023.6.1.23

Shezad, F., Goswami, R., Shaheen, A., & Khan, I. (2025). AI in teacher training and professional development: A tool for continuous learning and skill enhancement. *Review of Education. Administration & Law, 8*(1), 179–191. DOI: 10.47067/real.v8i1.416

Smith, A., & Chen, L. (2024). Artificial intelligence in teaching and teacher professional development: A systematic review. *Computers and Education: Artificial Intelligence, 5*, 100589. Advance online publication. DOI: 10.1016/S2666-920X(24)001589

Taipalus, T. (2024). Vector database management systems: Fundamental concepts, use-cases, and current challenges. *Cognitive Systems Research, 85*, 101216. Advance online publication. DOI: 10.1016/j.cogsys.2024.101216

Tammets, K., & Ley, T. (2023). Integrating AI tools in teacher professional learning: A conceptual model and illustrative case. *Frontiers in Artificial Intelligence, 6*, 1255089. Advance online publication. DOI: 10.3389/frai.2023.1255089 PMID: 38130325

Tan, X., Cheng, G., & Ling, M. H. (2024). Artificial intelligence in teaching and teacher professional development: A systematic review. *Computers and Education: Artificial Intelligence, 8*, 100355. Advance online publication. DOI: 10.1016/j.caeai.2024.100355

Teach, F. X. (2024). *TeachFX: Conversation analytics for reflective practice* [White paper]. https://teachfx.com/

Triwicaksana, M. B. S., & Oktavia, T. (2023). Building a retrieval-augmented generation system for enhanced student learning: Case study at private university. *Journal of Theoretical and Applied Information Technology, 101*(22), 7234–7245.

Vassileva, J. (2008). Social learning environments: New challenges for AI in education. In Luckin, R., Koedinger, K. R., & Greer, J. (Eds.), *Artificial intelligence in education* (pp. 532–539). Springer., DOI: 10.1007/978-3-540-69132-7_5

Villamizar Castrillón, L. J. (2017). The effects of Vygotsky's sociocultural theory on second language acquisition and language input. *Espiral. Revista de Docencia e Investigación*, *7*(1), 91–114. DOI: 10.15332/erdi.v7i1.1780

Vygotsky, L. S. (1978). *Mind in society: The development of higher psychological processes* (Cole, M., John-Steiner, V., Scribner, S., & Souberman, E., Eds.). Harvard University Press.

Williams, P., & Fowler, A. (2023). Accelerating feedback cycles with AI annotations in micro-teaching. *Computers & Education*, *205*, 104903. Advance online publication. DOI: 10.1016/j.compedu.2023.104903

Yu, W. (2022). Retrieval-augmented generation across heterogeneous knowledge. In *Proceedings of the 2022 Conference of the North American Chapter of the Association for Computational Linguistics: Human Language Technologies* (pp. 207–217). Association for Computational Linguistics. DOI: 10.18653/v1/2022.naacl-srw.7

Zawacki-Richter, O., Marín, V. I., Bond, M., & Gouverneur, F. (2019). Systematic review of research on artificial intelligence applications in higher education: Emerging trends and patterns. *International Journal of Educational Technology in Higher Education*, *16*(1), 39. Advance online publication. DOI: 10.1186/s41239-019-0171-0

Zhang, J., Wang, B., Yang, H. H., Chen, Z., Gao, W., & Liu, Z. (2022). Assessing quality of online learning platforms for in-service teachers' professional development: The development and application of an instrument. *Frontiers in Psychology*, *13*, 998196. Advance online publication. DOI: 10.3389/fpsyg.2022.998196 PMID: 36275249

Zhao, L., Wu, X., & Luo, H. (2022). Developing AI literacy for primary and middle school teachers in China: Based on a structural equation modeling analysis. *Sustainability (Basel)*, *14*(21), 14549. Advance online publication. DOI: 10.3390/su142114549

Compilation of References

Abdalkader, S. M. A. (2023). *The impact of using artificial intelligence on enhancing EFL language fluency and self-regulation for the preparatory stage students in distinguished governmental language schools*. PhD thesis. Ain Shams University.

Abdulayeva, A., Nazym, Z., Yerlan, A., & Farzana, B. (2025). Fostering AI literacy in pre-service physics teachers: Inputs from training and co-variables. *Frontiers in Education*, *10*, 1505420. Advance online publication. DOI: 10.3389/feduc.2025.1505420

Abrams, Z. (2025). Classrooms are adapting to the use of artificial intelligence. *Monitor on Psychology*, *56*(1). https://www.apa.org/monitor/2025/01/trends-classrooms-artificial-intelligence

Adeshina, A. E. (2024). From Theory to Practice: A Framework for Inclusive Technology Integration in Education. *International Journal of Instructional Technology and Educational Studies*, *5*(1), 1–6. DOI: 10.21608/ihites.2024.380764

Aguilera, E., & Salazar, C. (2023). *Critical Digital Pedagogy in the Platform Society*. Oxford Research Encyclopedia of Education. DOI: 10.1093/acrefore/9780190264093.013.1888

Agustini, N. P. O. (2023). Examining the role of ChatGPT as a learning tool in promoting students' English language learning autonomy relevant to Kurikulum Merdeka Belajar. *EDUKASIA: Jurnal Pendidikan Dan Pembelajaran*, *4*(2), 921–934. DOI: 10.62775/edukasia.v4i2.373

Akcan, A. T., Yıldırım, B., Karataş, A. R., & Yılmaz, M. (2023). Teachers' views on the effect of STEM education on the labor market. *Frontiers in Psychology*, *14*, 1184730. Advance online publication. DOI: 10.3389/fpsyg.2023.1184730 PMID: 37377702

Akhmetova, A. I., Sovetkanova, D. M., Komekbayeva, L. K., Abdrakhmanov, A. E., Yessenuly, D., & Serikova, O. S. (2025). A systematic review of artificial intelligence in high school STEM education research. *Eurasia Journal of Mathematics, Science and Technology Education, 21*(4), em2623. Advance online publication. DOI: 10.29333/ejmste/16222

Allington, R. L. (2002). *What really matters for struggling readers: Designing research-based programs*. Allyn & Bacon.

Ally, M. (2019). Competency Profile of the digital and online teacher in future Education. *International Review of Research in Open and Distance Learning, 20*(2). Advance online publication. DOI: 10.19173/irrodl.v20i2.4206

Anderson, L. W., Krathwohl, D. R., & Bloom, B. S. (2001). *A taxonomy for learning, teaching, and assessing : a revision of Bloom's taxonomy of educational objectives* Longman.

Anderson, J. R., Corbett, A. T., Koedinger, K. R., & Pelletier, R. (2014). Cognitive tutors: Lessons learned. *Journal of the Learning Sciences, 4*(2), 167–207. DOI: 10.1207/s15327809jls0402_2

Andrade, H. L., & Brookhart, S. M. (2019). Classroom assessment as the co-regulation of learning. *Assessment in Education: Principles, Policy & Practice, 27*(4), 350–372. DOI: 10.1080/0969594X.2019.1571992

Antonenko, P., & Abramowitz, B. (2022). In-service teachers' (mis)conceptions of artificial intelligence in K-12 science education. *Journal of Research on Technology in Education, 55*(1), 64–78. DOI: 10.1080/15391523.2022.2119450

Antropic. (2025). MagicSchool transforms K-12 education for 3 million educators and their students with Claude. Anthropic. https://www.anthropic.com/customers/magicschool

Armstrong, P. (2010). *Bloom's Taxonomy*. Vanderbilt University Center for Teaching. https://cft.vanderbilt.edu/guides-sub-pages/blooms-taxonomy

Ayanwale, M. A., Adelana, O. P., Molefi, R. R., Adeeko, O., & Ishola, A. M. (2024b). Examining artificial intelligence literacy among pre-service teachers for future classrooms. *Computers and Education Open, 6*, 100179. Advance online publication. DOI: 10.1016/j.caeo.2024.100179

Ayanwale, M. A., Frimpong, E. K., Opesemowo, O. A. G., & Sanusi, I. T. (2024a). Exploring factors that support pre-service teachers' engagement in learning artificial intelligence. *Journal for STEM Education Research*. Advance online publication. DOI: 10.1007/s41979-024-00121-4

Ayeni, O. O., Al Hamad, N. M., Chisom, O. N., Osawaru, B., & Adewusi, O. E. (2024). AI in education: A review of personalized learning and educational technology. *GSC Advanced Research and Reviews, 18*(2), 261–271. DOI: 10.30574/gscarr.2024.18.2.0062

Azzam, A., & Charles, T. (2025). K-12 STEM Teachers' Experiences with Artificial Intelligence. *TEM Journal*, 463–468. https://doi.org/DOI: 10.18421/tem141-41

Bahadir, F., & Dikmen, M. (2022) The Effect of 5E Learning Model on Students' Academic Achievement: A Meta-analysis Study. *İstanbul Aydın Üniversitesi Sosyal Bilimler Dergisi, 14(4),* 532-552.

Baker, R. S. J. d., & Siemens, G. (2022). Educational data mining and learning analytics. In Spector, J. M. (Eds.), *Handbook of research on educational communications and technology* (5th ed.). Springer., DOI: 10.1007/978-3-030-23206-8

Baker, R. S., & Hawn, A. (2021). Algorithmic bias in education. *International Journal of Artificial Intelligence in Education, 32*(4), 1052–1092. DOI: 10.1007/s40593-021-00285-9

Bali, M. (2014). *Critical pedagogy: Intentions and realities.* Hybrid Pedagogy.

Bandura, A. (1993). Perceived self-efficacy in cognitive development and functioning. *Educational Psychologist, 28*(2), 117–148. DOI: 10.1207/s15326985ep2802_3

Barrett, A., & Pack, A. (2023). Not quite eye to A.I.: Student and teacher perspectives on the use of generative artificial intelligence in the writing process. *International Journal of Educational Technology in Higher Education, 20*(1), 59. Advance online publication. DOI: 10.1186/s41239-023-00427-0

Barsoum, S. S., Elnagar, M. S., & Awad, B. M. (2022). The Effectiveness of Using a Cognitive Style-based Chatbot in Developing Science Concepts and Critical Thinking Skills among Preparatory School Pupils. *European Scientific Journal, 18*(22), 52. DOI: 10.19044/esj.2022.v18n22p52

Bautista, A., Estrada, C., Jaravata, A. M., Mangaser, L. M., Narag, F., Soquila, R., & Asuncion, R. J. (2024). Preservice teachers' readiness towards integrating AI-based tools in education: A TPACK approach. Educational Process. *International Journal (Toronto, Ont.), 13*(3), 40–68. DOI: 10.22521/edupij.2024.133.3

Bell, S. (2010). Project-Based Learning for the 21st Century: Skills for the Future. *The Clearing House: A Journal of Educational Strategies, Issues and Ideas, 83*(2), 39–43. DOI: 10.1080/00098650903505415

Bennett, V., & Royce, C. A. (2024, Dec. 9). AI and Culturally Relevant Pedgogy: A Great pAIr. *NSTA: Chalkboards to AI.* https://www.nsta.org/blog/ai-and-culturally-relevant-pedagogy-great-pair#:~:text=By%20using%20AI%2Dpowered%20learning,their%20cultural%20and%20eductional%20needs

Biesta, G. (2007). Why "what works" won't work: Evidence-based practice and the democratic deficit in educational research. *Educational Theory*, *57*(1), 1–22. DOI: 10.1111/j.1741-5446.2006.00241.x

Billingsley, B. S. (2004). Promoting teacher quality and retention in special education. *Journal of Learning Disabilities*, *37*(5), 370–376. DOI: 10.1177/00222194040370050101 PMID: 15460345

Binns, R. (2018). Fairness in machine learning: Lessons from political philosophy. *Proceedings of the 2018 Conference on Fairness, Accountability, and Transparency,* 149-159.

Bit.AI Editorial Team. (2019). *11 Best Content Curation Tools for Marketers!* Bit. AI Blog. https://blog.bit.ai/best-content-curation-tools/

Boateng, N. O., & Boateng, N. B. (2025). Algorithmic bias in educational systems: Examining the impact of AI-driven decision making in modern education. *World Journal of Advanced Research and Reviews*, *25*(1), 2012–2017. DOI: 10.30574/wjarr.2025.25.1.0253

Borg, S., & Al-Busaidi, S. (2012). Teachers' beliefs and practices regarding learner autonomy. *ELT Journal*, *66*(3), 283–292. DOI: 10.1093/elt/ccr065

Boud, D., Keogh, R., & Walker, D. (1985). *Reflection: Turning experience into learning*. Kogan Page.

Bower, M., Torrington, J., Lai, J. W. M., Petocz, P., & Alfano, M. (2024). How should we change teaching and assessment in response to increasingly powerful generative Artificial Intelligence? Outcomes of the ChatGPT teacher survey. *Education and Information Technologies*. Advance online publication. DOI: 10.1007/s10639-023-12405-0

Braaten, E., & Farnsworth, K. (2024). Educators' perspectives on generative AI in K-12: Informing AI in education guidance. *Friday Institute for Educational Innovation, North Carolina State University.* https://fi.ncsu.edu/resource-library/perspectives-ai-in-k12/

Brisk Labs Co. (2025). Brisk teaching [Large language model]. https://www.briskteaching.com/

Brisk Teaching. (2025). *The simple ai teaching assistant that works wherever you do.* https://www.briskteaching.com/

Brookhart, S. M., & Chen, F. (2014). The quality and effectiveness of descriptive rubrics. *Educational Review, 67*(3), 343–368. DOI: 10.1080/00131911.2014.929565

Bruner, J. (1986). *Actual Minds, Possible Worlds.* Harvard University Press. DOI: 10.4159/9780674029019

Burner, T., & Svendsen, B. (2020). A Vygotskian perspective on teacher professional development. *Education, 141*(1), 24–32.

Bybee, R. W. (2013). *The case for STEM education: Challenges and opportunities.* NSTA Press.

Bybee, R. W. (2015). *The BSCS 5E Instructional Model: Creating Teachable Moments* (1st ed.). National Science Teachers Association.

Çakıcı, D. (2015). Autonomy in language teaching and learning process. *İnönü Üniversitesi Eğitim Fakültesi Dergisi, 16*(1), 31–42.

Cakır, N. K. (2017). Effect of 5E learning model on academic achievement, attitude and science process skills: Meta-Analysis Study. *Journal of Education and Training Studies, 5*(11), 157. DOI: 10.11114/jets.v5i11.2649

Campello de Souza, F. C., Rangel, I. A., & Batista, R. C. (2024). The generative AI revolution and sophotechnic mediation. *AI & Society*. Advance online publication. DOI: 10.1007/s00146-023-01833-3

Canva, A. I. (n.d.). Canva [Large language model]. https://www.canva.com/your-apps/ai-powered

Cao, W., Wang, Q., Sbeih, A., & Shibly, F. (2020). Artificial intelligence based efficient smart learning framework for education platform. *Inteligencia Artificial, 23*(66). Advance online publication. DOI: 10.4114/intartif.vol23iss66pp112-123

Carbonell, J. R. (1970). AI in CAI: An Artificial Intelligence approach to computer-assisted instruction. *IEEE Transactions on Man-Machine Systems, 11*(4), 190–202. DOI: 10.1109/TMMS.1970.299942

Carreon, A., Criss, C., & Mosher, M. (2023). Classroom virtual reality for students with disabilities: A preliminary guide to available virtual content. *Journal of Special Education Technology, 0*(0), 1–8. DOI: 10.1177/01626434231170593

Carver-Thomas, D., & Darling-Hammond, L. (2019). The trouble with teacher turnover: How teacher attrition affects students and schools. *Education Policy Analysis Archives*, *27*(36), 36. DOI: 10.14507/epaa.27.3699

Carver-Thomas, D., & Darling-Hammond, L. (2022). *Teacher turnover and the teacher shortage: Why teachers leave and why it matters*. Learning Policy Institute.

CAST. (2018). *Universal Design for Learning Guidelines version 2.2*. http://udlguidelines.cast.org

Celce-Murcia, M. (2001). Language teaching approaches: An overview. *Teaching English as a Second or Foreign Language*, *2*(1), 3–10.

ChatGPT Pro. (2025, June 19). *Student engagement practices*. ChatGPT Pro. https://chatpro.ai-pro.org/chat/new

ChatGPT. (2025). OpenAI. https://chatgpt.com/

Cheng, G. (2017). The impact of online automated feedback on students' reflective journal writing in an EFL course. *The Internet and Higher Education*, *34*, 18–27. DOI: 10.1016/j.iheduc.2017.04.002

Cheng, G., Law, E., & Wong, T.-L. (2016). Investigating effects of automated feedback on EFL students' reflective learning skills. *2016 IEEE International Conference on Teaching, Assessment, and Learning for Engineering*, 226–230. DOI: 10.1109/TALE.2016.7851798

Chen, L., Chen, P., & Lin, Z. (2020). Artificial intelligence in education: A review. *IEEE Access : Practical Innovations, Open Solutions*, *8*, 75264–75278. DOI: 10.1109/ACCESS.2020.2988510

Chinta, S. V., Wang, Z., Yin, Z., Hoang, N., Gonzalez, M., Quy, T. L., & Zhang, W. (2024). FairAIED: Navigating fairness, bias, and ethics in educational AI applications. *arXiv (Cornell University)*. https://doi.org//arxiv.2407.18745DOI: 10.48550

Chiu, M., Hwang, G., Hsia, L., & Shyu, F. (2022). Artificial intelligence-supported art education: A deep learning-based system for promoting university students' artwork appreciation and painting outcomes. *Interactive Learning Environments*, *32*(3), 824–842. DOI: 10.1080/10494820.2022.2100426

Chiu, T. K. F. (2024). Future research recommendations for transforming higher education with generative AI Future research recommendations for transforming higher education with generative AI. *Computers and Education. Artificial Intelligence*, *6*, 100197.

Christou, P. A. (2023). The use of artificial intelligence (AI) in qualitative research for theory development. *The Qualitative Report*, *28*(9), 2739–2755. DOI: 10.46743/2160-3715/2023.6536

Cochran-Smith, M., & Lytle, S. L. (2009). *Inquiry as stance: Practitioner research for the next generation*. Teachers College Press.

Cook, A. M., & Hussey, S. M. (2002). *Assistive technologies. Principles and practice*. Academic Press.

Cook, V. (2014). How do people learn to write in a second language? In *Key topics in second language education* (pp. 73–88). MM Textbooks. DOI: 10.2307/jj.26931996.9

Cooper, M. M. (1986). The ecology of writing. *College English*, *48*(4), 364–375. DOI: 10.58680/ce198611607

Creswell, J. W. (2014). Research design: Qualitative, quantitative and mixed methods approaches. *Sage (Atlanta, Ga.)*.

Cummings, K. D., Atkins, T., Allison, R., & Cole, C. (2008). Response to intervention; Investigating the new role of special educators. *Teaching Exceptional Children*, *40*(4), 24–31. DOI: 10.1177/004005990804000403

Curipod, A. S. (2025). Curipod [Large language model]. https://curipod.com/

Damioli, G., Van Roy, V., & Vertesy, D. (2021). The impact of artificial intelligence on labor productivity. *Eurasian Economic Review*, *11*(1), 1–25. DOI: 10.1007/s40821-020-00172-8

Dam, L. (1995). *Learner autonomy: From theory to classroom practice*. Authentik Language Learning Resources.

Daniels, H. (2001). *Vygotsky and pedagogy*. Routledge.

Darling-Hammond, L. (2000). Teacher quality and student achievement: A review of state policy evidence. *Education Policy Analysis Archives*, *8*(1), 1. Advance online publication. DOI: 10.14507/epaa.v8n1.2000

Darling-Hammond, L., Flook, L., Cook-Harvey, C., Barron, B., & Osher, D. (2019). Implications for educational practice of the science of learning and development. *Applied Developmental Science*, *24*(2), 97–140. DOI: 10.1080/10888691.2018.1537791

Davis, F. D. (1989). Perceived usefulness, perceived ease of use and user acceptance of information technology. *Management Information Systems Quarterly*, *13*(3), 319–339. DOI: 10.2307/249008 del Carmen Salazar, M. (2013). A humanizing pedagogy: Reinventing the principles and practice of education as a journey toward liberation. *Review of Research in Education*, *37*(1), 121–148. DOI: 10.3102/0091732X12464032

Demszky, D., Liu, J., Hill, H. C., Jurafsky, D., & Piech, C. (2023). Can automated feedback improve teachers' uptake of student ideas? Evidence from a randomized controlled trial in a Large-Scale online course. *Educational Evaluation and Policy Analysis*, *46*(3), 483–505. DOI: 10.3102/01623737231169270

Dewey, J. (1933). *How we think: A restatement of the relation of reflective thinking to the educative process*. D.C. Heath & Co Publishers.

Diana, N. (1882). Yohannes, & Sukma, Y. (2021). The effectiveness of implementing project-based learning (PjBL) model in STEM education: A literature review. *Journal of Physics: Conference Series*, (1), 12146. DOI: 10.1088/1742-6596/1882/1/012146

Diffit. (2025). *Learning resources for all.* https://web.diffit.me/

Diffit. (n.d.-a). Diffit for teachers [Large language model]. https://web.diffit.me/

Diffit. (n.d.-b). Diffit in the ELA classroom. https://docs.google.com/presentation/d/16a8ZTmea0AWCGnljjDTmnZrqMA5EAxHkvQfz6yjJM5Q/edit?slide=id.g2ee86109b2d_0_0#slide=id.g2ee86109b2d_0_0

Digital Learning Institute. (2022, November 21). AI's transformative effect on curating digital learning content. https://www.digitallearninginstitute.com/blog/ai-transformative-effect-on-curating-content

Ding, A.-C. E., Shi, L., Yang, H., & Choi, I. (2024). Enhancing teacher AI literacy and integration through different types of cases in teacher professional development. *Computers and Education Open*, *6*, 100178. Advance online publication. DOI: 10.1016/j.caeo.2024.100178

Doshi-Velez, F., & Kortz, M. (2017). Accountability of AI under the law: The role of explanation. *Harvard Law School Report*.

DreamBox Learning. (2024). *DreamBox Learning Math: Adaptive learning for student growth.*https://www.dreambox.com

Edyburn, D. L. (2001). Models, theories, and frameworks: Contributions to understanding special education technology. *Special Education Technology Practice*, *4*(2), 16–24.

Enabling Learning, L. L. C. (2024a, March 15). *Enhancing AI interactions in teacher education*. Enabling Learning LLC. https://www.enablinglearning.com/enhancing-ai-interactions-in-teacher-education/

Enabling Learning, L. L. C. (2024b, January 8). *Veronica*. Enabling Learning LLC. https://www.enablinglearning.com/veronica/

Engeström, Y. (1987). *Learning by expanding: An activity-theoretical approach to developmental research.* Orienta-Kosultit Oy.

Erdem Coşgun, G., & Savaş, P. (2024). Enhancing teaching skills of in-service English teachers through online professional development. *Journal of Learning and Teaching in Digital Age*, *9*(1), 58–72. DOI: 10.53850/joltida.1248625

Facer, K., & Selwyn, N. (2021). Digital technology and the futures of education—Towards 'non-stupid' optimism. *Educational Research*, *63*(2), 130–141. DOI: 10.1080/00131881.2021.1907327

Family Educational Rights and Privacy Act (FERPA) of 1974, 20 U.S.C. § 1232g

Floridi, L., Cowls, J., Beltrametti, M., Chatila, R., Chazerand, P., Dignum, V., Luetge, C., Madelin, R., Pagallo, U., Rossi, F., Schafer, B., Valcke, P., & Vayena, E. (2019). The Ethical Framework for a Good AI Society: Opportunities, Risks, Principles, and Recommendations. *Minds and Machines*, *29*(4), 689–707. DOI: 10.1007/s11023-018-9482-5 PMID: 30930541

Frank, A. (1989). *The diary of Anne Frank*. Longman.

Freeman, S., Eddy, S. L., McDonough, M., Smith, M. K., Okoroafor, N., Jordt, H., & Wenderoth, M. P. (2014). Active learning increases student performance in science, engineering, and mathematics. *Proceedings of the National Academy of Sciences of the United States of America*, *111*(23), 8410–8415. DOI: 10.1073/pnas.1319030111 PMID: 24821756

Freire, P. (2005). Pedagogy of the Oppressed. *Continuum.*

Frontline Research & Learning Institute. (2024). *Empowering K-12 Districts: Navigating AI Adoption for Enhanced Educational Efficiency and Effectiveness | Frontline Research & Learning Institute*. https://www.frontlineinstitute.com/reports/what-is-artificial-intelligence-ai-in-education/

Furtak, E. M. (2023). *Formative Assessment for 3D Science Learning: Supporting Ambitious and Equitable Instruction*. Teachers College Press.

Fu, Y., & Weng, Z. (2024). Navigating the Ethical Terrain of AI in Education: A Systematic Review on Framing responsible Human-Centered AI Practices. *Computers and Education Artificial Intelligence*, *100306*, 100306. Advance online publication. DOI: 10.1016/j.caeai.2024.100306

Giroux, H. A. (1994). *Disturbing pleasures: Learning popular culture.* Routledge.

Goldman, S. R., Taylor, J., Carreon, A., & Smith, S. J. (2024). Using AI to support special education teacher workload. *Journal of Special Education Technology*, *39*(3), 434–447. DOI: 10.1177/01626434241257240

Google Cloud. (n.d.). *What is artificial intelligence (AI)?* https://cloud.google.com/learn/what-is-artificial-intelligence?hl=en#common-types-of-artificial-neural-networks

Grabe, W., & Kaplan, R. B. (1996). *Theory and practice of writing*. Pearson Education Limited.

Graesser, A. C., Chipman, P., Haynes, B. C., & Olney, A. (2005). AutoTutor: An intelligent tutoring system with mixed-initiative dialogue. *IEEE Transactions on Education*, *48*(4), 612–618. DOI: 10.1109/TE.2005.856149

Guan, L., Zhang, Y., & Gu, M. M. (2025). Pre-service teachers preparedness for AI-integrated education: An investigation from perceptions, capabilities, and teachers' identity changes, Computers and Education. *Artificial Intelligence*, *8*, 100341. Advance online publication. DOI: 10.1016/j.caeai.2024.100341

Gunawan, K. D. H., Liliasari, L., Kaniawati, I., & Setiawan, W. (2021). Implementation of Competency Enhancement Program for science teachers assisted by artificial Intelligence in designing HOTS-based integrated science learning. *Jurnal Penelitian Dan Pembelajaran IPA*, *7*(1), 55. DOI: 10.30870/jppi.v7i1.8655

Guskey, T. R. (2002). Does it make a difference? Evaluating professional development. *Educational Leadership*, *59*(6), 45–51.

Hannan, B., & Eynon, R. (2025). Widening the Digital Divide: The mediating role of Intelligent Tutoring Systems in the relationship between rurality, socioeducational advantage, and mathematics learning outcomes. *Computers & Education*, *233*, 105312. DOI: 10.1016/j.compedu.2025.105312

Han, T., & Sari, E. (2022). An investigation on the use of automated feedback in Turkish EFL students' writing classes. *Computer Assisted Language Learning*, 1–24. DOI: 10.1080/09588221.2022.2067179

Hardcastle, J. M., Herrmann-Abell, C. F., & DeBoer, G. E. (2021). Validating a Claim-Evidence-Science Idea-Reasoning (CESR) framework for use in NGSS assessment tasks [Conference presentation]. *NARST Virtual Annual Conference, Online*. https://files.eric.ed.gov/fulltext/ED612227.pdf

Hattie, J., & Timperley, H. (2007). The power of feedback. *Review of Educational Research*, *77*(1), 81–112. DOI: 10.3102/003465430298487

Hein, G. E. (1991). *Constructivist learning theory*. Institute for Learning.

Herrmann-Abell, C. F., & DeBoer, G. E. (2022). Using Rasch measurement to develop 3D assessment tasks to measure students' understanding of energy. *Journal of Research in Science Teaching*, *59*(9), 1543–1568. DOI: 10.1002/tea.21798

Herrmann-Abell, C. F., Hardcastle, J., & DeBoer, G. E. (2023). Exploring the comparability of multiple-choice and constructed-response versions of scenario-based assessment tasks. *Journal of Research in Science Teaching*, *60*(1), 3–27. DOI: 10.1002/tea.21829

Hmelo-Silver, C. E. (2004). Problem-Based Learning: What and How Do Students Learn? *Educational Psychology Review*, *16*(3), 235–266. DOI: 10.1023/B:EDPR.0000034022.16470.f3

Hmelo-Silver, C. E., & Barrows, H. S. (2006). Goals and strategies of a problem-based learning facilitator. *The Interdisciplinary Journal of Problem-Based Learning*, *1*(1), 21–39. DOI: 10.7771/1541-5015.1004

Hodges, T. S. (2017). Theoretically speaking: An examination of four theories and how they support writing in the classroom. *The Clearing House: A Journal of Educational Strategies, Issues and Ideas*, *90*(4), 139–146. DOI: 10.1080/00098655.2017.1326228

Holec, H. (1981). *Autonomy and foreign language learning*. Pergamon.

Holicza, B., & Kiss, A. (2023). Predicting and comparing students' online and offline academic performance using machine learning algorithms. *Behavioral Sciences (Basel, Switzerland)*, *13*(4), 289. DOI: 10.3390/bs13040289 PMID: 37102803

Holmes, W., Bialik, M., & Fadel, C. (2019). *Artificial intelligence in education: Promises and implications for teaching and learning*. Center for Curriculum Redesign.

Holmes, W., Bialik, M., & Fadel, C. (2019). *Artificial Intelligence in Education: Promises and Implications for Teaching and Learning*. Center for Curriculum Redesign.

Holmes, W., Porayska-Pomsta, K., Holstein, K., Sutherland, E., & Baker, R. S. (2022). The promises and challenges of artificial intelligence for education: A critical review. *Learning, Media and Technology*, *47*(1), 1–20.

Hopman, J. A., van Lier, P. A., van der Ende, J., Struiksma, C., Wubbels, T., Verhulst, F. C., Maras, A., Linda, D., Breeman, L. D., & Tick, N. T. (2018). Impact of the Good Behavior Game on special education teachers. *Teachers and Teaching*, *24*(4), 350–368. DOI: 10.1080/13540602.2017.1379389

Huang, L. (2023). Ethics of Artificial intelligence in Education: Student privacy and data protection. *Science Insights Education Frontiers*, *16*(2), 2577–2587. DOI: 10.15354/sief.23.re202

Hyland, K. (2003). *Second language writing*. Cambridge University Press. DOI: 10.1017/CBO9780511667251

Ikumapayi, N. A. (2023). Automated front-end code generation using OpenAI: Empowering web development efficiency. SSRN *Electronic Journal*. DOI: 10.2139/ssrn.4590704

Individuals with Disabilities Education Improvement Act (IDEA), 20 U.S.C. § 1400 (2004).

Inkpen, K., Chappidi, S., Mallari, K., Nushi, B., Ramesh, D., Michelucci, P., Mandava, V., Vepřek, L. H., & Quinn, G. (2023). Advancing human-AI complementarity: The impact of user expertise and algorithmic tuning on joint decision making. *ACM Transactions on Computer-Human Interaction*, *30*(5), 74. Advance online publication. DOI: 10.1145/3534561

Işcan, Y. V. V., & Seyhan, H. G. (2021). The Effect of the 5E Learning Model Supported with Material Ensuring Conceptual Change on Science Achievement: The Example of "Heat and Temperature.". *Mimbar Sekolah Dasar*, *8*(3), 250–280. DOI: 10.53400/mimbar-sd.v8i3.33044

Javed, M., Juan, W. X., & Nazli, S. (2013). A study of students' assessment in writing skills of the English language. *International Journal of Instruction*, *6*(2), 129–144.

Jiao, P., Ouyang, F., Zhang, Q., & Alavi, A. H. (2022). Artificial intelligence-enabled prediction model of student academic performance in online engineering education. *Artificial Intelligence Review*, *55*(8), 6321–6344. DOI: 10.1007/s10462-022-10155-y

Johnson, D. W., Johnson, R. T., & Smith, K. A. (2014). Cooperative Learning: Improving University Instruction by Basing Practice on Validated Theory. *Journal on Excellence in College Teaching*, *25*(3–4), 85.

Kallio, M., & Harju, P. (2023). *Technology-enhanced learning in Finland: A case study*. Finnish National Agency for Education.

Kamalov, F., Santandreu Calonge, D., & Gurrib, I. (2023). New era of artificial intelligence in education: *Towards a Sustainable Multifaceted Revolution. Sustainability (Basel)*, *15*(16), 12451. DOI: 10.3390/su151612451

Karaci, A., Akyuz, H. I., & Bilgici, G. (2018). Effects of web-based intelligent tutoring systems on academic achievement and retention. In *International Journal of Computer Applications* (Vol. 181, Issue 16, pp. 35–36). https://files.eric.ed.gov/fulltext/ED588768.pdf

Karakaya, F., & Yılmaz, M. (2022). Teachers views on assessment and evaluation methods in STEM education: A science course example. *Journal of Pedagogical Research*. DOI: 10.33902/JPR.202213526

Karan, E., & Brown, L. (2022). Enhancing Students' Problem-solving Skills through Project-based Learning. *Journal of Problem Based Learning in Higher Education, 10*(1).

Karata¸, F., & Yüce, E. (2024). AI and the future of teaching: Preservice teachers' reflections on the use of artificial intelligence in open and distributed learning. *International Review of Research in Open and Distance Learning*, *25*(3), 304–325. DOI: 10.19173/irrodl.v25i3.7785

Kasneci, E., Sessler, K., Küchemann, S., Bannert, M., Dementieva, D., Fischer, F., Gasser, U., Groh, G., Günnemann, S., Hüllermeier, E., Krusche, S., Kutyniok, G., Michaeli, T., Nerdel, C., Pfeffer, J., Poquet, O., Sailer, M., Schmidt, A., Seidel, T., & Kasneci, G. (2023). ChatGPT for good? On opportunities and challenges of large language models for education. *Learning and Individual Differences*, *103*, 102274. Advance online publication. DOI: 10.1016/j.lindif.2023.102274

Kauffman, J. M., Hallahan, D. P., Pullen, P. C., & Badar, J. (2018). *Special education: What it is and why we need it*. Routledge. DOI: 10.4324/9781315211831

Kavitha, K., & Joshith, V. P. (2024). Pedagogical incorporation of artificial intelligence in K-12 science education: A decadal bibliometric mapping and systematic literature review (2013-2023). *Journal of Pedagogical Research*. DOI: 10.33902/JPR.202429218

Keppler, S., Sinchaisri, W., & Snyder, C. (2024). Backwards Planning with Generative AI: Case Study Evidence from US K12 Teachers. SSRN *Electronic Journal*. DOI: 10.2139/ssrn.4924786

Khan, W. N. (2024). Ethical Challenges of AI in Education: Balancing Innovation with Data Privacy. *Journal of AI in Education: Innovations, Opportunities, Challenges, and Future Directions*, *1*(1), 1–13.

Kim, J., Lee, H., & Cho, Y. H. (2022). Learning design to support student-AI collaboration: perspectives of leading teachers for AI in education. *Education and Information Technologies, 27*(5), 6069. http://dx.doi.org.proxy.tamuc.edu/10.1007/s10639-021-10831-6

Kim, M. S. (2019). Developing a competency taxonomy for teacher design knowledge in technology-enhanced learning environments: A literature review. *Research and Practice in Technology Enhanced Learning*, *14*(1), 18. Advance online publication. DOI: 10.1186/s41039-019-0113-4

Kim, Y.-S. G., & Park, S.-H. (2019). Unpacking pathways using the direct and indirect effects model of writing (DIEW) and the contributions of higher-order cognitive skills to writing. *Reading and Writing*, *32*(5), 1319–1343. DOI: 10.1007/s11145-018-9913-y

Koh, E., & Doroudi, S. (2023). Learning, teaching, and assessment with generative artificial intelligence: Towards a plateau of productivity. *Learning Research and Practice*, *9*(2), 109–116. DOI: 10.1080/23735082.2023.2264086

Kolb, D. A. (2015). *Experiential learning: Experience as the source of learning and development* (2nd ed.). Pearson Education.

Koper, R. (2014). Conditions for effective smart learning environments. *Smart Learning Environments*, *1*(1), 5. DOI: 10.1186/s40561-014-0005-4

Kop, R., Fournier, H., & Mak, J. S. F. (2011). A pedagogy of abundance or a pedagogy to support human beings? Participant support on massive open online courses. *International Review of Research in Open and Distance Learning*, *12*(7), 74–93. DOI: 10.19173/irrodl.v12i7.1041

Kotsis, K. T. (2024). Significance of experiments in inquiry-based science teaching. *European Journal of Education and Pedagogy*, *5*(2), 86–92. DOI: 10.24018/ejedu.2024.5.2.815

Krall, B., Fagan, C., Schwartz, N., & Boguslav, A. (2024, May). *AI in professional learning: Navigating opportunities and challenges for educators* [Report]. Annenberg Institute at Brown University.

Lankshear, C., & Knobel, M. (2015). Digital literacy and Digital Literacies:-policy, pedagogy and research considerations for education. *Nordic Journal of Digital Literacy, 10*(Jubileumsnummer), 8-20.

Lewis, R. B. (1993). *Special education technology: Classroom applications*. No Title.

Li, K. C., & Wong, B. T. (2023). Artificial intelligence in personalised learning: A bibliometric analysis. *Interactive Technology and Smart Education, 20*(3), 422–445. DOI: 10.1108/ITSE-01-2023-0007

Li, L., Chen, C. P., Wang, L., Liang, K., & Bao, W. (2023). Exploring Artificial Intelligence in Smart Education: Real-Time Classroom Behavior Analysis with Embedded Devices. *Sustainability (Basel), 15*(10), 7940. DOI: 10.3390/su15107940

Lin, C. C., Huang, A. Y. Q., & Lu, O. H. T. (2023). Artificial intelligence in intelligent tutoring systems toward sustainable education: A systematic review. *Smart Learning Environments, 10*(1), 41. Advance online publication. DOI: 10.1186/s40561-023-00260-y

Lincoln, Y. S., & Guba, E. G. (1985). Naturalistic inquiry. *Sage (Atlanta, Ga.).*

Littlejohn, A. (1985). Learner choice in language study. *ELT Journal, 39*(4), 253–261. DOI: 10.1093/elt/39.4.253

Liu, G. L., & Wang, Y. (2024). Modeling EFL teachers' intention to integrate informal digital learning of English (IDLE) into the classroom using the theory of planned behavior. *System, 120*, 103193. DOI: 10.1016/j.system.2023.103193

Liu, J., Aziku, M., Qiang, F., & Zhang, B. (2024). Leveraging professional learning communities in linking digital professional development and instructional integration: Evidence from 16,072 STEM teachers. *International Journal of STEM Education, 11*(1), 56. Advance online publication. DOI: 10.1186/s40594-024-00513-3

Luckin, R., & Esparrell, F. (2024). *Artificial intelligence in education: Adapting to individual needs*. Universitepark Press. Retrieved from ERIC Database.

Luckin, R., & Cukurova, M. (2019). Designing educational technologies in the age of AI: A learning sciences-driven approach. *British Journal of Educational Technology, 50*(6), 2824–2838. DOI: 10.1111/bjet.12861

Luckin, R., Holmes, W., Griffiths, M., & Forcier, L. B. (2016). *Intelligence Unleashed: An Argument for AI in Education*. Pearson Education.

Luckin, R., Holmes, W., Griffiths, M., & Forcier, L. B. (2016). *Intelligence unleashed: An argument for AI in education*. Pearson.

MacDowell, P., Moskalyk, K., Korchinski, K., & Morrison, D. (2024). Preparing educators to teach and create with generative artificial intelligence. *Canadian Journal of Learning and Technology, 50*(4), 1–23. Advance online publication. DOI: 10.21432/cjlt28606

Magallanez, M. (2025, May 15). AI Meets the Science of Reading and Writing Skill Development. CSTA Voice Blog. https://csteachers.org/ai-meets-the-science-of-reading-and-writing-skill-development/

Magic School AI. (2025). *Magic School AI.* https://www.magicschool.ai/

MagicSchool AI. (2025). Privacy & Security. *Anthropic.* https://www.magicschool.ai/privacy

MagicSchool AI. (2025). Understanding Force and motion lesson plan. MagicSchool AI. https://app.magicschool.ai/tools/lesson-plan-generator?thread=78103107

MagicSchool.ai. (n.d.). MagicSchool.ai [Large language model]. https://www.magicschool.ai

Malik, A. R., Pratiwi, Y., Andajani, K., Numertayasa, I. W., Suharti, S., Darwis, A., & Marzuki, . (2023). Exploring artificial intelligence in academic essay: Higher education student's perspective. *International Journal of Educational Research Open*, *5*, 1–11. DOI: 10.1016/j.ijedro.2023.100296

Marlina, R., & Giri, R. A. (2014). *The pedagogy of English as an international language: Perspectives from scholars, teachers, and students.* Springer., DOI: 10.1007/978-3-319-06127-6

Martin, F., Zhuang, M., & Schaefer, D. (2023). Systematic review of research on artificial intelligence in K-12 education (2017–2022). *Computers and Education Artificial Intelligence*, *6*, 100195. DOI: 10.1016/j.caeai.2023.100195

Martin, M., & Sun, J. (2022). AI-augmented video reflection and its impact on novice teachers' questioning strategies. *Teacher Education Quarterly*, *49*(2), 67–90.

McGehee, N. (2024). *Breaking Barriers: A Meta-Analysis of Educator Acceptance of AI Technology in Education.* Michigan Virtual. https://michiganvirtual.org/research/publications/breaking-barriers-a-meta-analysis-of-educator-acceptance-of-ai-technology-in-education/

McLeskey, J. (2017). *High-leverage practices in special education.* Council for Exceptional Children, & Collaboration for Effective Educator Development, Accountability and Reform. Council for Exceptional Children: Arlington, VA.

Mishra, P., & Koehler, M. J. (2006). Technological Pedagogical Content Knowledge: A Framework for Teacher Knowledge. *Teachers College Record, 108*(6), 1017-1054. (Original work published 2006)DOI: 10.1111/j.1467-9620.2006.00684.x

Mittelstadt, B. D., Allo, P., Taddeo, M., Wachter, S., & Floridi, L. (2016). The ethics of algorithms: Mapping the debate. *Big Data & Society, 3*(2). Advance online publication. DOI: 10.1177/2053951716679679

Moore, R., Vitale, D., & Stawinoga, N. (2018). The digital divide and educational equity. Insights in Education and Work, 1-10.

Murtaza, M., Ahmed, Y., Shamsi, J. A., Sherwani, F., & Usman, M. (2022). AI-Based Personalized E-Learning Systems: Issues, challenges, and solutions. *IEEE Access : Practical Innovations, Open Solutions, 10*, 81323–81342. DOI: 10.1109/ACCESS.2022.3193938

National Education Association. (2024). *The role of artificial intelligence in professional learning.* [White paper]. National Education Association.

National Geographic Society. (2025). National geographic kids. https://kids.nationalgeographic.com/

National Reading Panel. (2000). *Teaching children to read: An evidence-based assessment of the scientific research literature on reading and its implications for reading instruction.* National Institute of Child Health and Human Development.

National Research Council. (2012). *A Framework for K-12 Science Education: Practices, Crosscutting Concepts, and Core Ideas.* National Academies Press.

National Science Board, National Science Foundation. (2024). U.S. STEM workforce: Size, growth, and employment (NSB-2024-5). *National Center for Science and Engineering Statistics.* https://ncses.nsf.gov/pubs/nsb20245/u-s-stem-workforce-size-growth-and-employment

Neelakandan, N. (2019). The Impact of Content Curation in eLearning. https://elearningindustry.com/content-curation-impact-in-elearning#:~:text=Content%20curation%20in%20eLearning%20is,to%20get%20what%20they%20need

Nguyen, H., Gardiner, E., & McGowan, J. (2021). AI Tools and Accessibility in Education: Enhancing Inclusivity. *Journal of Educational Technology, 18*(2), 45–62.

Nja, C. O., Idiege, K. J., Uwe, U. E., Meremikwu, A. N., Ekon, E. E., Erim, C. M., Ukah, J. U., Eyo, E. O., Anari, M. I., & Cornelius-Ukpepi, B. U. (2023). Adoption of artificial intelligence in science teaching: From the vantage point of the African science teachers. *Smart Learning Environments, 10*(1), 42. Advance online publication. DOI: 10.1186/s40561-023-00261-x

Obermeyer, Z., Powers, B., Vogeli, C., & Mullainathan, S. (2019). Dissecting racial bias in an algorithm used to manage the health of populations. *Science*, *366*(6464), 447–453. DOI: 10.1126/science.aax2342 PMID: 31649194

OECD. (2023). *AI in education: A pathway to innovation*. OECD Education Working Paper Series.

Okonkwo, U. (2011). Computer assisted language learning (CALL) software: Evaluation of its influence in a language learning process. *UJAH: Unizik Journal of Arts and Humanities*, *12*(1), 76–89. DOI: 10.4314/ujah.v12i1.4

Open, A. I. (2023). ChatGPT (Mar 14 edition) [Large language model]. https://chat.openai.com/chat

Open, A. I. (2023, November 30). *ChatGPT: Optimizing language models for dialogue*. OpenAI Blog. https://openai.com/blog/chatgpt

Open, A. I. (2024a). *Embeddings – OpenAI API*. OpenAI. https://platform.openai.com/docs/guides/embeddings

Open, A. I. (2024b). *Fine-tuning – OpenAI API*. OpenAI. https://platform.openai.com/docs/guides/fine-tuning

Orakcı, Ş., & Gelişli, Y. (2017). Learner autonomy scale: A scale development study. *Malaysian Online Journal of Educational Sciences*, *5*(4), 25–35.

Otto, F., Kling, N., Schumann, C.-A., & Tittmann, C. (2023). Conceptual approach to an AI-based adaptive study support system for individualized higher education. *International Journal of Advanced Corporate Learning*, *16*(2), 78–89. DOI: 10.3991/ijac.v16i2.35699

Ouyang, F., & Jiao, P. (2021). Artificial intelligence in education: The three paradigms. *Computers and Education: Artificial Intelligence*, *2*, 100020. Advance online publication. DOI: 10.1016/j.caeai.2021.100020

Pack, J. (2024, April 1). Using AI to Enhance Universal Design for Learning. *Edutopia* https://www.edutopia.org/article/using-ai-in-universal-design-for-learning/r/ChatGPT

Panadero, E., & Jonsson, A. (2013). The use of scoring rubrics for formative assessment purposes revisited: A review. *Educational Research Review*, *9*, 129–144. DOI: 10.1016/j.edurev.2013.01.002

Pane, J. F., Griffin, B. A., McCaffrey, D. F., & Karam, R. (2013). Effectiveness of Cognitive Tutor Algebra I at scale. *Educational Evaluation and Policy Analysis*, *36*(2), 127–144. DOI: 10.3102/0162373713507480

Pardo, A., Jovanovic, J., Dawson, S., Gašević, D., & Mirriahi, N. (2019). Using learning analytics to scale the provision of personalised feedback. *British Journal of Educational Technology*, *50*(1), 128–138. DOI: 10.1111/bjet.12592

Patiño, A., Ramírez-Montoya, M. S., & Buenestado-Fernández, M. (2023). Active learning and education 4.0 for complex thinking training: Analysis of two case studies in open education. *Smart Learning Environments*, *10*(1), 8. Advance online publication. DOI: 10.1186/s40561-023-00229-x

Pearson, P. D. (2004). The reading wars. *Educational Policy*, *18*(1), 216–252. DOI: 10.1177/0895904803260041

Pedró, F., Subosa, M., Rivas, A., & Valverde, P. (2019). *Artificial intelligence in education: Challenges and opportunities for sustainable development.* UNESCO. https://unesdoc.unesco.org/ark:/48223/pf0000366994

Peña, E. V., & James, A. L. (2024). Transmediating with AI: Literacies, design, and justice in teacher learning. *Learning, Media and Technology*.

Penuel, W. R., Van Horne, K., & Bell, P. (2020). Steps to Designing Three-Dimensional Assessments that Connect to Students' Interests, Experiences, and Identities. *STEM Teaching Tools Practice Brief #29*. https://STEMteachingtools.org/link/2900

Perplexity, A. I. (2023). Perplexity [Large language model]. https://www.perplexity.ai

Pimthong, P., & Williams, J. (2018). Preservice teachers' understanding of STEM education. *Kasetsart Journal of Social Sciences*. Advance online publication. DOI: 10.1016/j.kjss.2018.07.017

Prince, M. (2004). Does active learning work? A review of the research. *Journal of Engineering Education*, *93*(3), 223–231. DOI: 10.1002/j.2168-9830.2004.tb00809.x

Qu, J., Zhao, Y., & Xie, Y. (2022). Artificial intelligence leads the reform of education models. *Systems Research and Behavioral Science*, *39*(3), 581–588. DOI: 10.1002/sres.2864

Rakap, S. (2024). Chatting with GPT: Enhancing individualized education program goal development for novice special education teachers. *Journal of Special Education Technology*, *39*(3), 339–348. DOI: 10.1177/01626434231211295

Ramirez, R., & Fuentes Esparrell, F. (2023). *Multi-agent systems and adaptive learning environments*. Universitepark Press.

Rehman, N., Huang, X., Mahmood, A., AlGerafi, M. M., & Javed, S. (2024b). Project-Based learning as a catalyst for 21st-Century skills and student engagement in the math classroom. *Heliyon, 10*(23), e39988. DOI: 10.1016/j.heliyon.2024.e39988 PMID: 39660178

Retzlaff, C. O., Das, S., Wayllace, C., Mousavi, P., Afshari, M., Yang, T., Saranti, A., Angerschmid, A., Taylor, M. E., & Holzinger, A. (2024). Human-in-the-loop reinforcement learning: A survey and position on requirements, challenges, and opportunities. *Journal of Artificial Intelligence Research, 79*, 349–415. DOI: 10.1613/jair.1.15348

Reynders, G., Lantz, J., Ruder, S. M., Stanford, C. L., & Cole, R. S. (2020). Rubrics to assess critical thinking and information processing in undergraduate STEM courses. *International Journal of STEM Education*, *7*(1), 9. Advance online publication. DOI: 10.1186/s40594-020-00208-5

Reza, H. M., Deng, C., Justin, J. K., Zhou, P., Kwon, Y. D., Ahmed Hosny, S. M., Tlili, A., Bassanelli, S., Bucchiarone, A., Gujar, S., Nacke, L. E., & Pan, H. (2023). *Exploring User Perspectives on ChatGPT: Applications*. Perceptions, and Implications for AI-Integrated Education.

Riessman, C. K. (2008). Narrative methods for the human sciences. *Sage (Atlanta, Ga.)*.

Rizk, N., Taylor, S., & Taylor, N. (2024). Remote classroom modelling: A professional development model for in-service generalist primary teachers of science. *Australian Educational Researcher*, *51*(1), 287–309. DOI: 10.1007/s13384-022-00594-5 PMID: 36568710

Robins, A., Hunt, T., Robertson, D., & Carter, R. (2022). Amazon Alexa Skills as a Novel Modality for In-service Professional Micro-Development (WIP). *Association for Computing Machinery*, *284–288*, 284–288. Advance online publication. DOI: 10.1145/3491140.3528314

Rose, D. H., & Meyer, A. (2002). *Teaching Every Student in the Digital Age: Universal Design for Learning* (Alexandria, V. A., Ed.).

Rubin, A. (2012). *Dragons love tacos*. ENH Penguin Young Readers Group.

Rubin, A. (2013). *Secret pizza party*. Dial Books for Young Readers.

Rudolph, J., Tan, S., & Tan, S. (2023). War of the chatbots: Bard, Bing Chat, ChatGPT, Ernie and beyond: The new AI gold rush and its impact on higher education. *Journal of Applied Learning and Teaching*, *6*(1), 364–389. DOI: 10.37074/jalt.2023.6.1.23

Rui, Z., & Badarch, T. (2022). Research on Applications of Artificial Intelligence in Education. *American Journal of Computer Science and Technology*, *5*(2), 72. DOI: 10.11648/j.ajcst.20220502.17

Russel, S. J., & Norvig, P. (2010). *Artificial intelligence: A modern approach*. Pearson Education.

Sahota, N. (2023). *Precision Education: How K-12 schools are embracing AI*. Forbes. https://www.forbes.com/sites/neilsahota/2023/12/15/precision-education-how-k-12-schools-are-embracing-ai/

Salinas-Navarro, D. E., Vilalta-Perdomo, E., Michel-Villarreal, R., & Montesinos, L. (2024). Designing experiential learning activities with generative artificial intelligence tools for authentic assessment. *Interactive Technology and Smart Education*, *21*(4), 708–734. DOI: 10.1108/ITSE-12-2023-0236

Sanusi, I. T., Ayanwale, M. A., & Tolorunleke, A. E. (2024). Investigating pre-service teachers' artificial intelligence perception from the perspective of planned behavior theory. *Computers and Education: Artificial Intelligence*, *6*, 100202. Advance online publication. DOI: 10.1016/j.caeai.2024.100202

Scott, L., Bruno, L., Gokita, T., & Thoma, C. A. (2022). Teacher candidates' abilities to develop universal design for learning and universal design for transition lesson plans. *International Journal of Inclusive Education*, *26*(4), 333–347. DOI: 10.1080/13603116.2019.1651910

Seale, J. (2014). *E-learning and disability in higher education: Accessibility research and practice*. Routledge.

Seliger, H. W., & Shohamy, E. (1989). *Second language research methods*. Oxford University Press.

Selwyn, N. (2010). Looking beyond learning: Notes towards the critical study of educational technology. *Journal of Computer Assisted Learning*, *26*(1), 65–73. DOI: 10.1111/j.1365-2729.2009.00338.x

Selwyn, N. (2019). *Should Robots Replace Teachers? AI and the Future of Education*. Polity Press.

Sharma, R. C., & Sharma, Y. (2022). Augmenting learning through virtual reality applications in education. *Tenth Pan-Commonwealth Forum on Open Learning*, 1–6. DOI: 10.56059/pcf10.7986

Shata, A., & Hartley, K. (2025). Artificial intelligence and communication technologies in academia: Faculty perceptions and the adoption of generative AI. *International Journal of Educational Technology in Higher Education*, *22*(1), 14–22. DOI: 10.1186/s41239-025-00511-7

Shezad, F., Goswami, R., Shaheen, A., & Khan, I. (2025). AI in teacher training and professional development: A tool for continuous learning and skill enhancement. *Review of Education. Administration & Law*, *8*(1), 179–191. DOI: 10.47067/real.v8i1.416

Siemens, G., & Long, P. (2011). Penetrating the fog: Analytics in learning and education. *EDUCAUSE Review*, *46*(5), 30–32.

Siew, N. M., & Ambo, T. (2021). Assessing creativity in elementary science project-based learning using rubrics. *Journal of Baltic Science Education*, *20*(1), 120–134. DOI: 10.33225/jbse/21.20.120

Slavin, N. (2022). The datafication of education: Surveillance, privacy, and power. *Surveillance & Society*, *20*(1), 85–102.

Smith, A., & Chen, L. (2024). Artificial intelligence in teaching and teacher professional development: A systematic review. *Computers and Education: Artificial Intelligence*, *5*, 100589. Advance online publication. DOI: 10.1016/S2666-920X(24)001589

Song, Y., Weisberg, L. R., Zhang, S., Tian, X., Boyer, K. E., & Israel, M. (2024). A framework for inclusive AI learning design for diverse learners. *Computers and Education. Artificial Intelligence, 6*, 100212-. https://doi.org/DOI: 10.1016/j.caeai.2024.100212

Sotáková, I., & Ganajová, M. (2023). The effect of the 5E instructional model on students' cognitive processes and their attitudes towards chemistry as a subject. *Eurasia Journal of Mathematics, Science and Technology Education*, *19*(9), em2317. DOI: 10.29333/ejmste/13469

Staff, N. A. E. S. P. (2023, August 26). 5 Strategies for Success in Bringing AI to Schools. *NAESP National Association for Elementary School Principals Blog*. https://www.naesp.org/resource/5-strategies-for-success-in-bringing-ai-to-schools/

Stanja, J., Gritz, W., Krugel, J., Hoppe, A., & Dannemann, S. (2022). Formative assessment strategies for students' conceptions—The potential of learning analytics. *British Journal of Educational Technology*, *54*(1), 58–75. DOI: 10.1111/bjet.13288

Stano, E. (2024). Attending to Bias, Accessibility, and Ethical Concerns in the Use of AI in Education. *EdTech Digest*. https://www.edtechdigest.com/2024/11/20/attending-to-bias-accessibility-and-ethical-concerns-in-the-use-of-ai-in-education/#:~:text=One%20of%20the%20most%20pressing,negative%20outcomes%20for%20marginalized%20groups

Stommel, J. (2014). Critical digital pedagogy: A definition. *Hybrid Pedagogy: The Journal of Critical Digital Pedagogy.*

Stommel, J., & Morris, S. M. (Eds.). (2018). *An Urgency of Teachers: The Work of Critical Digital Pedagogy*. Hybrid Pedagogy Incorporated.

Su, L., & Xie, Y. (2022). Artificial intelligence applications in teacher education: A systematic review. *Journal of Research on Technology in Education.* Advance online publication. DOI: 10.1080/15391523.2022.2078694

Sun, Y., & Yan, Z. (2025). Factors influencing teachers' technology adoption in technology-rich classrooms: Model development and test. *Educational Technology Research and Development*. Advance online publication. DOI: 10.1007/s11423-025-10454-5

Taipalus, T. (2024). Vector database management systems: Fundamental concepts, use-cases, and current challenges. *Cognitive Systems Research*, *85*, 101216. Advance online publication. DOI: 10.1016/j.cogsys.2024.101216

Tammets, K., & Ley, T. (2023). Integrating AI tools in teacher professional learning: A conceptual model and illustrative case. *Frontiers in Artificial Intelligence*, *6*, 1255089. Advance online publication. DOI: 10.3389/frai.2023.1255089 PMID: 38130325

Tapalova, O., & Zhiyenbayeva, N. (2022). Artificial Intelligence in Education: AIEd for Personalised Learning Pathways. *Electronic Journal of e-Learning*, *20*(5), 639–653. DOI: 10.34190/ejel.20.5.2597

Tarisayia, K. S. (2024). A theoretical framework for interrogating the integration of artificial intelligence in education. *Research on Education and Media, 16*(1), 38-44. DOI: 10.2478/rem-2024-0006

Teach, F. X. (2024). *TeachFX: Conversation analytics for reflective practice* [White paper]. https://teachfx.com/

TeachFlow.AI. (2023). *The evolution of AI in education: Past, present, and future*. TeachFlow.AI.

Tegegne, T. A., & Kelkay, A. D. (2023). Comparative study of using 5E learning cycle and the traditional teaching method in chemistry to improve student understanding of water concept: The case of primary school. *Cogent Education, 10*(1), 2199634. Advance online publication. DOI: 10.1080/2331186X.2023.2199634

Tomlinson, C. A. (2000). *Differentiation of instruction in the elementary grades* (ED443572). ERIC. https://files.eric.ed.gov/fulltext/ED443572.pdf

Tomlinson, C. A. (2001). *How to Differentiate Instruction in Mixed-Ability Classrooms*. ASCD.

Topsakal, İ., Yalçın, S. A., & Çakır, Z. (2022). The effect of problem-based STEM education on the students' critical thinking tendencies and their perceptions for problem solving skills. *Science Education International, 33*(2), 136–145. DOI: 10.33828/sei.v33.i2.1

Treve, M. (2024). Integrating Artificial Intelligence in Education: Impacts on Student Learning and Innovation. *International Journal of Vocational Education and Training Research, 10*(2), 61–69. DOI: 10.11648/j.ijvetr.20241002.14

Triwicaksana, M. B. S., & Oktavia, T. (2023). Building a retrieval-augmented generation system for enhanced student learning: Case study at private university. *Journal of Theoretical and Applied Information Technology, 101*(22), 7234–7245.

U.S. Department of Education, Office of Educational Technology. (2023). *Artificial intelligence and future of teaching and learning: Insights and recommendations.* Author.

UNESCO. (2021). *AI and Education: Guidance for Policy-Makers.* UNESCO Publishing.

Vassileva, J. (2008). Social learning environments: New challenges for AI in education. In Luckin, R., Koedinger, K. R., & Greer, J. (Eds.), *Artificial intelligence in education* (pp. 532–539). Springer., DOI: 10.1007/978-3-540-69132-7_5

Vesin, B., Mangaroska, K., & Giannakos, M. (2018). Learning in smart environments: User-centered design and analytics of an adaptive learning system. *Smart Learning Environments, 5*(1), 24. Advance online publication. DOI: 10.1186/s40561-018-0071-0

Viberg, O., Hatakka, M., Bälter, O., & Mavroudi, A. (2018). The current landscape of learning analytics in higher education. *Computers in Human Behavior, 89*, 98–110. DOI: 10.1016/j.chb.2018.07.027

Villamizar Castrillón, L. J. (2017). The effects of Vygotsky's sociocultural theory on second language acquisition and language input. *Espiral. Revista de Docencia e Investigación, 7*(1), 91–114. DOI: 10.15332/erdi.v7i1.1780

Vygotsky, L. (1978). *Mind in society: The development of higher mental processes.* Harvard University Press.

Vygotsky, L. S. (1978). *Mind in society: The development of higher psychological processes* (Cole, M., John-Steiner, V., Scribner, S., & Souberman, E., Eds.). Harvard University Press.

Vygotsky, L. S. (1986). *Thought and language* (Kozulin, A., Trans.). MIT Press.

Vygotsky, L. S., & Cole, M. (1978). *Mind in society: the development of higher psychological processes.* Harvard University Press.

Wang, F., Fang, W., & Tang, Y. (2020). Human-AI collaboration in education: Strengthening outcomes through balance. *Journal of Educational Technology Research, 38*(4), 601–620.

Wang, K., Ruan, Q., Zhang, X., Fu, C., & Duan, B. (2024). Pre-service teachers' genAI anxiety, technology self-efficacy, and TPACK: Their structural relations with behavioral intention to design genAI-assisted teaching. *Behavioral Sciences (Basel, Switzerland), 14*(5), 373. DOI: 10.3390/bs14050373 PMID: 38785864

Waterfield, D. A., Watson, L., & Day, J. (2024). Applying artificial intelligence in special education: Exploring availability and functionality of AI platforms for special educators. *Journal of Special Education Technology, 39*(3), 448–454. DOI: 10.1177/01626434241257237

Webb, N. (2002). *Depth-of-knowledge: Levels for four content areas.* Wisconsin Center for Educational Research.

Wei, L. (2023). Artificial intelligence in language instruction: Impact on English learning achievement, L2 motivation, and self-regulated learning. *Frontiers in Psychology, 14*, 1–14. DOI: 10.3389/fpsyg.2023.1261955 PMID: 38023040

Wertsch, J. V. (1991). *Voices of the mind: A sociocultural approach to mediated action.* Harvard University Press.

West, D. M. (2019). *The Future of Work: Robots, AI, and Automation.* Brookings Institution Press.

Whittaker, M., Alper, M., Bennett, C. L., Hendren, S., Kaziunas, L., Mills, M., Morris, M. R., Rankin, J., Rogers, E., Salas, M., & West, S. M. (2019). *Disability, bias, and AI.* AI Now Institute. https://ainowinstitute.org/wp-content/uploads/2023/04/disabilitybiasai-2019.pdf

Williams, P., & Fowler, A. (2023). Accelerating feedback cycles with AI annotations in micro-teaching. *Computers & Education*, *205*, 104903. Advance online publication. DOI: 10.1016/j.compedu.2023.104903

Williams, R. T. (2024). The ethical implications of using generative chatbots in higher education. *Frontiers in Education*, *8*, 1331607. DOI: 10.3389/feduc.2023.1331607

Wu, S., & Yang, K. (2022). The effectiveness of teacher support for students' learning of artificial intelligence popular science activities. *Frontiers in Psychology*, *13*, 868623. Advance online publication. DOI: 10.3389/fpsyg.2022.868623 PMID: 35719487

Xu, W., & Ouyang, F. (2022). The application of AI technologies in STEM education: A systematic review from 2011 to 2021. *International Journal of STEM Education*, *9*(1), 59. Advance online publication. DOI: 10.1186/s40594-022-00377-5

Yan, D. (2023). Impact of ChatGPT on learners in a L2 writing practicum: An exploratory investigation. *Education and Information Technologies*, *28*(11), 1–25. DOI: 10.1007/s10639-023-11742-4 PMID: 37361815

Yang, S., & Evans, M. A. (2022). AI-supported personalized learning: A conceptual framework. *Educational Technology Research and Development*, *70*(1), 5–28. DOI: 10.1007/s11423-022-10039-3

Yildiz, Y., & Yucedal, H. M. (2020). Learner autonomy: A central theme in language learning. International. *Journal of Social Sciences and Educational Studies*, *7*(3), 208–212. DOI: 10.23918/ijsses.v7i3p208

Yılmaz, Ö. (2024). Personalised learning and artificial intelligence in science education: Current state and future perspectives. *Educational Technology Quarterly*, *2024*(3), 255–274. DOI: 10.55056/etq.744

Yu, W. (2022). Retrieval-augmented generation across heterogeneous knowledge. In *Proceedings of the 2022 Conference of the North American Chapter of the Association for Computational Linguistics: Human Language Technologies* (pp. 207–217). Association for Computational Linguistics. DOI: 10.18653/v1/2022.naacl-srw.7

Zagona, A. L., Kurth, J. A., Lockman Turner, E., Pace, J., Shogren, K., Lansey, K., Jameson, M., Burnette, K., Mansouri, M., Hicks, T., & Gerasimova, D. (2022). Ecobehavioral analysis of the experiences of students with complex support needs in different classroom types. *Research and Practice for Persons with Severe Disabilities : the Journal of TASH*, *47*(4), 209–228. DOI: 10.1177/15407969221126496

Zamel, V. (1982). Writing: The process of discovering meaning. *TESOL Quarterly*, *16*(2), 195–209. DOI: 10.2307/3586792

Zawacki-Richter, O., Marín, V. I., Bond, M., & Gouverneur, F. (2019). Systematic review of research on artificial intelligence applications in higher education: Emerging trends and research agenda. *International Journal of Educational Technology in Higher Education*, *16*(39). Advance online publication. DOI: 10.1186/s41239-019-0171-0

Zhang, C., Schießl, J., Plößl, L., Hofmann, L., & Gläser-Zikuda, M. (2023). Acceptance of artificial intelligence among pre-service teachers: A multigroup analysis. *International Journal of Educational Technology in Higher Education*, *20*(1), 49. DOI: 10.1186/s41239-023-00420-7

Zhang, J., Wang, B., Yang, H. H., Chen, Z., Gao, W., & Liu, Z. (2022). Assessing quality of online learning platforms for in-service teachers' professional development: The development and application of an instrument. *Frontiers in Psychology*, *13*, 998196. Advance online publication. DOI: 10.3389/fpsyg.2022.998196 PMID: 36275249

Zhang, K., & Aslan, A. B. (2021). AI technologies for education: Recent research & Future directions. *Computers and Education: Artificial Intelligence*, *2*, 100025. DOI: 10.1016/j.caeai.2021.100025

Zhang, L., & Ma, Y. (2023). A study of the impact of project-based learning on student learning effects: A meta-analysis study. *Frontiers in Psychology*, *14*, 1202728. Advance online publication. DOI: 10.3389/fpsyg.2023.1202728 PMID: 37564309

Zhao, L., Wu, X., & Luo, H. (2022). Developing AI literacy for primary and middle school teachers in China: Based on a structural equation modeling analysis. *Sustainability (Basel)*, *14*(21), 14549. Advance online publication. DOI: 10.3390/su142114549

Zheng, W., Cheng, H., Yu, J. X., Zou, L., & Zhao, K. (2019). Interactive natural language question answering over knowledge graphs. *Information Sciences*, *481*, 141–159. DOI: 10.1016/j.ins.2018.12.032

About the Contributors

Juan J. Araujo is Director and Professor in the School of Education within the College of Professional Education at Texas Woman's University. He holds a Doctor of Philosophy in reading with a minor of anthropology from University of North Texas, a Master of Bilingual Education from Southern Methodist University and a Bachelor of Science in electrical engineering from New Jersey Institute of Technology. Dr. Araujo has been a co-editor/lead editor for the ALER yearbook from 2016-2020, and Co-editor with the LRI Journal for the past term. He has also been on the review boards with the Journal of Adolescent and Adult Literacy since 2013, on the LRA Review board from 2012-2016, and with the TESOL Journal from 2017 to the present. Methodological expertise includes case study, narrative inquiry, ethnographic, and survey research.

Sharla Snider is Professor and Division Head of Early Childhood Education in the School of Education at Texas Woman's University. She holds a Doctor of Philosophy and Master of Arts in Early Childhood Education from Texas Woman's University and a Bachelor of Science in Elementary Education from the University of North Texas. Dr Snider has served in various faculty and administrative roles, including former interim Chair of the Department of Literacy and Learning. She has published in peer-reviewed journals, presented at major conferences, and secured over $1 million in external funding from sources including the U.S. Department of Education and Intel Corporation. She teaches at all levels in early childhood education, technology integration, and research methods, including direction of doctoral work. Methodological expertise includes case study, ethnographic, narrative inquiry, and mixed methods research.

***

Nancy Anderson is a Professor of Literacy and Language at Texas Woman's University. Her publications include articles in The Reading Teacher and the book Linking Assessment to Reading Comprehension Instruction: A Framework for Actively Engaging Literacy Learners, K-8. Her areas of research include the relationship between language and literacy and teacher education. Nancy works extensively in school settings connecting research and theory to effective teaching practices with leaders and teachers.

Michaine Ashley is an Assistant Professor at Texas Woman's University, specializing in experiential learning within STEM education, fostering positive learning communities, and leveraging instructional technology to enhance K-12 classrooms. With over a decade of experience teaching science to students in grades 4-12, Dr. Ashley focuses on integrating hands-on, technology-enhanced approaches that promote depth and complexity in learning. Her expertise includes supporting at-risk and diverse learners through innovative STEM practices and personalized instructional strategies. Dr. Ashley is dedicated to advancing teacher knowledge by providing accessible methods for implementing experiential, technology-enhanced learning models that improve educational outcomes and inspire student engagement in STEM disciplines.

Selami Aydin is a full professor in the Department of English Language Teaching at Istanbul Medeniyet University, Istanbul, Turkey. He researches EFL writing, testing, affective states, technology use, and social media effects on language learning and teaching processes. Currently, he teaches ELT-related courses at BA and MA programs.

Teresa Cardon is an educator and a dually certified speech pathologist and behavior analyst. She has worked with individuals with differing abilities for over 25 years. Dr. Cardon is currently a Senior Lecturer at the University of North Texas. Her research interests include interprofessional practice, video modeling, autism in the media, and collaboration bias. Dr. Cardon serves on editorial boards for prominent journals, volunteers in various capacities for professional organizations, and enjoys supporting educators and clinicians who work with unique populations.

Heather Cato, Ph.D., is a literacy educator and researcher with a deep commitment to classroom practice. Her career spans roles as a classroom teacher, curriculum director, and professional learning facilitator. She holds a Ph.D. in Reading Education from Texas Woman's University and an EC–12 Principal Certification. Her research focuses on the validity and reliability of literacy assessments and the development of teacher expertise in evidence-informed instruction.

Kathleen Crawford, Ed.D., is currently an Associate Professor at Georgia Southern University, where she teaches elementary literacy courses at the undergraduate and graduate levels. Prior to joining the faculty at Georgia Southern, she was a K–5 literacy coach and fourth and fifth grade English language arts teacher. Her research interests include engaging literacy experiences, enhancing elementary teacher education, artificial intelligence in education, mentoring beginning teachers, exploring the emotional dynamics involved in teaching and learning, and designing effective online teaching practices.

Shivnath Ghosh is a Professor and Head of the Department of Computer Science and Engineering at Brainware University. With 19 years of academic experience, he has made significant contributions to research and development. His work includes 52+ research papers, 7 patents, 11+ books, and 13 book chapters. He is currently guiding 6 Ph.D. scholars, with 2 having already completed their degrees under his supervision.

Luis Hernandez is an instructional designer and educational consultant with over 20 years of experience in bilingual education, instructional technology, and teacher preparation. He is the co-founder of Enabling Learning LLC, where he develops AI-powered tools and hybrid professional development models to support multilingual educators. His work integrates constructivist approaches with emerging technologies to foster inclusive, effective learning environments for preservice and in-service teachers.

Catherine S. Howerter is an Associate Professor at Texas Woman's University. She earned her PhD in Special Education from the University of Nevada, Las Vegas, her master's in Educational Psychology from New York University, and B.A. from Carlow University (Pittsburgh, PA) as a double major in Elementary and Special Education. She was an Associate Professor of Elementary and Special Education at Georgia Southern University. She taught in a K-5 resource room in Washington, D.C., and co-taught at the middle school level (6-8) in Brooklyn, NY. She was an Intervention Specialist at a middle/high school in Las Vegas. She has taught a variety of graduate and undergraduate courses and supervised teacher candidates at different levels.

Heather M. Huling, Ed.D., is currently an Assistant Professor in the Elementary Education Program at Georgia Southern University where she teaches courses in arts integration and children's literature, language arts methods, and supervises preservice teachers in their senior level field experiences. She was an elementary educator in the public school system before moving into higher education to work with preservice teachers as a teacher educator and mentor. Her research interests focus on literacy education, mentoring preservice teachers, online learning, artificial intelligence in education, teacher education, and best practices in teaching.

Uvaldina Janecek is a retired bilingual education professor and researcher with decades of experience in multilingual teacher preparation and culturally responsive pedagogy. Now working as an independent consultant, she continues to support educators through her expertise in language development, equity-focused instruction, and the integration of best practices for diverse classroom settings.

Sena Könez is an instructor at the School of Foreign Languages at Turkish National Defense University, Istanbul, Turkey. She researches on EFL writing, learner autonomy and technology use in language learning and teaching. She currently teaches EFL lessons at prep school programs.

Tami Morton is a Professor and Assistant Department Head in the Curriculum and Instruction department at East Texas A&M University (formerly Texas A&M Commerce). She has been at the university for over 13 years, and has a passion for reading foundations and multicultural children's and young adult literature. Tami is a member of the ILA primary book award committee. Tami also teaches undergraduate, masters, and doctoral level courses.

Christina Salazar is an early-career lecturer of Teacher Education whose work centers on critical digital pedagogy, humanizing practices, and the preparation of equity-oriented educators. Her research explores how emerging technologies, including artificial intelligence, intersect with culturally responsive teaching and reflective praxis. With a background in language and literacy, Dr. Salazar draws on over a decade of K–12 teaching experience to inform her scholarship and support future teachers in diverse, urban educational contexts.

Index

Symbols

A

B

C

D

E

F

G

H

I

K

L

M

P

R

S

T

V

www.ingramcontent.com/pod-product-compliance
Ingram Content Group UK Ltd.
Pitfield, Milton Keynes, MK11 3LW, UK
UKHW052003051026
15624UKWH00003B/540

9 798337 311227